D1257824

STUDIES IN
SLAVIC LINGUISTICS
AND POETICS

Boris O. Unbegaun

STUDIES IN
SLAVIC LINGUISTICS
AND POETICS

in Honor of
BORIS O. UNBEGAUN

EDITORIAL COMMITTEE:
Robert Magidoff, *New York University*
George Y. Shevelov, *Columbia University*
J. S. G. Simmons, *Oxford*
Kiril Taranovski, *Harvard University*
SECRETARY:
John E. Allen III, *New York University*

New York · New York University Press
London · University of London Press Ltd.
1968

Copyright © 1968 by New York University Press
Library of Congress Catalog Card No. 68-28005
Printed in the United States of America

491.7
S933

CONTENTS

FOREWORD   ix

JOHN E. ALLEN III
The T:ŠČ, D:ŽD Alternations in the Russian Verb   I

ROBERT AUTY
A Note on the Indeclinable Nouns of Modern Czech   11

CHARLES E. BIDWELL
The Adjective and Pronoun Systems of Bulgarian   15

HENRIK BIRNBAUM
On Deep Structure and Loan Syntax in Slavic   21

JOHN L. I. FENNELL
The Ermolinskij Chronicle and the Literary Prelude
to "The Tale of the Murder of Mixail of Tver'"   33

JAMES O. FERRELL
The Phonology of East Slavic at the Period Preceding
the Loss of the *Jers*   39

SUNRAY C. GARDINER
Russian Participles   47

WILLIAM E. HARKINS
The Symbol of the River in the Tale of Gore-Zločastie   55

RADO L. LENČEK
Čupa, Čupus, 'enodebelni čoln' — v ruščini in slovenščini   63

HORACE E. LUNT
On the *Izbornik of 1076*   69

455614

ROBERT MAGIDOFF
The Recurrent Image in Doctor Živago   79

OLEG A. MASLENIKOV
Disruption of Canonical Verse Norms in The Poetry
of Zinaida Hippius   89

THOMAS F. MAGNER
Jagić and the Varaždin Kajkavian Dialect   97

KARL H. MENGES
Weitere slavisch-orientalische Lehnbeziehungen   107

GRIGORE NANDRIŞ
Moldova — The name of the River and the country   119

ANNE PENNINGTON
Some High-Style Elements in Seventeenth-Century
Russian   129

RICCARDO PICCHIO
On the Textual Criticism of Xrabr's Treatise   139

J. B. RUDNYCKYJ
Un Cas de Bilinguisme Regional   149

W. F. RYAN
Some Observations on the History of the Astrolabe and
of Two Russian Words: *astroljabija* and *matka*   155

Л. РЖЕВСКИЙ
Образ рассказчика в повести Солженицына «Один
день Ивана Денисовича»   165

MICHAEL SAMILOV
Kartavoe R in Russian   179

WILLIAM R. SCHMALSTIEG
Labialization in Old Prussian   189

GEORGE Y. SHEVELOV
On the Lexical Make-Up of the Galician-Volhynian
Chronicle   195

JOHN S. G. SIMMONS
Homage Volumes in Slavic Linguistics: A Tentative List   209

CONTENTS

EDWARD STANKIEWICZ
The Etymology of Common Slavic *skot'ъ* 'cattle' and
Related Terms   219

GLEB STRUVE
Some Observations on Pasternak's Ternary Metres   227

VICTOR SWOBODA
Some Problems of Belorussian Vocabulary   245

KIRIL TARANOVSKY
Certain Aspects of Blok's Symbolism   249

LAWRENCE L. D. THOMAS
Toward a Contrastive Study of Word-Usage:
Mickiewicz and Puškin   261

GERTA H. WORTH
Über Redewendungen und Figurative Bedeutungen im
Russisch-Kirchenslawischen   271

DEAN S. WORTH
Notes on Russian Stress, 2: любовь, вошь, etc.   279

FOREWORD

BORIS O. UNBEGAUN was born in Moscow on the 23rd of August, 1898. A cadet at the Constantine Artillery School in St. Petersburg in 1917, he served in the Russian Army as an officer during the First World War and in the White Army during the Civil War. He was twice wounded in action.

During the twenties, Professor Unbegaun was a student, first at the University of Ljubljana, Yugoslavia and, later, at the Sorbonne. During his Paris studies, he served as Librarian of the Institute d'Etudes Slaves of the University of Paris.

After receiving his Docteur ès-Lettres from the Sorbonne in 1935, Professor Unbegaun was appointed Professor of Slavonic Philology at the Institute de Philologie et d'Histoire Orientales et Slaves de l'Université Libre de Bruxelles. He simultaneously held a professorship in Slavonic philology at the University of Strasbourg, France.

Professor Unbegaun's academic career was interrupted by World War II. Arrested by the Gestapo in 1943, he was deported to Germany and spent two years in the infamous Buchenwald concentration camp.

Professor Unbegaun, a Visiting Professor at Oxford after 1948, accepted the post of Professor of Comparative Slavonic Philology in 1953 at Brasenose College, Oxford, which he held until retirement in 1965.

Professor Unbegaun visited the United States several times before moving here in 1965. His first visit was in 1938 when he was Visiting Professor at Columbia University. Later, in 1959 and in 1964, he held visiting professorships at Columbia again, Yale and New York University.

Since 1965, Professor Unbegaun has been Professor of Slavic Linguistics at New York University where he continues teaching on this, his seventieth birthday.

Professor Unbegaun's scholarly writings, over his career, number in the hundreds. Among his book-length works, *La langue russe au XVIe siècle (1500–1550)*, I, *La flexion des noms* (1935), *Grammaire russe* (1951), later translated into English as *Russian Grammar* (1957), *A Bibliographical Guide to the Russian Language* in collaboration with J. S. G. Simmons (1953), *Russian Versification* (1956), and his critical edition of *Henrici Wilhelmi Ludolfi Grammatica Russica, Oxonii, A.D. MDCXCVI* (1959) are particularly well known and esteemed.

Professor Unbegaun has been honored often during his lifetime. He is an Associate Member of the Académie Royale de Belgique, a Corresponding Member of the Akademie der Wissenschaften und der Literatur of Mainz, West Germany, and a Member of the Bureau of the Institut d'Etudes Slaves in Paris. Additionally, he holds the post of Commandeur de l'Ordre de la Couronne (Belgium), and is a Chevalier de la Légion d'Honneur (France). He also holds the rank of Chevalier de Ordre de Léopold (Belgium). Upon his retirement from Oxford in 1965, the honorary degree of Doctor of Letters was conferred upon him.

In 1967, a group of Professor Unbegaun's American and British colleagues formed a committee to create an homage volume of essays in Slavic linguistics and poetics for presentation on the occasion of his seventieth birthday. The authors represented in this collection are among the first rank of Slavic scholars from the English-speaking nations. They represent former students, current colleagues and personal friends.

A European group is preparing a second homage volume representing Slavic scholars from the non-English-speaking nations. The simultaneous issue of two homage volumes on the same occasion is a rare and impressive event.

To Boris O. Unbegaun, on the happy occasion of his birthday, this volume is respectfully and affectionately presented.

STUDIES IN
SLAVIC LINGUISTICS
AND POETICS

The T: ŠČ, D: ŽD Alternations in the Russian Verb

JOHN E. ALLEN III

Two abiding interests of Professor Boris O. Unbegaun during his scholarly career have been the broad area of Slavic morphology generally and the place of Old Church Slavonic in modern standard Russian. The present paper, in his honor, describes an area that spans both these interests.

The inventory of Old Church Slavonic and Church Slavonic (hereafter OCS and CS) elements in Russian (R) has been a major topic of Slavic linguistics since the beginnings of such research.

Within the R verb system, there are a number of items that can be designated "recognizable" CS elements that may be listed apart from normal R verbs. The basis for the "recognizability" is morphological in that certain verbs manifest a type of consonantal alternation distinct from R norms.

Typically, in R verbs, a stem final *t* or *d* in the perfective infinitive alternates with *č* or *ž*, respectively, in the imperfective infinitive. In CS verbs with the suffix *-a-*, however, the alternation takes a recognizably different shape:

PERFECTIVE	IMPERFECTIVE	
—*t* (R and CS)	—*č* (R)	—*šč* (CS)
—*d* (R and CS)	—*ž* (R)	—*žd* (CS)

Compare, for example,

	PERFECTIVE		IMPERFECTIVE	
R	dopla*t*ít'	:	doplá*č*ivat'	(Suffix: *-iva-*)
CS	vozvra*t*ít'	:	vozvra*šč*át'	(Suffix: *-a-*)
R	prilá*d*it'	:	prilá*ž*ivat'	
CS	utver*d*ít'	:	utver*žd*át'	

I

A verb such as *nuždát'sja* would not be listed by us here in its unprefixed form since it does not have a contrasting perfective formation **núdit'sja* to give it recognizability. The presense of the cluster *-žd-* is not *per se* evidence of OCS or CS origin (cf. *podoždát'*, etc.). In prefixed formations, however, such pairs as *prinuždát'—prinúdit'* are normal and may be considered recognizably CS.

Shevelov points out that there are many cases in modern Russian where a single root has both R and CS morphological features, usually with different prefixes.[1] For example,

R   proglotít' : proglátyvat'
CS   poglotít'   : pogloscát'

Shevelov makes the important observation that the aspect-forming suffix of the imperfective is the key to the delineation of the two types of alternation. Speaking of the consonantal alternation between the infinitive and the 1st person singular present tense of the perfective verb, Shevelov states:

> In Wirklichkeit liegt der Schlüssel im imperfektiven Aspekt.
> Die Verba auf *-it'*, die den unvollendeten Aspekt mit dem
> Suffix *-a-* bilden, haben *šč* in allen vier obenerwähnten
> Formen; nicht ein Verb, das den imperfektiven Aspekt mit
> dem Suffix *-iva-* bildet, hat *šč* in irgendeiner Form. Vgl.
> *progloču—proglatyvat'* neben *pogloščú—pogloščat'* ... (p. 100).

Shevelov presents a list of seventeen roots which follow the *t:šč* type of alternation with various prefixes. The roots are: *-bogatít'*, *-glotít'*, *-kratít'*, *-krotít'*, *mutít'*, *-plotít'*, *-pretít'*, *-rabotít'*, *-ščitít'*, *-ščutít'*, *setít'*, *svetít'*, *svjatít'*, *-sýtit'*, *-tjagotít'*, *-vratít'*, and *-xitít'*.[2]

Shevelov points out that all but three of the above listed roots are used only with prefixes, and all but two have suffix stress. He also shows that the three roots which may occur without prefixes (*mutít'*, *svetít'*, and *svjatít'*) may, when used without prefixes, have only the normal R alternation *t* : *č* (*mučú*, *svečú*, and *svjačú*) and that the two formations with root stress (*nasýtit'* and *poxítit'*) can probably be shown to have secondary stress from original suffix stress (cf. *vosxitít'* and semantically differentiated *sytít'*). Shevelov continues by asking the obvious question; are there any verbs in—*tít'* that do not have the *t* : *šč* alternation? His answer is, only three, *otvétit'*, (*za*)*métit'*, and *vstrétit'* (p. 101).

Our own evidence, below, does not contradict Shevelov, but it is possible for us to find a slightly differentiated formulation which will reduce the exceptional forms to two or zero.

Shevelov has shown that the stress position in these verbs is (or can be reconstructed as) suffixial. If we add this criterion to a rule, then *otvétit'*, *(za)métit'*, and *vstrétit'* would be automatically excluded by virtue of their root stress. The difference between two or zero has to do with the status of *nasýtit'* and *poxítit'*; these two verbs are exceptional in R only synchronically, diachronically they will fit the rule via their reconstructable stress position.

Therefore, if we reformulate Shevelov's rule to include stress position, we can make the statement that perfective verbs in *-tit'* with prefixes always have the *t : šč* alternation when the imperfective suffix is *-a-*; verbs in *-tit'* without prefixes and verbs in *-tit'* with or without prefixes, have only the *t : č* alternation, regardless of imperfective suffix.

The situation with *d : žd* is more complicated. Shevelov presents a list of nineteen roots which follow the *d : žd* type of alternation, with various prefixes. The roots are: *-bedit'*, *bludit'(sja)*, *budit'*, *-čredit'*, *čudit'*, *godit'*, *-gradit'*, *núdit'*, *-predit'*, *rodit'*, *sadit'*, *-sladit'*, *sudit'*, *-svobodit'*, *-trudit'*, *tverdit'*, *vodit'*, *vredit'*, and *xladit'* (pp. 103–104).[3]

If we attempt to apply the same distinctive criteria here that we did for the *t : šč* type, we find that at least ten of the roots may be used without prefixes (*budit'*, *godit'sja*, etc.); we also find that one verb, *prinúdit'*, has root stress, but it is not possible here to show convincingly that the original stress position was **prinudít'*. Also, there are at least ten roots (Shevelov's figure) with prefixes and suffix stress that do *not* show the *d : žd* type alternation. Shevelov states:

> Die Gesetzmäßigkeiten der negativen Ordnung—d.h. welche Verben nicht *žd* haben können—sind hier dieselben, wie auch im Falle *šč*. Alle präfigierten Verben, die den imperfektiven Aspekt mit dem Suffix *-iva-* oder überhaupt nicht bilden, alternieren ihr *d* nicht mit *žd*. Beispiele für die ersteren mögen sein: *pogládit'*—*pogláživat'* .... Die Schwierigkeit liegt jedoch darin, daß es eine ziemlich erhebliche Menge von Verben gibt, die allen oben aufgestellten Bedingungen für die Alternation *d : : žd* entsprechen und dennoch *d* und *ž* alternieren.... *snabdit'* ....*snabžát'* [etc.] (p. 104).

The basis for our own studies was a computerized sample of 1,356,528 Russian words in sentences, selected in equal proportions from the periods 1860–1870 and 1950–1960. The size and orientation of the sample permitted characterization of the situation of this verbal area and several others in synchronic slices one hundred years apart and a comparison of the dynamics of the category over the one-hundred-year time span.

Summarizing a large body of detailed statistical information, we may say that, despite the large body of evidence our study found no examples of roots with the *t* : *šč* or *d* : *žd* alternations not already listed by Shevelov. On the other hand, we were able to add a number of prefixes that are used with the various roots.

The basic information for the CS type alternations may be found in four places in the R paradigms: 1) the past passive participle; 2) the 1st person singular present perfective; 3) the deverbal substantive; and 4) the entire imperfective paradigm. (In the case of the *d* : *žd* type, the *žd* expected in the 1st person singular present perfective has been uniformly replaced by normal R *ž*). Our evidence consisted solely of the verbal information. Accordingly the deverbal substantive was not considered for either type.

The following summary list presents the attestations of imperfective verbs with *šč* and *žd* in our two time periods.

ROOT (WITH PREFIXES)	1950–60	1860–70
t : *šč*		
-bogaščát'sja		
o-	5	2
-gloščát'sja		
po-	2	4
-kraščát'(sja)		
pre-	11	5
so-	6	2
-kroščát'		
u-	1	2
-muščát'(sja)		
s-	12	13
voz-	3	7
-ploščát'(sja)		
vo-	5	1
-preščát'(sja)		
vos-	1	1
za-	—	11
-ščiščát'(sja)		
za-	16	27
-ščuščát'(sja)		
o-	22	4
-seščát'		
po-	3	16

ROOT (WITH PREFIXES)	1950–60	1860–70
-sveščát'(sja)		
o-	16	4
-svjaščát'(sja)		
o-	1	1
po-	10	6
-tjagoščát'		
o-	—	2
-vraščát'(sja)		
iz-	1	—
ob-[4]	57	105
ot-	1	3
pre-	19	9
raz-	1	1
voz-	64	51
-xiščát'(sja)		
po-	1	1
vos-	4	7

$$d : žd$$

	1950–60	1860–70
-beždát'		
po-	8	3
predu-	—	1
u-	13	13
-bluždát'(sja)		
za-	3	3
-buždát'(sja)		
po-	4	2
pro-	5	6
voz-	5	16
-čreždát'(sja)		
u-	—	1
-čuždát'(sja)		
ot-	—	1
-goždát'		
u-	1	4
-graždát'(sja)		
na-	2	4
o-	1	2
vozna-	2	6
za-	—	1

ROOT (WITH PREFIXES)	1950–60	1860–70
-nuždát'(sja)		
po-	—	3
pri	3	8
vy-	2	—
-preždát'		
predu-	9	13
u-	1	1
-roždát'(sja)		
na-	—	1
pere-	—	1
po-	8	3
voz-	1	1
vy-	1	—
za-	1	4
-saždát'(sja)		
o-	1	2
-slaždát'(sja)		
na-	7	15
u-	—	4
-suždát'(sja)		
o-	4	5
ob-	18	2
poras-	—	1
predo-	—	1
pri-	1	—
ras-	13	38
-svoboždát'(sja)		
o-	11	3
-truždát'(sja)		
u-	1	2
-tveoždát'(sja)		
pod-	7	8
u-	1	2
-voždát'(sja)		
sopro-	13	15
pro-	—	1
-vreždát'		
po-	—	1
-xlaždát'(sja)		
o-	1	3
pro-	—	1

There are a number of prefixed formations that are attested in the 1860–1870 sub-set that are not attested in the 1950–1960 sub-set. To ascertain the vitality (or lack thereof) of such forms in the contemporary language, we checked four sources for each formation. These sources were the *Academy Dictionary*, Avanesov-Ožegov, Ožegov, and Ožegov-Šapiro.[5] The specific items are (order follows above lists): *zapreščát'(sja)*, *otjagoščát*, *predubežát'*, *učreždát'*, *otčuždát'sja*, *zagraždát'*, *ponuždát'(sja)*, *naroždát'sja*, *pereroždát'sja*, *uslaždát(sja)*, *porassuždát'*, *provoždát'*, *proxlaždát'sja*.

All the forms listed are admitted by all four sources in standard usage with the following specific exceptions:

1) *predubeždát'*—is not listed in any of the sources in verbal form; Avanesov-Ožegov lists the participle *predubeždénnyj* but does not distinguish it from adjectival listings. We checked the Ušakov dictionary to determine if the formation was admitted during the middle portion of the hundred-year time span we considered; the formation is listed but annotated "bookish—antiquated." We can safely assume that this formation has lost all verbal vitality in the contemporary language.[6]

2) *predosuždát'*—is not listed in any of the sources. The formation is listed in the Greve and Kroesche dictionary (IV, 221) but this source is not the most reliable since it neither annotates nor dates its entries.[7]

3) *provoždát'*—is not listed by any of the modern sources. As early as 1935, Ušakov lists the imperfective formation corresponding to perfective *provodít'* only as *provožát'*.

Since, with our large corpus, it was possible to expand Shevelov's list of prefixed formations, we may take note of formations found by us not listed by Shevelov and vice versa. Not attested in the present sample but cited by Shevelov are: *poraboščát'*, *nasyščát'*, *pregraždát'*, *dosaždát'*, and *nasaždát'*. All five formations were checked in the four named sources and all are admitted in normal usage except that Ožegov considers *poraboščát'* "high."

Items attested in our corpus but not listed by Shevelov are: *izvraščát'*, *otvraščát'*, *posvjaščát'*, *pobuždát'*, *vozbuždát'(sja)*, *vynuždát'*, *upreždát'*, *vyroždát'sja*, *zaroždát'sja*, *osaždát'*, *obsuždát'(sja)*, *prisuždát'*, *rassuždát'*, *podtverždát'(sja)*.

In summary, considering the large size of our sample, it seems safe to say that Shevelov's list of roots is exhaustive. While we have expanded the list of possible prefixations on these roots, we do not suggest that our list exhausts such prefixations.

The following facts are clear. Only those verbs that have the imperfective suffix -*a*- may have the *šč* and *žd* corresponding to perfective *t* and *d*. Conversely, any verb with imperfective *šč* and *žd* and any other suffix but -*a*- will not have a corresponding *t* or *d* in the perfective. Further, Shevelov's rule, as reformulated herein, can eliminate the *t* : *šč* category as a fluid area since it can be defined by an unambiguous rule.

Unfortunately, we are not able to improve the characterization of the *d* : *žd* group. Shevelov himself gives a list of ten verb formations, all prefixed perfectives and all but one with suffix stress, that have perfective—*dít'* and imperfective—*žat'*. We may add to this list the verbal pair *provožát'*—*provodít'*. This formation is attested once in the 1860–1870 period in the form *provoždát'* and eighteen times in the form *provožát'*. The 1950–1960 period has thirty-three attestations, all *provožát'*. This is quite interesting because if a verb of this CS type is to be "Russianized," we could expect that not only the morphophonemic consonantal alternation but also the aspect-forming suffix would be affected, yielding a formation **prováživat'* (cf. *výprovodit'*—*vyprováživat'*). Such, however, is not the case.

The anomalous position of *provožát'* can be seem most clearly when contrasted with purely CS and R type formations:

	IMPERFECTIVE	PERFECTIVE
CS	soprovož*dát'*	soprovo*dít'*
	provož*át'*	provo*dít'*
R	vyprová*živat'*	výprovo*dit'*

The nineteen roots that have the *d* : *žd* were considered at length from many points of view, not excluding the semantic. In the final analysis, however, it is necessary to agree with Shevelov that there seems to be no criterion or set of criteria whereby the *d* : *žd* vs. *d* : *ž* types can be delineated by exhaustive rule.

New York University

NOTES

1. A. Šaxmatov and G. Y. Shevelov, *Die kirchenslavischen Elemente in der modernen russischen Literatursprache* (Wiesbaden, 1960), pp. 100 ff. All page references, *ibid*.

2. The hyphen before the root indicates 'only with prefixes'; note the two stresses in -*xítít'* and compare *poxítit'* and *vosxítít'*.

3. The (*sja*) reflexive suffix is listed with *bludít'* because Shevelov gives *only* a reflexive example. In principle, nearly all of these roots, and those of the preceding list (*t* : *šč*), can be reflexive with a given prefix.

4. In the form *obraščát'sja* with morphophonemic loss of root-initial *v*.

5. *Academy Dictionary* — V. I.Černy-šev, *et al, Slovar' sovremennogo russkogo literaturnogo jazyka* ([Moscow—Leningrad, 1950] only complete through letter S at the time the original materials were compiled); R. I. Avanesov and S. I. Ožegov, *Russkoe literaturnoe proiznošenie i udarenie* (Moscow, 1955, 1959, 1960); S. I. Ožegov, *Slovar' russkogo jazyka* (Moscow, 1949); S. I. Ožegov, and A. B. Šapiro (eds.), *Orfografičeskij slovar' russkogo jazyka* (fourth ed.; Moscow, 1957).

6. D. N. Ušakov (ed.), *Tolkovyj slovar' russkogo jazyka* (4 vols.; reprint of 1935 ed.; Moscow, 1947).

7. R. Greve and B. Kroesche, *Russisches rückläufiges Wörterbuch* (6 vols.; Wiesbaden, 1957–59).

A Note on the Indeclinable Nouns of Modern Czech

ROBERT AUTY

In 1947 BORIS UNBEGAUN published an admirable study on the indeclinable nouns of Russian,[1] a subject which, as he rightly noted, is
rather neglected by descriptive grammars of that language. At the end
of his article he briefly compared the facts of Russian with the
situation in the other Slavonic languages, notably Serbocroatian,
Bulgarian, Czech, Polish, and Ukrainian. Noting that Russian, at one
extreme, tends to resist the assimilation of foreign loanwords to the
native inflexional system, while Serbocroatian, at the other, encourages
the greatest possible degree of assimilation, he observed that Czech,
while on the whole closer to Serbocroatian in this respect, nevertheless
occupies something of an intermediary position between the two poles.
The present article aims to supplement Unbegaun's remarks about the
indeclinable nouns of Czech; it is based on an examination of all the
nouns indicated as indeclinable in the official Czech orthoepic manual
Pravidla českého pravopisu (Prague, 1957). The word-list of this work
contains approximately 230 nouns designated as indeclinable. In about
twenty cases, declinable forms are given as existing side by side with
the indeclinable ones.[2]

Unbegaun's remarks dealt mainly with loanwords ending in a vowel.
On the whole the characteristics and tendencies he noted in 1947
are confirmed by the current *Pravidla*. Thus nouns in *-o* enter the
native o- stem paradigm. It is noteworthy that there is some uncertainty in the classification of French loans in [-o] (orthographi-
cally *-eau, -ot*, etc.) While the indeclinable *byró, roló, rondó, tabló* are
given as the most usual forms, the declinable alternatives *byro,*[3] *rolo,
rondo, tablo* are also listed. Moreover, while the *Pravidla* list only
ševró (from *chevreau*) the *Slovník spisovného jazyka českého* [*SSJČ*]

(III, Prague, 1966) lists also the colloquial form *ševro*. While this may indicate a tendency toward the assimilation of this class to the native inflexional system the strength of the indeclinable *-ó* model is shown by the fact that, while the *Příruční slovník jazyka českého* [*PSJČ*] (VIII, Prague, 1955–1957) shows only. *žabot*, gen. *žabotu* the current *Pravidla* show only the indeclinable *žabó*.[4]

Nouns in *-i* still seem to follow the pattern recorded by Unbegaun. Animates are assimilated to the adjectival declension (*dandy*, gen. *dandyho*, *kuli*, gen. *kuliho*[5]), while inanimates remain indeclinable (*alibi*, *Bari*, *Gori*, *khaki*, *Nairobi*, etc.[6]). Nouns in *-u*, as noted by Unbegaun, remain declinable, with genitives in *-ua*, e.g., *kakadu*, gen. *kakadua*, *marabu*, gen. *marabua*. Nouns in *-é* are still indeclinable (*kliše*, *nargilé*).[7] Nouns in *-e* may be declined, but the instability of the present situation seems to be shown by the fact that for *aloe* the *Pravidla* gives the indeclinable form as the more common, but for *kánoe* (*kanoe*) the declinable feminine form with gen. *kánoe*.

"Il va de soi," Unbegaun wrote, "que des monosyllabes, comme *gnu*, ou des noms de notes (*do*, *re*, *mi*, etc.) ne sont pas fléchis ...''; and this remains true. In this connection we may note the curiosity that the Russian loanword *ščí*, for which one might reasonably predict gen. **ščí*, dat, **ščím*, etc., is nevertheless too exotic to enter the native inflexional system and remains indeclinable.

We may add a few notes on some classes of words not dealt with by Unbegaun. Very striking is the fact that a number of foreign place-names ending in a consonant are not assimilated to the masculine *o*-stems and remain indeclinable. Among these are *Cannes*,[8] *Göttingen*, *Lausanne*, *Los Angeles*, *Marseille*. There seems no obvious reason why these words should not be assimilated in the same way as *Lyon*, gen. *Lyonu*, *Manchester*, gen. *Manchestru*, *New York*, gen. *New Yorku*. In the case of *Cannes* the unfamilar orthography, making it uncertain whether the genitive should be pronounced [kanu] or]kanzu] has perhaps helped to resist the process of assimilation. It is possible that the presence of a native, albeit obsolescent, form *Gotinky* has tended to define *Göttingen* as in all respects a foreign word and thus indeclinable.[9] It is, however, legitimate to surmise that in words of this kind we have an indication of an extension of the area of indeclinability similar to, and possibly even influenced by, the situation in Russian. Some common nouns of this type are also listed as indeclinable, e.g., *imprimatur*, *exequatur*, *placet*, *rekviem*. All these are technical or learned words; and it may be that, in the first three cases, consciousness of their verbal origin has helped them to resist inflexion.

A new class of indeclinable neuter noun has been introduced to the written language as a result of the tendency toward phonetic spelling of foreign words which characterizes the orthoepic recommendations of the 1957 *Pravidla*—that of nouns in *-má*, representing French nouns in *-ment*. The *Pravidla* lists the following: *abonmá, angažmá, apartmá, aranžmá, etablismá, reglamá*, all of them except the last with declinable alternatives in *-ment*, gen. *mentu* [mánu]. *gouvernement*, however, appears only in the form *gouvernement*, either indeclinable or with gen. *-mentu*. It seems probable that the indeclinable forms will here ultimately oust the inflected ones.

A rather heterogeneous class of nouns is that of the neuters in *-a*. Greek loanwords such as *dogma, drama, klima, schéma* decline with genitive in *-atu*, etc. According to B. Havránek and A. Jedlička, *revma* is the only noun of this class which is normally indeclinable.[10] Nevertheless, the *Pravidla* of 1957 list both *aróma* and *fantasma* as more usually indeclinable though existing also in the alternative declinable form with genitive in *-atu*. It is perhaps not without significance that the *Pravidla* of 1924, while agreeing with those of 1957 over *aróma* (then spelt *aroma*) give *fantasma* exclusively in the declinable form. In addition to these words of Greek origin, a number of other foreign loanwords, of varied provenance, have resisted assimilation to the *a*-stem declension. We find, for instance, *alinea, gala, havana, hosana, kuba, malaga, moka, panama*.[11] No doubt most of these words are either learned or of recent origin. It is at first sight surprising to see here the familiar *moka*, and to note that while *malaga* is an indeclinable neuter, the no less exotic *madeira* is a regular *a*-stem feminine. In both these cases it may be that resistance to the introduction of a new root with velar termination, implying dative/locative forms *malaze, *moce, has helped to retain them in the class of indeclinables.

The examples that have been discussed would seem to justify the belief that modern Czech shows a slightly greater tendency to retain loanwords in an unmodified form than was the case in the nineteenth and early twentieth century. If this is so, it is no doubt a sign of the "Europeanization" of the Czech literary language under the influence of what Unbegaun called "ses contacts suivis avec le monde occidental," but also of the more intimate contacts with Russian which have marked the history of Czech in recent times.

The present article has made no attempt to assess the degree to which the usage reflected in, or recommended by, the *Pravidla* represents the usage of educated conversation (*hovorová čeština*). The writer would be surprised if the tendencies toward assimilation were not greater in the spoken language than in the written standard. Nevertheless, it is clear that the situation is unstable, and it is to be hoped that the intensified study of all varieties of Czech speech that is being carried out in Czechoslovakia will eventually provide us with the material on which a more detailed and accurate picture of the state and tendencies of the present-day language can be built up, both in the sphere that has been touched on in the present article and in many others.

Oxford

NOTES

1. B. O. Unbegaun, "Les substantifs indéclinables en russe," *Revue des études slaves*, XXIII (1947), 130–45.

2. As the excerption has been done by the methods of the pre-computer age, only approximate accuracy can be claimed for the figures given.

3. B. Havránek and A. Jedlička, *Česká mluvnice* (Prague, 1963), p. 172, state: "Nová podoba *byro*, která se v češtině skloňuje, je podporována i vlivem ruštiny." It is difficult to understand this remark. Russian *bjuro* is indeclinable, and one would have expected its influence to work against the assimilation of *byro* to the Czech inflexional system.

4. No doubt the length of the final -ó results from the reinterpretation of the final stress (impossible in Czech) as quantity. I am indebted to Professor G. Y. Shevelov for this suggestion.

5. F. Trávníček, *Mluvnice spisovné češtiny*, I (Prague, 1948), 510, notes *kuli* as indeclinable.

6. The word *gummi*, cited by Unbegaun (*op. cit.*, p. 142), seems to have been wholly replaced by the declinable feminine form *guma*. *PSJČ* characterizes it as "little used"; *SSJČ* does not list it at all.

7. There seems to be no trace in the present-day language of assimilated forms such as the gen. pl. *klišat* (*clichat*) noted by Unbegaun in Machar (*op. cit.*, p. 142).

8. Cf. "V Cannes bez nás," "filmový festival v Cannes," etc. in *Literární noviny*, XVI, No. 20 (20 May 1967), 8.

9. I recently heard an educated Czech use the form *v Göttingách*, thus clearly indicating that the German word is felt as a plural. It may be that this is also true of *Cannes* and *Los Angeles*: in these cases the singular declension is inhibited, but assimilation to the plural pattern has not yet taken place.

10. *Op. cit.*, p. 169.

11. In the sense of 'panama hat'; in certain other senses this word is declinable.

The Adjective and Pronoun Systems of Bulgarian

CHARLES E. BIDWELL

1.0 The Adjective.

1.1 Adjectives are inflected to agree with their phrase head in number and, in the singular, in terms of gender. In the plural of the adjective the category of gender is neutralized.[1] Adjectives show the following endings:

SINGULAR			PLURAL
masc.	*neuter*	*fem.*	
Ø ~ -i	-o (~ -e)	-a	-i (-e only in *tezi*, etc.)

The neuter ending -e occurs in adjectives with the suffix -*j*-, preferred in those where the suffix is realized as /j/, optionally in those where it is realized as substitutive softening of the stem.[2] It also occurs optionally in some other adjectives, particularly those with stems in /š/. Thus,

m. kózi	*f.* kózja	*n.* kóze *or* kózjo	'of a goat' (cf. *kozá* 'goat')
vráži	vráža	vrážo *or* vráže	'hostile' (cf. *vrág* 'enemy')
bífš	bífša	bífšo *or* bífše	'former'
or bífši			

In the masculine singular, the typical distribution of endings, except in vocative phrases, is occurrence of zero when no article is attached and of the extended ending -*i* in the presence of the enclitic article.[3] In vocative phrases the extended ending -*i* is usual, though the article does not occur: *míli bráte* 'dear brother.' In set phrases as *velíki četvártək* 'Holy Thursday' and place-names as *béli lóm* (literally 'White Lom') the extended ending *-i* may occur. However, there are adjectives which always show *-i*, notably with the suffixes *-sk-* (*žénski* 'feminine') and *-j-* (cf. *kózi, vráži* above) and loans (from Russian) with *-ov-* plus stressed ending (*polkoví* 'regimental'). A few others such as *bífš, bífši* 'former,' and *svét, svetí* 'holy' show free alternation Ø ∼ *i* in the absence of the article.

There are also adjectives which never show the extended ending *-i*. Such are: the possessives *mój* 'my,' *tvój* 'thy,' *svój* 'one's own,' and adjectives which are never articulated, such as *tája* and *ónja* 'that,' *kój* 'which,' *takáv* 'such,' *kakáv* 'what kind,' etc.

1.2 Bulgarian grammarians cite two kinds of adjectives (both loanwords from Turkish) which do not show the above distribution of endings. One type consists of undeclined stems: *serbéz* 'daring,' *tazé* 'fresh,' *safí* 'pure,' while the other has the stem-suffix *-lij-* and the endings *-a* (singular, all genders) and *-i* (plural): *dertlíja* 'afflicted,' *kibritlíja* 'violent tempered,' *zavalíja* 'wretched,' *kəsmetlíja* 'lucky.' It is questionable whether these are adjectives; in terms of syntactic function it might be better to class them as a special set of nouns, usually occuring in apposition (*kibritlíja čovék* 'a hot-tempered man') or more rarely as phrase heads (*šte e begál zavalíjata* 'He will have fled, the wretch'). Morphologically the latter type is identical with such *a/i* type nouns as *juzbašíja* '(Turkish) captain.'

1.3 Stem modifications of the adjective. The phonemic shape of the adjective is, of course, subject to all the phonotactic constraints of the language and to all automatic morphophonemic changes resulting therefrom. These include, in addition to those mentioned in note 1, loss of /j/ before front vowel (cf. above *kózj-a*, but *kóz-e, kóz-i*). Certain non-automatic changes also occur. Metathesis of šwa and liquid is rare (RəC$_{\#}^C$ ∼ əRCV; cf. *práv* ∼ *párvi* 'first'). The alternation represented by the morphophoneme ᴇ (/ja/ under stress and not followed by /š ž č j/ or a syllable containing front vowel is replaced by *e* when either of those conditions is not met) is widespread (*bjál, bjálo, bjála*, but *béli* 'white').

Alternation of vowel and zero.[4] Stems terminating in consonant cluster (when followed by a vocalic ending) usually intercalate a vowel before the final consonant when followed by a zero ending. The vowels are *ə* (always inserted before final /l r m v/ and before suffixal /k/), *e* (typically before suffixal or non-suffixal /n/), and *i* (two examples only: *nej(i)n-* 'her' and *ed(i)n-* 'one'; note that the vowel /i/ also occurs in the articulated form of the latter, *edínijət*):

dobór, dobrá   'good'
dólǝg, dólga   'long'
bístǝr, bístra   'clear'
slábičǝk, slábička   'weakish'
pólen, pólna   'full'
čéren, čérna   'black'
zémen, zémna   'earthen'
néin, néjna   'her'

1.3.1 Stress is fixed in all forms of the Bulgarian adjective; typically as stem stress, rarely as ending stress. Ending stress, of course, automatically shifts to the final stem syllable in the event the ending is zero. Examples follow; stem stress: *kózi, brátov, bjál, bístǝr*; ending stress: *polkoví, sveti* ~ *svét svetá, dobór dobrá, kój kojá*.

1.4 A special subclass of adjectives is constituted by the deictics, which include *tózi* 'this,' *ónzi* 'that,' *takóv* 'such,' *onakóv* 'that kind,' *kój* 'which,' *kakóv* 'what kind,' *fsíčki* 'all,' *fséki* 'every,' and some others, plus the article, which is an enclitic deictic adjective.[5] Beside the article, some of these, namely *tója, tóz(i)* 'this'; *ónja, ónzi* 'that,' have irregular forms, as listed below. These are formed on the stems *t-* and *on-* followed by partially irregular endings and terminated by the postfixes *-ja* (~ *-j* after neuter ending *-u*) and *-zi* (~ *-va* after neuter *-o*). Final /i/ of *-zi* is often elided after vowel.[6]

	POSTFIX *-zi* ~ *-vá*		POSTFIX *-ja* ~ *-j*	
masculine	tóz(i)	ónzi	tója	ónja
neuter	tová	onová	túj	onúj
feminine	táz(i)	onáz(i)	tája	onája
plural	téz(i)	onéz(i)	tíja	oníja

The deictics *takóv* and *onakóv* have the stems *t-ak-(ǝ)v-* and *on-ak-(ǝ)v-* plus zero ending in the masculine form (cf. *k-ak-(ǝ)v-* in *kakóv, kakvó, kakvá*) and *t-ak-* and *on-ak-* plus ending and postfix *-va* in the remaining forms (cf. n. *takóva*, f. *takáva*, pl. *takíva*).

1.4.1 The forms of the article are as follows:
(a) *(j)ǝ(t)* with initial /j/ after the masculine adjective ending *-i*; without initial /j/ after zero ending of the masculine adjective and noun. Occurrence or absence of final /t/ varies freely in colloquial speech.
(b) *-ta* after the ending *-a* of whatever gender or number and after zero ending of feminine singular nouns; also after numerals ending in *a*.

(c) *-to* after neuter singular nouns of whatever ending and after the ending *-o* or *-e* of whatever gender in the singular.

(d) *-te* after the plural endings *-i*, *-e*; after numerals not ending in *a*.

2.0 The Pronoun.

The pronoun in Bulgarian is the only form class which retains in the current spoken language a distinction of oblique cases (accusative and dative) *vs.* nominative.[7] The oblique forms of the personal pronoun occur in both full (accented) and short (enclitic) forms. The third person singular pronoun distinguishes the three genders. In the reflexive pronoun the categories of person and number are neutralized. The remaining personal pronouns distinguish only number, person, and case. Beside the personal pronouns, the only pronouns properly speaking are the animate interrogative *kój* 'who' and its affixed derivatives *njákoj* 'someone,' *níkoj* 'no one,' *fsjákoj* 'everyone.'[8] The inanimate interrogative *štó* 'what' is indeclinable and not of frequent occurrence, being usually replaced by the neuter singular of the interrogative adjective *kakǝ́v*, namely *kakvó*. The forms of the remaining pronouns are given in the table below.

PRONOUNS

person	SINGULAR				reflexive		PLURAL			
	1st		2nd				1st		2nd	
	full	enclitic	full	encl.	full	encl.	full	encl.	full	encl.
nominative	ás	—	tí	—	—	—	níe	—	víe	—
accusative	{ mén(e)	me	{ téb(e)	te	{ sébe	se	nás	{ ni	vás	{ vi
dative	{	mi	{	ti	{	si	nám	{	vám	{

THIRD PERSON[9]	masc.		neuter		fem.		plural		animate
	full	encl.	full	encl.	full	encl.	full	encl.	*interrogative*
nominative	tój	—	tó	—	tjá	—	té	—	kój
accusative	négo	go			néja	ja	tjáx	gi	kogó
dative	nému	mu			néi	i	tjám	im	komú

In current usage, the stressed dative forms (including *komú*) are obsolete and replaced by the preposition *na* plus the appropriate stressed accusative form, as is the accusative *sébe* by the pronominal phrase *sébe si*. The variant accusative/dative forms of the first and second person singular pronoun without final *e* are characteristic of both colloquial and poetic style, but are absent in formal literary prose. Colloquial usage tends to replace *kogó* by *kój*, such a replacement, if consistent, would make *kój* indeclinable, like *štó*.

Normative handbooks also list oblique case forms for certain items that I have listed as adjectives, but these do not belong to the colloquial language. The dative forms in particular are archaic and obsolete in current language. For the sake of completeness I list them here:

NOMINATIVE	GENITIVE	DATIVE	
tózi	togózi, togóva	tomúzi	'this'
ónzi	onogózi, onogóva	onomúzi	'that'
drúg	drúgigo	drúgimu	'another'
edín	ednogó	ednomú	'one'

These above-listed oblique case forms occur only as phrase heads (not as attributes) and refer to masculine persons.

University of Pittsburgh

NOTES

1. The following sources were consulted in this study: F. Sławski, *Gramatyka języka bułgarskiego* (Warsaw, 1954); L. Andrejčin, N. Kostov, and E. Nikolov, *Bɔlgarski ezik* (Sofia, 1962); S. Stojanov, *Gramatika na bɔlgarskija knižoven ezik* (Sofia, 1964); A. Teodorov-Balan, *Nova Bɔlgarska gramatika* (Sofia, 1940); C. T. Hodge, *Bulgarian basic course* (Washington, 1961). All Bulgarian examples cited in the text are in quasi-morphophonemic transcription which does not indicate the following automatic morphophonemic changes: voicing assimilation, replacement of voiced by voiceless consonant before juncture, simplification of consonant clusters (including geminates) and replacement of low by high vowels in unstressed position. The phonemic analysis underlying the transcription is that used in my *Slavic historical phonology in tabular form* (Pittsburgh, 1959; The Hague, 1963), pp. 20–21.

2. The suffix *-j-*, indicating appurtenance, is realized as substitutive softening of stem-final velars and /c/ (i.e., /k→č, g→ž, x→š, c→č/), and addition of /j/ elsewhere.

3. Some writers refer to the articulated adjective or noun as the "definite" form of adjective or noun. This however is not quite correct. Definiteness versus indefiniteness is not a category pertaining to the individual noun or adjective, but to the noun phrase, and is signalled by the presence of the article, an enclitic deictic, which normally occurs but once in a phrase and is appended to

the first stressed constituent of the phrase (see C. E. Bidwell, "Bulgarian syntax," 29:5–33 [1967] in *Linguistics*).

4. See H. Aronson "Vowel/zero alternations in the Bulgarian inflection," *SEEJ*, 6:34–8 (1962).

5. Interrogative words (including interrogative pronouns and adjectives) postfix the particle *-to* to form the respective relative word. Thus, *kakśv* 'what kind,' *kakśv-to*. See my "Bulgarian Syntax," 29:5–33 (1967) in *Linguistics*.

6. The forms *túj* and *onúj*, though colloquial, are considered slightly substandard.

7. I classify as adjectives many words traditionally classified as pronouns (e.g., the possessives *mój*, *číj*; the deictics, etc.). Word classes should be based on likeness of morphological form and syntactic function, and on this basis such items are to be classified as adjectives. Cf. G. H. Fairbanks's comment in reviewing Lunt's *Grammar of the Macedonian literary language* (*Language*, 30:127 [1954]).

8. More usual than *ſsjákoj* 'everyone' is *ſséki*, masculine of the adjective *ſsjak-*, which has the oblique forms, accusative *ſsékigo*, dative *ſsékimu*, analogous to those listed in the final paragraph below.

9. Alternate dialect forms for the nominative of the third person pronoun exist: m. *ón* n. *onó* f. *oná* pl. *oní*.

On Deep Structure and Loan Syntax in Slavic

HENRIK BIRNBAUM

IN ONE OF HIS EARLY essays, Boris Unbegaun sketched the foundations of a comparative study of loan translations (calques) encountered in the Slavic literary languages, classifying basic types, identifying fundamental problems, and suggesting potentially fruitful approaches to further detailed explorations on the basis of a sample list of pertinent items selected from various Slavic languages.[1] Following some of his suggestions, valuable contributions have been made to this field of lexical (including semantic as well as phraseological) innovation in several individual Slavic languages, thus preparing the ground for a comprehensive and thorough treatment of this complex phenomenon of linguistic borrowing and copying, bound to reveal some of the general principles and mechanisms underlying an important creative—or, rather, regenerative—aspect of language contact and bilingualism.[2] Another, kindred problem, namely that of loan syntax, remains, so far, more obscure as regards the basic principles governing this sort of function and structure transfer or imitation, in spite of the fact that a sizable amount of pertinent linguistic data, notably also from the Slavic field, has already been gathered and analyzed. The following remarks, contributed in honor of one of the outstanding authorities on the development of the Slavic literary languages, are offered here merely by way of comment on the margin of an ongoing discussion.

In its application to Slavic linguistic material, much of the theoretical discussion on loan syntax has in recent years centered around the "penetrability" of syntax, i.e., the degree of its susceptibility to the influence of foreign models. In addition, it has been pointed out that a clear-cut distinction must be made between two degrees of loan syntax: the mechanical transfer of syntactic functions characteristic of certain morphological categories (such as a case or tense form) to the nearest equivalent forms of the influenced language, these forms being originally altogether alien to such particular meanings; and, on the other hand, the mere activation of inherently latent or less-developed functions of certain forms under the impact of foreign patterns. The same applies, *mutatis mutandis*, also to grammatically well-formed word strings of various length and complexity, from the simplest, two-membered word combination (syntagm) to sentences of deep and multiple "embedding." As for the "penetrability" of syntax in comparison with other components or levels of language (phonology, morphology, vocabulary, etc.), some linguists—among them the present writer—have argued that syntax belongs to the most "penetrable" parts of linguistic structure while others, minimizing the mechanical function and syntagm-to-sentence transfer just mentioned, have taken the opposite view, maintaining that syntax is largely resistant, i.e., that it is a non-susceptible or only weakly susceptible domain of language.[3]

This discussion on the "penetrability" of syntactic structures may come into a somewhat different light if we introduce the notion of deep structure or, to be more exact, the distinction between surface and deep structure currently much emphasized in transformational-generative theory.[4] Put in terms of this (or some similar) distinction, it turns out to be more appropriate to speak about the (relative) stability (or its opposite, the instability) of syntax rather than about its "penetrability" (or "impenetrability"). When it comes specifically to loan syntax, it can be shown that in the surface structures of different origin (e.g., Slavic and non-Slavic, respectively) it may be quite feasible to single out syntactic foreignisms from such linguistically "mixed" structures. On the other hand, the underlying deep structure of two languages (with one of them syntactically influencing the other) may very well be roughly the same, especially if the two languages involved are genetically and/or typologically related.[5] This holds true even if "deep structure" is limited to the syntactic component proper (i.e., the base and transformational subcomponents), as is the case in transformational-generative theory, or, in other words, even without going still deeper and attempting to analyze also the semantic component of language in terms of a finite (and, indeed, fairly limited) set of invariant elements (which could perhaps be termed "semantic primes"), as has been more or less explicitly suggested in the so far only tentatively formulated linguistic theory of A. Bogusławski.[6] Thus the deep structure of loan syntax is often reducible to a model largely identical with, or at any rate not too different from, that which underlies the syntactic surface structure of the affected (primary) language.

In this specific sense, then, syntax (in its deep structure aspect) can actually be considered a fairly stable component of language also when viewed in the context of bilingualism and language intererfence.

As applied to a set of genetically related natural languages, one could therefore, for example, venture to say that much of the deep structure underlying the surface data of most if not all of the recorded ancient Indo-European languages displays a considerable degree of uniformity, thus suggesting a new, promising approach to the problem of reconstructing Proto-Indo-European syntax.[7] Similar considerations can be shown to apply, among other things, also to the syntactic relationship of Greek and Slavic, Greek loan syntax in Old Church Slavic (and, indirectly, in other literary Slavic languages, notably Russian) being a much, though still far from sufficiently investigated field of Slavic linguistics.[8]

It goes without saying that the methods of transformational-generative grammar can be applied to Old Church Slavic linguistic data only to a very limited extent. Thus, the primary criterion for determining "grammaticalness" or "well-formedness" resorted to in the theory of N. Chomsky and his followers, namely, intuition, applicable, in principle at least, to any currently spoken (i.e., directly observable) language, can clearly not be used for a strictly literary language which went out of use many centuries ago and which, even when used, seems to have reflected the structural properties of Slavic as actually spoken in the ninth through eleventh centuries primarily in Macedonia and Bulgaria only to a certain degree. As is well known, Old Church Slavic linguistic structure in other respects represents rather an artificial, imposed norm, largely patterned after foreign (Greek, Latin in the case of the *Kiev Leaflets*; indirectly also Semitic) models. Moreover, Old Church Slavic linguistic evidence cannot be conceived of as representing an "open text," i.e., an infinite set of well-formed sentences, but rather it must be considered a highly limited corpus of linguistic data, i.e., a "closed text," containing, incidentally, a great number of anacoluthically constructed or, in other words, ill-formed sentences. Yet it is this finite set of sentences that must serve as a basis for devising a generative (if incomplete) grammar of Old Church Slavic, capable of generating (or predicting) not only all actually encountered sentences of Old Church Slavic but also all potentially conceivable (though unattested) sentences of that language.[9] In this context we disregard, incidentally, the controversial issue of the extent to which Church Slavic texts of a somewhat later date (written after roughly A.D. 1100 but copied from earlier, strictly Old Church Slavic manuscripts) should be utilized for providing data to be accounted for in the framework of Old Church Slavic syntax, as many of those texts,

while displaying phonological, morphological and/or lexical features of
a specific, local, and more recent, nature, frequently, in terms of their
syntactic structure, in no way differ from that found in the classical
("canonical") Old Church Slavic texts. To give just a few examples,
this could apply to such texts as the extant copies of the Lives of
St. Cyril and St. Methodius (known also as the so-called Pannonian
legends), of the writings of John the Exarch (of Bulgaria), many
biblical texts (Gospels, Psalters, etc.), as well as a great number of
Church Slavic manuscripts of the *Sbornik* and *Izbornik* type.[10] Finally,
it is obvious that, given the scantiness of transmitted Old Church
Slavic linguistic data, the variants, though of limited range (allowing
for some actual verification of possible transformations in Old Church
Slavic), are of primary significance and will be instrumental for formu-
lating at least some fragmentary transformational rules in a (necessarily
incomplete) generative grammar of Old Church Slavic.[11]

Under the difficult, not to say adverse, circumstances indicated it
may seem legitimate to question whether a transformational-generative
approach to Old Church Slavic syntax, and in particular to the
specific problems of Greek loan syntax in the earliest Slavic writings,
is at all feasible. The recent study by Růžička, utilizing such an
approach, seems clearly to show that, in spite of the particular
difficulties, the application of this method is both possible and re-
warding. Thus, by applying a set of transformational rules, Růžička has
succeeded in establishing the underlying relationship among such Old
Church Slavic constructions as *accusativus cum infinitivo* (type: *vy
že kogo mę g[lago]lete byti*, translating the Greek τίνα με λέγετε
εἶναι, Matth. XVI. 15, *Zogr.*), *accusativus cum participio* (type: *is
že ěko viдě jǫ plačǫštǫ sę* for Greek Ἰησοῦς οὖν ὡς εἶδεν αὐτὴν
κλαίουσαν, J XI. 33), and the frequent rendering of Greek *accusativus
cum infinitivo* constructions by Slavic *dativus cum infinitivo* phrases
(type: ... *gl[agolj]ǫšte vъskrešenьju ne byti*, Greek ... λέγοντες ἀνά-
στασιν μὴ εἶναι, Lk XX. 27, *Zogr.*). Various degrees of "grammaticalness," essential for defining the very notion of loan syntax (as
well as loan semantics), can thus be set up. Semantic connotations
(e.g., of modality), found in some of these constructions when used
independently and according to the rules of Slavic syntax (e.g., in
the dative-infinitive phrase), are frequently lost in the process of
embedding, patterned after Greek models, and so forth.[12] Likewise,
the *dativus absolutus* construction—implying such transformations of
the deep structure as $\text{Nom}_{\text{subj}} \Rightarrow \text{Dat}_{\text{subj}}$ and $\text{Vb}_{\text{fin}} \Rightarrow \text{Part}_{\text{pred}}$—
can be considered a grammatical variation of the corresponding
transformation underlying the *genetivus absolutus* construction
($\text{Nom}_{\text{subj}} \Rightarrow \text{Gen}_{\text{subj}}$, etc.) of Greek (cf., e.g., *i prišedъšemъ imъ* for Greek

καὶ ἐλθόντων αὐτῶν, Matth. XVII. 14, *Mar.*). On the other hand, it does occasionally occur that a Greek absolute genitive construction is slavishly rendered in Old Church Slavic by means of the same (genitive) construction (e.g., *vrěmene zovǫšta*, Greek καιροῦ προσκαλοῦντος, *Supr.* 332. 21–22), which must be considered a violation even of the "mixed" syntax of Old Church Slavic, i.e., of the syntactic rules as extended to include those of Greek loan syntax.[13] This is not the place to elaborate any further on the usefulness of a transformational-generative approach to phenomena subsumable under Greek loan syntax in Old Church Slavic; yet, at the same time, it may also by appropriate to voice a word of warning against any exaggerated expectations with regard to the results of this method as applied to Old Church Slavic linguistic data.[14]

There is still another aspect of loan syntax, applicable also to Slavic, which, although frequently overlooked, covers some items of particular interest. I am referring to the three-language relationship by which a particular syntactic usage or construction can be carried over from one language to another by way of an intervening language. Examples of phenomena of this sort can be found in Old Church Slavic where some of the syntactic foreignisms can be traced to Semitic (Hebrew or Aramaic) origins, with Greek—primarily the Greek language of the Septuagint—as the mediating vehicle. A few such "pseudo-Grecisms" of Old Church Slavic syntax were briefly mentioned in an earlier study of mine: the use of perfective presents for the imperative in quotations from the Old Testament, rendering Greek future tense forms which, in turn, were used to translate Hebrew jussive forms; the preference for progressive periphrases by means of a form of the copula verb and the present participle, to indicate durative mode of action; and the nearly delexicalized use of the verb for 'begin' as an auxiliary.[15]

On the other hand, there are also examples of Hebraisms in Slavic which may have entered the language of later Bible translations directly from Hebrew without passing through the medium of Greek (although such syntactic foreignisms have sometimes been erroneously attributed to Greek influence). A case in point is the so-called *dativus auctoris* (a variety of the *dativus agentis*), i.e., constructions of the type *blagoslavenъ estъ gospodevi* (*blahoslovena ty hospodu*, etc.) occasionally found in East Slavic (Russian Church Slavic, early Ruthenian) Bible texts where the agent or originator is in the dative. In Greek the Indo-European ablative/instrumental (denoting, among other things, the point of departure and the means, respectively) had been syncretized with the dative which therefore regularly expresses also some of the functions originally characteristic of the ablative or the instrumental.

As a result, the Greek translators of the Hebrew *dativus auctoris* constructions (as the pertinent phrases with a prepositional *lamed* are
frequently termed) would simply use the dative capable of having the
very same connotation.[16] In Old Church Slavic such datives (as well as
the far more frequent equivalent prepositional phrases, usually ὑπό +
genitive) are rendered either by the instrumental or by an *otъ* phrase,
the distribution of these two ways of translation being governed by
specific rules.[17] The constructions of the type *blagoslovenъ gospodevi*
(*gospodu*) as encountered in Slavic Bible translations of a somewhat
more recent date which were at least partly made directly from
Hebrew (rather than from Greek or Latin) can be explained best if
they are considered imitations of Hebrew phrases of the type
bārūkh ladōnay (the prepositional *l-* being conceived as the dative
marker) and not necessarily as patterned after the corresponding
Greek dative phrase εὐλογητός (or εὐλογημένος) τῷ κυρίῳ or even its
occasional Latin counterpart *benedictus deo*.[18]

The case of Hebrew-Greek-Slavic syntactic structure "mixing," as
exemplified by the phenomena referred to in the preceding, is interesting also from a theoretical point of view. While a fragment of "mixed"
Greek-Slavic syntax, heterogeneous at the surface level, can often be
accounted for or rather resolved within the framework of a largely
homogeneous syntactic structure at a deeper level (a deep structure
which, with some qualifications, one may choose to term Indo-European in a typological rather than genetic sense), the matching of
Hebrew and Slavic grammatical categories will but exceptionally yield
any underlying homogeneous syntactic structure. Where it does, however, such an agreement in terms of a fragmentary generalized deep
structure seems to point to a set of certain language universals
(within the syntactic component) rather than to any ascertainable
typologically conditioned deep-structure features underlying Slavic as
well as Semitic.

Whereas the, to be sure, very limited impact of Hebrew on Slavic
(Old Church Slavic, Russian Church Slavic) syntax was conveyed
either by the medium of Greek or directly, the syntactic influence that
Greek has exerted on the Russian literary language, particularly in the
earlier phases of its evolution, is inconceivable without the intermediary
role played in the history of Russian by Old Church Slavic and its
local recension. This view gains support by the—though partly belated
—recognition that the earliest *literary* language of ancient Russia was
indeed but a slightly Russianized variety of Old Church Slavic and
not any genuinely East Slavic idiom, altogether unaffected by the
linguistic (and stylistic) standards set by the tradition of Old Church
Slavic writing.[19] Thus, the mention that during the rule of Jaroslav the

Wise "many scribes translated from Greek to Slavic" in Kievan Russia does not have to be interpreted as anything else but referring to translations into the Russian variety of Old Church Slavic which at that time still was the predominant standard literary language of the educated segment of the population.[20] Space prevents any discussion of the individual syntactic features of literary Russian (at different stages of its development) which ultimately can be traced back to Greek models. Needless to say, a comprehensive study of Russian historical syntax from this particular angle is bound to yield interesting new insights.[21]

Some of the theoretical considerations made here with regard to the Greek (and Hebrew) impact on (Old) Church Slavic and Russian find their application, *mutatis mutandis*, to other instances of foreign influences on Slavic syntax. This applies in particular to the impact made by Latin and German syntactic models on such literary languages as Czech, Polish, Slovenian, and the Croatian variety of Serbocroatian.[22] In the case of the two South Slavic languages mentioned, the influence exerted by Italian (especially in the largely Italianized literature of Dubrovnik and the rest of Dalmatia during the Renaissance) would also deserve further investigation. However, to derive some important new theoretical insights from such data, much basic philological and linguistic work—of a kind such as A. Wierzbicka's recent penetrating and sophisticated study on the syntactic and stylistic structure of Polish Renaissance prose (greatly influenced by classical Latin patterns)—still needs to be done.[23]

University of California, Los Angeles

NOTES

1. Cf. B. O. Unbegaun, "Le calque dans les langues slaves littéraires," *RÉS*, XII (1932), 19–48.
2. Among relevant publications see, e.g., K. Schumann, *Die griechischen Lehnbildungen und Lehnbedeutungen im Altbulgarischen*(Wiesbaden,1958), cf. esp. p. xiii; G. Hüttl-Worth, *Die Bereicherung des russischen Wortschatzes im XVIII. Jahrhundert* (Vienna, 1956), cf. esp. pp. 4 and 70–72; see also her papers "Problemy mežslavjanskix i slavjano-neslavjanskix leksičeskix otnošenij," *American Contributions to the Fifth International Congress of Slavists*, I (The Hague, 1963), 133–52; esp. pp. 140–42, and "Zu den Quellen des russischen Wortschatzes (Insbesondere über den Izbornik Svjatoslavov von 1073)," *WslJb*, XII (1965), 18–25; J. Dambrovský, "Sdružená pojmenování francouzského typu v polštině," *Studia językoznawcze*

poświęcone ... *Stanisławowi Rospondowi* (Wrocław, 1966), pp. 105–14 (esp. pp. 106–107).

3. Cf. my remarks in *Scsl*, VIII (1962), 119–20, esp. n. 19, as well as my reply to question 18: "Kakvi sa genezisăt i xarakterăt na čuždite sintaktični vlijanija v slavjanskite ezici ?" *Slavjanska filologija*, I (Sofia, 1963), 126–28, with further references.

4. Cf., e.g., N. Chomsky, *Aspects of the Theory of Syntax* (Cambridge, Mass., 1965), pp. 16–18, 64–106, 128–47, 198–99; for some criticism of the surface/deep structure concept as being inconsistent and "quasi-stratificational," see S. M. Lamb's forthcoming review of Chomsky's *Current Issues in Linguistic Theory* (The Hague, 1964), and *Aspects* ..., as well as the pertinent remarks in Lamb's *Outline of Stratificational Grammar* (Washington, D. C., 1966), pp. 34–40; cf. further M. A. K. Halliday, "Some notes on 'deep' grammar," *JLing*, 2:1 (1966), 57–67. To me, in spite of the criticism, the notion of "deep structure" seems quite valuable even if I interpret it as having typological connotations definable in terms of what L. Hjelmslev called "category function"; cf. L. Hjelmslev, *Sproget. En introduktion* (Copenhagen, 1963), pp. 88–93, esp. p. 92 (French version: *Le langage. Une introduction* [Paris, 1966], pp. 123–29, esp. p. 128).

5. For discussion of the partial universality of deep structure as compared to the specific individuality of surface structures, see also, e.g., R. Růžička, *Studien zur Theorie der russischen Syntax* (Berlin, 1966), pp. 19–20; N. Chomsky, *Aspects* ..., pp. 117–18.

6. A preliminary outline of Bogu-sławski's intriguing linguistic theory is buried as Part One in his monograph on the Russian numeral, *Semantyczne pojęcie liczebnika i jego morfologia w języku rosyjskim* (Wrocław-Warsaw-Cracow, 1966), pp. 11–48, esp. pp. 23–38, on semantics. For some additional information on this theory, I am indebted to Dr. A. Wierzbicka. See further A. Wierzbicka, "O smyslovyx ograničenijax dlja pravil množestvennogo sinteza pri automatičeskom perevode," *Naučno-texničeskaja informacija* (Moscow, 1966), No. 5, and "On the Semantics of the Verbal Aspect in Polish," *To Honor Roman Jakobson* (The Hague-Paris, 1967), III, 2231–49; and I. Bellert, "A Semantic Approach to Grammar Construction," *To Honor Roman Jakobson*, I, 165–73. Considerable further progress in developing and refining the theoretical framework of this semantic conception has since been reported. To a certain degree, the boundaries between syntax and semantics remain fuzzy also in transformational-generative grammar; cf. N. Chomsky, *Aspects* ..., pp. 148–63.

7. For some comparative evidence and further discussion see, e.g., C. Watkins, "Preliminaries to the Reconstruction of Indo-European Sentence Structure," *Proceedings of the Ninth International Congress of Linguists* (The Hague, 1964), pp. 1035–42; V. V. Ivanov, *Obščeindoevropejskaja, praslavjanskaja i anatolijskaja jazykovye sistemy* (*sravnitel'no-tipologičeskie očerki* [Moscow, 1965]), pp. 185–289 ("Rekonstrukcija sintaksičeskix struktur"). The deep-structure concept is particularly being used in much of the (as yet largely unpublished) pertinent writings of P. Kiparsky.

8. Cf. among earlier studies in this field, e.g., St. Słoński, *Die Übertragung der griechischen Nebensatzkonstruktionen in den altbulgarischen Sprachdenkmälern* (Kirchhain, 1908). Of the many thorough works on Old Church Slavic syntax published in more recent years cf. esp. H. Bräuer, *Der persönliche Agens beim Passiv im Altbulgarischen. Eine syntaktische Untersuchung* (Wiesbaden, 1952); H. Birnbaum, *Untersuchungen zu den Zukunftsumschreibungen mit dem Infinitiv im Altkirchenslavischen. Ein Beitrag zur historischen Verbalsyntax des Slavischen* (Stockholm, 1958); R. Večerka, *Syntax aktivních participií v staroslověnštině* (Prague, 1961); R. Růžička, *Das syntaktische System der altslavischen Partizipien und sein Verhältnis zum Griechischen* (Berlin, 1963); *Issledovanija po sintaksisu staroslavjanskogo jazyka. Sbornik statej* (Prague, 1963); Cz. Bartula, *Związki czasownika z dopełnieniem w najstarszych zabytkach języka staro-cerkiewno-słowiańskiego* (Warsaw-Wrocław-Cracow, 1964); A. Sjöberg, *Synonymous Use of Synthetical and Analytical Rection in Old Church Slavonic Verbs* (Stockholm-Gothenburg-Uppsala, 1964); all these studies take into account the impact of Greek patterns on Old Church Slavic syntax. Other recent research in the field deliberately (although in my view without sufficient justification) disregards the Greek influence; cf., e.g., I. K. Bunina, *Sistema vremen staroslavjanskogo glagola* (Moscow, 1959); K. I. Xodova, *Sistema padežej staroslavjanskogo jazyka* (Moscow, 1963); recently, however, Xodova seems to recognize the necessity of taking into consideration the Greek originals; cf. her latest contributions "Sintaksis predloga *u* s roditel'nym padežom v staroslavjanskom jazyke," *Scsl*, XII (1966), 96–114, and "Mesto predložno-padežnyx form v strukture predloženija" (in the preliminary version of the volume *Strukturni typy slovanské věty a jejich vývoj* [Brno, 1966]; the same volume contains also two further papers on Old Church Slavic syntax, by Cz. Bartula, "Uwagi o zasobie struktur zdania pojedynczego w języku staro-cerkiewno-słowiańskim," and R. Večerka, "K problematice vět s jmenným a sponově jmenným přísudkem v staroslověnštině"). Several studies have been devoted specifically to the methods of identifying and defining elements of Greek origin in Old Church Slavic syntax: J. Bauer, "Vliv řečtiny a latiny na vývoj syntaktické stavby slovenských jazyků," *Československé přednášky pro IV. Mezinárodní sjezd slavistů v Moskvě* (Prague, 1958), pp. 73–95, esp. pp. 75–82; H. Birnbaum, "Zur Aussonderung der syntaktischen Gräzismen im Altkirchenslavischen. Einige methodische Bemerkungen," *Scsl*, IV (1958), 239–57; R. Růžička, "Griechische Lehnsyntax im Altslavischen," *ZfSl*, III (1958), 173–85. Recently methods of transformational-generative grammar have been applied to problems of Greek loan syntax in Old Church Slavic by R. Růžička in his article "Beziehungen zwischen altslavischer und griechischer Syntax im Lichte der Transformationsgrammatik," *Wiss. Zschr. der Karl-Marx-Univ. Leipzig*, 15, Jg. (1966), *GSR*, 3, pp. 539–47; Russian version; "O ponjatii 'zaimstvovannyj sintaksis'

v svete teorii transformacionnoj grammatiki," *VJa* (1966), 4, pp. 80–96; for discussion and some additional viewpoints, cf. also my paper "Obščeslavjanskoe nasledie i inojazyčnye obrazcy v strukturnyx raznovidnostjax staroslavjanskogo predloženija," in the *American Contributions to the Sixth International Congress of Slavists*, I (The Hague, 1968). For a brief account of Greek loan syntax in Russian, see A. Stender-Petersen and K. Jordal, "Das griechisch-byzantinische Erbe im Russischen," *Acta Congressus Madvigani, Proceedings of the Second International Congress of Classical Studies*, V (= *TCLC*, 11 [1957]), 163–218, esp. pp. 201–17 ("Griechisch-russische syntaktische Beziehungen").

9. Cf. R. Růžička, "Beziehungen ...," p. 539; *VJa* (1966), 4, pp. 80–81.

10. For partial descriptions (in traditional terms) of the syntax of the oldest extant version of the "Life of St. Methodius" and of another text contained in the Russian-Church Slavic *Uspenskij Sbornik*, see my respective essays: "Zur Sprache der Methodvita," *Cyrillo-Methodiana* (Cologne-Graz, 1964), pp. 329–61, and "Linguistische Beobachtungen an einem altrussischen Text: Einige syntaktische Erscheinungen des *Skazanie* von Boris und Glěb nach der Handschrift des sog. *Uspenskij Sbornik*," *IJSLP*, III (1960), 45–68. An extensive study on the syntax of the writings of John the Exarch (now available in R. Aitzetmüller's and L. Sadnik's excellent critical editions) is being prepared by the present writer.

11. Variant readings within the Old Church Slavic "canon" (in a narrow sense) are largely limited to a few texts, notably the gospels (transmitted in four major manuscripts); cf. also a few parallel passages, e.g., in *Supr.* and *Cloz.* For a thorough inquiry into the syntax of Old Church Slavic one will therefore have to go beyond the narrow scope of "classical" texts; on this methodological point cf. also J. Kurz' remarks in *Issledovanija* ..., pp. 7–8, and K. I. Xodova's comments in *Scsl*, XII (1966), 100. On the linguistic significance of studying Old Church Slavic variants cf. further H. Birnbaum, *Untersuchungen* ..., p. 59 (with the references in note 2, p. 290).

12. Cf. R. Růžička, "Beziehungen...," esp. pp. 54 ff.; *id.*, *VJa* (1966), 4, pp. 83 ff.; see further also *id.*, *Das syntaktische System* ..., pp. 238 ff.

13. Cf. R. Růžička, "Struktur und Echtheit des altslavischen dativus absolutus," *ZfSl*, VI (1961), 588–96; H. Birnbaum, *Scsl*, IV (1958), 245.

14. For further discussion of this approach, see my forthcoming paper "Obščeslavjanskoe nasledie. ..."

15. Cf. *Scsl*, IV (1958), 246–48, with further references.

16. Cf., e.g., O. Grether, *Hebräische Grammatik für den akademischen Unterricht*, 3. unver. Aufl. (Munich, 1962), pp. 200–201, § 74 f and k; J. Humbert, *Syntaxe grecque* (2e éd.; Paris, 1954), pp. 287–88, § 479. In New Testament Greek usually a ὑπό + genitive phrase is used instead of the dative alone; cf. F. Blass and A. Debrunner. *Grammatik des neutestamentlichen Griechisch*, 8. Aufl. (Göttingen, 1949, or any later edition), pp. 88–89, § 191.

17. Cf. H. Bräuer, *op. cit.*, esp. p. 5 (for a summary confrontation of the

pertinent facts in Greek and Old Church Slavic).

18. My attention was drawn to this phenomenon by Professor M. Altbauer of the Hebrew University, Jerusalem, who has treated it in a separate study: "O niezauważonym słowiańskim *dativus auctoris*" (forthcoming); see also his contribution "O technice przekładowej Szymona Budnego," *Studia . . . Rospondowi*, pp. 85–96 (esp. pp. 91–92: "Naśladowanie konstrukcji biblijnej: *Passivum + Dativus*").

19. Cf. L. P. Jakubinskij, *Istorija drevnerusakogo jazyka* (Moscow, 1953), esp. pp. 87–118, 273–84; A. V. Isačenko, *Voprosy teorii i istorii jazyka. Sbornik v čest' . . . B. A. Larina* (Leningrad, 1963), pp. 153–54 (in his contribution "K voprosu o periodizacii istorii russkogo jazyka"). Cf. also B. O. Unbegaun's recent statement: "Daß die heutige russische Hochsprache ihrem Ursprung nach ein unvollständig russifiziertes Kirchenslavisch ist, dürfte seit Šachmatovs Zeiten wohl außer Zweifel stehen" (*Aus der Geisteswelt der Slaven* [Koschmeider Festschrift (Munich, 1967)], p. 5). Among

the most significant studies attempting to prove the indigenous origins of the Russian literary language is S. P. Obnorskij's monograph *Očerki po istorii russkogo literaturnogo jazyka staršego perioda* (Moscow and Leningrad, 1946).

20. Cf. *Povest' vremennyx let*, I (Moscow and Leningrad, 1950), 102, 302 (*sub anno* 1037).

21. For a summary account of the Greek impact on Russian syntax, see A. Stender-Petersen and K. Jordal, *op. cit.* (*TCLC*, 11 [1957], 201–17).

22. For some pertinent remarks on the influence of Latin syntax on the Slavic literary languages, and especially on Czech, cf. J. Bauer, *op. cit.*, pp. 83–94; for Polish see also the reference in note 23, below.

23. Cf. A. Wierzbicka, *System składniowo-stylistyczny prozy polskiego Renesansu*, "Instytut Badań Literackich PAN. Historia i Teoria Literatury." Studia. Teoria Literatury, 5 (Warsaw, 1966), pp. 5–278; cf. further, e.g., T. Brajerski, "Latynizmy w Kazaniach Gnieźnieńskich," *Studia . . . Rospondowi*, pp. 97–104.

The Ermolinskij Chronicle and the Literary Prelude to "The Tale of the Murder of Mixail of Tver'"

JOHN L. I. FENNELL

In the complex textological tangle presented by fourteenth- and fifteenth-century Russian chronicle writing, the *Ermolinskij Chronicle* (the origins of which have never been exhaustively investigated) again and again poses peculiarly tantalizing textual problems. In spite of the clearly abbreviated nature of so many of its documentary entries and *povesti* prior to the 1420's, it is often tempting, owing to the seemingly unique nature of some of the items, to look on the *Ermolinskij Chronicle* as the source of other compilations rather than as a derivative work itself. This is indeed the case with the account of the events of the year 1317 found in the *Ermolinskij Chronicle* (abbr. E)[1].

The text runs as follows (phrases and sentences are numbered for the purpose of easy reference):

> [In the year 6825–1317] (1) Prince Jurij Danilovič [of Moscow] came from the Horde to [assume] the grand principality; (2) he brought with him Kavgadij and Astrabyl (3) and he marched to Tver' (4) and got to within 40 versts; (5) here at Bortenevo Prince Mixajlo [of Tver'] and his army met him. (6) And Prince Mixajlo won, (7) and Prince Jurij fled to Novgorod; (8) and his brother Prince Boris was captured and his princess Končaka, who was the sister of the khan, and they took her to Tver' and there she was killed by poison; (9) and they carried her to Rostov and buried her in the cathedral church; her [christian] name was Agafija. (10) But [Mixail] forbade [the Tverites] to slaughter Kavgadij's Tatars, but he brought them to Tver' and rendered to Kavgadij and his Tatars much honour, but they were deceitful, saying:

33

"We marched against you unjustly with Jurij, without the permission of the khan." And he dismissed them with honour. (11) And Prince Jurij summoned the Novgorodians (12) [and] came to the Volga, (13) and Prince Mixajlo met him near Senev'skoe and there was nearly a battle between them; (14) and they kissed the cross and made peace on condition that both went to the Horde. (15) And Prince Jurij dismissed the Novgorodians (16) and went to Moscow, and it was already spring.

Now if we compare the above with the versions found in the *Rogožskij* (*R*), *Novgorod First* (*N-I*), and *Trinity* (*T*) *Chronicles*, all of which can be considered to reflect closely the primary versions of the local Tver', Novgorod, and Moscow chronicles respectively,[2] it will be seen that, while there are textological similarities, there are also considerable divergences. The Tver' account (*R*), which contains much information not found in the other two primary sources (e.g., Mixail's relinquishment of the grand princely title to Jurij at Kostroma and the pre-battle parleys between Mixail and Kavgadij) and studiously avoids mentioning Končaka's fate, has very little in common with *E*: all that can be said is that some episodes in *E* (1, 2, 10, 12, 14) are reminiscent of *R*. The main similarities between *E* and the Novgorod account (*N-I*), which is largely concerned with explaining away the inglorious behaviour of the Novgorod army prior to the battle of Bortenevo, occur in 1, 3, 4, 11, 12, 14, 15, and 16.[3] The Moscow account (*T*), which ends with Končaka's burial in Rostov, is textually close to *E* only in 1, 2, 5–9.[4]

From this it can be seen that all but two passages of *E* (10 and 13) derive from the primary Moscow and Novgorod sources via the later hypothetical compilations known as the "Vladimirskij Polixron of 1418" and the "*svod* of 1448":[5] where *E* is closest to *N-I* it derived from the "*svod* of 1448"—this can be seen by comparing *E* with the two major fifteenth-century compilations which are known to have been based on the "*svod* of 1448," namely the *Sofijskij First* (*S-I*) and the *Novgorod Fourth* (*N-IV*) *Chronicles*;[6] where *E* is closest to *T*, it derived from either the "Vladimirskij Polixron of 1418" or the "*svod* of 1448."[7]

But what of the remaining two passages of *E*, 10 and 13? They are not found in any of the secondary sources stemming from the "*svod* of 1448." They are, however, closely reflected in the following: a) the two expanded redactions of the "Tale of the Murder of Mixail" contained in the *Sofijskij First Chronicle* (*S-I(a)*) and the *Moscow svod of 1479* (*M(a)*)[8]; b) the sixteenth-century *Nikon Chronicle*'s version of the events of 1317 (N)[9]:

10.

E	s-1(*a*)	м(*a*)	N
Tatar že Kavgadyevyx izbivati ne povelě no prived ix v Tferь, i mnogu čestь vъzdastь Kavgadyju i Tatarom ego, a oni lьstjaxu, glagoljušče: "my prixodili na tebe [ne] pravedno sь Jurьem bez povelěnija careva." I otpusti s čestьju.	a okannago že Kavgadyja s drugy ego ne povelě knjaz' izbivati, v nemъze poslědnjaja pogybelь. Si ze poběda sъtvorisja měsjaca dekabrja 22. ... [Mixail] privede okaannago Kavgadyja v grad svoj, i mnogo čestiv i odariv ego, i otъpusti ego; on že mnogo s lestiju rotjašesja ne vaditi na nь ko carju, glagolja: "zaneže voevali esmi vlastь tvoju bez careva slova i povelěnija."	a okaanogo Kavgadyja i Tatar ego ne povelě knjazь Mixail izbivati, v nem ze bolšaja posledi bystь pogybelь. Si že poběda stvorisja měsjaca dekabrja vo 22.... A okaannogo Kavgadyja privede knjazь Mixailo v grad svoj i mnogo čьstiv i dariv otpusti ego. A on s lestьju rotjašesja ne vaditi na nь ko cesarju, voevali bo esmja i vlast' tvoju bez cesareva slova i povelěnija.	Knjaz' Mixajlo že Jaroslavičь Tverskij Tatar Kavgadyjevyx izbivati ne povelě, no privede ix vo Tverь, i mnogu čestь vъzdade Kavgadyju i Tatarom ego, a oni lstjaxu, glagoljušče: "my otnyně tvoi esmja, a prixodili esmja na tebja so knjazemь Jurьem bez povelěnia careva i v tom esmja vinovati, i boimsja ot carja opaly čto esmja takovo dělo sotvorili i mnogu krovь prolili." Knjazь že Mixajlo Jaroslavičь jat věry im, i mnogimi dary odari ix, i otpusti ix s čestiju.

13.

i srěte ego knjazь Mixajlo protivu Senevьskogo, tu malo ne bystь boju mežu ix...	i srěte ego knjazь Mixajlo protivu Siněevskogo, i paky ne xotja viděti drugago krovoprolitija za tolь maly dni...	i srěte ego knjazь Mixajlo protivu Siněevъskago, i tu malo ne bystь drugavo krovoprolitьja...	i srěte ego knjazь Mixajlo Jaroslavičь Tverskij, i tu malo boj ne bystь...

From the above comparison the following points emerge:

1.) In both cases N derives indirectly from E (E is clearly an abbreviated text, therefore, it is unlikely that N derived directly from
it), and *not* from S-$I(a)$ or $M(a)$. Now Nasonov has shown that there
must have been a *svod* of the mid-fifteenth century which served as the
direct source of E and which contained information not found in either
the "*svod* of 1448" or in the "Vladimirskij Polixron of 1418."[10] It
has also been shown that this *svod* was influenced by both the above
compilations and therefore must have been written between 1448 and
1472 (the date of the compilation of E) and that it served as a source
both for N and for M.[11] On this occasion, therefore, N used the
"*svod* of 1448–1472" as its main source.

2.) In 10, $M(a)$ is nothing more than an abbreviated version of
S-$I(a)$ and *not* of E. In 13, however, "i tu malo ne bystь drugavo
krovoprolitьja" is an amalgam of E and S-$I(a)$. Thus we can assume
that $M(a)$ used, and abbreviated, S-$I(a)$ as its main source, but also
had access to the "*svod* of 1448–1472."[12]

Careful comparison of E and S-$I(a)$ shows that E (or E's source) is
an abbreviated version of S-$I(a)$ rather than that S-$I(a)$ is an expanded version of E. The words: "a oni lьstjaxu, glagoljušče: my
prixodili na tebe [ne]pravedno sь Jurьem bez povelěnija careva" have
little meaning in the context of E. In S-$I(a)$, on the other hand,
Kavgadij's words are logically explained by his deceitful promise not
to accuse Mixail before the khan.[13]

The following general conclusions can now be drawn:

1.) The text found in the *Ermolinskij Chronicle* was not the source,
direct or indirect, of any of the Russian chronicle accounts known to
have been compiled before the first half of the fifteenth century.

2.) The immediate source of the *Ermolinskij Chronicle* was a *svod*
compiled between 1448 and 1472.

3.) This "*svod* of 1448–1472" was used both by the redactor of the
"Tale of the Murder of Mixail" found in the *Moscow svod of 1479* and
by the compiler of the sixteenth-century *Nikon Chronicle*.

4.) The compiler of the "*svod* of 1448–1472" used on this occasion as
sources: a) the "Vladimirskij Polixron of 1418"; b) the "*svod* of
1448"; and c) the independent "Tale of the Murder of Mixail" found
in the *Sofijskij First Chronicle*.[14]

Oxford

NOTES

1. *Polnoe sobranie russkix letopisej* (abbr. *PSRL*), XXIII, 98. See also the almost identical *"L'vovskij Chronicle," PSRL*, XX, 174–75.

2. See *Rogožskij letopisec* in *PSRL*, XV, cols. 36–38 (the version of the *Tverskoj sbornik* in *ibid.*, cols 409–10, is virtually the same); *Novgorodskaja pervaja letopis' staršego i mladšego izvodov* (Moscow–Leningrad, 1950), pp. 95–96, 337–38; *Troickaja letopis'*. Ed. M. D. Priselkov (Moscow–Leningrad, 1950), pp. 355–56 (cf. *PSRL*, XVIII, 88). Though it can not be said for certain that any of the above versions are identical with the original versions, they clearly contain no later interpolations. However, a certain amount of pruning may have been done in the ten or twenty years following the events.

3. In both versions 7, 8 and 9 are fairly close; but in *N-I* Jurij's flight to Novgorod (7) comes after the report of Končaka's death.

4. Note that none of the primary sources mentions Astrabyl in 2. However, it must have been in one of them originally as it appears in the various derivatives of the *"svod* of 1448."

5. The most widely accepted hypothesis is that the "Vladimirskij Polixron of 1418" was a re-edition of the all-Russian *"svod* of 1408" (= *T*) and that the *"svod* of 1448" (the date and origin are subject to considerable dispute) is an amalgam of a re-edited "Vladimirskij Polixron" and the so-called "Sofijskij Vremennik of 1418" (i.e., the *Novgorod First Chronicle* taken as far as 1418). See M. D. Priselkov, *Istorija russkogo letopisanija XI–XV vv.* (Leningrad,

1940), pp. 149 ff.; D. S. Lixačev, *Russkie letopisi i ix kul'turno-istoričeskoe značenie*. AN SSSR (Moscow, 1947), Ch. 17, Sec. 2.

6. *PSRL*, V, 207; IV, issue 1, 257.

7. It is hard to say to what extent *T* was incorporated into the *"svod* of 1448" via the "Vladimirskij Polixron." *N–IV* and *S–I* are certainly much closer to *N–I* than to *T*, but there is evidence of a synthesis of *T* and *N–I* in the Moscow *svod* of 1479 (*M*) (*PSRL*, XXV, 161), which is known also to have derived from, *inter alia*, the *"svod* of 1448." The passage: "A brata ego knjazja Borisa rukami jaša i knjaginju Jurьevu Končaka jaša i povedoša ix vo Tferь, i tamo zelьem umorena bystь velikaa knjagyni Jur'eva Končak..." is an amalgam of the two. Note that *N–IV* shows a curious hesitation between the two sources in the same passage: "a brata ego Borisa i knjaginju ego jaša rukami i v Tferi umoriša. A Končaka vedoša na Tferь, i umre tamo."

8. *PSRL*, V, 207–15; XXV, 161–66. These two expanded versions of the "Tale," which *include an account of the events of the year preceding the murder*, are quite distinct and separate from the accounts of the events of 1317 which are found in the same compilations (i.e., *S–I* and *M*). Hence they are not considered to have been in the *"svod* of 1448." Note that *R*, *E*, and *N* also have contracted versions of the "Tale," but all three begin with Jurij's departure to the Horde in 1318.

9. *PSRL*, XX, 180–81.

10. A. N. Nasonov, "Moskovskij svod 1479 i ego južnorusskij istočnik,"

Problemy istočnikovedenija, IX (Moscow, 1961), 350–85; "Moskovskij svod 1479 i Ermolinskaja letopis'," *Voprosy social'no-èkonomičeskoj istorii i istočnikovedenija perioda feodalizma v Rossii. Sbornik statej k 70-letiju A. A. Novosel'skogo* (Moscow, 1961), pp. 218–22. Nasonov evidently considered this *svod* to have been a metropolitan *svod* of Feodosij Byval'cev (1461–1465). I am obliged to Professor Ja. S. Lur'e for this information.

11. J. L. I. Fennell, "The Tver' Uprising of 1327: a Study of the Sources," *Jahrbücher für Geschichte Osteuropas*, Heft 2 (June, 1967), 168–69.

12. From other passages it is evident that *N*'s second main source for the events of 1317 was *R*. For *N*'s use of a fifteenth-century redaction of the Tver' chronicle, see A. N. Nasonov, "Letopisnye pamjatniki Tverskogo knjažestva," *Izvestija AN SSSR. Otdel gumanitarnyx nauk* (Leningrad, 1930), No. 10, Sec. 4.

13. Note that the author of *N* attempts, by expanding the Tatars' speech, to make *E* more intelligible: "from now on we are your subjects. . . ."

14. Čerepnin suggested 1431–1432 as a date for the composition of *S–I(a)*. L. V. Čerepnin, *Obrazovanie russkogo centralizovannogo gosudarstva v XIV–XV vekax* (Moscow, 1960), p. 472. A textological study of the relationship between *S–I(a)*, *M(a)*, and the "archetypal MS Tale" (now in the Lenin Library) might enable us to obtain a more accurate date both for *S–I(a)* and for the "*svod* of 1448–1472."

The Phonology of East Slavic at the Period Preceding the Loss of the *Jers*

JAMES O. FERRELL

THE LOSS of the *jers*, the reduced vowels ь and ъ, in weak position belongs in large part to the historical period in East Slavic. The summary of the evidence given by V. I. Borkovskij and P. S. Kuznecov in their *Istoričeskaja grammatika russkogo jazyka* (Moskow, 1965), 99 ff., appears to be sober. However, an attempt to analyze the phonological system of East Slavic for a period which was, perhaps, not too long before the appearance of writing in the Russian area offers a number of problems, some with respect to the aims of the construct one is making and some in the assessment of the evidence at our disposal.

One can, for instance, set out to describe a system that will accord well enough with the evidence of the oldest texts and state that certain dialect variants are attested and others are not improbable or one can attempt to construct an optimally differentiated phonology from which dialect differences can be derived, i.e., a restoration of the general type that the young grammarians attempted for Indo-European. The latter alternative is attractive in view of the relatively few variants which seem to require our attention, yet it will, as we shall see, confront us with several major questions to which no certain answer will be given. We shall, in principle, adopt the course of attempting to set up this sort of universal construct, but in some instances we will content ourselves with mentioning the existence of problems without trying to arrive at a definitive solution. This will result in part from the desire to approximate a reasonably late period in the history of East Slavic and from a feeling of not being obligated to account for every morphologically motivated atypicality reflected in the older texts and the contemporary dialects.

The most obvious difficulty presented by the earliest texts from Russia which we have is that, though they are old, they are, for the most part, Church Slavic in a Russian recension and the East Slavic elements must be isolated item by item. Moreover, as we have previously noted, the oldest layer of texts, though reflecting the *jers* in approximate accordance with etymological expectation, show, nevertheless, certain disturbances. However, these problems offer difficulties no greater for our purposes than ambiguities in the writing system. The Cyrillic alphabet, in which the documents were written, was designed for Church Slavic. When it was taken over by the East Slavs, more than one sign for a single sound certainly resulted and, not improbably, multiple values for a single sign. Moreover, there are no signs for the suprasegmental values. Possible multiple values and the lack of suprasegmental signs, of course, are crucial limiting features for the overall value of our system. We must content ourselves with silence or with a notation of possibilities or, at best, probabilities in matters where these factors played a role.

East Slavic can with reasonable certainty be assigned the following simple vowels *i, ь, e, ä, a, o, ъ, y, u*. The addition of a phoneme *ü* will allow us to dispense with two consonant phonemes (*ś* and *ź*) which would otherwise be necessary.[1] Furthermore, we must posit a vowel or diphthong *ě* or *ie* and perhaps a corresponding back vowel or diphthong *ô* (or *uo*) as reflex of *o* under a neoacute accent, which is still differentiated from that of *o* not so accented in a number of Great Russian dialects and which may have been differentiated in former times in some White Russian ones as well, cf. Borkovskij and Kuznecov's, *Istoričeskaja grammatika*, 142. Similarly, reflexes of the neoacute on the second vowel of pleophonic complexes, whether deriving from **TeRT* or **ToRT*, give evidence of differentiation from other types within the Ukrainian area: e.g., *horód* but *boríd*, cf. L. A. Bulaxovskij, *Movoznavstvo* (1936), No. 2, 65 ff. and *Voprosy jazykoznanija*, VII (1958), No. 2, 87 ff. How we treat these problems within the phonological system of East Slavic will depend *inter alia* on the type of suprasegmentals we assume. I am inclined to believe, though by no means certain, that the facts of the contemporary dialects can be explained without assuming the maintenance of pitch and length into the era we are describing. However, the negative assumption would minimally demand a qualitatively differentiated *o* phoneme for our period, at least for Great Russian, cf. dialectal *nôs'iš*. Whether it would be reasonable simultaneously to treat the Ukrainian phenomenon in terms of **meréžь > meréž* but **čeredь > čeríd* (the spellings at this point are more or less conventional), requires further investigation.[2]

At this point let us turn to the asyllabics. Here at least part of the inventory would seem to be beyond dispute: the stops *p*, *b*, *t*, *d*, *k*, *g*, the spirants *s*, *z*, *x*, the nasals *m*, *n*, and the liquids *l* and *r*. Our inventory of syllabics has rendered *ś* and *ź* otiose, but *c* requires a solution. One could enter it as a separate phoneme *c* and add an item to the inventory, one could analyze it as *ts*, which would probably be phonetically unobjectionable, but would represent a type of consonant sequence otherwise unattested in the language, or one could represent it by *k* before a front vowel, which, though phonetically inferior to the *ts* solution, is not unreasonable (a view its origin in Slavic, *inter alia*, tends to support), adds no new item to the inventory, and finds support in the morphophonemic alternations of the language. This last solution is the one we will favor. It is possible in East Slavic because of the presence of the syllabics *ä* and *ü* (and because the corpus we assume precludes borrowed words of the type *kitъ* and analogical dialectal forms such as the dative *Dъmъkě*). Thus we would handle the declension of the word for "father" in terms of *otъkъ*, *otъkä*, *otъkü*, etc. as opposed to *sokъ*, *soka*, *soku*, etc.

Whatever the realization of the grapheme *v* may have been at the period under consideration, the evidence that it was a separate phoneme and not a variant of *u* or any other syllabic is decisive. Not only must we reckon with words such as *uime mъ*, where the problem might allow solution at another level, but *lovlenija*, where interpreting the first syllable in terms of a falling diphthong would do violence to the overall system. There seems to be no such serious objections to treating asyllabic *i* as a positional variant of the *i* we have already posited among the vowels, but it would require a special device to mark off prefixes, cf. *priučenъ*. Hence there would seem to be no real gain in economy by preferring that solution to the establishment of a phoneme *j*.

In East Slavic the palatal graphemes *š*, *ž*, *č* are subject to rather special distributional restraints. While *č* occurs only before vowels, *š* and *ž* can occur both before vowels and before other palatals. Thus we find the grapheme sequences *šč*, *žč*, and *žg*. The latter two, as Roman Jakobson has pointed out in his *Selected Writings* (The Hague, 1962), I, 247–53, are both best assessed as representations of a sequence varying in value from *šč* only in voicing, i.e., *žǯ*, with the choice of grapheme dependent on other factors within the representational requirements of the dialect. As far as the evidence of the early documents is concerned, there is no reason to believe that an affricate *ǯ* occurred outside of this environment. In literary Ukrainian and in the Ukrainian dialects, however, there are a number of examples in which *ǯ* does occur as a reflex of Protoslavic **dj* where no *ž* precedes, e.g., *sadžaty* (Russian *sažát'*). Whether this Ukrainian trait represents an ancient survival or a morphologically motivated innovation is a subject of argument and one which, though of consequence to us in the application of our phoneme inventory since we are seeking an overall system, we are not obligated to solve here. The reader will find materials and a history of the question by M. F. Nakonečnyj in the collection of articles *Pytannja istoryčnoho rozvytku ukrajins'koji movy* (Kharkov, 1962), 145–50. However, though it would seem extremely doubtful in view of the information we receive from the earliest documents that the dialects used in them realized *ž* outside of the mentioned sequence, one cannot with real certainty preclude it from all the East Slavic dialects.[3] Our inventory will have the means of writing *ž*, which it must in any event for the sequence *žž*. For the sake of economy we shall treat all four palatals mentioned so far as sequences of plain consonant plus *j* except that in groups of palatals we shall write groups of plain consonants plus *j*: e.g., *sjirokъ* 'broad,' *zjenu* 'I reap,' *tjьrnъ* 'black,' *jezdjü* 'I ride' *jestje* 'still' (and, possibly, *sadjäti* 'set'). This solution seems distributionally and phonetically acceptable.

There is some doubt how widely palatal *ř*, *l'*, *ň* existed as phonologically distinct from plain *r*, *l*, *n* before front vowels in East Slavic even at a period prior to the loss of the *jers*.[4] It is true, as L. L. Vasil'ev, *Russkij filologičeskij vestnik* (1913), LXIX, 182–223, has observed, that some schools of Russian copyists of the eleventh and twelfth centuries distinguished rather well between palatal and non-palatal *l* and *n* in their Church Slavic manuscripts. One will find analyses of their work in Horace Lunt's *The Orthography of Eleventh-Century Russian Manuscripts* (Ann Arbor, 1961 [microfilm]), and especially in A. E. Kalnyn''s article in *Učenye zapiski Instituta slavjanovedenija*, XIII, (1956) 135–50. Kalnyn' states, p. 145, that in the best manuscripts, which are characterized by the use of a palatal-marking hook or by such a hook plus a jotated vowel, the instances of marking of palatal *l* and *n* in general exceeds those of failing to do so; moreover, the marking of non-palatal consonants with a palatal hook is rare. (The manuscripts which denote palatalized consonants by means of a jotated vowel are less consistent in marking palatalized consonants and also contain rather numerous examples of non-palatal consonants followed by a jotated vowel.) These data are considered by some scholars as reasonable proof that East Slavic still maintained a distinction of palatal and palatalized (or, *mutatis mutandis*, palatal consonants and plain consonants before front vowels) because in general the Russian schools of Church Slavic copyists tend to ignore or confuse those features of Church Slavic phonology and, to a less extent, morphology, that are not paralleled at some level in East Slavic, e.g., the differentiation of back nasal vowel and *u*, of the group *žd* and *ž*, and of the instrumental singular masculine-neuter in *-omъ* and *-ъmъ*. Though the documents in which the palatals are marked are almost exclusively Church Slavic copies, at least one East Slavic original, a deed of the Grand Prince Mstislav Volodimirovič and his son Vsevolod of about 1130, shows, as Kalnyn' has pointed out, reasonable consistency in using jotated vowels to differentiate palatal *n* from plain (or, more probably, palatalized) *n*; of four cases in which marking would be etymologically expected, three are marked.

Yet evidence of this type remains inconclusive. The manuscripts tend to mark palatal *r* only sporadically. Nikolaj Durnovo, *Slavia* (1923–24), II, 604, has attributed this trait to the South Slavic originals, pointing to the loss of palatality of *r* in Serbocroatian. The statistical material which Josef Kurz has gathered in respect to the *Codex Zographensis* indicates the comparative rarity of the marking of palatal *r* before front vowels, cf. *Rocznik slawistyczny*, X (1931), 150–51. The *Codex Suprasliensis* is quite striking in this respect and tends to ignore palatal marking of *r* before back as well as front vowels, cf. Štěpán Kul'bakin, *Mluvnice jazyka staroslověnského* (Prague, 1948), 72–73. This trait in the Russian manuscripts would seem to point to a rather careful following of South Slavic originals since there is no other indication that in the East Slavic of this period palatal *r* had undergone a development different from that of palatal *l* or *n*. The specifics of the implementation of the marking of palatal consonants, the use of the hook in the manuscripts which show the best consistency, may help explain the relative rarity of historically non-palatal consonants that were marked as palatal. The scribe was not under the same sort of pressure, as, say, in making a choice between *ǫ* and *u* where something had in every instance to be written. Here the choice was between hook and zero and, if one grants that a South Slavic manuscript was being copied and that among certain schools of copyists it was accepted practice to transmit these hooks, the results seem less than decisive in respect to establishing the existence of a distinct palatal series in the dialect of the copyist. I am uncertain what value one should attach to the coexistence in manuscripts of East Slavic scribes of forms of the type of the first person singular *myšlju* and *myslju*. First, there is uncertainty attendant on the disengagement of Church Slavic and East Slavic forms. If one grants that both forms were coexistent in East Slavic, then their dialect relationship poses problems to which we can find no ready answer. It is tempting to see in forms of the type *myslju* a leveling of palatal with non-palatal liquid or *n* before a front vowel with a resultant depalatalization of the group as a whole, at least in some of the dialects. On the other hand, the very fact that palatalization of the group would be dependent on palatalization of its final member might lead to the sort of situation that exists in contemporary Russian where *spet'* 'to sing' can in the same ideolect be realized as *s'p'et'* or *sp'et'* and, in this latter case, there would be no evidence of the loss of the palatal quality of the liquid or *n* in this double treatment. Moreover, the occurrence of palatalization of *s* in *pošlju* < *posъlju* offers a substantial difficulty (though, perhaps, not a completely insuperable one) to the contention of a universal or very widespread loss of palatal liquids and *n* before the final loss of the *jers*.

For the type of predialectal phonemicization of East Slavic we are attempting, the differentiation of palatal liquids and *n* from their plain equivalents before front vowels would seem to be required. However, the same aim would point to indicating the palatal value of the total cluster by indicating the palatal value of the final liquid or *n*. Thus, we would write *moljü, mysljü, merjü, sъmotrjü, vonjä, kaznjenъ*, etc.

In fine we would suggest the use of a system involving the following phonemes: *i, ü, ь, e, ä, a, o, ъ, y, u* (treating *ě* as *ie* and *ô* as *uo*), *p, b, t, d, k, g, s, z, x, m, n, l, r, v*, and *j*. As we have noted, further study of pleophony and its relationship to the historical neoacute in Ukrainian might require a modification of the preceding inventory (we tentatively posit no suprasegmentals of the type of length and intonation for the system though stress must, in any case, be assumed).

The relatively low inventory of phonemes implies, of course, the use of a phoneme sequence to denote what another system might treat as a unit and hence economy at one level is, to some extent, purchased at the expense of extravagance at another. However, a lean basic inventory would seem to be generally regarded as a desideratum, and the representation of further analyzable sequences as unit phonemes[5] must normally be defended with special arguments.

It is of some interest that even with a relatively lean inventory, considerable phonemic intersection still occurs. This statement holds true both for paired sets that include most of the vowels when they occur immediately after *j* and for a number of the consonants occurring alone or in clusters before *j*. Vowel pairs include *y* and *i* (*tjisty* 'clean' ins. pl. masc. and neu. and *kosti* 'bones' gen. sg. etc. but only *nistji* 'poor' ins. pl. masc. and neu., etc.), *ъ* and *ь* (*tjistъ* nom.-acc. sg. masc., *kostь* nom.-acc. sg., but only *nistjь* nom.-acc sg. masc.), *e* and *o* (*tjisto* nom.-acc. sg. neu., *tjiste* voc. sg. masc., but only *nistje* nom.-acc. sg. neu. and voc. sg. masc.), *a* and *ä* (*tjista* nom. sg. fem. etc., *rostä* 'raising' nom. sg. masc. and neu. pres. part. act., but only *nistjä* nom. sg. fem., etc.), *u* and *ü* (*tjistu* dat. sg. masc. and neu., *kənäzü* 'prince' dat. sg., but only *nistjü* dat. sg. masc. and neu.). Consonant intersection includes *s* and *x* (*pisati* 'write' inf., *dyxati* 'push' inf., but *pisjä* and *dysjä* (nom.-acc. sg. masc. and neu. pres. part. act.), *g*, *d*, and *z* (*ləgati* 'lie' inf., *voditi* 'lead' inf., *voziti* 'haul,' but *ləzjü* and *vozjü* pres. 1st. pers. sg. for both the latter verbs), *t* and *k* (*təpətati* 'trample' inf. and *plakati* 'weep' inf., but *təpətjü* and *platjü* pres. 1st pers. sg.), and any labial consonant and the same labial consonant plus *l*. The preference for particular writings, e.g., *jä* rather than *ja* in instances of such intersections can be justified only on the basis of probable phonetic realization.

The paper indicates a need for additional studies to determine how deeply the process of palatalization affected the phonology and morphology of the Balto-Slavic languages both individually and in their collective groupings.

University of Michigan

NOTES

1. The decision is justified by the simultaneous softening of the consonant and fronting of the following vowel.

2. Bulaxovskij himself observes that realizations do not always accord with his expectations. In any case, this leaves still unsolved the central problem of why the second vowel in Ukrainian pleophonic forms did not normally undergo the same treatment in closed syllables as *o* and *e* of other origins. The solution proposed by George Shevelov, *A Prehistory of Slavic* (Heidelberg, 1964), pp. 410–12, offers an out, but requires assumptions in respect to chronology that are disturbing though not impossible. His solution would, of course, require our assuming the maintenance of the old intonational distinctions. I am uncertain whether a solution based on tautomorphemic *oro*, etc. would work.

3. I should regard the case for secondary, morphological motivation of the contemporary Ukrainian occurrences as very strong. See the bibliography in Nakonečnyj for discussions of the problem. One should add the extremely interesting observations on parallel matters contained in Roman Jakobson's, "The Phonemic and Grammatical Aspects of Language in their Interrelations," *Actes du Congrès International des Linguistes à Paris, juillet, 1948* (Paris, 1949), pp. 5–18, 601.

4. The possiblity of coexistence of palatal and palatalized liquids and nasals seems to have been conclusively shown by Émile, Petrovici, *International Journal of Slavic Linguistics and Poetics*, I–II (1959),

184 ff., to which Jakobson and Halle have appended some materials of importance on Slavic.

5. The representations of written *š*, *č*, etc. by *sj*, *tj* need not imply that the phonetic realization *sj* coexisted with the realization *š* in East Slavic of the period under consideration as it does in contemporary English word sandhi. However, in view of the frequency of the displacement of *sj* by *š*, etc. as a wide-spread historical phenomenon and in view of the type of coexistence we find in English, the utilization of *sj*, etc. in this function would seem appropriate where it is justified at some level by the morphology of the language.

Russian Participles

SUNRAY C. GARDINER

IN HIS ARTICLE "Le russe littéraire est-il d'origine russe?"[1] Professor Unbegaun outlines the stages of the process of interpenetration of the Russian and Church Slavonic components which resulted in the formation of the Russian literary language: Russian Church Slavonic was from the first adapted to the pronunciation of its users; therefore, RCS has no phonetic system of its own. At the other extreme, the vocabulary shows a constantly changing interplay of various factors involving subject matter, genre, and style; this state of flux can continue and the most diverse elements can co-exist in this open system without disrupting linguistic unity. But "la morphologie forme un système fermé, et toute forme insolite dans ce système fait dresser l'oreille et contribue au sentiment de différenciation."[2] Differences became more marked owing to diverging Russian developments, and the gap was made wider by the "second South Slavonic influence"; when the two languages were once more brought closer together, this was due in part to the decay of RCS grammatical structure, which led to its gradual Russification.[3] By the seventeenth century this process was so advanced as to justify the phrase "effondrement du système slavon de déclinaison et de conjugaison."[4]

The participial system is a case in point, which illustrates Professor Unbegaun's thesis that the Russian literary language is a continuation of RCS, as it presents "tout un système slavon maintenu dans le russe littéraire."[5] The participial system (if we exclude the past passive participle) can be regarded as a set of forms, although it happens that only the present active contrasts with the Russian form. Comparison with the type *mogučij, gorjačij*, however, leads us no further than the obvious statement that divergence in function made the coexistence of both forms possible. It can also be treated as the use of a category that had no parallel in Russian, and also as a question

47

of syntax (unlike, e.g., the use of the aorist which does not affect clause structure).

A. Stender-Petersen and K. Jordal[6] mention several constructions, ultimately derived from Greek through OCS, which were in use in RCS, among others: certain uses of the genitive, that of the predicative nominative and accusative, and the dative absolute, all of which were eliminated in the process which led to the formation of the Russian literary language. The authors come to the conclusion that

> Wenn wir es aber nichtsdestoweniger [i.e., in spite of the fact that Russian has inherited a great deal from Greek as far as vocabulary and syntax are concerned] nicht wagen zu behaupten, die russische Literatursprache sei aus dem Geist der griechischen geboren, so beruht das darauf, daß die russische Sprache ihre Syntax nur wiederstrebend dem Einfluß der griechischen Sprache aussetzte und sobald sie in die Periode des Europäismus eintrat, die Resultate dieses Einflusses rasch wieder abstreifte.[7]

This is also true, *mutatis mutandis*, of the influence of CS syntax in general.

Within the participial system itself, RCS originally had several constructions which are not found in modern Russian:[8]

1. The participle as nominative complement of certain verbs:
(a) The present active participle (PrA) as complement of *byti*, e.g., *sutь že kosti ego i doselě tamo ležače* (*Lavr. Let.*, p. 87). There is nothing to show that this construction was not also possible in OR, and it is probable that its loss is a development within the history of Russian, connected with the elimination of tense distinctions. It is still found as an archaism in sixteenth-century RCS: "oboi že *b'jaxu služašče* i dani *dajušče* russkomu carstvu do Batyja carja" (*Kazanskij Letopisec*, p. 191). The examples without copula of the PrA, and those, also without copula, of the PaA given by Nikiforov do not belong to this construction, although they may have been influenced by it.[9]
(b) The PrA as complement of various verbs requiring a verbal complement: "I jako *skonča žiža*, ukrasi ju ikonami" (*Lavr. Let.*, p. 52). This was replaced in Russian by an infinitive phrase. There are also examples where the participial phrase indicates the cause of a state of mind denoted by the main verb: "Danilo . . . *sožalisja otslavъ* syna" (*Ip. Let.*, p. 190). This construction was no longer possible in later RCS owing to its homonymy with the gerundial phrase.
(c) The participle is the obligatory complement of a reflexive verb: "*mnimsja* Boga *ljubjašče*" (*Lavr. Let.*, p. 129). In Modern Russian (MR)

the adjective in the nominative of the nominal form was replaced by the adjective in the instrumental (pronominal form), and since the function of the participle is that of an adjective, the MR construction (e.g., "on *kazalsja spjaščim*") may be derived from Russian syntax.

2. The PrA is the complement of a verb requiring the accusative; this construction is very frequent in RCS. In MR the instrumental was substituted for the accusative, so that the MR construction is again rather the extension of a Russian development made possible by the existence of the participle.

These constructions were therefore not carried over into MR, either because some of them had already been lost in RCS, or because they were part of a more general construction (predicative nom. or acc.) which was superseded by an equivalent Russian construction (predicative instr.). All of them involve the nominal form of the participle which was eliminated in connection with the increasing restriction of the use of the nominal form of the adjective.

The participles in question could also be used, either alone or with elements depending on them, as a participial phrase (PP) which was an adjunct of a noun. Two types of PP can be distinguished:

1. The PP (nominal form) forms a kind of subordinate predicate (Potebn'ja's "secondary predicate") dependent on the subject, therefore, invariably in the nominative. Here there is no break in continuity between the use of the participle in OR and the MR construction. The participle became a gerund, and the gerundial phrase is a feature both of the administrative language and of RCS, where the corresponding ChSl form was often used, invariably owing to Russian influence. This resulted in the opposition of R forms in *-če, -či* to CS forms in *-šče, -šči*, besides a form which was common to both, in *-a*. It is significant that the specifically R and ChSl forms were eliminated, whereas the "common" form prevailed. The past gerund shows a different compromise, R *-v* paralleled by ChSl *-vši* after vowel. The form in *-ši* after consonants in ChSl was later replaced in some cases by the R form in *-a*, cf. *prišedši* (N.B. with *e* not *ě*), OR *prišod*, MR *pridja* like *prinesja*. This construction is therefore entirely Russian, and in MR the ChSl element is limited to the forms in *-ši*.

There was, however, another participial construction of the same type, which provided for the event when the subject of the PP was not the same as that of the finite verb: the dative absolute. Although there was no equivalent construction in Russian (the nominative absolute is not frequent in the administrative language; by the seventeenth century it may have been colloquial, or dialectal or in some other way not acceptable), this construction has also been eliminated. This cannot be attributed to the fact that the participle in nominal form made way for the pronominal form, as the pronominal form was already used in the plural, the nominal form being exclusively singular by the seventeenth century. The reason lies rather in the clear distinction made between adjectival function (to which participles were assigned) and adverbial function (reserved for gerunds), as the gerundial phrase became part of the predicate.

2. The PP modifies a noun (which itself may occupy any position in the sentence). This construction had, of course, no Russian equivalent, and it was carried over *in toto* from RCS. But the participial constructions were in an advanced state of decay by the seventeenth century. The invariable participle (or gerund) in *-šče, -šči* has already been mentioned. We often find the dative absolute used when the subject is the same as that of the finite verb (this occurs already in OCS), or when the noun is in the dative, but is accompanied by a gerund. There are long strings of PP, or, more often gerundial phrases without finite verb, or loosely connected to a main clause by a conjunction. The constructions tend to be hypotactic only externally, but are in fact a variant of the paratactic or semi-paratactic constructions of OR.

A participial construction does not merely consist in the use of participial phrases grouped round a finite verb. In his paper on Latin influence on European syntax, F. Blatt defines it as follows: "a fine system of subordination which allows the possiblity of grouping a very large number of facts, indicating their mutual relations, in one syntactical unity," and reminds us of the distinction made by Aristotle between the "strung-together style ... which has no end in itself, unless the subject-matter comes to an end" and the "periodic style ... which returns on itself." But then "there is no need of grouping and classifying facts linguistically, if you have no complicated thought to express."[10] The examples of involved periods given by Stender-Petersen and Jordal are of the pseudo-hypotactic kind, and it is significant that the authors in each case are able (or rather, have to) cut the citations short by an "etc." This would be impossible when quoting a properly constructed period. This style can hardly have been the model for the secular works of the age of Peter the Great, let alone for the new Russian literature, and the elimination of most RCS constructions from the literary language is not surprising. The survival of some participial constructions seems therefore to call for investigation. An explanation is suggested by Stender-Petersen and Jordal: "Im altrussischen Schrifttum durch den dauernden Einfluß des Altkirchenslavischen aufrechterhalten, war dieses System zu Lomonosovs Zeit schon ganz ausgesprochen antiquiert, wurde aber dann dank dem neu einsetzenden sprachlichen Einfluß der westeuropäischen Sprachen dermaßen wieder-belebt, daß es jetzt frei und ungehemmt in der Literatursprache ... benutzt wird."[11] "Der Strom der Rede des modernen Russisch ist prinzipiell der gemeinsame Strom der lateinischen Syntax."[12]

This would seem to imply that the participial system was carried over from ChSl as a category, but its syntactic use was inspired by, if not directly calqued upon, West European models (in this case only Latin and German would come into consideration, unless we move this influence forward to the second half of the eighteenth century). This view could be supported by the fact that the constructions which were thus "revived" are those which have Latin parallels. The dative absolute would thus be a remarkable exception, as its correspondence with the ablative absolute would be certain to make it eligible. This construction does, in fact, occur as a conscious archaism in the eigh-teenth century, e.g., in the works of Radiščev. As a matter of fact, although there seems to have been a Latin influence, this was neither direct nor the only factor involved.

The solution to the problem must obviously be sought at a point where the RCS tradition and the living Russian language meet. One such point is the language of the historical and other non-ecclesiastical genres, but here RCS was a passive element disintegrating not under the impact of a conscious attempt to bring the literary language closer to the vernacular, but owing to the crisis being undergone by tradi-tional culture, which eventually led to its collapse. The point of contact to be studied is that at which RCS was an active element cons-ciously (and literately) employed where new circumstances created a vacuum which the administrative language was unable to fill. Just such a juncture is found in the language of the diplomatic correspondence with Western powers, particularly the letters exchanged between the Tsar and the Emperor. Professor Unbegaun pointed out the importance of the Russian translations of these documents, some of which are virtually entirely written in RCS in an attempt to reproduce the style and syntax of their Latin originals,[13] and stressed the point that their language played an important part in the development of the ad-ministrative language by fostering the rise of a special style in the *Posol'skij Prikaz*.[14]

An examination of these texts shows that after a period (roughly to the end of the sixteenth century) when ChSl elements of all kinds are fairly frequently used, these elements become less marked during the first half of the seventeenth century, but are once more in the ascendant after 1656, and increase considerably toward the end of the century. This is particularly true of the lexical element, for the mor-

phological and syntactic elements tend to be confined to certain
contexts, and indeed some syntactic features such as the predicative
accusative are not found after the sixteenth century. The use of the
participles, however, presents a different picture: they are frequent in
translations, but this may be due to the original Latin or German.[15]
In the earlier non-translated documents the present active participle
(PrA) occurs only in set phrases already current in the administrative
language, e.g., *carstvujuščij grad*, but it becomes increasingly frequent in the second half of the seventeenth century. The present
passive participle is much rarer and entirely confined to translations.
In these texts the participles are used in constructions similar to those
of MR. The dat. abs. is not found at that period, except for one
example where it occurs in conjunction with a nominative absolute,
and in the phrase *Bogu pomogajušču* which translates Lat. *Deo juvante*.
One may also note the adjectives *nastojaščij, buduščij* (and *predbudu-
ščij*), *slědujuščij*, and the substantivized adjective *grjaduščee*. The PrA
has *-ščij* in the nom. masc. sing., with two exceptions where it is *-jaj*.

The participles, as well as the other ChSl forms, are used correctly,
although the result is often a terribly long, involved, and obscure
sentence. One feels that the translators were at great pains to render
the elegant Latin of the Imperial chancery with inadequate means, but
it was the resources of ChSl itself which were insufficient, and not their
command of the language. This ChSl, however, was not that of the
contemporary Russian *literati*, but of the Ukrainian and Belorussian
translators who had probably been educated in "Lithuania" and, in
collaboration with some Russians and some West Europeans employed
in a similar capacity in the *Posol'skij Prikaz*, produced the comedies
of Aleksej Mixajlovič's reign and the technical translations of the age
of Peter the Great. The result, however, was not the creation of a new
style, but, as G. Shevelov put it, a mixture of *slavenščizna, polites s
manira pol'skogo*, and *graždanskoe posredstvennoe narečie*.[16] One of the
elements of this mixture was invariably the PrA: it is significant that in
the *Vedomosti*, which contain few ChSl elements, this is a regular feature.
However, this product of the administrative language with alien
elements marked an endpoint, not the beginning of a new development.

At the same time as the administrative language was losing its
homogeneity, in an entirely different sphere Ukrainian and Belorussian
scholars were exercising a powerful influence on Russian learning and
civilization, and their background must have been similar to that of
the translators of the *Posol'skij Prikaz*. They brought with them a
ChSl tradition which had been cultivated with the aim of rivalling that
of Polish Latin, borrowing, at least indirectly, from Latin in the
process.

In the sermons of Feofan Prokopovič there is, as might be expected, a high proportion of ChSl elements, and the participial phrases occupy a prominent place. In the first sermon there are several constructions of the Latin type (e.g., predicative acc. with *byti*, from the Latin *acc. cum. inf.*), including long participial phrases placed before the noun they qualify. The masc. sing. nom. is in *-yj* or *-jaj*. There are relatively few examples of the PrA in nominal form, and these forms are used only with the dat. abs. and the pred. acc., but with the latter construction the participle is often in pronominal form: "edinago sebe pomyšljaja *byti nepobedima*, i ujazvitisja ne *mogušča*"[17] but: "vidim bo tebe . . . vsja ugodija *otvergšago*, var i znoj *nosjaščago*, mnogija i dalekija puti *podъ emljuščago*."[18] In the last sermon there are no Latin-type constructions, indicating greater integration into the pattern of Moscow ChSl. There is only one dat. abs. and one pred. acc., both with nominal forms of the participle: "i *umeršu emu*, aki by *živu sušču*, mir i tišina i del ego krepkoe sostojanie prebyvalo";[19] "znali *ego* vo vsem *dejstvujušča* i *pekuščasja*."[20]

The style of these sermons differs sharply from that of seventeenth century RCS works, not, however, in the syntactic means of expression, but in the organization of the period, where the use of participial phrases (or of hypotaxis, for that matter) is only one element. Cf. a fairly involved period such as the following:

> Budi nam ne v primer drevnij Ellinskix i Rimskix i pročiix slavoljubnyx ljudej obyčaj, kotorye velikim iždiveniem sooružali stolpy, i vrata, i obeliski, i piramidy, i inyja trofei, ili pobedonosnyja znamenija, eže by v nix ne umirajuščuju slavnyx del svoix pamjatъ poslednim vekom: xotja i nam takovago popečenija niktože vozbranjaet; no i vopreki, čelovek o slave otečestva svoego neradjaščij vsegda u mužej mudryx v ne dorogoj cene xodit, jako malodušnyj i grubyj; odnakože, budi ne v obrazec nam, jako Xristianom i k vyššej i ne suetnoj nebesnoj bo slave prostirajuščimsja, ne vo obrazec, ne v priklad nam, glagolju, budi obyčaj jazyk slavy istinnyja nepoznavšix."[20]

In such a sentence it is not hypotaxis as such, but the use of figures made possible by hypotaxis, which creates the impression of a period "which returns upon itself." Here these figures are variety of subordination (*kotoryj . . . , xotja . . . , no i vopreki . . . , jako . . . , odnakože . . .*), repetition and inversion (budi nam ne v primer . . . obyčaj/budi ne vo obrazec nam/ne vo obrazec, ne v priklad nam . . . budi . . . obyčaj), which serve as a counter to the centrifugal tendencies introduced by other figures such as accumulation of words and clauses which are designed to convey an impression of spontaneity and conceal the contrived structure of the sentence. This is the part of syntax which belongs to rhetoric rather than to grammar, and although OR literature ultimately derived its stylistic devices from the same source as Ukrainian CS, the latter had been subjected to the influence of the Renaissance—of classical style as interpreted by modern scholars and writers—whereas the Muscovite tradition was still medieval.

We have thus seen, as far as it it possible to see from such a brief and insufficiently documented sketch, that the participial system was the only ChSl morphological and syntactic feature to be used without a break in continuity and which spread to a great variety of styles and contexts. By the time Lomonosov wrote his grammar, it was definitely a ChSl element, but it was accepted as normal (if limited to verbs which can occur in ChSl) and not regarded as an archaism to be rejected (e.g., the nominal form of the participles), or whose obsolescence was lamented (cf. his regret on the subject of the dative absolute).

Manchester

NOTES

1. *Revue des Études Slaves*, T. 44 (1965), pp. 19–28.
2. *Ibid.*, p. 20.
3. *Ibid.*, p. 22.
4. *Ibid.*, p. 23.
5. *Ibid.*, p. 28.
6. "Das griechische byzantinische Erbe im Russischen," in *Acta Congressus Madvigiani*, V (Copenhagen, 1957), 163–218.
7. *Ibid.*, p. 218.
8. The actual origin of the participial constructions in RCS and their relation with existing Russian forms cannot be dealt with here. It seems a priori unlikely that OR ever made use of the involved constructions which are characteristic of the classical languages. The examples (e.g., in the chronicles) of participles in Russian form does not prove the existence of a given construction.
9. S. D. Nikiforov, *Glagol, ego kategorii i formy v russkoj pis'mennosti vtoroj poloviny XVI veka* (Moscow, 1952), pp. 243–46.
10. *Acta Congressus Madvigiani*, V, 36.

11. *Op. cit.*, p. 211.
12. *Ibid.*, p. 218.
13. *La langue russe au XVIe siècle* (Paris, 1935), p. 26.
14. *Ibid.*, pp. 27 and 28.
15. Actual calques are rare: "po vzjatyx Navarinax" (*Pamjatniki diplomatičeskix snošenij drevnej Rossii s Rimskoju Imperijeju*, VI (St. Petersburg, 1862), col. 1332, 1685; "pri buduščix vas" (*ibid.*, col. 641, 1685). This construction "po nekotoryx dnex prošedšix," also occurs in "Gistorija o Vasilii Koriotskom," *Russkie povesti pervoj treti XVIII veka*, ed. G. N. Moiseeva (Moscow–Leningrad, 1965), p. 193.
16. A. Šaxmatov-G. Y. Shevelov, *Die kirchenslavischen Elemente in der modernen russischen Literatursprache* (Wiesbaden, 1960), p. 80.
17. *Sočinenija* ed., I. P. Eremin (Moscow–Leningrad, 1961), p. 24.
18. *Ibid.*, p. 28.
19. *Ibid.*, p. 141.
20. *Ibid.*
21. *Ibid.*, pp. 48–49.

The Symbol of the River in the Tale of Gore-Zločastie

WILLIAM E. HARKINS

THE ROLE played by the nameless river in the Russian seventeenth-century Tale of Gore-Zločastie is a complex one, and to date it has not been elucidated. The hero of the Tale is pursued by the "unclean" Gore (Misery), a spirit of ill fortune. As a result of his own bragging and the temptations of Gore, he loses all he has in a drinking bout in a tavern, and wanders on, in borrowed rags, till he comes to a river which blocks his further progress. His destination at this point in the Tale is uncertain: it is clear only that he is fleeing from the scene of his failure, as he had done once before after a spree. Having no money to pay the ferrymen, he sits for three days by the river, disconsolate and hungry. He resolves to end his misfortunes by hurling himself into the river, when Gore again appears to him from behind a rock and abjures him to accept his misery, remain cheerful, and make the best of his lot; then, providing only that he make obeisance to Gore, he will be ferried across the river and fed and clothed by "good people." The youth does as he is bidden, sings a song in which he recalls his home and his mother, and characterizes his misfortunes as already predestined in childhood. He is ferried over by the ferrymen, who are ostensibly touched by his singing. But once he is across the river, Gore appears to him again. In spite of his earlier obeisance to Gore and presumed resolve to accept his misfortunes, he now struggles desperately to escape: his efforts take the form of zoomorphic transformations. But no matter what magical form he assumes, Gore transforms itself into an appropriate pursuer: the youth becomes a falcon and Gore a gerfalcon; the youth becomes a dove and Gore a hawk; the youth a wolf and

55

Gore a huntsman with hounds; the youth a blade of grass and Gore a reaper with a scythe; the youth a fish and Gore a fisherman with nets. Finally, giving up his attempts at escape, "the youth recollects the path of salvation" and enters a monastery; the unclean spirit Gore remains outside at the gates.

The dual nature of Gore is apparent: on one hand Gore is a physical demon, naked but girded in bast, who dwells behind the stove like a *domovoj* or behind a rock by the river; on the other hand, Gore serves as an inner *alter ego*, the youth's own psychic and spiritual weakness, leading him to drink and self-destruction (Gore first appears to the youth in a dream, and never appears to any other personage in the Tale). Buslaev already emphasized this duality.[1]

The symbolic role of the river is unclear. Presumably it might represent a trauma or crisis in the youth's *Seelendrama*, resolved by his worship of Gore, i.e., by his acceptance of his own limitations and his unhappy lot. But this explanation is contradicted by the youth's rebellion against Gore on the other side of the river. Elsewhere, in what is perhaps an excessively subjective interpretation of the Tale, I have tried to argue that crossing the river does symbolize the youth's reconciliation to his unhappy fate, but that this resolution of one conflict only permits another to emerge; the spiritual conflict within himself as to the future use of his miserable life: shall he become a beggar or a brigand as Gore wishes, or shall he transcend this manifest destiny and enter a monastery? Hence, there are in fact two conflicts, the first symbolized by the river and its crossing; the second, by the zoomorphic transformations and their futile outcome.[2] The interpretation is at least plausible, but it fails to explain those folk versions of the narrative in which both crossing the river and the zoomorphic transformations occur,[3] for in most of these the youth's "escape" from Gore takes the form not of entrance into a monastery, but of death.

Regardless of the relation of the Tale to the versions of the same narrative which have survived in modern Russian oral tradition, it is clear that its main sources are in folklore. The figure of Gore-Zločastie itself derives from the numerous East Slavic lyric songs about Gore and Dolja, spirits that pursue young people, often to their death.[4] The Tale is also related to Russian narrative songs or ballads,[5] folk tales,[6] *duxovnye stixi*,[7] as well as to proverbs about misfortune (see below). The literary elements of the Tale are few and are largely confined to the prologue and the ending (even here they may have been transmitted via the *duxovnye stixi*[8]). So it is to Russian and East Slavic folklore that we should look first for an explanation of the symbol of the river.

It is well known that crossing a river by bridge or ferry, or being transported across by boat in general, symbolizes a young girl's marriage. Potebnja has culled the Slavic song material to demonstrate this point.[9] The examples he presents, including ritual wedding songs, are convincing.[10] It is worth noting, however, that certain later nonritual lyrics use the motif in a kind of inverted parody: a fisherman or ferryman refuses to convey a girl across *unless* he marries her.[11] Yet this distortion is perhaps to be expected: once the original symbolic significance of the crossing was lost, the journey, still loosely associated with the fact of marriage, is now explained, somewhat humorously, as blackmail. The extreme of this is reached in a song in which a maiden, fleeing from captivity under the Tartars, spurns the ferryman who demands her hand for conveying her over, and hence perishes.[12] This ballad is generally regarded as a "historical song" of Tartar times, but the Tartars appear as an arbitrarily chosen enemy used to motivate the situation; the real subject of all these songs is virginity and marriage.

Kolpakova lists crossing a river as a symbol of marriage as one of a group of symbols of luck or happiness (*sčast'e*), and failure to cross among the symbols of unhappiness (*gore*).[13] But marriage could inspire a feeling of ambivalence, at least for the peasant bride, particularly in the North, where lamenting was common. Hence there seems to be no reason (and apparently no supporting evidence from songs themselves) for regarding the symbol as one of general good luck, prosperity, or happiness. Indeed, the choice of the symbol itself obviously suggests connotations of risk, fright, and separation from maiden happiness and freedom.

True, the river is a barrier, which can serve either to expose a hero to danger (as in the "Tartar" ballad described above), or preserve him from danger, cf. the proverb, "Živi, kolotilo, za rekoju, da k nam ni nogoju" ('Stay across the river, clapper, and don't come near us!')— the clapper here suggests trouble or disturbance, perhaps an alarm sounded.[14] But the meaning of the river symbol here is hardly very deep or ancient (it is metonymic rather than metaphoric), and we find this proverb contradicted by another, in which misfortune seems rather to be intimately associated with crossing a river: "Ty ot gorja za reku, a ono už stoit na beregu" ('You try to escape misfortune by crossing the river, but it's already waiting for you on the bank'),[15] a situation strikingly similar to the one in the Tale, in which Gore reappears to the youth on the bank of the river near the ferry.

Hence we must reject any interpretation of the river symbol that would connect it with marriage, good fortune, or even escape from ill fortune. The first symbolization seems to be reserved for women in any case, and our hero is a young man, one who earlier in the Tale had rejected marriage. This is not to say, however, that no shade of this type of symbolic meaning is present in the Tale: the youth at least seems to believe that he can escape from Gore, and that crossing the river may change his luck.

A second meaning of the symbol of the river in folklore is death. It may seem strange to suggest such a meaning for Russian folklore, which contains no obvious parallel to the classical Styx. But nonetheless there are parallels. In Russian fairy tales a river of water or fire may serve as a barrier separating the hero from the realm where he is to pursue his quest; a ferry is often provided to convey him across, and he, like the ferrymen in our Tale, demands his fare. In one fairy tale there are three such rivers: the hero must pay with an arm, a leg, and his head as the toll for crossing them.[16] These mutilations, like those of tribal initiation ceremonies, symbolize death, as Propp has shown, a death which is preparatory to rebirth for adult or future life.[17] The magic world beyond the river where the hero's quest is to be carried out is the world of death, into which the hero crosses only at the greatest risk.[18] Russian *duxovnye stixi* show Heaven and Hell as separated from earth by a river of fire, across which a ferryman conveys departed souls. This image, though probably derived from classical mythology by way of popular Christian beliefs, turns up with amazing frequency, and had evidently been assimilated into Russian popular consciousness.[19] Not only a river, but other bodies of water, may of course separate the world of the living from that of the dead: in the Arthurian legend the land of Avalon, where King Arthur is taken, is located across the sea. Russian *byliny* such as those about Sadko and Vasilij Buslaev suggest a similar conception.

Is not Gore itself a spirit of death? This theory, proposed by Markov,[20] can be at least partly confirmed. Markov pointed to the symbolic image, found in most of the folk songs about Gore as well as in the Tale, of Gore as a reaper: this is a traditional image of death, one evidently less characteristic of Slavic folklore than Germanic because of the feminine gender of the word for death (in Russian *smert'*). The image, migrating into the East Slavic world, was presumably transferred to this "secondary" spirit with a name in neuter gender.

All but one of the narrative folk songs about Gore, and even some of the short lyric songs, end with the death of the hero, who kills himself in his attempt to escape from Gore. Indeed, this seems to be Gore's purpose: it hounds men to their death. The hero may escape the persecutions of Gore through death (usually suicide), but this "escape," of course, is only an irony: Gore's real end is attained when its victim is dead, e.g.,

> Už ja ot gorja vo syru zemlju—
> Gore za mnoj so lopatkoju;
> Stoit gore, usmexaetsja,
> Soboj gore poxvaljaetsja:
> "Dokonal, dokonal krasnu devicu!
> Vognal, vognal vo syru zemlju!"[21]

In turn, Gore itself may possibly be connected with rivers and with water. In the Tale it reappears to the youth beside a river, when it leaps out from behind a rock. This rock by the river also appears in some of the narrative folk songs, and in several of these Gore makes its *initial* appearance there, i.e., the rock may perhaps be regarded as Gore's "home."[22] In the Tale, Gore promises that the youth will be ferried across the river if he does obeisance to it: thus Gore seems to possess some power over the ferry and its operation.

At least one proverb reflects this close association of Gore and the river: "Čto za gore, koli u reki bez xleba ne sižival?" (Dal' adds: "t.e. na perevoze").[23] This proverb may even stem from the Tale itself (or from a common source), in which the youth sits for three days by the river without food. Another, also probably a reflection of the Tale narrative, has already been quoted: "Ty ot gorja za reku, a ono už stoit na beregu." The rhyme of *gore-more* ('misery-sea') has inspired a number of related proverbs, such as "Po gore ne za more" and "Ot gorja xot' v more, ot bedy v vodu."[24] These may be explained by the rhyme, but their sense was conceivably reinforced by a prior association between Gore and water. Normally Gore drives the youth "into the ground" (i.e., into his grave), but in one ballad version he drowns himself in the sea to escape Gore.[25] This is hardly a part of the original myth, but again, it may have been suggested by the sense of Gore's association with water.[26]

The youth's passage across the river is followed by his attempts to escape Gore by zoomorphic transformation. Are not these transformations likewise symbols of death, or more precisely, of his attempts to escape death? That the voluntary crossing of the river should represent passage into the realm of death, and that this passage is followed by an effort to escape from death, is not so inconsistent as it might at first seem. The myth is no longer completely alive in the oral and written versions that have come down to us; it is largely vestigial. And mythic images themselves are not literal; they do not state, but only suggest. One of the purposes of such magical transformations, known

in English folklore terminology as shape-shifting, is to avoid death, and
as such the motif is common in folk tales, where it often takes the
form of transformation of the hero by himself or by a friendly spirit
when he is fleeing from an enemy: a dragon, ogre, or other pursuing
spirit belonging to the world of the dead (e.g., Afanas'ev, Nos. 208,
219, 220, 249, etc.).

Transformation combats, resembling that of the youth with Gore,
are well known in folklore.[27] In a Scottish ballad "The Twa Magi-
cians" (Child, No. 44), a smith vows to gain a lady's maidenhead: to
escape from him she turns herself successively into an eel, a hare, a
mare, etc.—he assumes the same form or one appropriate to pursuit:
a trout, a hound, a saddle, etc. The chase is over when the two
finally take the form of bedclothes. The images are fairly close to those
of the Tale, and one pair (beast-hound) is the same.[28] True, there is no
death here, but Child's note to the ballad suggests the likelihood of a
grimmer origin of the subject.

Finally, at least one of the transformations itself suggests death:
the youth turns himself into a blade of grass, and Gore into a reaper
with a scythe, a traditional image of death.[29] Yet the hero of the Tale
escapes death by entering a monastery; does not this end contradict
the mythic interpretation we have given?

Presumably the monastery is a later addition, and it is found only in
the written Tale and one folk version (Rybnikov, No. 48), probably
influenced by the written Tale. This strongly suggests that it is a literary accretion, a reworking by an author for whom the significance of
the original myth had been lost, or who wished to transcend the pagan
myth with a Christian resolution. For this author the motif of crossing
a river and the magical transformations become dynamic symbols of an
inner, spiritual struggle of the hero with himself, or with an *alter ego*,
Gore, standing for his own baser self. It is just possible that the
changed ending is a deliberate one, embodying in symbolic form the
Christian's triumph over death.

It is difficult today to determine which elements of the original
myth are essential ones. Neglect of parental advice, drinking,
boasting, rejection of one's bride—all these motifs, so important in the
written Tale, are perhaps later additions, designed to rationalize or to
give a didactic signification for contemporary hearers of an older
mythic tale concerning the inevitability of misfortune and death. Yet
it may be significant that all these motifs (except that of drink) are
suggested in variants of another ballad, one long associated with the
Tale and its own ballad variants, in which crossing a river (of death)
also plays a crucial role: "Molodec i reka Smorodina."[30] (The name of
this river is the same as that of most of the folk narratives about

the youth and Gore.) These motifs and the style and references to *realia* suggest a myth of mid-Muscovite times, hardly much older than our written Tale. How this was combined with a presumably much more ancient myth—the inevitable death of man, perhaps a man cast off by family or clan, at the hands of a pursuing demon of fate and death, we can only speculate.

Columbia University

NOTES

1. See F. Buslaev, "Povest' o Gore i Zločastii," *Istoričeskie očerki russkoj narodnoj slovesnosti i iskusstva* (St. Petersburg, 1861), I, 538–43. See also my articles, "The Pathetic Hero in Russian Seventeenth-Century Literature," *American Slavic and East European Review*, XIV: 4 (December, 1955), 514–19; and "The Mythic Element in the 'Tale of Gore-Zločastie,'" *For Roman Jakobson* (The Hague, 1956), pp. 201–206.

2. Harkins, "The Mythic Element...," *loc. cit.*

3. Especially significant in this respect is the version published in *Pesni sobrannye P. N. Rybnikovym*, I (Petrozavodsk, 1864), No. 48 (this version is closest to the seventeenth-century Tale, and, unlike other folk versions, even retains the youth's end in a monastery); also the two variants published in V. Varencov, *Sbornik russkix duxovnyx stixov* (St. Petersburg, 1860), pp. 127–33. For a listing of the related East Slavic folk-song material, see V. Ržiga, "Povest' o Gore i Zločastii i pesni o Gore," *Slavia*, X (1931), 288–90.

4. See Ržiga, *op. cit.*, pp. 40–66, 288–315.

5. *Ibid.*

6. See A. Sonni, "Gore i Dolja v narodnoj skazke," *Kievskie Uni-*

versitetskie Izvestija, XLVI: 10 (October, 1906).

7. See A. V. Markov, "Povest' o Gore-Zločastii," *Živaja starina*, XXII: 1–2 (1913), 17–24.

8. *Ibid.*

9. A. A. Potebnja, *Ob"jasnenija malorusskix i srodnyx narodnyx pesen*, II (Warsaw, 1887), 271, 446–53; see also his *Perexod čerez reku kak predstavlenie braka* (Moscow, 1867), which unfortunately has not been available to me.

10. Potebnja's opinion is confirmed by N. P. Kolpakova, *Russkaja narodnaja bytovaja pesnja* (Moscow-Leningrad, 1962), pp. 210, 220, and, more superficially, by V. M. Sidel'nikov, *Poètika russkoj narodnoj liriki* (Moscow, 1959), p. 75.

11. A. I. Sobolevskij (ed.), *Velikorusskie narodnye pesni*, II (St. Petersburg, 1896), No. 206; *Pesni sobrannye P. V. Kireevskim*, Nov. ser. (Petrograd, 1917[?]), vyp. 2, č.1, No. 1507.

12. "Krasnaja devica iz polonu bežit," *Ètnografičeskij sbornik*, vyp. 6 (1864), p. 92; reprinted in *Narodnye ballady* (Biblioteka poèta, Bol'š. ser. [Moscow-Leningrad, 1963]), pp. 205–206.

13. Kolpakova, *op. cit.*

14. V. Dal' (ed.), *Poslovicy russkogo naroda* (Moscow, 1957), p. 148.

15. *Ibid.*, p. 159.

16. A. N. Afanas'ev (ed.), *Narodnye russkie skazki* (Moscow, 1957), I, Nos. 138, 173.

17. V. Propp, *Istoričeskie korni volšebnoj skazki* (Leningrad, 1946), *passim*, especially Chapter 3.

18. *Ibid.*, *passim*, especially pp. 184, 327.

19. See P. Bessonov (ed.), *Kaliki perexožie* (Moscow, 1863), Part V, pp. 162–63, 166, 169, 226, *passim*.

20. A. V. Markov, *op. cit.*, pp. 21–24. Note also Ždanov's theory that references to Gore in incantations are symbolic of death—see *Sočinenija I. N. Ždanova*, I (St. Petersburg, 1904), 726.

21. The ending of a lyric song about Gore, first published in *Pesni sobrannye P. V. Kireevskim*, Nov. ser. (Moscow, 1929), vyp. 2, č. 2, No. 2624. Reprinted in V. I. Černyšev (ed.), *Russkaja ballada* (Leningrad, 1936), 295–96.

22. The closer association of the river with Gore is stressed by Markov, *op. cit.* Both variants published by Varencov, *op. cit.*, open with the scene of a river, otherwise quite unexplained.

23. Dal', *op. cit.*, p. 151.

24. *Ibid.*

25. A. F. Gil'ferding (ed.), *Onežskie byliny*, II (Moscow-Leningrad, 1938), No. 177.

26. It is possible that the association of Gore as a death spirit with the river has its inner connection in the act of suicide. It is to suicide, of course, that Gore drives its victims in the folk songs. The folk belief (probably not ancient) that *rusalky* were spirits of the girls who had committed suicide also connects suicide and water. In this case Gore might be regarded as that death spirit which drives man to suicide through hardship and persecution. But we must not forget that in the written Tale (which may not give us as authentic evidence on this point as the folk versions) Gore frustrates the youth's resolve to drown himself; Gore rather prefers that he end on the gallows as a brigand.

27. See *Funk and Wagnalls Standard Dictionary of Folklore, Mythology and Legend*, II (New York, 1950), 1122.

28. In French versions of the same song, Child (No. 44) describes correspondences that are even closer, and mentions such pairs as quail-sportsman, carp-angler, and hare-hound.

29. The dove into which the youth transforms himself may also represent a departed spirit (see F. J. Oinas, "Russian Golubec 'Grave Marker, etc.' and Some Notions of the Soul," *International Journal of Slavic Linguistics and Poetics*, VIII [1964], 79–86), but this symbolization would contradict the motif of *escape* from death.

30. The basic version, in which the youth is apparently cast off by his family, is Kirša Danilov, No. 33. North Russian variants rather describe him as running away from an unloved wife—see the discussion in *Drevnie rossijskie stixotvorenija sobrannye Kiršeju Danilovym* (Akademija nauk, Moscow-Leningrad, 1958), pp. 619–20.

Čupa, čupus 'enodebelni čoln'— v ruščini in slovenščini

RADO L. LENČEK

NA FORMALNO in semantično podobnost ruskih in slovenskih izrazov *čúpa*, *čúpka*, *čúpočka* (f.), *čúpus*, *čúpas* (m.)—in *čúpa*, *čúpca*, *čúpka* (f.), v osnovnem pomenu 'v les izdolbena posoda, korito', doslej še ni opozoril noben slovanski etimološki slovar. V obeh jezikih so ti izrazi dialektični in arhaični, še zlasti ko gre za njihov ožji pomen, ki ga imata osnovna izraza z izvedenkami kot apelativa za 'enodebelni čoln (alveus monoxilus)' Že v osnovnem pomenu skladnost preseneča, kajti—vsaj kot se zdi—kompleksa ne izhajata iz skupnega praslovanskega korena, ampak sta po izvoru vezana na neslovansko sredo; še bolj presenetljiva pa je njuna skladnost v drugem pomenu, kajti kot je znano (cf. Moszyński, 672; Niederle, 446–62), za primitivni monoksil v slovanskih jezikih doslej ni ugotovljenega skupnega naziva. Namen sopostavitve gradiva, ki sledi, je opozoriti na ta dokaj nenavadni paralelizem dveh apelativov z istim pomenom, ki bi lahko služil kot lep primer potencialne konvergence v leksikalni strukturi jezikov s paralelnimi evolucijami, s katero mora lingvist vsaj teoretično pri etimologiziranju vedno računati.

1. V ruskih leksikalnih virih najdemo sledeče tri zapise: 1. za rjazanjsko in moskovsko področje: *čúpka*, *čúpočka* z gloso 'nebol'šaja derevjannaja čaška, stavnik' (cf. Dal'; prvič: Vostokov 1852); 2. za bivšo oloneško gubernijo: *čúpa* z opisom: 'dva uzkix dolblenyx koryta, skreplennye vmeste dlja ezdy po malym rekam i ozeram (Kanakša)', in *čúpus* z gloso: 'vydolblennaja dlja čelnoka osinovaja koloda, poka v nee ne vstavleny špangouty (Rjazovskaja oblast')' (cf. Kulikovskij); 3. za

bivšo vologodsko gubernijo: *čupas* z opisom: 'širokoe koryto s dvumja doskami po bokam, pridelannymi v gorizontal'nom položenii v rode kryl'ev; čupas zamenjaet soboju lodku na malen'kix rečkax i ozerax (Kadnikovski uezd)' (cf. Šajtanov, 398).

V slovenskih virih je besedo prvič zapisal K. Štrekelj v obliki *čopa* z gloso: 'Art Kahn aus einem ausgehöhlten Baumstamme (Devin, Nabrežina)' (cf. Štrekelj, 456; cf. also Pleteršnik), ki jo veže z izrazom *čoba* 'ein Baumstrunk'. Kasneje je bila beseda znova zapisana kot *čupa*, *čupca*, *čupka* v pomenu 'korito, koritce, enodebelni čoln' (cf. Lenček) z razločnim *-u-* v korenu. Ta *-u-* je verjetno tudi Štrekelj slišal, a je hotel dati besedi "pravilnejšo" obliko z *-o-*, kajti bil je prepričan, da je *čupa* iz lat. *copa* 'navicula' in da mora biti v etimološki zvezi s *čoba* 'ein Baumstrunk'. Ta poslednji izraz v pomenu 'drevesni panj z delom korenin v zemlji' je bil kasneje ponovno registriran kot *čopa* [čûǫpa] (cf. Lenček).

V živi govorici na slovensko-italijansko-furlanski jezikovni meji v okolici Trsta in vzdolž Soče se za čupo 'enodebelni čoln' uporabljata *ciòpolo* in *zòppolo* (m). Beneška oblika *zoppolo* je našla pot v veliki etimološki slovar italijanskega jezika (Battisti—Alessio, *DEI*). Furlanski slovar (*Il Nuovo Pirona*) ima registrirane oblike starih tekstov v beneškem zapisu: *zopolèt*, *zòpul* in *zopi* (pl.) s sledečim komentarjem: "Barche per i passi dell'Isonzo (sec. XV)" (za zapise cf. Corgnali). Od živih oblik omenja Pirona obliki *ciàup*, *zàup* [čaup] (m) v pomenu 'korito za svinje ali za napajanje živine'. Zdi se, da je ta beseda z objektom vred še v živi rabi, medtem ko je prva le zgodovinsko dokumentirana (*zopo* prvič 1356); obe sta geografsko vezani na vzhodnofurlansko področje.

Za dalmatinsko Jadransko obalo in otoke imamo izpričano besedo *zopolo* (m.) v italijanski obliki v zapisu nekega beneškega dokumenta že za l. 1419; dokument se nanaša na otok Korčulo. Kasneje, 1597, je beseda zapisana v statutih otoka Raba v dveh oblikah: *çaupo* in *zaupo* (m.). Alberto Fortis jo je v svojem "Viaggo in Dalmazia" (Venezia, 1774, p. 156) opisal pod imenom, kakršno je slišal ob Krki, Cetini in Neretvi, kjer so jo v njegovem času še uporabljali: *ciopula*. Tako je besedo registriral tudi Della Bella: *cjopula* 'barca tutta d'un pezzo di tronco scavato, monoxylum linter'.

2. Doslej sta bili postavljeni dve različni etimologiji te besede. Obe sta vezani na geografsko ločena področja in predpostavljata penetracijo besede v znamenju "kulturne difuzije" med Slovane.

Za rusko *čupus* M. Vasmer sprejema razlago, kot jo je postavil T. I. Itkonen, po katerem je beseda mlajša izposojenka iz lapščine. Itkonen jo izvaja iz lapskih narečnih form: *sùves*, *so'ppaz*, *suβpas* v pomenu

'Kiel', gredelj, s sledečim komentarjem: "Genetisch ist der Kiel aus einem flachen kiellosen Einbaume entstanden, welcher allmählich enger wurde, dem entsprechend wie die Seiten durch immer neue Bretter in die Höhe wachsen" (Itkonen, 61). Lingvistično Itkonen podpira svojo etimologijo s primerom korespondence *č : s* (e.g.: čibaki < sivakka 'krplje') in s sklicevanjem na morfem *-us ~ -as*, ki se v njegovem gradivu javlja dokaj pogosto.[1] Za izolirano obliko *čupus* utegne biti taka argumentacija prepričljiva. Toda vprašanje je, ali smemo ločiti *čupus* od *čupas* in *čupa*, ko osnovni pomen vse tri druži v eno samo semantično skupino in ko v isto skupino spadata tudi *dubás* in *dub* (m.) 'enodebelni čoln' (cf. Vasmer, *REW*), morfemska struktura katerih je veliko zgovornejša.

Slovensko *čupa* je K. Štrekelj na podlagi asociacije s *čoba* popravil v *čopa* in primerjal s srednjeveško-latinskim *copa* 'navicula' (cf. Du Cange) in s furlanskima *ciaup, zaup*.[2] Implikacija je jasna: *čopa* je mlada izposojenka iz latinščine, morda preko furlanščine. Lingvističnih argumentov za tak razvoj Štrekelj ne navaja, dasi bi jih lahko, če bi hotel biti ekspliciten. N. pr. za /č/: furl. *çocc* /čok/, ben. *zòco*, sle. *čok* (dial. čữok); furl. *zuètt* (< čott), ben. *zòtto*, sle. *čot* (dial. čữot); za /p/, katerega ohranitev v furlanščini kaže, da je bila beseda kasneje sprejeta, prim. furl. *çhapp* /čap/, ben. *ciapo*, sle. *čap* 'čreda' (cf. Šturm). Vendar se zdi, da je bila Štreklju etimologija *čupa < copa* tako jasna, da ni čutil potrebe po ugotavljanju glasovnih korespondenc.

Furlansko-italijanske razlage kompleksa *ciaup-zaup-zòppolo* 'korito, enodebelni čoln' ne izhajajo naravnost iz latinščine. Furlanski Pirona, n.pr., le ugotavlja zvezo med beneškim *zopo, zoppo* 'enodebelni čoln' starih dokumentov (1356, 1371, 1434, etc.; cf. Corgnali) in furlanskim *ciaup, zaup* 'korito'; fonološko oba ustrezata korenu [*čaup*-]. Za kasnejše oblike kot *zòpolo, zòpolèt*, Pirona ugotavlja, da so prav tako prešle v furlansko pisano besedo iz beneškega dialekta.—Battisti-Alessio (*DEI*) obravnava beneške *zoppo, zòpolo* starih dalmatinskih zapisov, ki so se ohranili v dveh formah: *çaupo* ali *zaupo* (fonološko: čaupo); o njih pravi: "latinizate in *zaupum*; la voce scomparse nel XVI sec." (*DEI*, 421a). Zanimivo razlago daje A. Prati v članku posvečenem furlanskim krajevnim imenom (129–130), kjer opozarja na sorodnost s padovanskim dialektičnim *zuoppo* 'štor, panj', ki ga na podlagi vzorca korespondenc: *paucus* (lat.) vs. *puoco* (padov., it.: *poco*), *pauper* vs. *puovero* (*povero*), rekonstruira v *zaupo z gloso 'deblo'. Dalje te etimologije ne vodijo.

3. Ni namen teh vrstic iskati etimologijo besede v jezikovnih plasteh, ki segajo globlje v indoevropsko preteklost. Kompleks *čupa—zòpolo* je na neki ravni gotovo povezan s srednjeveško-latinskim (bolje lati-

niziranim) *caupulus, -i* (m.) 'navicula,' izvor katerega sam pa ostaja
še vedno temen, nepojasnjen (cf. Walde, *LEW*). Ako bi smeli iti za
asociacijo z rekonstruiranim **zaupo*, imamo verjetno opravka z ger-
mansko (morda langobardsko) izposojenko v romanskih jezikih iz
korena **topp-*, a hkrati s kompleksom besed, katerih refleksom je
inogoče slediti v mnoge indoevropske in neindoevropske jezike (cf.
Wartburg, 181) in ki prav tako niti najmanj niso etimološko jasni.

Morda je vredno poudariti, da se je kompleks *čupa - zòpolo* razvil ali
ohranil le v vzhodnojadranskem prostoru, na slovansko-romanski jezikovni meji. Ali tudi ruske *čupa, čupus, čupas* spadajo v ta isti krog, bi
bilo ob današnji dokumentaciji tvegano domnevati.

LITERATURA:

Battisti, C., and Alessio, G. *Dizionario Etimologico Italiano*. Florence,
1957.

Corgnali, G. B., "Ciaup o ciopule,"
Patrie dal Friul, III (Udine, 1948),
2; 5-6.

Dal', V. I. *Tolkovyj slovar' živogo
velikorusskogo jazyka*. 3rd ed. St.
Petersburg-Moscow, 1903-1909).

Della Bella, A. *Dizionario Italiano-
Latino-Illirico*. Venice, 1728.

Du Cange, Ch. du Fresne. *Glossarium
mediae et infimae latinitatis*. Ed. L.
Favre. I–VII. Paris, 1883-87.

Itkonen, T. I. "Lappische Lehnwör-
ter im Russischen," *Annales Acad.
Scient. Fennicae*, Ser. B., XXVII
(Helsinki, 1932), 47-65.

Kulikovskij, G. *Slovar' oblastnogo
oloneckogo narečija*. St. Petersburg,
1898.

Lenček, R. "Poročilo o čupi,"
*Izvestje srednjih šol v brit.-amer.
pasu STO* (Trieste, 1950), 1-12.

Moszyński, K. *Kultura ludowa
Słowian. I.* Cracow, 1929.

Niederle, L. *Život starých Slovanů,
III, 2.* Prague, 1925.

*Il Nuovo Pirona, Vocabolario Friu-
lano*. Udine, 1935.

Pleteršnik, M. *Slovensko-nemški slovar*. Ljubljana, 1894-95.

Prati, A. "Spiegazioni di nomi di
luoghi del Friuli," *Révue de Linguistique Romane, XII* (Paris, 1936),
44-140.

Šajtanov, G. "Osobennosti govora
kadnikovskogo uezda vologodskoj
gubernii," *Živaja starina*, V (St.
Petersburg, 1895), 383-99.

Štrekelj, K. "Beiträge zur slavischen
Fremdwörterkunde, I," *AslPh*, XII
(Vienna, 1890), 451-74.

Šturm, F. "Romanska lenizacija
medvokaličnih konzonantov in njen
pomen za presojo romanskega ele-
menta v slovenščini," *Časopis za
slovenski jezik, književnost in zgodo-
vino, VII* (Ljubljana, 1928), 21-46.

Vasmer, M. *Russisches Etymologisches Wörterbuch*. I–III. Heidelberg,
1953-1958.

Vostokov, A. H. (ed.). *Opyt oblastnogo velikorusskogo slovarja.* St.
Petersburg, 1852.
Walde, A. *Lateinisches Etymologisches Wörterbuch,* I–III. Heidelberg,
1938–56.

Columbia University

Wartburg, W. "Le FEW: évolution
et problèmes actuels," *Linguistics
Today* (= *Publications of the Linguistic Circle of New York, 2*), ed.
A. Martinet. New York, 1954.

NOTES

1. Sufiks -*as* bi utegnil predstavljati
germanski -*az*, ki je bogato zastopan
v baltijskih jezikih, odkoder se je
razširil tudi v vzhodno-finske go-
vore. Cf. J. Kalima, "Etymologisches," *Annales Acad. Scient. Fennicae,* Ser. B, XXVII (Helsinki,
1932), 76.

2. Štrekelj omenja tudi sle. *kópanj,
kopánja* 'korito' (Pleteršnik tudi s
pomenom 'ein Kahn aus einem
Baumstamm ausgehöhlt'), ki se mu
zdi prevzeto iz beneškega *copano,* za
katerega latinski izvor *copána* 'navicula' glej v Du Cange, 588.

On the *Izbornik of 1076*

HORACE G. LUNT

A NEW EDITION of the third-oldest dated Slavic manuscript, the famous *Izbornik of 1076*, now makes it possible to examine its language with confidence.[1] The pertinent questions are what norms can be discerned, and what relation the norms have to classical Old Church Slavonic on the one hand and to East Slavic dialects—insofar as we can reconstruct them—on the other.[2]

The manuscript is in a pitiable state, for its faded ink was restored more than once during the middle ages and treated chemically by nineteenth-century investigators. The editors have done an admirable job of finding the original spellings by using the latest techniques of examination and photography under special lighting conditions, but as their footnotes tell us, they found it difficult or impossible in many cases to reach a decision. One feels that many of their unqualified decisions must have caused them considerable agony. This means that one must still approach individual spellings with caution, and the reader should be warned that the edition is not without its blunders and inconsistencies.[3]

The most important discovery for the linguistic investigator is that the manuscript was written by two scribes, the "sinful Ioan" of the colophon, who did most of the text and all of the red headings and initials, and a subordinate (to be referred to here as 76b) who copied the text of pages 606–668.9. (I cite the pages of the *edition*; the folia are garbled, and it is an extraordinary inconvenience that all references in the edition are to the folia.) Despite the opinion of the editors, neither Ioan nor his presumed pupil was a good scribe: they made all sorts of errors (misspellings, omissions, repetitions), some of which they caught and corrected, but many of which remain to plague the investigator.

The two had somewhat different habits. Ioan is less consistent and more conservative, which is to say that his text has much more of an OCS aura about it. Thus he much prefers the combination шт to the unit letter щ by about ten to one, although he makes a number of errors (e.g., 292.5, 540.5) and his pronunciation of the щ is revealed when he divides the word пооуш|чениюмь. The use of шт is shared with the OCS tradition of the *Suprasliensis* type (but not the *Savvina kniga*), and a small number of early East Slavic manuscripts. The consistent use of ю after ш, ж, шт/щ, and ц is like *Sav.* but not *Supr.*

Ioan retains all four *jusy*, but their distribution has nothing to do with etymology. ѩ (only two examples) and ѧ are used after vowel-letters and in initial position, while ѧ is regular after consonant-letters, although there are exceptions. A unique feature among the eleventh-century manuscripts is that both ѫ and ѭ serve as equivalents of ю—over 150 times in post-consonantal position and about 20 times after vowels. Only twice does ѫ stand for ESl *u* (пѫтьмь 163, пѫстыни 515). The iotized ѭ is found only in initial or post-vocalic position.

The *jer*-letters are used conservatively, despite many deviations from the hypothetical norms scholars set up on the basis of etymology. The overwhelming predominance of correct spellings like *lъžьnъ, lьvъtь, sъnьmъše,* or *pravьdьnъ,* and the conventional nature of most of the deviations (especially in view of the faulty quality of Ioan's work in general) are entirely in keeping with the usage of other early East Slavic manuscripts which are under strong South Slavic influence. It seems to me most likely that the *jers* were still ordinarily pronounced as units different from *e/o* in all positions, although doubtless they could be reduced to phonetic zero under some conditions.

Russian scribes tended to reject OCS spellings with ѣ under certain specific conditions, most importantly in the combination *CrěC* (< *CerC*) where all ESl dialects had *CereC*. Here Ioan's norm was the South Slavic type (брѣмѧ), which he wrote in about 250 examples, opposed to the phonetic ESl 16 times (type веремѧ) and the curious hybrid *CreC* 17 times (type времѧ). The parallel *ClěC/ColoC* type occurs rarely, 5 in SSl shape and one ESl (*polovela*). For *ColC*, only SSl *ClaC* is found (over 50 examples), while for *CorC* about 160 cases of normal SSl *CraC* and a distorted отворѧть (for OCS *ot[ъ]vratętъ*) are contrasted to pleophonic forms in each of six roots plus ten examples in the root *norov-*. Obviously, then, Ioan preferred the traditional OCS spellings, except that he believed that *nrav-* was somehow incorrect.

Russian scribes usually replaced the OCS *ě* of the imperfect suffix with the letters ѧ or ѧ. The evidence for 1076 is sparse, but the

forms бАше and хотАше indicate that Ioan followed the Russian
norm.[4] He hesitates in the suffixes where Russian has ѧ or ѧ for
OCS ѣ before nasal: мѣѧдн-, плътѧн- and багрѧниц-, but нинєвь-
гитѣн- and скитѣнин-. In the root 'eat,' ѣ is written twice at the
beginning of a line and once following a ѧ and once with the unique
occurrence of a "iotized ѣ," a letter otherwise known only in the
Izbornik of 1073. In fourteen other instances the traditional spelling
with ѧ is found. The Russian desinence *-ě* occurs in nouns (*vlъčьcě
vъdovicě, pijanicě, pъticě, sračicě, larě* 4 ×) and in the personal pronoun
(ѣ, ѥѣ). There are approximately twice as many counter-examples
with the normal SSl nominal desinences.

In the reflexes of earlier *CьrC, Ioan preferred the typical ESl
spellings, but while the types *CьrC* and *CъrC* clearly predominate
(roughly 60 per cent and 90 per cent of possible cases), examples with
CъlC make up but slightly over half. Compromise forms are also
found (*CьrьC* about 5 per cent, *ъrь/ъrъ* 5 per cent, *ръlьn-* and *obъlъčen-*).[5]
Ioan obviously did not feel strongly that any one spelling was necessary;
he writes with equal inconsistency *dlъgotьrpělivъ* and *dъlgotrъpělivyi*.

The reflexes of *dj are slightly more frequently spelled with ж than
the SSl жд, while only жд appears for the rare *zdj and *zgj. On the
other hand, Ioan was relatively partial to his native *č* for *tj. He
prefers ч in the present system of *xotěti* (21 × ч ∼ 11 × шт/щ) and,
curiously, in the participles *klokoču-, groxoču-, trepeču-*, and the present
pošъrъčetь. Like many other Russian scribes, he uses only *č* at the
beginning of the root **tjudj-* (OCS *štjužd-/štužd-/stužd-/tužd-*). (Ioan is
not averse to hybrid forms: чюжд-; съкрачаѥши for *sъkraštaj-* or
sъkoročaj-.) Yet all these examples total less than fifty and are in-
significant in the face of several hundred SSl spellings.

One might note a few morphological innovations which are not
typical of OCS (third-person verb-forms in *-tь* and instrumentals in
-ъmь/-ьmь are taken for granted). Adjectival datives in *-omu/-emu* are
frequent but not normal (13 *vs.* 32 in *-umu/-uumu*). Thus the *Izbornik*
is more conservative than a newly discovered western Bulgarian text
of about the same period, the *Enina Apostle*, in which *-omu/-emu* is the
only possible type. (This is one of the features which make it unwise
to call the Enina manuscript OCS, as does Mirčev.) Only the Russian
aorists *umьre, umьroša* occur (not the SSl *umrě, umrěšę*). Extension of
the old *u*-stem genitive plural to soft stems is found not only in
voždevъ and *plištevъ* (comparable to exceptional OCS *vračevъ, zmijevъ,
znojevъ*), but also to the exclusively ESl *larevъ*. This last form indicates
the productivity of the desinence.

Ioan uses the ESl dative *tobě* once, and the numeral 'seven' (OCS
sedm-) appears in Russian form in *semid(ь)nъje* 'week.'

The second scribe makes many errors, but it is clear that he aims at a rather more Russian norm than his senior colleague. He has completely abandoned the letters ѫ, ѭ and ѧ; as well as the combination шт. Nor does he use the combination ъі, an occasional variant in Ioan's system. The use of ы is unusual until much later, although it has a tradition reaching back into OCS (the *Zograph Folia*; the scribe of *Supr.* 131, 218) and including the great *Izbornik of 1073*. A decidedly un-Russian trait is the occurrence of ъ after ш, ж and ч (no cases with щ occur, and ь is written after ц), although 76b is not really consistent. The traditional *CraC* forms are much preferred by 76b to the native pleophonic type (9× vs. *norov-, ogorožajutъ, voroga*), but the front-vowel equivalent has only eighteen SSl *CrěC* examples opposed to twenty-four hybrid spellings with *CreC* and two unexpected cases of the preposition черсъ. This is an important trait of the rapidly developing Russian literary standard, for the *CreC* formula becomes the norm (i.e., used in at least 85 per cent of possible cases) in the *Archangel Gospel* of 1092, the first part of the *Novgorod Minei* of 1097, and increasingly in the manuscripts of the twelfth century.

In the *CъrC* type there are no spellings with the *jer* only following the liquid: *CъrC* 18× vs. *CъrъC* 7×; *tъrg-* 2×, *mъlva* and *pъln-* with no counter-examples.

The Russian ж for *dj* predominates (7× vs. 2× жд), while ч for *tj* is found only once in the stem чюж- and once in a participle, ищюче.

No imperfects occur in the text; the Russian *ä* is found in прѩмо (OCS *prěmo*), плътан-, and самарѧниню, with no counter-examples. Where Ioan correctly spelled the stem *těles-* (9×), 76b wrote *teles-* both times he had the opportunity. Other early Russian scribes had trouble with the shape of this stem (Durnovo, *JF* 6. 41), which, we may conclude, was unfamiliar to them.[6]

The orthographies of Slavonic manuscripts from eleventh-century Rus' range from the very conservative style of the second scribe of the *Ostromir Gospel* of 1056 (Grigorij) to the innovating and therefore "Russian" usage that is typified by the second scribe (Mičьko) of the *Archangel Gospel*. The former is essentially a regional variant of the kind of classical Southern Slavonic found in the *Suprasliensis*, differing only by its systematic revision of the use of the *jer*-letters (manifested chiefly as a preference for the -*tъ* of third-person verb forms, and -*ъmь*/ -*ьmь* of instrumental singulars), plus the few nonsystematic East Slavic details which are to be regarded as errors in terms of the norms the scribes were obviously trying to follow. In this scale Ioan is on the conservative side, but stands in a rather neutral place, while the second scribe is very close to the most distinctively Russian pole.

This is an important observation, for it shows that this kind of norm was not a product of the very last years of the century, but was well on its way to achievement by 1076.

It is wrong to suppose that such markedly Russian orthography has anything to do with the place of the translation of a given text. The underlying linguistic systems of South and East Slavic must have been very much alike at this time; the written language is a compromise, or rather a series of compromises, in which many of the most pervasive elements seem to be South Slavic, but many details are Eastern. We must assume that well-trained bookmen would strive to adapt every text that passed through their scriptoria to the particular norm they had learned or consciously elaborated.

It seems quite reasonable to suppose that this particular selection, primarily from the works of popular church fathers, was compiled "from the princely books" of Kiev, rather than Bulgaria. It is not a translation of a known Greek miscellany, but many of the components can be demonstrated to have been available in Slavonic by 1073. The Greek texts in the new edition plus those recently published by Ihor Ševčenko of Dumbarton Oaks (Agapetus for the *Nakazanije bogatymъ*, the *Life of St. Niphon* for the story of Sozomenus, plus the lines mentioned in Ševčenko's footnote 33) account for a full two-thirds of the *Izbornik*, and the rest is of such patent Byzantine origin that it seems certain the Greek sources will eventually come to light. The alleged originality of the "authors of the *Izbornik*" has been greatly exaggerated (see especially the literature cited by Ševčenko), yet the fact remains that the passages whose sources we know have been modified in varying measure.

Two characteristic motives are obviously at work, and a close examination of the whole manuscript may well reveal more. The first aim of the adapter is to produce a text generally suitable for the secular reader, who is of course a Christian and probably relatively well-to-do. Thus, St. Basil's tract on how a *monk* should act is consistently changed to say what a *man* should do (as Dubrovina points out, 719). Ševčenko has noted that all references to the princes have been taken out of passages from Agapetus, thus making the admonitions pertinent to any well-placed person. In the story of Sozomenus, too, there have been modifications. The first sentence of the *Life of Niphon* in the Slavonic translation (which clearly was made in Bulgaria) is garbled so as to make it sound as though Sozomenus was a cleric to start with. In the *Izbornik*, Sozomenus is merely "a man." At the end, the story departs purposefully from the original. In the Greek (and its faithful translation, preserved even in the late form published by Tschižewskij) Sozomenus becomes a monk; in the

Izbornik he merely becomes "very merciful to the poor" and his renown rests only on his generosity. The last twenty lines of the tale, with their pious, somewhat commonplace moralizing, can easily be attributed to the Kievan compiler.

The other aim of the compiler is to bring the messages clearly to his Kievan reader. Thus a number of mildly confusing details are removed from the Sozomenus story. For the Byzantine, a eunuch is an entirely appropriate guide to a magnificent palace. But in the dream of Sozomenus in the *Izbornik*, the *kaženikъ* of Niphon becomes simply a youth (*unoša*). The *kovъčezi* become *larě*, presumably because a *larь* was the sort of container a Kievan would keep his costly garments in, as opposed to the "chests" or "arks" or "coffins" vaguely associated with the word *kovъčegъ* in various familiar church texts. Now, long ago Vostokov remarked that οἶνος, ordinarily translated *vino*, was rendered in the *Izbornik* by *medъ* 'mead' (Sreznevskij, s.v. *medъ*).* There is a reason.

Vino in the *Izbornik* is the blood of Christ (237) and the blessing of the vine (524), but St. Paul warns against its misuse (*ne upivaite sę vinъmь*, Ephes. 5:18), Neilos of Sinai emphasizes that it, like food, must be taken in moderation (622 ff.), and Ecclesiasticus cautions against drinking it in the presence of someone else's wife (Eccl. 9:9; 372). The *Izbornik*'s adapter is well aware of the Russian love of drink, but he draws a line between wine and mead. Wine is a good thing, but not without its dangers. Mead, on the other hand, is unqualifiedly bad. Thus Ecclesiasticus inveighs against drinking mead (31:25, 29, 31; *Izb.* 403–4, then Eccl. 31:29 and 25, 26:8; *Izb* 685 ff.), while "the prophet Joel"—actually St. Basil—paints a black picture of the results of *bezměrije medvьnoje*, even changing Paul's warning (ne upivaite se *medъmь* 682). Even in rather neutral contexts, cautions against wine are changed to apply specifically to mead (Neilos, 280; Basil, 469). In all these cases the Greek text has οἶνος; it is likely that the same is true in the responses of Athanasius (599), although the original has not yet come to light.

Most of these changes I believe to have been made by the adapter who picked out the selections and arranged them for the original

* On reading the draft of this article, G. Y. Shevelov, as editor, kindly called my attention to the article by Jacques Lépissier, "Une source de l'*Izbornik* de 1076," *RES* 45.38–47, which gives the Greek and Slavonic texts of the tale of Sozomenus. In his short commentary, Lépissier anticipated all the remarks and conclusions I have made in the foregoing two paragraphs. Both disconcerted and heartened by this agreement, I have decided to let my text stand nonetheless, as an introduction to my final paragraphs.

Kievan miscellany. Yet the scribe Ioan may have carried the matter further. At 280.11, the neuter accusative *je* has to refer to *medъ*; surely this shows us that a Slav, working from a Slavonic text, has changed the expected "wine" to "mead" and failed to adjust the gender of the pronoun.[7] Here I suspect Ioan. Now, M. N. Speranskij has amply demonstrated that a complete Slavonic Ecclesiasticus was at the disposal of the Kievan compiler (cf. Dubrovina, 754), who did not hesitate to rearrange the verses and even to adapt some passages to suit his own purposes. In the long excerpts from Eccl. (309–427), verses 25, 29 and 31 of Ch. 34 appear with a heading *o medu* (403–4), while 25 and a paraphrase of 27 occur much later among sayings attributed to St. Paul (686). The compiler has thus, surely with purposeful tendentiousness, omitted the praise of wine measurably drunk from verses 27 and 28, and seriously modified 27.[8] We read: *Medъ bo vъ veselije dano bystь b(o)gъmь, a ne na pijanьstvo sъtvoreno.*[9] Here again, I submit, the Kievan compiler-adapter had a text reading *vino . . . dano bystь.* He, or more likely the hasty copyist Ioan, substituted *medъ* as subject but did not adapt either participle to fit the new gender.

Harvard University

REFERENCES

Izbornik 1076 goda. Pod redakciej S. I. Kotkova; izdanie podgotovili V. S. Golyšenko, V. F. Dubrovina, V. G. Dem'janov, G. F. Nefedov. Moscow, 1965. (The Slavonic text runs from 151 to 701.)

Durnovo, Nikolaj. "Russkie rukopisi XI i XII vv. kak pamjatniki staroslavjanskogo jazyka," *Južnoslovenski filolog,* 4 (1923–1924), 72–94, 5 (1925–1926), 93–117, 6 (1927), 11–64.

——. "Staroslavjanskoe pravopisanie XI–XII vv.," *Slavia,* 12 (1933–1934), 45–82.

Lunt, Horace G. *The Orthography of Eleventh-Century Russian Manuscripts.* Ann Arbor: University Microfilms, 1949.

Eninski Apostol, starobъlgarski pametnik ot XI vek. Sofia, 1965.

Ševčenko, Ihor. "On some sources of Prince Svjatoslav's *Izbornik* of the year 1076," *Orbis Scriptus, Festschrift für Dmitrij Tschiževskij zum 70. Geburtstag* (München, 1966), pp. 723–38.

Tschiževskij, Dmitrij. *Zwei russisch-kirchenslavische Texte.* Wiesbaden, 1956.

NOTES

1. Bibliographical references are given at the end of the paper.
2. On the question of orthographical norms in early Slavic manuscripts, see Durnovo and Lunt.
3. The word-index is particularly vulnerable to criticism, since it contains a number of ghost-words, several incorrect grammatical identifications (e.g., *tysęšti* 168ᵛ is nom. sg. despite the Greek, the *sebe* at 80ᵛ13 is not dative but acc.), an uneven attitude toward doubtful forms to be labeled with question marks or exclamation points (e.g., *lěpovati* is a perfectly reasonable infinitive, but *otъčavjutъ* is an impossible form), and omits some easily recognizable though distorted words (like *umletъ* 123ᵛ–p. 504, surely *ujemljetъ*, from *uimati*), displaying in general a distressing lack of lexicographical consistency. One of the most curious entries is *obъdъ?* (52ᵛ–p. 253), defined as past active participle feminine (sic!) nominative of *obъěsti*, and its corollary *rža* "n. sg. fem." The passage has therefore been construed "rust having eaten up thy pride." But even at first glance it is obvious that no emendation is necessary, for this is the ordinary aorist, impeccably spelled, *obъdъrža*: "(the grave) has embraced thy pride." Indeed, the whole passage is quoted in Sreznevskij s.v. *obъdъržati*.
4. The editors' introductory remarks about the language and spelling of the *Izbornik* are inadequate and often based on misunderstandings. Thus the note about imperfects (p. 116) cites normal OCS forms as significant for the Russianess of the scribes.

5. Note that the root **sъln-* 'sun' is written out, in SSl shape, only twice. The ESl form is not found, but the root appears *pod titlom* seven times. Could it not be a way to avoid the painful decision which way to spell this difficult combination? Note that none of the early SSl manuscripts abbreviate this stem.
6. G. Y. Shevelov informs me that there is some evidence that Kievans had a living form *teles-* beside the general ESl *těl-*; cf. the *Ivasyk Telesyk* of the folk tales.
7. The *Izbornik* contains two translations of the same bit of advice by Neilos: Πίνε τὸν οἶνον ἐλάχιστον· ὅσον γὰρ κολοβοῦται, εὐεργετεῖ τοὺς πίνοντας (♯ 59, p. 712).

280: Pii medъ po malu.
jeliko bo je sъkračaješi.
to bl(a)g(o)dětъ ti je.

622: Pii vino po malu.
jeliko bo skudo pijetъ sę.
toliko bo bl(a)go tvori
pijuščimъ.

The first is in the series of *kephalaia* identified by Dubrovina, but its second clause is less felicitous a rendering than the second version, while the last clause is so free as to scarcely correspond to the Greek. It might be noted that as a rule the *Izbornik* reads easily and naturally; the translations have none of the awkwardness or downright incoherence that characterize a number of early Slavic efforts. Most of the difficulties appear to be due to poor copying, and I am therefore strongly inclined to believe that the adaptation was not done by Ioan.

8. It may indeed be the case that this whole section (685–86) is excerpted from a yet unidentified sermon that includes St. Paul's remarks on drunkeness, since most of the maxims are paraphrases or allusions rather than accurate translations of the parallels adduced by Dubrovina (824).

9. The current Slavonic is close to the Greek: Polezno vino životu člověču, ašče pieši je v měru ego. Kij životъ poběždaemomu vinomъ ? Sie bo na veselie človēkomъ sozdano estъ. ἔφισον ζωῆς οἶνος ἀνθρώποις [var. ἀνθρώπῳ] ἐὰν πίνῃς αὐτὸν [ἐν] μέτρῳ αὐτοῦ. τίς ζωὴ ἐλασσουμένῳ οἴνῳ; καὶ αὐτὸς ἔκτισται εἰς εὐφροσύνην ἀνθρώποις. *Septuaginta* II (ed. A. Rahlfs, [Stuttgart, 1950]), 431.

The Recurrent Image in Doctor Živago

ROBERT MAGIDOFF

IN THE WRITING of *Doctor Živago*, Pasternak skillfully exploited many of the devices open to the lyric poet, as well as those which properly belong to the sphere of prose. The one poetic device that he used with particular readiness and spontaneity is metaphoric language, and his figures of speech do indeed pulsate with the concentrated power and suggestiveness of poetry, at the same time retaining the evaluating quality and realism of detail so vital to the functioning of imagery in prose. The profusion of tropes in Pasternak's novel, their uniqueness and dynamism, establish him beyond doubt as one of the most prolific and original creators of imagery among Russian prose writers.

Pasternak's lifelong preoccupation with figurative language, both in his prose and poetry, stems from his profound understanding of the power and magnificence of this poetic device. "Images," he once said, "that is, miracles in words."[1] And again, on another level but no less significantly:

> Metaphorical language is the result of the disproportion between man's short life and the immense and long-term tasks he sets himself. Because of this, he needs to look at things as sharply as an eagle and to convey his vision in flashes which can be immediately apprehended .... Outsize personalities use metaphor as a shorthand of the spirit.[2]

In conveying his vision by means of metaphoric language, in "looking at things as sharply as an eagle," the writer throws a revelatory light on himself, his attitudes, his approach to reality, and

79

his philosophic and aesthetic concepts. The very areas from which he selects the objects which he brings together in the associative process contribute to that revelation. The omissions may be no less illuminating than the inclusions. The truth of this emerges with particular clarity from a comparison of one significant aspect of the imagery in Shakespeare and Pasternak. Whereas the former turns his powers of imagination on all of life's manifestations, including evil, fear, corruption, illness, and decay, Pasternak reserves his figures of speech almost exclusively for what he cherishes as beautiful and lifegiving. This is no accident, for Pasternak deliberately refuses to dignify evil and ugliness with the aura of imagery. In the course of an interview with Professor Ralph Matlaw in June, 1959,

> Pasternak went on to say that for him the inchoate or the ugly can never matter for art, that art is reserved for the beautiful. Only, perhaps, the ugly can be used for contrast, as in the figure of the lawyer Komarovsky.[3]

Such an approach could not but drastically restrict the scope of Pasternak's imagery, if only because cruelty, ugliness, illness, and death are so much a part of many aspects of man's existence, and of the struggle for survival in all animal life. The imagery in *Doctor Živago* concerns itself primarily with the life-giving inanimate nature, with the comfortingly familiar details of daily life, and with a radiant human being named Lara. Throughout the novel, with very few and very pallid exceptions, Pasternak ignores opportunities to employ figurative language in connection with animal life and the many characters portrayed. His consistency in the matter is truly amazing, for neither an impressionistic stroke, nor flight of metaphoric fancy invade the straightforward prose of Pasternak's depictions of men and women in *Doctor Živago*. The one exception is its heroine, Lara. The imagery associated with her is second in quantity only to the novel's nature imagery, and second to nothing in variety and evocativeness. As though attempting to demonstrate his adherence to his dictum that "art is reserved for the beautiful," Pasternak portrays Lara, from the moment she appears early in the novel to her final exit, as the very epitome of radiance, purity, and beauty. Thus:

> She moved with a silent grace. (25)*

* Quotations from *Doctor Živago* are in my own translation of the Russian original as published by University of Michigan Press, Ann Arbor, 1959. The page number, placed in parentheses, immediately follows each such citation.

> Her soul, her inner being fitted harmoniously into her con-
> tours and strained with a responsive eagerness toward the
> future. (25)

> She was incomparable in her spritual radiance. Her arms
> were astonishing the way sublime thought astonishes. Her
> shadow on the wallpaper of the hotel room was like the
> outline of her innocence. (46)

> She was lovely in that incomparably simple and swift line
> the Creator had drawn around her at a single stroke, and in
> this divine form had handed her over to his soul, like a
> child tightly wrapped in a sheet after having been bathed.
> (377)

Lara remains pure even after her seduction by Komarovskij when still a very young girl, so pure that the boy Antipov, who was in love with her, suspected nothing and rejoiced at the sight of her "as if she were a grove of birch trees, untrodden green grass and clouds" (50).

Toward the end of the book, when Lara had already gone through the purgatory of life in a country ravaged by upheavals of unprecedented cruelty, Pasternak still finds it possible to describe her as "effortlessly beautiful" (506).

In the imagery which comes bursting forth at practically every mention of Lara, she is associated with all that he prizes as noble, radiant, compassionate, and life-giving. She is compared and identified with the rowan tree which feeds hungry birds in the dead of Siberian winters; with light and air; with water and the sea; with Russia and the countryside; with the miracle of life itself. In some instances, the association is established explicitly, but in most cases Pasternak relies on the suggestive power of metaphors, similes, metonymies, and even epithets which he otherwise uses very sparingly.

A unique and paramount aspect of the figures of speech connected with Lara is their domination by *recurrent imagery*.

The onetime image appears lightning-like, illuminating a character trait, setting a nature scene in relief, or stressing the mood of the moment. The cumulative force of the reiterated image sustains and strengthens the imaginative process within the reader, as the author weaves the image in and out of the text, exploiting its metaphoric potentialities a little further with each step.

In *Doctor Živago*, recurrent imagery is reserved exclusively for Lara. This striking peculiarity of the novel's figurative language is still further underscored by the frequency with which Pasternak associates her with water in his iterated metaphors. Lara's "moist voice" is mentioned three times (292, 405, 450). Her room after a violent rain is "a sea, a real sea, a whole ocean" (152). Živago and Mademoiselle Fleury have a vision of her standing outside the house "in the form of a watery wraith" (152). Years later, Živago again sees an apparition resembling Lara, and this time, too, she is associated with water:

> A blurred, greatly magnified image of an adored, astonishing head was stretched in the air from one side of the forest glade to the other, like a huge banner extended across a street from one house to another. And the apparition wept, and the rain, now grown more intense, kissed and watered it. (378)

Lara's nearness is to Živago like "the first wave of the sea which rolls up to meet you as you run toward it over the sandy beach in the dark" (314). When he and Lara are alone in the darkness of the night, they exchange "secret words, great and quiet like the name of the Asian ocean" (437), which in the original (*tajnye slova, velikie i tixie*) suggests the Pacific Ocean. When the two lovers are separated, never to see each other again, Živago describes Lara in a striking series of images associating her with the sea, the first of which reads as follows:

> I'll trace your features on paper as the most powerful, farthest-reaching wave traces its lines on the sand after a fearful storm that churns up the sea to its very depths. (464)

One of the poems in the novel attributed to Živago, "Parting" (551–52), contains six stanzas wherein the recurrent sea imagery associated with Lara is echoed and reechoed in unforgettable lines of mourning and lament.

Pasternak's concentration on water imagery is no surprise to anyone acquainted with his early work, which is saturated with figures of speech associated with this life-giving element.[4] There, however, each such trope appears in isolation, existing, so to speak, *an sich*, whereas in *Doctor Živago* practically all the water imagery is connected with one person, thereby gradually acquiring the cumulative force inherent in the recurrent image.

The other iterated images which, as already stated, are always associated with Lara, do not occur nearly so frequently as the tropes linking her with water, with the sea, nor are their potentialities as fully exploited. There are, for instance, three passages connected with the rowan tree. Lara is not mentioned by name in any of them, but all three passages are so inescapably associated with her that the rowan emerges in the reader's mind as the very symbol of Lara. She readily comes to mind as one reads the first passage in which Pasternak describes the rowan's unfading beauty and motherliness:

> Just at the edge of the camp and of the autumnally naked forest through which one could see as though a gate were open into its bareness, a solitary, beautiful, rusty-leaved rowan grew, which alone among all the trees had kept its foliage.... Something of a living intimacy had grown between the birds and the tree. It was as though the rowan had been watching them, and had resisted stubbornly and for a long time, but then gave in, took pity on the birds and, like a nurse giving breast to a baby, unbuttoned her blouse. (363).

The second description of the rowan contains an explicit reference to Lara. Živago is making his escape from the partisans in order to find her, and he comes upon the tree which stands half-buried in snow:

> ... and it held out two snow-covered branches toward him. He remembered Lara's long white arms, round and generous, took hold of the branches and pulled the tree toward him. As if responding, the rowan shook snow all over Živago. Distraught and oblivious of what he was saying, he kept muttering to himself: "I'll find you, my radiant beauty, my cherished little rowan, my life's blood." (385)

The identification of Lara with the rowan in the concluding sentence is doubly poignant to the reader of the original because of the use of stylistic devices which are deeply rooted in the Russian lyrical folk song. The sentence reads: *Krasota moja pisanaja, knjaginja moja rjabinuška, rodnaja krovinuška.* The choice of words and their reiteration, the diminutives, the rhyme, the rhythmic pattern are all reminicent of the folk song where the rowan tree is the traditional symbol of "the suffering of the married woman . . . the image of the grieving woman."[5] Lara, we will recall, is a loving and devoted mother whose duty, as she sees it, is "to stay close to the ground and to shelter my young with my wings" (446). In her own way, and in the complex and tortured way of those times, she is also the

loving and devoted wife to a husband who abandoned her in order to
fight for the revolution which, as Lara foresees, "will one day show
no mercy toward him" (412). When that day comes, he commits suicide. Pasternak's description of the dead body of Lara's husband
contains only one figure of speech, and in it he alludes to the rowan
for the third time, evoking an association of it with the widow:

> The small drops of blood that had spurted on to the snow
> had mixed with it to form red beads resembling rowan-
> berries. (476)

As has been mentioned, Pasternak's recurrent imagery associates
Lara with light and air, with Russia and the Russian countryside, and
with the miracle of life itself. These elements are so interconnected
that it would be inadmissible to discuss them in isolation from one
another. It should, however, be emphasized at this point that light
appears more frequently than the other components, alone and in
combination with them, so frequently indeed that it seems to accom-
pany Lara, and also Živago, like a trusted old friend, through much
of the book. Thus, "a soothingly rosy light followed them across the
field, calming them and filling them with hope" (276). Or:

> The light in the room was exactly as outside, the fresh,
> un-aged evening light of early spring.... The transparency of
> spring's all-pervading evening light seemed to him a pledge
> of distant hopes. (393)

In its transparency, light unveils Russia's immeasurable expanse,
unveils the vistas of life itself "for many years to come" (188)—light
and Russia and life merging into a vision of Lara. The vision glows
with particular luminosity in two of the novel's passages crowded with
the recurrent imagery cannected with her.
The first starts simply enough, but then, almost immediately, bursts
forth in impatient complexity and imaginative force:

> Ever since childhood, Živago loved the evening forest pierced
> with the fire of the sunset. At such moment it was as though
> shafts of light were passing also through him, as though the
> gift of the living spirit flooded his breast, cut through his
> whole being, emerging from under his shoulder in the form of
> wings. The archetype which is formed in every person at a
> tender age, and remains with him forever after, seeming to
> be his inward being, his personality, now came to life in

Živago in all its primordial strength, compelling nature, the forest, the glow of the sunset and every single thing he could see to be transfigured into a similarly primordial and all-embracing likeness of a girl. "Lara," he half-whispered, closing his eyes, invoking in his mind his whole life, all of God's earth, the entire sunlit expanse stretched out before him. (353)

Later in the book, when Živago is beset by sadness and uncertainty because he cannot find Lara upon his return to her apartment after a long separation, he asks himself "the question he can always answer," the question of Lara's meaning to him. Živago's ready answer is here cited in the original to prevent loss of imagery, particularly the sound orchestration and the noun-epithets, those rarest of all figures of speech, which are the despair of the translator:

Vot vesennij večer vo dvore. Vozdux ves' razmečen zvukami. Golosa igrajuščix detej razbrosany v mestax raznoj dal'nosti, kak by v znak togo, čto prostranstvo naskvoz' vse živoe. I èta dal'—Rossija, ego nesravnennaja, za morjami našumevšaja znamenitaja roditel'nica, mučenica, uprjamica, sumasbrodka, šalaja, bogotvorimaja, s večno veličestvennymi i gibel'nymi vyxodkami, kotoryx nikogda nel'zja predvidet'! O, kak sladko suščestvovat'! Kak sladko žit' na svete i ljubit' žizn'! O, kak vsegda tjanet skazat' spasibo samoj žizni, samomu suščestvovaniju, skazat' èto im samim v lico!
  Vot èto-to i est' Lara. S nimi nel'zja razgovarivat', a ona ix predstavitel'nica, ix vyraženie, dar sluxa i slova, darovannyj bezglasnym načalam suščestvovanija. (401–402)

Wind, rain, snow, light, and other phenomena from the realm of nature dominate the imagery in Pasternak's pre-*Doctor Živago* writings as they do in the novel, but there they appear in isolation—swift, striking, and only very rarely developed. They lack, therefore, the cumulative force of the recurrent image, and they never culminate in a complex master metaphor, such as in the passage just quoted, or in the one associating Lara with the sea.
  It might be argued that *Doctor Živago* is Pasternak's only novel, and that recurrent imagery is likely to thrive more readily in a longer work than in a shorter one. True, of course, but it is no less true that Pasternak had ample opportunity to create recurrent images in his several series of verses devoted to one theme, or in his long narrative poems, or in his short stories. He did not avail himself of these

opportunities, but he did so in *Doctor Živago*. This seems most unusual in a writer whose stylistic devices underwent very little change in the course of nearly half a century of creative activity.[6]

One possible explanation, and the one that seems most convincing to me, emerges out of the fact that the years Pasternak spent on the writing of his novel (from the late thirties to the middle fifties) roughly coincided with the period of his most intense preoccupation with Shakespeare, that incomparable master of the recurrent image.

As is well known, official Soviet hostility to Pasternak had compelled him to earn his living by doing translations. Among the writers whom he translated were Goethe, Schiller, Verlaine, Byron, Keats, and Shelley. But that it was Shakespeare who attracted him most is apparent from the list of Pasternak's published translations.[7] And Shakespeare alone moved him to write an extended commentary which leaves little doubt that he was aware of the impact that the Bard was making on him. In daily progressing through the text, writes Pasternak,

> ... the translator finds himself reliving the circumstances of
> the author. Day by day he reproduces his actions and he is
> drawn into some of his secrets, not in theory but practically,
> by experience.[8]

The result is thus not necessarily imitation, conscious or subconscious, but possibly also the more complex and profound process of absorbing the author's "secrets," a process that is imperceptible and organic, capable of enriching the translator's own creative potentialities.

It seems logical to assume that recurrent imagery in *Doctor Živago* is one such "secret" which Pasternak mastered and made his own in the course of his work on translations from Shakespeare. As already stated, the latter was an incomparable master of the recurrent image. Moreover, this type of figurative speech plays a vital role in Shakespeare's works, a role aptly summed up by Caroline Spurgeon:

> There is no question but that the most striking function
> of the imagery as background and undertone in Shakespeare's
> art is the part played by *recurrent images* in raising and
> sustaining emotion, in providing atmosphere or in emphasiz-
> ing a theme.[9]

One finds a number of arresting similarities between the reiterated figures of speech in Shakespeare and Pasternak, and also one significant difference. First, about the difference. Like all of Shakespeare's tropes, his recurrent ones may be found in association with heroes and villains alike, and with things benevolent or evil, whereas Pasternak reserves his use of recurrent imagery exclusively for the heroine of his novel. This, as already pointed out, is in keeping with his general tendency to avoid figures of speech when writing about human beings except Lara.

The similarities are especially pronounced when comparing the recurrent images in *Doctor Živago* with those in *Romeo and Juliet* and *Antony and Cleopatra*, plays which, like Pasternak's novel, are centered around star-crossed lovers. The associations common to all three works, which are made most frequently and consistently, are those that link the leading characters with light. We have already seen how ubiquitously light permeates the metaphoric language connected with Lara. Similarly, in *Romeo and Juliet*, "the dominating image is light, every form and manifestation of it," to cite Spurgeon.[10] Compare, for instance, Shakespeare's

> her beauty makes
> This vault a feasting presence full of light.
> (V–3–85)

with Pasternak's

> ...whenever she entered a room, it was as though a window were flung open and the room filled with light and air. (473)

Imagery connected with light, sun, stars, and various light-emitting objects, such as torches and lamps, also dominate *Antony and Cleopatra*. Wolfgang H. Clemen observes:

> Just as Antony himself is conceived of as partaking in the nature of light, so does his death appear as the quenching of this light.[11]

Likewise with Cleopatra. Antony sees her as "day o' the world" (IV–8–13), and exclaims when thinking her dead: "The torch is out" (IV–14–46). When lamenting his loss of Lara, Živago resorts to the kindred image of a light extinguished: "My bright sun has set" (463).

Less abundant than light images, but occurring frequently in both Shakespearean tragedies, are figures of speech based on associations with sea, rain, "and waters sighs and tears," especially in *Antony and Cleopatra*, from which the metaphor is drawn (I–2–153). Sea imagery is indeed so prevalent in that tragedy that Clemen speaks of its "omnipresence,"[12] just as one may speak of the water element as being ever present in Pasternak's tropes connected with Lara. Antony is compared with the "grand sea" (III–12–10), and the water imagery that crowns

Capulet's speech to Juliet calls to mind the cited passage which crowns Pasternak's water imagery associated with Lara:

> How now! a conduit, girl? what! still in tears?
> Evermore showering? In one little body
> Thou counterfeit'st bark, a sea, a wind;
> For still thy eyes, which I may call the sea,
> Do ebb and flow with tears; the bark thy body is,
> Sailing in this salt flood; the winds, thy sighs;
> Who, raging with thy tears, and they with them,
> Without a sudden calm, will overset
> Thy tempest-tossed body. (III–5–130–38)

To conclude: Shakespeare's magnificent examples of recurrent imagery seem to have prompted Pasternak's use of that poetic device, and some of the dominating associations in both authors are analogous, to the point of occasional use of the same words. Still, it would, in my opinion, be unjust and untrue to speak of imitation or borrowing on Pasternak's part. The supreme degree to which his recurrent images are integrated with the context points, rather, to a meeting of kindred minds, in which the lesser adopts for his own purposes an effective device mastered in the course of day-to-day contact with works of genius.

New York University

NOTES

1. Boris Pasternak, *The Last Summer* (New York, 1958), p. 101.
2. Boris Pasternak, *I Remember* (New York, 1959), p. 126.
3. Ralph Matlaw, "A Visit With Pasternak," *The Nation* (September 12, 1959), p. 134.
4. For a detailed discussion of the extent and significance of the water element in Pasternak's works, see "*Vodjanoj znak*" by V. S. Frank in *Sbornik statej, posvjaščennyx tvorčestvu B. L. Pasternaka* (Munich, 1962), pp. 240–52.
5. V. M. Sidel'nikov, *Poètika russkoj narodnoj liriki* (Moscow, 1959), p. 63.
6. Pasternak's consistency gave rise to a couplet I often heard cited in

Moscow during the thirties and forties. It is, I understand, well remembered to this day:
Vse menjaetsja pod znakom Zodiaka,
Ne menjaetsja liš' muza Pasternaka.
7. A complete list of translations by Pasternak will be found in George Reavey, *The Poetry of Boris Pasternak* (New York, 1959), pp. 252–53.
8. *I Remember*, p. 142.
9. Caroline Spurgeon, *Shakespeare's Imagery and What It Tells Us* (Cambridge, England, 1958), p. 213.
10. *Ibid.*, p. 310.
11. Wolfgang H. Clemen, *The Development of Shakespeare's Imagery* (London, 1953), p. 162.
12. *Ibid.*, p. 159.

Disruption of Canonical Verse Norms in The Poetry of Zinaida Hippius

OLEG A. MASLENIKOV

IN RUSSIAN literature one of the major achievements of the Modernist rebellion of the "Platinum Age" (i.e., the two decades preceding World War I) was the disruption of the established syllabotonic norms of nineteenth-century Russian verse. A major role, especially at the beginning of the rebellion, belongs to Zinaida Hippius (1869–1945), whose poetry shows remarkable metric and rhythmic variations from the norm.

As though responding to her husband's (D. S. Merezkovskij's) exhortation to explore "new, as yet undiscovered worlds,"[1] Hippius embarks upon a number of experiments involving the disruption of the metrical system of Russian canonic verse forms. Her attempts at discovering new forms characterize her poetry of the Symbolist era (1893–1910), and are seen in her first two books of verse.[2]

Hippius' opening poem "Pesnja" in her first book of verse (1893: I, 1–2) shows a free alternation not only of meters but of line lengths as well, with the odd-numbered lines repeating the final phrase of the preceding line.

> Mne nužno to, čego net na svete,
> Čego net na svete.

The very next poem, "Posvjaščenie" (1894: I, 3–4), features the "dol'nik" or "pauznyj trerdol'niks,"[3] essentially a lame trisemic verse with ternary feet alternating irregularly with binary feet:

> Nebesa unyly i nizki,
> No ja znaju—dux moj vysok.

89

The rhythm pattern may be depicted:

$$ooX \quad oXooXo$$
$$ooXo \quad XooX$$

Hippius was the first to explore extensively this particular irregular meter, which was later popularized by Blok and Axmatova. Already over 12 per cent of the ninety-eight poems comprising her first volume of verse feature this retreat from metrical tradition.

In her employ of the "dol'nik," Hippius frequently uses the pauses to convey a feeling of mystery that lies behind the visible physical reality of our world. Thus, in her "Cvety noči" (1898: I, 17–18):

O, nočnomu času ne ver'te	ooXo XooXo
On ispolnen zloj krasoty.	ooXo XooX
V êtot čas ljudi blizki k smerti	ooXooXo Xo
Tol'ko stranno živy cvety.	ooXo XooX

The pauses interrupting the regular beat of the anapest[4] established by the first line suggest some mysterious, evil essence lurking in the background—a trait typical of the "metaphysical" stream of decadent poetry.

On occasion, Hippius limits the pause positionally within the framework of the poem. One such example is her "Stuk" (1900: I, 69–70) in which an obligatory pause is found on the evenly numbered lines, while the odd-numbered lines appear in regular amphibrach:

Polnočnaja ten'. Tišina.	oXooXooX
Stuk serdca i stuk časov.	oXooX oX
Kak noč neponjatno černa.	oXooXooX
Kak tjažek eë pokrov.	oXooX oX

Another such example is the poem "Kak vse" (1901: I, 109):

Ne xoču, ničego ne xoču.	ooXooXooX
Prinimaju vsë tak, kak est'.	ooXooX oX
Izmenjat' ničego ne xoču.	ooXooXooX
Ja dyšu, Ja živu, ja molču.	ooXooXooX

Here, in the first two stanzas, the pause occurs only in the second and sixth lines immediately following the stressed syllable at the word boundary between the second and third feet. In the third stanza, the pause occurs in the same position within each of the four lines:

I k čemu ono vsë—Bog vest'.	ooXooX	oX
No da budet vsë tak, kak est'.	ooXooX	oX
Nerušimy zemlja i tverd'.	ooXooX	oX
Neizmenny i žizn' i smert'.	ooXooX	oX

In seven of the eight lines of her poem "Tetrad' ljubvi" (1901: I, 123), Hippius once more employs the pause after a stressed foot at the word boundary. In six cases the "lame" foot occurs after the second stressed syllable. In line seven, the pause occurs after the third foot. Line two is deficient in the initial short syllable of an otherwise essentially amphibrachic pattern:

Segodnja zarja vstaët iz-za tuč.	oXooX oXooX
Pologom tuč ot menja ona sprjatana.	XooXooXooXoo
Ne svet i ne mgla . . . I tëmen surguč,	oXooX oXooX
Kotorym "Ljubov" moja zapečatana.	oXooX oXooXoo

On several occasions Hippius, contrary to accepted usage, resorts to a variable anacrusis. One example is seen in her poem "Mgnovenie" (1898: I, 62), in which such irregularity of meter is further disrupted by use of internal pauses:

Skvoz' okno svetitsja nebo vysokoe,	ooX	XooXooXoo
Večernee nebo, tixoe, jasnoe.	oXooXo	XooXoo
Plačet ot sčastija serdce moe odinokoe,	XooXoo	XooXooXoo
Rado ono, čto nebo takoe prekrasnoe.	XooX o	XooXooXoo

In her second book of verse, Hippius continues to employ the "dol'nik." In the poem "Svoboda" (1904: II, 19–20):

Ja ne mogu pokorjat'sja ljudjaęm	XooXooXo	Xo
Možno li rabstva xotet'?	XooXooX	

the lame foot occurs regularly only at the end of the third foot, immediately before a feminine (Xo) end foot. In the fourth stanza, however, in the first and third lines, the pause occurs at the word boundary between the second and third feet:

Tol'ko vzyvaju imenem Syna	XooXo XooXo
K Bogu, Tvorcu Bytija:	XooXooX
Otče, vovek da budet edino	XooX oXooXo
Volja tvoja i moja	XooXooX

Of interest also is Hippius' use of the caesura. In two poems
written in 1902, "P'javki" (I, 133) and "Časy stojat" (I, 135–36),
she employs a hypermetric caesura in a trochaic ("P'javki") and an
iambic ("Časy stojat") hexameter.

> Tam, gde zavod' tixaja, gde molčit reka,   XoXoXoo/ /XoXoX
> Lipnut p'javki černye, k kornju trostnika. XoXoXoo/ /XoooX
> (I, 133)

> Časy ostanovilis'. Dvižen'ja bol'še net.   oXoooXo/ /oXoXoX
> Stoit, ne razgorajas', za oknami rassvet.   oXoooXo/ /oXoooX
> (I, 135)

   In a hexametric line the use of a hypermetric caesura was not
unknown in Russian verse; Hippius' application of it to a tetrameter,
however, was original. Her poems "Voz'mi menja" (1904: II, 63),
"Zemlja" (1905: II, 48–49), and "Neljubov'" (1907: II, 38–39), are
examples of iambic tetrameters, with a hypermetric caesura after the
second foot, dividing each line into two dimetric hemistichs. The
effect may be felt in the following two lines from "Neljubov'":

> Kak veter černyj, ty b'jëš'sja v stavni,   oXoXo/ /oXoXo
> Kak veter mokryj, poëš': ty moj!   oXoXo/ /oXoX

In her poem "Mudrost'" (1908: II, 41–43), Hippius modifies the
pattern. She employs the caesura regularly after the second foot and
introduces the hypermetric syllable thirty times, but only in the odd-
numbered lines:

> Sošlis' čertovki na perekrëstke   oXoXo/ /oooXo
> Na perekrëstke trex dorog.   oooXo/ / XoX

As a result of the rhythmic inertia established in the first line, the
syllable immediately following the caesura of the second line almost
demands a compensatory lenghthening of the third foot.
   Noteworthy also are Hippius' experiments with a regularly placed
paeonic line in lieu of two regular iambic feet. Thus in her poem
"Gluxota" (1901: I, 85–86):

> Časy stučat nevnjatnye,   oXoXoXoo
> Net polnoj tišiny.   oXoooX
> Vse goresti—ponjatnye,   oXoooXoo
> Vse radosti—skučny.   oXoooX

Except for the first line, which displays a regular iambic trimeter, the remaining nineteen lines show a regular metric "alleviation" on the second foot, yielding the following metric pattern:

oXoooX(oo)

In a later poem of sixteen lines, "Dóma" (1908: II, 36–37), Hippius repeats the pattern throughout the poem, except for one line (1. 12):

Zelënye, lilovye	oXoooXoo
Serebrjanye, alye	oXoooXoo

The one exceptional line (1. 12):

| Molčan'em Smert' zovuščie | oXoXoXoo |

has the key word *Smert'* disrupting the regularly established rhythmic inertia (oXoXoXoo for oXoooXoo) and, thus, emphasizes the thematic significance of the disruptive lexeme: *Smert'*.

Continuing her metrical experiments, Hippius, in one of her poems, "Xristu" (1901: I, 79–80), employs a regularly recurring bacchic monopodic line, lending a rare (for Russian prosody of that time) combination of two successive stressed syllables:

My ne žili i umiraem	oo Xoooo Xo
Sredi t'my.	oXX
Ty vernëš'sja ... No kak uznaem	ooXooXoXo
Tebja—my?	oXX

Of great interest to the prosodist are Hippius' experiments with allometric verse—poetry that fails to follow any single metrical pattern. Although most of her lines follow a fairly simple rhyme scheme, she is among the first Russian poets to employ free, unrhymed verse. Her first was the poem "Krugi" (1899: I, 63):

Ja pomnju: my sideli na skamejke.
Pred nami byl pokinutyj istočnik
 I tixaja zelen'.

In it, the inertia of the iambic rhythm of the first two lines, is disrupted by the amphibrachic pattern of the third line. The poem lacks rhymes except for the final four lines, which lend it a feeling of completeness:

> Tol'ko net bezvinno umeršix, nevoskresšix slov.
> I net doždëm smytyx,
>   Zemlëj skrytyx,
> Moix jasnyx krugov.

Two years later, "Krugi" was followed by a longer (fifty-eight lines) unrhymed, weird "Pesni rusalok" (1901: I, 87–89), in which allopodic feet and allometric lines appear in free alternation.

> My belye dočeri
> Ozera belogo
> Ot čistoty i proxlady my rodilis'
> Pena, i tina, i travy nas nežat.
> Lëgkij, pustoj kamyš laskaet:
> Zimoj podo l'dom, kak pod tëplym steklom,
> My spim i nam snitsja leto.
> Vsë blago: i žizn'! i jav'! i son!

Another example of Hippius' struggle for the liberation of Russian poetry from the confining rules of syllabotonic versification is her "Do dna" (1901: I, 90):

> Tebja privetstvuju moë poraženie   oXoXoooXooXoo
> Tebja i pobedu ljublju ravno   oXooXooXoX

In such lines Hippius appears as one of the first modernists to approach the "accentual" verse.

The rhythmic effect of her "Ne znaju" (1901: I, 101) parallels that produced by "Do dna."

Illustrative of Hippius' rhythmical virtuosity is the poem "Pereboi" (1905: II, 44–45) in which a stanza of a trimetric "dol'nik"

> Esli serdce vdrug ostanavlivaetsja   ooXo XooXoooo
> Na duše bespokojno i veselo . . .   ooXooXooXoo

is suddenly interrupted by a monopodic iamb:

> No vdrug

After which the poem proceeds in a catalectic trochee:

Net sveršen'ja, novyj krug   XoXoXoX

only to be interrupted by the same

I vdrug—

Whereupon the trochee yields to a lame allometric "dol'nik":

Serdce opjat' ostanavlivaetsja   XooXooXooo o
Vižu ja oči Tvoi, Bezmernaja   XooXooX oXoo

In her poem "Kamen" (1907: II, 75) Hippius successfully combines
yet another set of rhythmical and metrical patterns:

Kamen' tela davit dux   XoXoXo   X
Kryl'ja belye, šelestjaščie   XoXoo/ /ooXoo
Dumy lëgkie i tvorjaščie   XoXoo/ /ooXoo
Davit kamen' tela dux   XoXoXo   X

The second stanza maintains the word boundary pattern of the first:

Xo/Xo/Xo/X
Xo/Xoo/ /ooXoo
Xo/Xoo/ /ooXoo
Xo/Xo/Xo/X

The rhythm pattern of these two stanzas may be approached as a
trochaic tetrameter with a regular caesura after the second foot (with
a hypermetric syllable before a caesura in the middle two lines). Such
an approach can be supported by the boundary pattern of line six:

Radost' detskuju, s tajnoj svituju   XoXoo/ /XoXoo

Thus the foot directly following the caesura in line two may be seen as
the substitution of a pyrrhic foot for the expected trochee.

Other examples of Hippius' employment of allometric verse of
varying feet and line length are seen in such poems as "Rosnoe
imja" (1904: II, 78):

My včera govorili, govorili...   ooXooXoooXo
Prekrasnye, jasnye cvety vyrostali o XooXoooXooXo
Tonkie, strojnye travy vsxodili,   XooXoo XooXo
Vyrostali, vsxodili—i vjali...   ooXooXoo Xo

The poem "Ženskoe" (1907: II, 108–109) provides us with yet another illustration of allometric verse:

Gde gniët sedejuščaja iva,	ooXoXoooXo
Gde byl i nyne vysox ručeëk,	o XoXoXoooX
Devočka, na kraju obryva,	XooooXoXo
Plačet, svivaja venok.	XooXooX

Finally, the verses of "Žuravli" (1908: II, 103–104) once more exemplify Hippius' recourse to irregular verse.

We see that in her attempt to free Russian verse from old metrical norms, Hippius exploited various metrical irregularities, from the "dol'nik" ("pauznik"), the caesura, to the so-called "Accentual" verse ("akcentnyj stix"), and in a few instances an unrhymed free verse. Thus Hippius' metrical experiments, in many respects, foreshadowed the later developments in Russian versification.

University of California, Berkeley

NOTES

1. D. S. Merežkovskij, "O pričinax upadka i o novyx tečenijax sovremennoj russkoj literatury," *Polnoe Sobranie Sočinenij* (Moscow, 1914), XVIII, 217.
2. In my references, the Roman figure "I" will refer to her *Sobranie Stixov* (Moscow: Scorpion, 1904); and "II" will designate her second book of verse (Moscow: Musaget,

1910). The Arabic numeral following the Roman numeral will refer to the page of each volume.
3. Cf. A. P. Kvjatkovskij, *Poetičeskij slovar'* (Moscow, 1966).
4. Since canonic nineteenth-century Russian verse normally avoids variable anacrusis, I will continue to apply traditional nomenclature to the various meters.

Jagić and the Varaždin Kajkavian Dialect[1]

THOMAS F. MAGNER

Vatroslav jagić, the greatest Slavist of the past century, was born in the small city of Varaždin (northwestern Croatia) in 1838; after a long and productive life he died in Vienna in 1923 and was buried in Varaždin. Varaždin is located in the kajkavian dialect belt of Yugoslavia, and Varaždin kajkavian was the native speech of Jagić. Kajkavian was, in fact, the language of all of Jagić's ancestors: his father, Vinko, was born in a small village in Zagorje (the kajkavian area south of Varaždin) and as a youth came to Varaždin to learn the trade of *čizmar*, 'bootmaker.' Jagić's mother, Ana, was herself born in Varaždin; her father, Ivan Kraljek, the "dedek" of Jagić's youth, had also come to Varaždin from Zagorje.[2] The Jagić family, through the influence of the grandfather, was well-versed in kajkavian literature. As Jagić recalls in his memoirs (I, 4):

> ... my grandfather had a small complete library of kajkavian literature all of which even my mother had read. I still remember how every year around Christmas my grandfather would give me twenty cents to get him *Danicza Zagrebechka*, published in Zagreb by Ignac Kristianović, the last kajkavian writer.

Ana had gone to school in Varaždin with the Ursuline nuns and there had learned to read and write in kajkavian; she taught Jagić to read before he started to school and while still in elementary school he had read practically all of his grandfather's library (I, 7).

> I have already mentioned the kajkavian library of my grandfather, from which my mother supplied the whole neighbor-

hood with books. One part of those books which were not
carried away while I was off ... in Zagreb and Vienna later
became part of my library. Actually there were a lot more. I
am especially sorry about the disappearance of one manuscript in which sacred and secular songs had been written, all
in kajkavian dialect.

He also recalls an occasion during the holidays when the children from
his street gathered to hear a reading of Robinson [Crusoe] in kajkavian
translation (I, 11). Many years later, in his article analyzing the works
of Juraj Habdelić, a seventeenth-century kajkavian writer, Jagić is well
able to visualize the readers of Habdelić's chatty, moralistic prose:[3]

I envision particularly honest middle-class women and their
daughters as readers of his books, and that brings to my
mind the dear picture of my unforgettable mother who...
used to love to read pious or entertaining (e.g., Robinson)
books from the kajkavian literature of the time to the size-
able audience [which would gather] in our home on Sunday
evenings in the Winter.

Jagić's father often traveled through Zagorje selling his wares at
the village markets, and on such trips he would occasionally take his
son, Nacek, with him.[4] Of his father Jagić writes (I, 4):

He had a marvelous memory and could imitate very cleverly
local dialects of particular regions, especially those in Zagorje.
...These [imitations] were for me the earliest impressions of
discernible differences among the spoken dialects, in fact it
was a type of practical course in dialectology, which I once
took advantage of in citing the Krapina [town in Zagorje]
pronunciation of *kerv* instead of *krv*, which Miklošič rejected
in his grammar, but he was wrong....

Jagić grew up during the time of the Illyrian movement which
sought to unite all South Slavs (Slovenes, Croats, Serbs, and Bul-
garians) by means of a common literary language, to be called Illyrian. To achieve the widest possible representation for all these peoples,
the Illyrian leaders decided in 1836 (two years before Jagić's birth) to
abandon the then dominant kajkavian as a literary medium in favor of
the more widespread štokavian.[5] An *Ilirska čitaonica*, 'Illyrian reading-
room,' was established in Varaždin in 1838,[6] and in the early 1840's
Illyrian (štokavian) books began to appear in Jagić's house; around

1845 Jagić's home was known locally as *Ilirska kuća* 'Illyrian house' (I, 7). The Illyrian language (štokavian Croatian) was not introduced into the program of the Varaždin high school until 1860.[7] However, Jagić went to Zagreb in 1851 to complete his high school training, and there he had the good fortune to have Vjekoslav Babukić, "the Illyrian grammarian," as one of his teachers.

There seems to be no kajkavian text of any length by Jagić himself though he does quote kajkavian phrases in various places throughout his memoirs. He recalls (I, 7), for example, a Christmas song which Varaždin boys would sing, one line being: *Antonec pospanec naj duže ne spi, za osla i vola sena skerbi*, 'Anthony sleepy-head, don't sleep any longer, get hay for the donkey and the ox.' Another line in the same context is: *Ti Jana daj lana, Ti Dora purana, to malomu, malomu Jezušu bu*, 'You, Yana, give linen, You, Dora, give a turkey, that will be for the small, small Jesus.' Or Jagić will sum up a situation with a kajkavian proverb, e.g., *Napredi štalicu, onda kravicu*, 'First the stall, then the cow' (I, 49).

Though it is reported that Jagić "loved to speak in our soft Varaždin kajkavian" in later years,[8] there are no kajkavian letters in his published correspondence. One factor which limited his use of kajkavian in letters was the fact that during the years of his courtship and early married life he was striving to improve his wife's Croatian. She, as a young lady from one of "the better families" of Zagreb, spoke only German during her youth; during his student days in Vienna Jagić corresponded with her in German. At his wedding (1862) in Zagreb, the priest conducted the wedding service in German, not being able "to imagine that an elegant young lady from Zagreb could know the Croatian language" (I, 48). Jagić strove to make her a *prava Hrvatica*, 'a true Croatian woman,' succeeding to the extent that in one letter to her in 1868 he compliments her on her progress, "Actually you wrote as if you had studied eight years with old Babukić and he would have given you a mark of 'Excellent'" (I, 48).

Fortunately we do have some kajkavian letters, those of his mother who corresponded with him regularly while he was away in Zagreb and later in Vienna. Of her letters Jagić writes (I, 30):

> My mother's accounts in Varaždin kajkavian dialect with
> some mixture of štokavian words make a charming impression
> of an intelligent woman who knew how to sweeten her
> comments with an appropriate proverb or a wise saying.

These letters, of which only twelve have been published, provide students of kajkavian with excellent texts of everyday kajkavian of

Varaždin of the mid-nineteenth century.[9] The language in these letters shows the general characteristics of the kajkavian group;[10] it is the language of Jagić's mother but it also is, in a limited sense, Jagić's own mother tongue. Here follow two excerpts of letters which she wrote to her son Nacek while he was studying at the University of Vienna. These selections will provide a fair picture of her kajkavian speech and, with the translations, a glimpse into the student days of her famous son.[11]

Dragi Nacek!   1856
 Nam se vre jako dugu vidi, da nikakov glas od tebe nečujemo, zato se ja tak bojim, kajti svako noč od tebe senjam, i tatek je ovu noč senjal, da si se ti vu Terstu oženil. Taki me je trucal da ti naj pišem, morti si betežen. Je li si vre pisal kaj Ceneku, on je i letos kak i lani len pisati, stopram je 2. put pisal . . . . Je li ti je Cenek kaj pisal, kak je zagrebački gvardian naglo vumerl 27. ov. m.; ob 8. vuri je mešu služil, ob poldan je bil mertev i baš danas nam je Kešer došel povedat, da je nas Čorko postal gvardian zagrebački. Naši se patri veseliju, kaj se ga rešiju, a onim znam nebu drago osobitu našemu Nikuli. Pred jednim tjednom je došel k nam jeden Pongračićev pajdaš pitat za te, je li si ti dobil štipendium, tak nam se je priatelski pokazal. Rekel je da mu je Pongračić od naše hiže povedal i rekel je, da se ni mogel zderžati, da nas nebi pohodil. Tak sem ga zaderžala pri obedu i spal je pri nas, drugi dan je odišel poštel vagenu v Gracu, s Oseka, zove se Pavešić.
 Dragi Nacek ja bi jako rada, da bi i ti tam bolše svetke imal, zato ti pošlem za probu jednu puricu. Štela sem sirovu, več je bila spakuvana, bi si dal tam pri peku speči, pak se baš danas pošta seli v Lipolduve hiže, onda hajd ja ž njum v rolek, pak se je spekla. Piši, kak ti je drakše sirova ili pečena i piši gda si to dobil. Ja denem na poštu 31. to jest v petek ob 4.ti vuri popoldan. Kasnar je rekel, da one knjige ti bu dopelal. . . . Tečica si je sve ruke zežgala, jednu ima svu ranjenu a i drugu punu mehurov. Ona ti je rekla, da bi si ti tak po diaki gde bliže kvartir iskal, makar tiam podn cimer kaj nebi po zimi tak dalko hodil. Tak stiha, nemoraš predi odpovedati, dok drugdi nezakapariš, im nisi na leto pogojen, neg na mesec. Samo, dragi Nacek, budi dober i pazliv na se. Tim te svi lěpo pozdravlamo i ja tvoja matti.

A. Jagić

* * *

Dear Nacek!

It seems to us that we haven't heard a word from you in a very long time and I'm so afraid because every night I dream about you, and last night Dad dreamed that you had gotten married in Trieste. He immediately persuaded me to write to you [to see] if perhaps you were sick. Have you written yet to Cenek [Jagic's younger brother Ivan]; this year same as last he is lazy about writing, he's written only twice. Has Cenek written to you that the Zagreb [Franciscan] abbot died suddenly on the 27th of this month; at 8 he was saying Mass, at noon he was dead and just today Kešer came to tell us that our Čorko has become the Zagreb abbot. Our [Franciscan] fathers are happy to get rid of him but I know that this won't be welcome [news] to our Nikula. A week ago a friend of Pongračić came to ask about you, whether you had received a stipend, and he turned out to be very friendly. He said that Pongračić had told him about our house and he said that he couldn't restrain himself from coming to visit us. So I made him stay for dinner and he slept at our place; next day he went by the mail train to Graz; [he's] from Osijek, [and] his name is Pavešić.

Dear Nacek, I'd like very much for you to have more enjoyable holidays there, and so I'll send a turkey (for you) to try. I wanted [to send] an uncooked one, [in fact] it was already packed, [and] you could have given it to a cook there to be baked, but just today the postoffice was moved to Lipolds' house, so I put it into the oven, and [now] it's baked. Write [and tell me] whether you prefer it uncooked or baked and write when you have gotten it. I put it in the mail on the 31st, that is, on Friday at 4 in the afternoon. Kasnar said that he'll deliver those books to you, . . . Aunty has burned her arms all over, one is [seriously] burned, and the other is full of blisters. About you she said that you ought to look around among the students [to find] closer lodgings, even if [you get] only an attic room, so you won't have to walk so far in winter. So [do it] quietly, you don't have to announce it [the move] in advance, until you put down your earnest money at another place; you didn't promise them [to rent] for a year, but [only] by the month. Now, Nacek, be good and attentive about everything. With this your mother and all [of us] send you greetings.

                                                              A. Jagić

Dragi Nacek!   1860
   Pozdravlenja celi kup od Omašlnov. Kakvo si ti veselje
napravil s onim kokotum i kokošjum, ja ti nemrem spisati,
svakomu pokaže, koj tam dojde. Ja sem njoj dala tortu, bile
su ove dane pri nas i povedala je Fanika, kak te je Pečenik
falil i kak si se Toniki jako dopal. Opet jeden iberašung, a je
li si ti kaj na on list v Zagreb odgovoril, gde ti se opet tak
šmaihla. Oni prahi, kaj si mi ti poslal čisto drugač zgledaju
kak naši varaždinski. Ovi su čisto beli, a naši čisto plavi.
Ja sad neznam skoro za nikakvu hasen—jedni kak drugi.
Naš tatek je opet ostal cemešter,...
   Naš Pavlek se je zdal v pondelek ob roti vuri. Bili smo mi
z njim ja i tatek v cirkvi i potlam je bil obed, kupil njoj je
svilno opravu za zdavanje.... Bog te čuvaj još ovo zadnju
leto od betega i od druge bune, da buš mogel bes neprilike
kakve te ispite napraviti. Samo se naj preveč napinjati. Ovo
ti pošilamo jedno šunku, da buš si tak po večerah rezal, kad
buš duže čul, neg neznam, je li bu dobra, kajti smo vpučeni
naj nekuhamo, nego pečemo v testu zamotanu. Buš probal, je
li bu dobra.

                         Ostajem tebe ljubeča Mati

                                                        A. Jagi

                              * * *

Dear Nacek!   1860
   A whole lot of greetings from the Omašli. I can't describe
the merriment you caused with that rooster and chicken [a
drawing?]; she shows it to everyone who goes there. I gave
her a tart, they [women] were at our place these past days
and Fanika was telling us how Pečenik had praised you and
how much Tonika liked you. Again a surprise: have you
responded to that Zagreb letter [from Jagić's future wife] in
which they make such a fuss over you. These powders [medi-
cine], which you sent me, look very much different from our
Varaždin powders. These are completely white, [while] ours
are all blue. As of now I don't know if they are of any
use—one or the other. Our dad stayed on as guild master...
On Monday at 10 o'clock our Paul got married. Dad and I
were at the church with him and afterwards there was a
dinner; he bought her a silk gown for the wedding.... May
God continue to protect you this last year from sickness or

any harm, so that you will be able to complete your exams without trouble. Only don't overwork! I'm sending you a ham which you can slice in the evenings when you will be working late, but I don't know whether it'll be good, because we are instructed not to boil it but to bake it in a pastry shell. You'll try it [and see] whether it's good. . . .

I remain your loving mother,

A. Jagić

Though it is impossible to reconstruct the exact kajkavian speech of Vatroslav Jagić, it is possible to get a general idea of it by considering the language of his mother's letters as shown above and comparing it with the language of his younger brother, as shown below. In 1860 Ana Jagić was forty-two years old, her son, Vatroslav, was twenty-two, while her youngest son, Dragutin, was fourteen. In three of Ana Jagić's letters of this year there are short messages from Dragutin (Karlek); two of these are simply postscripts, but one is a longer text describing a local play in the jumbled fashion one might expect of a younger brother adding some lines to his mother's letter. All three passages are given below:

Na to ti pošiljem 1 fr. pak mi kupi očnik, daj mi to dobrotu učini. Žepiću sam povedal, da uči filologiu jedan Žepić. Pošli mi očnik kak bèrže. Tvoj brat

Dragutin

To sem si prešparal, gda sem devenice nosil.

* * *

I'm sending you 1 forint so you can buy me a telescope; do that favor for me. I told Žepić that there is a Žepić studying philology [in Vienna]. Your brother,

Dragutin

I saved that [forint] when I was delivering sausages.

———————

Hvala ti, da se nisi z mene spozabil. Daj mi pošli, ako ti je volja pěsme Kačičove, kajti ja bi rad někoje tabore turske napamet navčiti. Tvoj tebe ljubeči brat

Dragutin

* * *

Thank you for not forgetting me. Send me, if you will, the poems of Kačić, because I'd like to learn some Turkish battle scenes [literally, 'Turkish camps'] by heart. Your loving brother,

Dragutin

Dragi Nacek!

Mi smo čuli od Požgaja, da bude narodno kazalište prepovĕdano, zato kaj ti su jako proti vladi bèrblali, jeden je bil oblečen kak ti drotar, on je strašno šinfal, to je bil Halterov subjekt, on s dugimi lasmi. On je rekel, da on zna se zakèrpati, napriliku da ako ima vaga, na koji se pravica važe, pak ako je ona šalica od vage potèrta, da ju bu on zakèrpal, kaj nebi kaj pravice Hèrvatske van opalo. Onda mu je plemič rekel, da naj ide u Frankfurt, da se je tam jeden veliki lonec potèrl, koj se zove Deuč Bund, pak koj onoga lonca bude pokèrpal, on če dobiti 200 holbih pive i bude postal General od Flotte nemačke, a on je rekel, da neče on švabske ladje voditi, neg si bu on rajši s hèrvatskim olovom i sibirskim železom ruke zalejal. Da je to rekel, onda su ljudi tak s rukami pucali i kričali živio, da su ovi na bini več govorili: tiho, tiho. Još sem ti ne povedal, kaj je bilo predstavljano.

Plemič pervi put u Zagrebu i onda je dal šnofati policii, da ga je patrol vlovil v noči, da je štel jednoga gospona biti, pak mu je dal tringelta onomu, koj ga je vlovil. Onda ga je pustil, pak onda da se je pelal nuter u varaš, onda ga je pital ov na malti, je li vozi prepovedane robe sobom, onda je rekel, da on neje tèrgovec, kaj bi prepovedane robe pelal. Onda ga je pital, je li vozi duhana, onda je rekel, da vozi, onda mu je dal tringelta ov plemič, onda mu je rekel "dobro pazite, kaj ga nebi gdo videl."

Izpita sem napravil iz Geometrie i Mathematike dobro. Direktor je bil polek. Hvala ti za prešpektiv, lepi je, samo kaj je jako kratek. Za se dosta—drugi put više.

Tim ostajem tebe ljubeči brat
Dragutin

NB Kazalište bude pak danas, dopušteno je predstavljati.

* * *

Dear Nacek!

We heard from Požgaj that the national theater [presenta-tion] would be prohibited because they were sounding off against the government; one was dressed as a hobo, he was cursing something awful, that was a Halter [Ban Haler?] subject, he's the one with the long hair. He said that he knew how to mend [things], for example, if there is a scale on which justice is weighed and if the container of the scale is broken, then he will be able to mend it so that no Croatian justice would fall out. Then the nobleman told him that he should go to Frankfurt, that a great pot had been broken there, one called the Deutsches Bund, and whoever will mend that pot will receive 200 half-pints of beer and will become a General of the German navy, but he said that he didn't want to command Kraut ships but would sooner pour Croatian lead and Siberian iron over his hands. When he said that, the peo-ple were applauding and shouting bravo so much that those on the stage had to say: quiet, quiet. I haven't told you yet what was presented.

The nobleman is in Zagreb for the first time and seemed suspicious to the police so that a patrol caught him in the night [charging] that he wanted to beat up a certain gentle-man, but he gave a bribe to the one who had caught him. Then that one let him go and then [he wanted] to ride into the city, then this person at the toll-house asked him if he's carrying forbidden goods with him, then he said that he's not a merchant who might be transporting forbidden goods. Then he asked him if he's carrying any tobacco, then he said that he is carrying [some], then this nobleman gave that [official] a bribe who then told him "look out carefully, so that no one will see you."

I passed the exam in geometry and mathematics with a "Good." The director was present. Thanks for the telescope, it's nice, only its awfully short. For now enough—more next time.

I remain your loving brother

Dragutin

NB The theater will be on tomorrow, it's been permitted to show.

The only other family text in kajkavian or partially in kajkavian is a long, humorous "poem," written in 1859 by Ivan, Jagić's then nineteen-year-old brother, for their father's name day (II, 326–29); the language is a mixture of kajkavian and štokavian. In his memoirs Jagić quotes from later letters from both brothers, but the language of their letters is the štokavian of the time.

Pennsylvania State University

NOTES

1. In responding to an invitation to contribute to a *Festschrift* for Boris Unbegaun, one of the outstanding Slavists of our day, it seemed to be particularly fitting to write about Vatroslav Jagić, an outstanding Slavist of an earlier day.

2. This information will be found in Volume I, of V. Jagić, *Spomeni mojega života* (Srpska kraljevska akademija [Belgrade,1930]1–4); Volume II appeared in 1934. References to these memoirs will be given in the body of the article with a citation of the volume and page, e.g., (I, 4).

3. "Nochmals Juraj Habdelić und seine literar. Tätigkeit im XVII. Jahrhundert," *Archiv für slavische Philologie* XXXI (1910), 536–37.

4. Jagić was baptized Ignatius Jacobus; the kajkavian form of Ignatius is Ignac for which the diminutive is Nacek; in his early school years Jagić used both Croatian renditions of Ignatius, that is, Ognjoslav and Vatroslav, later settling on Vatroslav. To his parents and brother he was always Nacek.

5. As Barac points out, the choice of dialect was dictated by the arithmetic of the situation, i.e., there were only about 200,000 speakers of kajkavian; see Antun Barac, *Hrvatska knjiievnost* knjiga I. *Knjiievnost ilirizma* (Zagreb, 1954), 102.

6. Krešimir Filić, *Lik Vatroslava Jagića* (Varaždin, 1963), 14.

7. "The Croatian language, as a school subject, appears for the first time during the school year 1860 as 'Ilirische Sprache' and then later by the name 'Croatian language.' Josip Kraišćan, "Nekolike crtice iz života Varaždinske gimnazije od njezina osnutka do 1850," *Varaždin i Hrvatsko Zagorje* (Belgrade, 1936), 956.

8. Filić, p. 89.

9. Petar Skok (ed.), *Korespondencija Vatroslava Jagiča* knjiga 1, Jugoslavenska akademija znanosti i umjetnosti (Zagreb, 1953), pp. 23–36. In Volume I of *Spomeni*, Jagić quotes fragments from other letters from his mother; see pp. 31–37, 74–75. Only twelve of the estimated forty-four letters were released by Jagić's family because the others are assumed to contain unflattering references to Jagić's future wife, Sidonija Struppi; cf. *Korespondencija*, p. 23, and Filić, pp. 23–24.

10. For a discussion of characteristics of kajkavian dialects see my monograph, *A Zagreb Kajkavian Dialect*, Penn State Studies No. 18, (1966), pp. 3–7.

11. As one might expect from family letters, the style is elliptical and the references are not always clear. The background for many of these letters can be found in Jagić's *Spomeni* I. I plan to make a detailed analysis of the language of these letters of Ana Jagić when the as yet unpublished thirty-two letters become available.

Weitere slavisch-orientalische Lehnbeziehungen

KARL H. MENGES

DIE TÜRKISCH-SÜDSLAVISCHEN Beziehungen haben in den letzten Jahren glücklicherweise einige Beachtung gefunden, und dies vorerst und hauptsächlich auf dem Gebiet der lexikalischen Beziehungen. So erschien im Jahr 1957 in Sarajevo Abdula Škaljićs Buch *Turcizmi u narodnom govoru i narodnoj književnosti Bosne i Hercegovine*, ein etymologisches Lexikon von 810 ss. in Maschinenschrift, mit einer mir noch nicht zu Gesicht gekommenen Neuauflage von 1966, und 1962 in Meisenheim am Glan Anton Kneževićs *Die Turzismen in der Sprache der Kroaten und Serben*, 506 ss., das in seinem lexikalischen Teil, ss. 19–356, nicht nur, wie Škaljić, die türkischen Elemente eines speziellen Dialektgebietes, sondern die des gesamten Serbo-Kroatischen, d.h. der Schriftsprache, mit nur gelegentlicher Berücksichtigung der Dialekte — was an sich zu bedauern ist —, vorlegen will. Beide Bücher sind im philologisch-linguistischen Teil unbefriedigend und erfüllen ihren Zweck eigentlich nur als Materialsammlungen. Das Kneževićsche Buch ist stellenweise einfach unbrauchbar und oft für den in türkischen Dingen Unerfahrenen irreführend. All das wird ausführlich in meinem Rezensions-Artikel "Türkisches Sprachgut im Serbo-Kroatischen", der demnächst in Band XXXIX der *Ural-Altaischen Jahrbücher* erscheint, gesagt. An dem Škaljićschen Buch ist wenigstens zu erkennen, daß er sein Osmanisch recht gut und das hierzu notwendige Arabische und Persische einigermaßen kennt, — was ihn allerdings noch nicht zum Philologen und Linguisten macht, als der er aber auch nicht angesehen werden will. Es sei hier nur en passant erwähnt, daß auch in dem seit 1962 erscheinenden, von der Bulgarischen Akademie der Wissenschaften herausgegebenen, neuen *Bəlgarski Etimologičen Rečnik*, von dem mir bis jetzt die 2 ersten Hefte vorliegen, das Türkologische unter aller Kritik ist; Näheres hierüber findet sich in meiner Rezension, die ebenfalls in *UAJbb* XXXIX erscheint.

Von türkologischer Seite hat sich mit türkisch-südslavischen Beziehungen G. Hazai in einigen Arbeiten vornehmlich in den *Acta Orientalia Hungarica* und den *Studia Slavica der Ungarischen Akademie der Wissenschaften* befaßt, in denen er meist gewissen phonologischen Problemen des alten und älteren Osmanischen an Hand der Lehnformen osmanischer Wörter im Süd-Slavischen nachgeht. Kommt diese neue Phase der türkisch-slavischen Lehnwortforschung zur Entfaltung, wie sie es jetzt verspricht, dann wird sie einige Probleme der türkischen und altaischen wie auch der slavischen historischen Phonologie und Etymologie, aber auch der Grammatik, wenn auch in weit geringerem Umfang, lösen. Hierher gehören nicht nur Fragen des labialen Suffixvokals im Türkischen nach nicht-labialen Stamm- oder Wurzelsilben, über die Hazai gearbeitet hat, sondern auch Fragen der osmanischen Develarisierung, Palatalisierung, der Vokalfolge im Wort (Stamm wie Suffixen), des konsonantischen Lautwandels ($\gamma > \emptyset$, $g > j$), der stimmhafte Occlusiva im Anlaut, der langen Vokale und dgl. auf türkischem Gebiet und Probleme der Chronologie des Übergangs des reduzierten Vokals in starker Stellung zu *a*, der Vertretung von *ö* und *ü* im Slavischen, des Grundes für *ń* und *ł*, der Lautsubstitution (Tk. *y* > *a, i, e, ɨ*) und — last but not the least — das komplizierte Problem der Betonung und Quantität bei den türkischen Lehnwörtern im Serbo-Kroatischen — um einige der wesentlichsten hier zu nennen. Einige davon habe ich schon in meinem oben genannten Rezensionsartikel behandelt.

Die Rezension des Kneževićschen Buches hat mich dazu verleitet, die gesamten Etymologieen der türkischen und durch das Osmanische vermittelten arabischen und persischen Elemente des Serbo-Kroatischen zu revidieren und — Vieles davon neu zu schreiben. Dabei kommen einige über Einzelwörter weit hinausgehende, manchmal fast unerwartete, gelegentlich rätselhafte, immer aber erforschenswerte Wort- und Kulturzusammenhänge zum Vorschein. Einige davon habe ich für Sie, sehr verehrter Boris Genrixovič und Ihren Leserkreis ausgesucht.

I.

AKSl. коръда Sb - *čŏrda*, AIran. *Karəta-* 'Messer, Schwert'

Sb.-Kr. *čŏrda* 'Säbel' leitet Knežević (p. 92) ohne weitere Erklärung von Osman. *kārd* 'großes Messer' und dies aus dem fast gleichlautenden neu-persischen *kārd* 'a knife' ab. So einfach liegen die

Dinge aber nicht. Osman., arab., n.-pers. langes *ā* ergibt im Sb.-Kr. kein *ō*, auch werden in der Regel im Sb.-Kr. Fremdwörter mit konsonantischen Auslaut nicht in die Kategorie der *a*-Stämme überführt. Vuk verweist auf ђôрдаћ, hat daneben aber auch noch кôрда. Dies Letztere liegt allen serbo-kroatischen Formen zu Grunde und ist die älteste im Slavischen belegte Form dieses iranischen Lehnwortes, AKSl. коръда, ARuss. кордъ, Neu-Russ. кôрда 'kurzes Schwert' (cf. Berneker, *SlEtWb.*, s. 569; Vasmer, *RussEtWb.*, I, 624); *côrda* ist das Resultat einer Kreuzung, einer Kontamination des alt-slavischen Lehnworts mit einer später durch das Osmanische eingedrungenen Form, *kärd*, welche die Palatalisierung des Anlauts verursacht hat, neben der sich dann noch eine mit stimmhaftem Anlaut entwickelt hat. Allen Formen dieses Wortes liegt, wie schon längst bekannt, eine iranische zu Grunde; diese war aber wahrscheinlich nicht, wie bisher meist angenommen, das neu-pers. *kārd*, sondern eher eine mittel-nord(ost)-iranische, die dem neu-pers. *kārd*, Tāžīk *kǎrd*, *kōrd* id. sehr ähnlich gewesen sein muß. Das Alt-Iranische hat Jung-Āvestā *karəta-* 'Messer' (Bartholomae, *AltIranWb.*, kol. 454), zum Verbum *karət-*, Skr. *kr̥ntati* 'er schneidet' gehörig, *kartarī-* f. 'Jagdmesser', Pahlavī-Übersetzungen *kārt*, Oset'i *k'ard* 'Messer', *k'árd-ŷn* "schneiden, mähen", etc.; sein Aequivalent im Armenischen ist *k'ert'em*, I. sg. prs., '(Haut) abziehen; abschälen'. Das Wort wird auch in skythischen Namen wie κάρδιος und dem von Q. Curtius Rufus (VII, 7) erwähnten Namen des oder eines Bruders des Skythenherrschers zur Zeit Alexanders des Großen, *Cartasis*, *Carthasis*, angesetzt, in welch' Letzterem Abaev ein *kart-ās, 'meč azov', ein 'Schwert der Ās' (Alanen, Oset'i) sieht; es könnte natürlich auch einen 'Schwert-Ās, Schwert-Osseten' bedeuten (cf. ABAEV, "Skifo-alanskie ètjudy," in *Osetinskij jazyk i Fol'klor*, I, 171; Moscow-Leningrad, 1949).

Die Frage des Weges der Entlehnung dieses Wortes vom Mittel-Iranischen ins Slavische ist noch nicht gelöst. Berneker nimmt "eine frühe türkische oder finnische Vermittlung" an und weist dabei auf Ugro-Ostjak (Xanty) *karte*, Votjak (Udmurt) *kort* und Zyrjan (Komi) *kört* 'Eisen' hin; Vasmer ist der Meinung, das Wort sei über das Turko-Tatarische aus dem Mittel-Persischen oder Neu-Persischen entlehnt, und "die Annahme einer direkten Entlehnung aus dem Iranischen" — mit Verweis auf Rozwadowski und Berneker — sei "kaum berechtigt". Das ungarische *kärd* 'Schwert' hält Berneker mit Simonyi für eine Entlehnung aus dem Alanischen. Die oben zitierten permischen und ugrischen Wörter, zu denen auch noch Jurak-Samojed (Ňeneć) *har* 'Messer' (Castrén), *xar* 'id., Schnitzmesser' (Lehtisalo) zu stellen ist, dürften ebenfalls aus einer der Alanischen nahver-

wandten nord(ost)-iranischen Sprache der mittel-iranischen Epoche
entlehnt worden sein. Das wird in der nördlichen Steppengegend
zwischen Aral-See und dem Ural-Gebirge gewesen sein. Für die Annahme einer türkischen Vermittlung des Wortes ins Slavische fehlen
bis jetzt aber alle Anhaltspunkte, denn das Wort fehlt in den türkischen Sprachen bis auf das oben schon genannte recht seltene osmanische *kārd*, und da das Wort im Tāǯik gang und gäbe ist, wird es auch
in den özbekischen Stadtdialekten heimisch sein — obwohl die Lexika
nur das türkische *pičǎq* anführen. Gegen eine unmittelbare Entlehnung
aus dem Türkischen spricht auch der Accent in Russ. *kórda*, da die
türkischen Wörter bei der Übernahme ins Russische ihre Ultima-Beto-
nung beibehalten. Das iranische Wort mit der Sippe von dem ebenfalls ins Slavische eingedrungenen türkischen *qurč* 'spitz, scharf,
schneidend, stark, tapfer, scharfsinnig; Stahl' (Maḥmud al-Kāšɣarī;
Radloff' *WB*: Altaj, Teleut, Lebed', Sart, Ujɣur, Qarajīm von
Troki und Łuck; 'Stahl' im Sart und Qarajīm), *quruc*, Toboł 'Stahl' =
Mongol. *qurča*. Lit.-Mong. *xurca*, Burjat *xursa*, etc., 'scharf, schnell,
geschickt, flink, intelligent', AKSl. кръчин 'Schmied' (cf. K. H.
Menges in *UAJbb.*, XXXI, 179 ff.) zu verbinden, geht aus phoneti-
schen wie semantischen Gründen nicht an, denn das iranische Wort
wäre bei der Übernahme ins Türkische in die palatale Reihe gekommen, *ā* bleibt aber durchweg erhalten, wenigstens als *a*, *-t* wird nie zu
-č, und zudem bedeutet *qurč* nirgends 'Messer, Schwert', obwohl
dies semasiologische Argument durch die Bedeutung 'Eisen' in den fin-
nisch-ugrischen Sprachen bis zu einem gewissen Grade entkräftet werden könnte. Es ist deshalb doch wohl anzunehmen, daß das Wort aus
einer der nordwestlichsten alten nord-iranischen Sprachen, wie z.B. der
der Sauromatai, Sarmatai, viel wahrscheinlicher aber später aus einer
der nach Westen vorrückenden Alanoi und Aorsoi direkt ins Slavische
entlehnt wurde, wobei das iranische *ā* (später > *å̄*, *ō*) wie auch später
das altajische *a* der ersten Silbe im ältesten Slavischen durchweg als
o erscheint, — oder daß es zum Beginn der aksl.-alt-bulgarischen und
alt-russischen Sprachperiode, wohl in der zweiten Hälfte des IX.
Jhdts., den Slaven durch die Ungarn vermittelt worden ist.

Das iranische Wort ist noch weiter nach Westen gewandert, ins
West-Slavische, Litauische, Deutsche und Dänische. Während Berneker
das mittelniederdeutsche *korde* (> Dän. *kaarde*) aus dem Čechischen,
kord, und das litauische *kárdas* aus dem Polnischen, *kord*, ableitet,
hält Vasmer die mndd. Formen *korde*, *kurde*, *karde* für aus dem Ost-
Slavischen entlehnt; es sollte aber auch die Möglichkeit einer Entlehnung aus dem Ungarischen nicht ausgeschlossen werden.

Im West-Slavischen gibt es noch ein sehr ähnlich klingendes Form-
paar: Poln. *kordelas*, in Dialekten *kordylac* 'Jagdmesser', Če., alt,

korduláč, kortuláč 'breite Klinge', Slovak. *korteláč* 'gekrümmtes Hack-
messer (Berneker, *ibid.*), zu denen Berneker auch noch Če. *kudla*
'gewöhnliches Taschenmesser' und Russ. кóртик 'Hirschfänger' stellt.
Berneker führt sie alle auf Ital. (Dial. von Brescia) *cortelàs* (= Lit.-It.
coltellaccio, ein Augmentativ von *coltello*) 'Schlachtmesser' zurück, das
auch einer Reihe von nhd. Formen, wie *kartilatz, kardelast* 'Art Degen',
kordelasche, kortelatsch 'eine Waffe', holländ. *kortelas* 'kurzer, breiter
Degen', NE, alt, *curtlasse, cutlass* und Schwed., alt, *kurtelas* zu Grunde
liegt (Berneker, *ibid.*). Damit sind wir hier in die romanische Sippe
von Lat. *culter* gekommen, das mit dem Alt-Iran. *karəta-* urverwandt
ist. Ohne hier in eine Reihe von weiteren Problemen hineinzugehen,
möchte ich doch darauf hinweisen, daß sich die beiden urverwandten
Gruppen von Lehnwörtern, die iranische wie die romanische, auf west-
slavischem Gebiet getroffen und gegenseitig soweit beeinflußt haben,
daß sie nicht mehr klar und eindeutig von einander abgesondert
werden können; diese Kontamination konnte sowohl durch die Phonetik wie die Semantik nur gefördert worden sein.

II.

AKSl. **dъly*, Osm. *dolap*, N.-Pers. *dōl*, Arab. *dalw*, Lat. *dōlium*

Sb.-Kr. *dòlāp, dòlāf* und (Bosnien und Herzegovina:) *dòlāf, dùlāf*
(Škaljić)' Schrank; Schöpfmühle, Göpelwerk'. Es ist eines der wenigen
Wörter, von denen Knežević dialektologische Angaben gemacht hat:
dòlāp in Beograd, *dòlāf* in Sarajevo — wird von Knežević (p. 106) auf
Osman. *dolab* 'a thing which turns round, as a waterwheel, a tread-
mill etc., a turnstile or eastern turning-cupboard, etc.; a trick, plot,
intrigue; a trademan's or merchant's business; any vortex of affairs; a
cupboard; drumbelly, tympanitis; a giddiness, vertigo; a middling
sized spar of pine timber, a pole' (Redhouse, *A Turkish-English
Dict.*, s. 1260; cf. auch Radloff, *WB*, III, 1718) zurückgeführt, dies
aber mit Fragezeichen für arabischer oder persischer Herkunft gehalten.

Das türkische Wort kann sehr gut aus dem Türkischen etymologi-
siert werden, und zwar als eins der — allerdings recht seltenen —
Nomina auf *-p* von südwest-türk. (Oγuz) *dola-*, gesamt-türk. *tolγa-*
'drehen, wenden, winden, umgeben, einwickeln, etc.' (Kāšγarī; WB:
Čaγataj, Taranči, Qarajīm, Baraba, Qojbał, Saγaj, Sojon, Qazaq,
Qrym — in dieser Form Lehnwort aus einer qypčaqischen Sprache,
nur in der Bedeutung 'wahrsagen'; die echte süd-qrymische Form ist
dola-), im *WB* unnötigerweise getrennt in 3 Einträge, *tolγo-*. (*WB*:
Qyrγyz, Ojrot), *dola-* (*WB*: Osman., Qrym), jeweils mit einer Reihe
Ableitungen, in der Grundbedeutung von 'Sache, Ding, das sich dreht,

zum Drehen, Einwickeln, etc.', die eben auch auf die spezielle Bedeutung von 'Schöpfmühle, Göpelwerk' anwendbar ist. Nun findet sich das soeben postulierte, rein-türkische deverbale Nomen auf *-p* nur im Osmanischen und Süd-Qrymischen, in der zu erwartenden Form *doła-p*, wozu im Qrymischen noch die Nebenform *dołaf* vorliegt, wie in demjenigen osmanischen Dialekt, aus dem die Dialekte von Sarajevo, Bosnien und der Hercegovina ihr *dòlāf, dùlāf* entlehnt zu haben scheinen, falls es sich hier nicht um die in türkischen Lehn- und Fremdwörtern des Serbo-Kroatischen sporadisch auftretende Schwankung *p:f:v* handelt; aber auch diese Unsicherheit im Gebrauch dieser Labiale dürfte ihren Ursprung im Türkischen haben, in einer Korrektionstendenz der Mundarten, der Halb- und Ungebildeten, die sich in Hyperurbanismus oder, besser, Pseudorichtigkeit auswirkt, denn der im Türkischen und im Slavischen fehlende Laut *f* wird in den osmanischen Volksdialekten wie in einer Reihe von Türksprachen meist durch *p* ersetzt. Die obige Form aus dem Qrym-Türkischen ist ein Beispiel einer solchen Pseudorichtigkeit, das zudem die Auffassung dieses Wortes als Fremdwort im volkstümlichen Milieu erweist.

Die echt-türkische Herkunft von *dołap* wird weiterhin dadurch in Frage gestellt, daß es nur im Osmanischen und Qrymischen vorzuliegen scheint — es fehlt im Türkmenischen —, während *tołya-* und *doła-* im Türkischen mit zahlreichen Ableitungen —außer gerade dieser — recht verbreitet sind. Daß das Wort als fremd empfunden wird, ist außer an der Nebenform auf *-f* daran zu erkennen, daß einige osmanische Lexika *dołap* nur in der Form دولاب geben — so Beḏros Zekʿi Ġarabeḏjan —, während die meisten es auch oder nur als طولاب anführen, wie *doła* — und dessen Derivativa — so z.B. Redhouse — und es zudem als arabisch oder persisch bezeichnen. Historisch ist das Wort im Osmanischen schlecht belegt — jedenfalls bisher —: es findet sich in der Form *dołav* in einer ins Osmanische übersetzten Auswahl aus Saʿdī aus dem XIV. Jhdt., dann ist es aber nicht mehr bis auf eine osmanische Übersetzung des persischen Wörterbuchs Burhān-i Qāṭiʿ, die im XVIII./XIX. Jhdt. gemacht worden sein muß, festgestellt worden: *dołap maraży* 'Diabetes' (cf. *Taṅïklarïyle Tarama Sözlüğü*, II [1945], 312; *Tarama Sözlüğü*, II [1965], 1202). Das Wort fehlt in den beiden Dialekt-Wörterbüchern des Osmanischen. Im Arabischen und Persischen liegt das Wort in der Form دولاب *dūlāb* vor, mit einem gebrochenen arabischen Plural دواليب *dawālīb*. Im Persischen findet sich *dōlāb, dūlāb*, von Steingass (*Persian-English Dictionary*, s. 546) *dol-āb*, als Compositum, geschrieben, mit den Bedeutungen: 'a wheel, especially for raising water to overflow fields; a machine in the walls of monasteries, hospitals or lazarettos, into which people on the outside put victuals or other necessaries (sometimes also superfluities, as children), and then, turning it upon its axis, leave them to be carried off by them within; a storehouse, pantry, buttery, locker; a labyrinth; trick, fraud, machination; a drum; a ditch profit; commerce; hard usage; diabetes', auch die Nebenform *dōlāba*, aus denen man immer noch die Grundbedeutung 'Ding, das sich dreht, etc', wie oben, abstrahieren kann. Das erste Glied dieser (scheinbaren oder echten?) Kompositon ist *dōl, dūl* 'a bucket, milkpail, pitcher; the hopper of a mill; the sign Aquarius; a deceitful, shameless person; base, ignoble; the mast of a ship; a purse' (Steingass, *ibidem*) — bei der Bedeutung 'Schiffsmast' muß es sich um ein homonymes Etymon handeln — und die Nebenform *dōlā* 'pitcher, ewer, water-bucket', Dimin. *dōlča* 'leathern bucket' (dies > Osman. *dołǯa* 'Trinkgefäß', Dial. von Qars, Bursa, und 'Schöpflöffel', Dial. von Čaηqyry [*Söz Derleme Dergisi*, I, 1939, s. 455]); es findet sich auch im Tāǯīk, *dūl*, als 'Mehlkasten in der Mühle' (*Tadžiko-russkij slovar'*, s. 143), entlehnt in die südlichen Dialekte des Qyrɣyz, *dołu*, 'id.', und findet sich im Bartangī (Pamir) in der Form *dūr* und der gleichen Bedeutung (Sokołova, s. 107), dürfte iranischer Herkunft sein und im Neu-Persischen als die einheimische Form, möglicherweise auf Kontamination beruhend, für das arabische دلو *dalw*, Pl. أدل، دلاء *'adlā', dilā' 'a bucket, urn; letting down (a bucket) into a well; the sign Aquarius; a mark burnt upon camels; hardship, calamity; the hopper of a mill' (Steingass, s. 533) in Gebrauch sein.

Das Letztere hat eine fast totale phonetische wiesemantische Identität mit ARuss. *dьłу, Gen. *dьłъve (loc. sg., nom. pl. делви belegt, M.-Bulg. *dьłi (loc. sg. дьльви belegt) 'Faß', N.-Bulg. дéлва 'großer tönerner Topf mit zwei Henkeln'' und gehört in eine Gruppe von vorindogermanischen Wörtern alt-mediterran-vorderasiatischen Ursprungs, von der auch Lat. *dōlium* 'großes irdenes Gefäß für Korn, Wein, Öl; πίθος' herkommt. Intern-indogermanische Etymologieen für die indogermanischen Vertreter dieser Gruppe zu suchen, ist abwegig, wie leicht aus den Ableitungen — phonetisch wie besonders semantisch — bei Vasmer (I, 337) wie Berneker (s. 252), der es zu der slavischen Sippe von *dol'a* 'Anteil, Los' stellen möchte, zu ersehen ist. Beide stellen *dьłу* zu Lat. *dōlium*, dies aber dann irrigerweise zu *dolāre* 'tailler, équarrir, façonner le bois', wie auch Walde-Hofmann, *LatEtWb.*, I, 364, was Meillet und Ernout auf Grund der Semantik abgelehnt haben (*Dict. ét.*, 1932, s. 268), obwohl sie "un rapprochement lointain" mit der Gruppe von *dolāre* für möglich halten. Das irische *delb* 'Form' ist viel zu unscharf und vag, um einen solchen sehr konkreten Gebrauchsgegenstand zu bezeichnen. J. Hubschmid erwähnt in seiner wertvollen und sehr anregenden Monographie "Schläuche und Fässer" (in *Romanica Helvetica*, 32, Bern, 1955) *dōlium* eigentlich nur en passant (s. 156); er sagt, es "bedeutet ausschließlich tönerne Gefäße" und meint, der Vergleich mit idg. *del-/dol- 'spalten, kunstvoll schnitzen' (Pokorny, IdgWb., 194f.) würde für diese Gefäße die ursprüngliche Bedeutung 'Holzfaß' erweisen, "wenn er zu Recht besteht" — was aber, wie gesagt, nicht anzunehmen ist. Hubschmid erwähnt auch ARuss. делва (sicherlich nach Vasmer, I, 337), leider aber nicht arab. dalw.

Das zweite Kompositionsglied von dūl-āb, dōl-āb ist — at its face value — pers. āb 'Wasser'.

Das Oγuzische hat aus dem Persischen dōlāb entlehnt, wobei das Wort schon auf Grund seiner Semantik sofort mit der ganzen Sippe von Türk. tolγa-, dola- in engste Berührung gekommen ist und nach dem Verlust seiner Längen sich kaum noch von einem Derivativum von dola- unterschied. Immerhin scheint das Gefühl für die Fremdheit des Wortes im Türkischen nie vollkommen verlorengegangen zu sein.

III.

AKSl чрътогъ, Sb.-Kr, ђѐрдек Pers.-Arab čārṭāq, Qom. kärtäk

Das Sb.-Kr. djèrdek 'Schlafgemach; erste Brautnacht' — Škaljić hat auch gèrdek — führt Knežević (s. 112) richtig auf Osman. ǵárdäk 'id.' (cf. Radloff, WB: Osman., Āzarb.) zurück, wobei er möglichen persischen Ursprung annimmt. Die Ableitung bei Škaljić (s. 239) von Osm. ǵär- 'strecken' ist falsch. Das Wort ist in den Formen gärdäk wie girdäk, auch mit Suffix -lik, im Osmanischen vom XVI. Jhdt. ab belegt (cf. Tanĭklariyle Tarama Sözlüğü, III, 289, 299 und IV, 334). Es liegt auch in Bulg. Гердéк vor. Es hat sonst im Türkischen die Form kärtäk, Osman., Qrym 'id., Θάλαμος', ist aber im Oγuzischen mit einem sehr ähnlichen persischen Wort kontaminiert worden, girdak, von der idg. Wurzel *vert- 'drehen, wenden, etc.', 'a small circular thing; a small circular tent; a royal, private tent; a circular kind of sweet cake' (Redhouse), so daß Redhouse in der Bedeutung "Θάλαμος" ǵirdäk sowie ǵärdäk angibt; das Letztere bezeichnet er als eine Nebenform von ǵirdäk. Die irrige Annahme persischen Ursprungs findet sich auch in Radloffs WB (II, 1559), wo deshalb auch ein Verweis auf kärtäk fehlt. Wie aus dem Folgenden hervorgeht, wäre als echt-türkische Form auch im Osmanischen und Qrym-Türkischen kärtäk anzusetzen.

Das Wort ist natürlich nicht von AKSlav., ABulg. чрътогъ 'Θάλαμος, Schlafgemach' zu trennen, das sich im ASerb. чрьтогъ, чрьтагъ 'id.', im Russ. als чертóг 'Prunkgemach, Prachtsaal', pl. 'Palast', Ukr. чертóг 'innerer Teil eines Gebäudes' vorfindet (cf. Berneker, 171f.;

Vasmer, III, 328). Berneker hielt es für ein Lehnwort im Urslavischen, das "durch türkische Vermittlung" aus Pers. *čārṭāq* (< Pers. *čār* < *čahār* '4' und Arab. *ṭāq* 'Bogen, Gewölbe, Nische, Fenster'), im Osmanischen 'a chamber surrounded by four arches supported on four columns' (Redhouse) und im Persischen 'four columns, i.e., a principal room on the top of Eastern houses, open in front and supported by four pillars; a kind of quadrangular tent; a kitchen tent; the elements; the sky, the firmament' (Steingass) herstammt. Dasselbe Wort hat im Vulgär-Osmanischen wie im Qrym und Qarajīm *čardaq* 'an open stage built on the roof of a house for drying linen, etc.; a trellis, supported on posts' (Redhouse) ergeben und als solches Eingang ins Slavische gefunden: Russ. чердáк 'Speicher (im Haus), Dachstube, Erker', Sb.-Kr. *čārdāk* 'Söller, Obergemach; Balkon an türkischen Häusern; Wachthütte; Behältnis für Maiskolben', Bulg. чардáк, auch mit *e* oder *o* in der 1. Silbe, 'Vorhalle, hohes Gemach', Sloven. *čārdak* 'Wachhaus auf Pfählen, Blockhaus' — wofür Miklosich, *Türk. Elemente...*, I, 273 *čerdak* gibt — (cf. Berneker, l.c.; Vasmer, III, 319). Vasmer, l.c., bringt in Einklang mit Berneker und den weiterhin zitierten Arbeiten von Miklosich, Melioranskij, Korš, Mladenov und Lokotsch dieselbe Ableitung, aber hält das persische Wort, ohne Zweifel wegen der von der persischen recht beträchtlich abweichenden Lautgestalt, für "wahrscheinlich durch proto-bulgarische Vermittlung" eingedrungen.

Sicher ist diese Etymologie aber keinesfalls. Phonetisch ist einzuwenden, daß das *a* der ersten Silbe, das auch im Türkischen eine gewisse Zeit seine Länge bewahrt haben muß — so gibt z.B. Redhouse für die literatur-osmanische Aussprache *čārtāq*, lediglich für das bereits zum Lehnwort gewordene *čardaq* keine Längenbezeichnung, d.h. die Vokale sind anceps —, im Slavischen nicht nur als *e*, sondern als reduzierter Vokal, *ь*, erscheinen sollte, woraus dann im Süd-Slavischen Liquida sonans, im Ost-Slavischen Vokal + Liquida, hier *er*, entsteht. Auch ist das *o* der zweiten Silbe aus altem *ā* oder auch *a* < *ā*, wenn nicht unwahrscheinlich, so doch ganz unerwartet. Nun könnte ja das Wort an slavische Bildungen auf -*ogъ*, so selten sie auch sind, angelehnt worden sein, was zugleich das -*g* statt -*k* für das türkische und arabisch-persische -*q* "erklärte". Mit der Semantik steht es nicht viel besser: die ursprüngliche Bedeutung ist 'θάλαμος, νυμφών', wie sie im Süd-Slavischen erhalten ist; das ost-slavische hat bereits sekundäre Bedeutungen. Deshalb ist чрьтогъ nicht mit *čārṭāq*, sondern nur mit *kärtäk* zusammenzustellen, das ebenfalls ausschließlich 'θάλαμος' bedeutet, und dies schon im Qumanischen (*Codex Cumanicus*; cf. *WB* und Grönbech, *Komanisches Wb.*, s. 140). Ist *kärtäk* ins Urslavische entlehnt worden, so ist die Annahme der I. Palatalisation des

Anlauts vollkommen logisch, fraglich bleibt nur die Qualität des Wurzelvokals und die Form des Suffixes, die für das türkische Wort nicht das allein belegte -äk, sondern -ök oder -ük, resp. -ög oder -üg voraussetzte: *kärt-ök, *kärt-ük, resp. *kärt-ög, *kärt-üg, wobei die Regel zu beachten ist, daß ein konsonantisch auslautendes palatales türkisches Wort im Urslavischen nicht in die palatale Kategorie der jo-Stämme aufgenommen wird, sondern daß in diesem Fall der auslautende Guttural -k/-g, der im Türkischen palatal ist, im Slavischen nicht palatalisiert wird und daher diese Wörter im Slavischen als o-Stämme erscheinen. Urslav., ARuss. čъrtogъ setzt nicht unbedingt ein türkisches Suffix mit stimmhaftem Guttural voraus, da dieser im Türkischen, im Qypčaqischen (Nordwest-Türkischen) ganz allgemein, vor vokalischem Suffix erscheint, worauf ich schon früher hingewiesen habe. Der Vokal der türkischen Wurzelsilbe in kärtäk kann ä oder auch e [gewesen] sein, welch' Letzteres sich im Volga-Tatarischen (Qazan-Tatar. und Baškirischen) zu i verschoben hat, aber er ist kein reduzierter Vokal, und daher wäre seine slavische Vertretung durch ь nicht phonologisch, sondern psychologisch, durch Angleichung des türkischen Wortes an Ableitungen von der slavischen Wurzel čъrt-/čert- mit reduziertem Vokal zu erklären, zumal die slavische Wurzel, die ursprünglich, wie ihr indogermanischer Prototyp *(s)qert-, "schneiden" bedeutet (cf. infra), semantisch wie etymologisch mit der türkischen engverwandt ist.

Durch die Übereinstimmung der beiderseitigen Wurzeln läßt es sich nicht endgültig feststellen, ob das türkische Wort ins Urslavische oder das urslavische ins Türkische entlehnt worden ist. Man kann zur Stützung dieser letzten These die anscheinend doch außerordentlich geringe Verbreitung des Wortes im Türkischen anführen. Es ist zudem auch ganz unwahrscheinlich, daß ein Θάλαμος, d.h. kärtäk, in nomadischen Gesellschaften vorkommen sollte, da es eine seßhafte und dabei eine gewisse Stadtkultur voraussetzt. So fehlt das Wort bei Kāšγarī, und, soweit bis jetzt festgestellt, in den neu-osmanischen Volksdialekten. Aber es ist ebenfalls nicht aus der Sprache der für ihre fortgeschrittene städtische Kultur bekannten Ujguren belegt. Es findet sich im Türkischen also nur in einigen wenigen Sprachen, und zwar gerade in denjenigen, die den ost- und süd-slavischen benachbart sind. Für die Qumanen ist dabei noch mit einer Symbiose mit den südlicheren Ost-Slaven vom XI. bis XIV. Jhdt. oder noch länger zu rechnen.

Der türkische Verbalstamm kärt- (gesamt-Türk., auch Osman.) "Einschnitte machen (mit der Axt, dem Messer), hineinschneiden"; — semantisch läßt sich kärtäk mit D. Zimmer vergleichen — hat seine altajische Parallele im Mongolischen, kärči- 'to cut, mince, slice, carve;

to make incisions, notch' (cf. z.B. Lessing, 455) < *kärti-; das Tungusische hat: Manǯu *kerči-* 'Schlachtvieh zerschneiden' (v. d. Gabelentz, 131), Ewenki *kĕrči-*, Dial. von der Nerča, '(zer)teilen', *kĕrči-mĕ*, Dial. der Steinigen Tunguska, Ñepa, Ñorboko und Ilimpija 'getrocknetes Fleisch', Barguzin 'Nudelsuppe, лапша в супе' (Vasilevič, 231), Nānaj *kĕrči-* 'mit dem Messer in kleine Stücke zerschneiden (Fisch, Fleisch)' (Petrova, 71); dies Etymon ist wegen -*č*- im Ewenki und der speziellen Bedeutung als Lehnwort aus dem Mongolischen anzusehen. Es ist die altajische Parallele zu der indogermanischen Wurzel *(s)qert-/(s)qort-* 'schneiden', die im Urslavischen *čьrt-ǫ, Inf. *čers-ti, RKdl. чрътж, чрѣстн Skr. *kr̥ntati* 'er schneidet', Av. *kərəntaiti* '*id*.', Lit. *kertù* (1. sg. prs.), Inf. *kĩrsti* 'scharf sein, heftig schlagen', Lett. *cẽrtu, cirst* 'hauen, hacken', Lat. *cortex* 'Rinde', etc. (cf. Vasmer, III, 329; Berneker, 172) vorliegt; hierbei ist zu bemerken, daß das Baltische in der Semantik dem Altajischen in diesem Fall am nächsten steht. So hatte Alexander Brückner wahrscheinlich doch recht, wenn er *čьrtogь* als echt-slavisch ansah (*KZ* 46, 237), selbst wenn seine Auffassung zu einem gewissen Grad von seinem slavischen Patriotismus getragen war. Vasmer, l.c., zitiert Brückner, hält aber dessen Auffassung für "nicht wahrscheinlich". *Čьrtogь* ist echt-slavisch wie *kärtäk* echt-türkisch ist; sie sind beide urverwandt und haben sich in dieser speziellen Bedeutung länger auf dem Gebiet gehalten, auf welchem beide große Sprachfamilien nebeneinander und miteinander gelebt haben und noch heute leben. Dabei ist aber die spezielle Bedeutung Θάλαμος ohne Zweifel aus der den alten ponto-kaspischen Türkvölkern wie auch den Oγuzen im Westen benachbarten slavischen Kultur übernommen worden.

Das sb.-kr. *čĕrdāg* 'Schlafgemach' (XVII. Jhdt.; Berneker, s. 171 u. — von Knežević nicht erwähnt) ist eine Mischform aus *čärdāk* und einer auf Türk. *kärtäk* zurückgehenden Form.

Ableitungen von der türkischen Wurzel *kärt-*, die ins Slavische entlehnt wurden, sind Russ. кирка́ 'Spitzhacke, Pickel' < *kärt-ki/kirt-ki* (mit dem Suff. nom. instrumenti -*qy/-ki*), кирпи́ч 'Ziegel' = Kāšyarī *kärpič* < *kärt-pič/*kirt-pič* '*id*.' (cf. *Language* XX, ss. 66 ff.).

Columbia University

Moldova—the name of the River
and the country

GRIGORE NANDRIŞ†

> You're my friend—
> What a thing friendship is, world without end!
> How it gives the heart and soul a stir-up
> As if somebody broached you a glorious runlet,
> All poured out, all lovelily, sparklingly, sunlit,
> Our green Moldavia, the streaky syrop,
> Cotnar as old as the time of the Druids—
> Friendship may match with that monarch of fluids;
> Each supplies a dry brain, fills you its ins-and-outs,
> Gives your life's hour-glass a shake when the thin sand doubts
> Whether to run on or stop short, and guarantees
> Age is not all made of stark sloth and arrant ease.
> Robert Browning, "The Flight of the Duchess," XVII, 1–12.

Among the river names of the East Carpathian region, that of the river Moldova, which gave its name to the Rumanian principality of Moldavia, founded in the fourteenth century between the Carpathians and the river Dniester, has received less attention from students of onomastics than have the other hydronyms of the region. The names of the rivers Danube (Dunărea), Ister, Dniester, Prut, Siret have been repeatedly studied with the aim of penetrating into the dark arcana of prehistory—for onomastics and archaeology are the only archives of prehistoric times. They do not, however, always yield up their secrets; among these is the origin of the name Moldova, which we intend to submit to a historico-linguistic analysis.

The study of river names of Thraco-Dacia shows that this late Roman province (105–272) was a meeting place of the Dacians with

119

the Iranian Scythians, Celts, Teutons, and other peoples of the Pontic region.

The Scythians founded a state of their own in Dacia, which was destroyed by the Dacian king Buerebista.

The names of the rivers Dnieper, Dniester, Ister (Lower Danube), Prut, Siret and others are considered to be of Iranian origin.[1] The names of the rivers east of the Carpathians, as they appear in the òldest texts are: Borysthenes (Herodotus) = Dnieper; Hypanis (Herod.) = Don; Tyras (Herod.) = Dniester; Pyretos (Herod.), Porata, Poras = Prut; Tiarantos (Herod.), Hierasos (Ptolemy), Gerasos (Ammianus Marcellinus) = Siret. Among the tributaries of the Ister mentioned by Herodotus are: Aratos, Naparis and Ordessos as well as the Tiarantos and Porata.[2]

To the west of the Carpathians, in Transylvania, the river names present the following pattern: Tisianus (Iordanes, *Get.* 5), Tisia (*ibid.* 34), Pathisus (Ammianus Marcellinus, 17, 13, 4) = Theiss (Tisa); Grissia, Gressia (Iordanes, *Get.* 22), Gerassus (Ammianus Marcellinus, 17, 13, 1), = Crişul; Maris (Herod. 4, 49), Marisos, Marissus (Strabo, 7, 304.). In these sources the river is considered to be a tributary of the Danube.); Tibisis (Herod.), Tibissus (inscription), Tibiscus, Tibiskos (Ptol. 3, 8, 1), Tifesas (locality, Priscus), Tibisia (Iordanes, *Get.* 34), Timeses (Constantine Porphyrogenitus) = Rumanian Timiş; Gifil, Gilpil (Iordanes, *Get.* 22) = Rumanian Jiul, German Schyll, Schiul; Aluta, Alutas (Ptolemy, 3, 8, 3), = Rumanian Olt.

Other variants of these river names appear in texts as well. Thus, for example, the name of the river Siret appears as Sarát in Constantine Porphyrogenitus (apparently a Pecheneg form with Séretos as the Byzantino-Hungarian form). A river Sered, a leftbank tributary of the Dniester in Podolia, and the Seretets in North Podolia represent the same name. The form Sarat (Constantine Porphyrogenitus) is considered to reproduce the Thraco-Dacian pronunciation of the Irano-Scythian *čarant-*, a present participle of *čar-* 'to wander, graze' found in Avestan (Old Indian *carati*). Avestan has the participle *čarant-* (Bartholomae, *Altiran. Wörterb.*, col. 450), which was used for any kind of movement. For running water Avestan has *tak-* and *žar-*. The meaning 'rapid' is reached by assuming a pregnant sense 'really moving, swift' just as Old Indian *takva-* 'swift' from *tak-* 'run, flow.' If Herodotus used *ti-* for foreign *tš-*, the comparison Siret: Tiarantós seems very possible (communicated by Professor Sir Harold W. Bailey in a letter from Cambridge of 11 March 1955). This confirms V. Pârvan's etymology of Siret.

None of these names or their variants can be identified with the name of the river Moldova. The Rumanian scholar I. Iordan explains this hydronym through the name of the tree *molid, molift* 'fir-tree' (*picea excelsa*), because, at its source in Bucovina, he observed forests of coniferous trees. By syncope Iordan derives Moldova from a *molid-ova with a Slavonic suffix.[3]

A. I. Sobolevskij derives the name from the Slavonic etymon *moldŭ 'tender, soft, young,' which appears in Russian names Nemoldova, Molodova representing an original *mŭldova. Ernst Schwarz considers the name in its German form *Moldau* as resulting from a dissimilation in the Czech form *Vltava* 'swift mountain river, torrent.'[4]

The origin and history of the name of Moldova cannot be studied outside its geographical and historical context. On Rumanian territory this name appears as a toponym in widely separated regions: in Bucovina, in Eastern Transylvania, in the Banat, on the Danube, near the Iron Gates (Moldova Nouă, Moldova Veche). The diminutive Moldovița in Bucovina is the name of a locality and a brook. The relation of the above to Moldovișul (region of Vîlcea), Moldișul (region of Prahova), is doubtful. Archaic forms are Moldua,[5] Mulduva.

Outside ancient Dacia, the Rumania of today, the river Velikaja, near Pskov, is called Muldova in Polish sources.[6] It has been suggested that this form is derived from a Gothic *mulda 'powder, dust,' Old Nordic *mold* 'soil, dust,' Low German Muld-ow derived by means of a Polish ending. Basing his theory on those forms, O. Sabler affirms the presence of the Germans on the Baltic Sea in prehistory.[7] M. Vasmer rejects this theory with the remark that a Germanic loanword *multa* exists in Finnish, is found in Estonian as *muld*, and that from these forms are derived the Finnish (Multava) and Estonian (Muldav) names of the river Velikaja. This view eliminates the presence of the Germans on the Baltic in prehistory.[8]

For the formal analysis of toponyms, the context is perhaps as important as the phonetic laws. These show less regularity and conformity in the history of place names than in the history of other words. Folk etymology, sound substitutions, spellings, the effects of administrative and literary factors, complicate the history of single or isolated words by comparison with the history of appellatives which appear in speech associated with other words.[9] For this speech context, which cannot help us in our search for the meaning and changes of a toponym, we have to substitute the historical and archaeological backgrounds. Furthermore, anthropology can supply valuable information regarding the successive ethnical strata which may have contributed to the changes in place names.

Moldavia's toponymy reveals several prehistoric ethnic strata. There are Thracians and Iranians (i.e., Scythians, with their kinsmen the

Osseti or Assi, who probably gave their name to Iaşi, the capital of
Moldavia); Celts and Germans: Bastarnae, Sciri, driven eastwards in
200 B.C., lived for a longer or shorter time in Moldavia while the
Gepids occupied Transylvania and formed the ruling class of the
Romance population. The Gumans, the Pechenegs, and the Slavs, who
reached Moldavia in later historical times as immigrants or prisoners of
war, left their mark in place names like Comana, Peceneaga, Şchei,
Ruşi. However, such names may be misleading since they may represent late personal names in their stems.

The ending -ova/-ava, -jev/-jeva is a regular Slavonic suffix in appellatives and in proper names: Warszawa, Olchowa; Czech Sázava;
Ukrainian Sadžava; Old Russian Moldava (modern Moldavija), adjective Moldovskij, from Rumanian.[10] However, one should not overlook
the commonness of suffix substitution in the history of place names.
We find the same suffix in the name Suceava, a river and town in
Moldavia. The same suffix appears in the Czech name Vltava, which
in German is called Moldau (as is the Rumanian river Moldova).

Farther north is the Morafa, a tributary of the Dniester, whence
comes the Rumanian (Bessarabian) family-name Murafă. The suffix in
these formations represents the Germanic -ahwa and the prototype for
Morava would be *Mar-ahwa; cf. German March representing the Indo-
European radical *mer-/mor- 'dark colour.'[11] The Polish name
Pełtew, Ukrainian Poltwa, a leftbank tributary of the Bug and a
rightbank tributary of the Horyń in Volhynia are similar formations
and represent a pre-Germanic *plta, *polta, from which the attested
Modern German forms Fulda, Folda.[12]

The two hydronyms, Moldova and Vltava, both called in German
Moldau, should be etymologically associated against the background of
the history of the Celts, who moved eastward from the lower Rhine on
a broad front as far as the Dniester. Archaeological data show that, in
general, in the whole of Transylvania and on the entire territory of
Moldavia the Celts represent the northern wave of expansion, and not
the southern. The Celts inhabited the North-West and North-East of
present day Rumania. The La Tène pottery of Apahida, according to
Kovács, links this Celtic civilization with the North-West Celts of the
Upper Danube, Elbe, and Vistula valleys and not with the south-
western Alpine civilization. This is true for the fourth to first centuries B.C. The Celts founded a kingdom in Transylvania in about
60 B.C., which was destroyed by the Dacian king Buerebista, whose
empire stretched from Pannonia to the Dnieper. During the first to
second centuries A.D., the superior Roman civilization replaced the
Celtic in Dacia. It was, however, the Celts who introduced the
potter's wheel into Dacia.[13]

The Finnish scholar J. J. Mikkola rejects a Germanic origin for the name Fulda and, proceeding from the form Fuldaha found in the *Annales Fuldenses*, suggests that this hydronym has an identical origin with Vltava and Moldova, and with the hydronym Flutausis of Jordanes.[14] The form Flutausis[15] is not the only reading of the codex form. Closs accepts the reading 'fluvius Tausis' and quotes in the *appratus criticus* other forms of the name: Fluitans (Pall. Codices duo Palatini. ed. Paris), Fluvius Flantasis, Flanrasis (Geogr. Rav. IV, 14), Thausis (Epit. Aenae Silvii, *Hist. Gothorum*). He considers that the original reading was *fluvius Aluta dissecat* (Aluta = Olt river) and that this was corrupted scribally into *Fluta + usis*.[16] Mommsen, too, identifies the name with Aluta preceded by *fluvius*. The Aluta is mentioned by Jordanes.[17] In Migne the name is interpreted as Fluvius Tausis.[18] With another vowel, the ending *-ausis* appears in Celtic names like Nem-ausos. The Celts (third and second centuries B.C.) could have adapted to their language an older name of Scythian origin (seventh to fourth centuries B.C.). The presence of the Celts in the region of Moldova is attested by the names of their cities on the Dniester: Carrodunum; in the south on the Danube they built Noviodunum; the Britolagi are mentioned by ancient sources further eastwards.

The Gepids and other Germanic tribes occupied northern Dacia, including present-day Moldavia, for a long time. Taking from the Celts the form Tausis, the Teutons antefixed to it the stem represented in their language by **fleutan* 'fluere,' Alemannic *flout* 'a stream,' Germanic *Fluss*. Thus, a Teutonic intermediary changed the Celtic **Tausis* into Flutausis. For *-ausis*, the Germanic ending *-ahwa*, *-awa*, *-au* was substituted. From this form Moldova, Moldau and Fulda could be derived, bearing in mind also an interplay with Germanic Mulde. The change of *fl-* to *ml-* (Flutausis : Vltava : Moldova) is not unusual in this region.[19]

If these distant echoes, conveyed via a very imperfect rendition in various little-known languages can be considered as a substitute for the precise requirements of philological research, then a Celtic **-tausis *<tausos* is the prototype of Moldova, Vltava, Fulda. And even if some words, in the long chain of communication through time and space, are distorted or misunderstood, the messages as a whole conveys a meaning. Some Celtic scholars identify the stems **tauso* and **tam* in Celtic hydronyms.[20] They see in them a radical **tao/*tawos/*tausos* which appears in Middle Irish *to* 'still, schweigend,' *tevel* 'schweigen.' From the same Indo-European root derive Old Church Slavonic *po-tъxnǫti* 'quiescare, cessare,' Old Swedish *thyst-er* 'schweigend.'[21]

The identification of **tauso/*tam* would add the name of Moldova to the very large family of Celtic hydronyms. The rivers Tvesis and

Tava appear in Scotland on the map of Ptolemy.[22] In France, La Thève, a tributary of the Oise, has the same root,[23] and in Wales the following seem to belong to this group: Tâf (Engl. Taff), Towy, Tywi, Tawe, Teifi (Engl. Tivy), Tafwys (Engl. Thames), perhaps also Dyfrdwy (Engl. Dee), Dyfi (Engl. Dovey).[24]

The identification of *tauso/*tam greatly enlarges the kinship of Flutausis > Moldova. The *tam element appears in Tamaris, Tamara (in Hispania Tarraconensis) now called Tambre in Galicia, Tamar in Cornwall, the river Thames, whose name appears in a great variety of forms: Tamesis (Caesar, 51 B.C.), Tamesa (Tacitus, A.D. 115–117), Tamensis (Orosius, A.D. 417), Tamensis (Bede, ca. A.D. 730), Tamisa (56 Cartularium saxonicum, 681), Temis (65 Cart. sax., 681, A.D.), Temes (443 Cart. sax., 843), Trevisa-Temse.[25]

Since the stem *tam appears also in the Sanskrit támas 'darkness,' and in the name of a tributary of the Ganges, Tamasa 'dark, the dark river,' its presence in Iranian is probable. This would suggest a Scythian prototype for Flutausis-Moldova, and bring it into context of other Scythian hydronyms: Siret, Prut, Dniester, etc.

One can hardly trace appellatives of Scythian origin in Rumanian, though ţap 'he-goat,' vatră 'fire-place' have been explained through Iranian.[26] However, it is uncertain through which intermediary language the words were borrowed.

A similar argument can be used to support the hypothesis of a Celtic origin of Moldova < Flutausis by blending with Teutonic elements that occur in this region of ancient Germanic settlers. Stynawa, a tributary of the river Stryj in Galicia, corresponds to a Germanic Steinau; Żuława, in the delta region of the Vistula, is called in German Saalau.[27]

The lasting settlement of the Celts in north eastern Rumania is sufficiently proven by toponymy and by archaeology. The presence of appellatives of Celtic origin is less certain. One word which may claim such an origin is Rumanian braga 'a drink of fermented buckwheat.' The Celtic forms that correspond to this appellative are: Cymr. brag 'malt,' Old Irish braich, Welsh bragwr, Engl. brewer, Lat. frāces. The word also appears in the East Slavonic languages: Russ. braga; Ukr. braha; as a loanword in Polish (braha), and in Lithuanian, brãgas. The word spread from Dacia. The Celtic origin of the Slavonic word was accepted by M. Vasmer[28] who later rejected it and proposed a Turco-Tartar origin by associating it with the Chuvash word peraga 'small beer, Dünnbier.' Vasmer rejects a Rumanian origin for the Slavonic word because, he says, there are no other Common Slavonic loanwords of Rumanian origin.[29] However, the word does not appear in South Slavonic. A. Brückner does not accept a Celtic origin for the word in Slavonic on the grounds that there are no Celtic loanwords in this language.[30] J. Kuryłowicz considers *braga* as being of Celtic origin.[31]

Another enigmatic Celtic loanword is Polish *gunia* 'woolen overcoat of the Podhale mountaineers, rough woolen material.' The word appears in all Slavonic languages with soft *n* (Russ. and Bulg. also have forms with hard *n*). The word seems to be of Celtic origin like Lat. *gunna* and Engl. *gown*. In Daco-Rumanian the word is unknown, but Arumanian has *guna* 'fur-coat,' *gunar* 'donkey.' Because of the soft *n*, Vasmer identifies the word with Old Iranian *gaunya-*, whereas A. Belić considers it to be a Balkan word carried to the Carpathian region of Poland by shepherds.[32] It may have disappeared in Daco-Rumanian, and the softness of *n* in the Slavonic forms may be a secondary change. In this case the word would be of Latin origin, where it is a Celtic loanword.

In conclusion, we must confess that our exploration of philological conjectures has not revealed a clear etymology of the name Moldova, but it has at least eliminated a Slavonic origin for the hydronym. The explanation of the name of this river by reference to the trees that grow in the valley of its sources is not acceptable. The name is of pre-Roman origin, as the background sketched above justifies us in assuming, even if the geographical identification in the ancient texts is not certain. Jordanes says that: "ab Africo vero magnus ipse Danubius, ab eos (scl. Gepidi) Flutausis secat, qui rapidus ac verticosus in Istri fluenta fures divolvitur."[33] This lack of geographical precision is not unusual in ancient texts and maps.

The history of the name Moldova reveals influences of several linguistic strata superimposed in the prehistory of other hydronyms of Dacia, the picture of successive ethnographic changes, which obscured the form and by popular etymology or textual distortion confused the meaning of the word.

In the context of the prehistory of Eastern Europe, a Celtic origin is the more probable. As V. Pârvan puts it:

There were Celtic *oppida* at Carrodunum, Maetonium [Maiotes on the Sea of Azov], Vibantavarium and Eractum in Galicia and on the Dniester; and very important Celtic workshops at Munkačevo in Eastern Slovakia, whose products spread throughout Northern Getia. By the third century at the very latest, Galicia, Moldavia, Bessarabia and a portion of the Ukraine as far east as Olbia were covered by Celtic tribes.[34]

Post Scriptum

Et in Arcadia... nos

Many travellers have called Moldavia a marvel of natural beauty and have praised its inexhaustible riches.

This charming landscape of great variety, enhanced by its art-treasures and the people's skill in craftmanship is of puzzling interest for the philologist and archaeologist.

An example to the point is a name of the market-town where—without being aware of it until we compared notes at a later date—Boris Unbegaun was quartered simultaneously with myself during World War I, exactly half a century ago. The name of the place is Dorohoi. Some historians, misguided by philologists, found in this and other similar formations a proof of an East Slavonic ethnical influence featured by pleophonism. The only snag in this imaginative theory is that the word cannot be explained through any East Slavonic language and the historical theories, on which some historians have built up states and cities, remain pure abstractions. The word is a learned transposition of Dragoi which is based on the South Slavonic name Dragu with a Rumanian suffix.

Such professional problems did not then trouble the blue sky of our Arcadia. Our memories of that meeting *manqué* were enriched later by the realities of the Moldavian Arcadia, overshadowed by the ravages and destructions of the epidemics and starvation brought by the war over that country. When the storm of anarchy brought greater evils, my friend Boris unfolded his young wings and landed in places more favourable to the development of his spiritual aspirations—the universities of Ljubljana and later of Paris. Here I met him in the beehive of the Bibliothèque Nationale or among the disciples of Meillet, Mazon, Gilliéron, and others where we collected our nectar and distilled it. Since then I remained in touch with the joyful scholar who enlightened his deep knowledge with his humour.

126

We were separated and thrown where the force of destiny pleased. When the storm subsided, I met the same young and good-humoured friend and scholar, Boris Unbegaun, who repeated to his depressed friends the saying of a great teacher: "If I knew that tomorrow the world were to disappear I would plant today my apple tree." His youthful nature has not changed with the advancing years. I have seen many people old at forty but very few young at seventy like Boris Unbegaun, whose anniversary we are celebrating.

In these hours of happiness for him and for his family, we extend to him hearty congratulations in the form of happy memories:

Quod Felix, Faustus, Fortunatumque Sit!

University of London (Emeritus)

NOTES

1. Cf. V. Pârvan, *Consideraţiuni asupra unor numiri daco-scite*. Acad. Rom., Mem. Secţ. Ist., Seria III, T. I (1923).
2. Cf. A. Forbiger, *Handbuch der alten Geographie* (1877), p. 775, note 90.
3. Iorgu Iordan, *Toponimia Romînească* (Bucharest, 1963), p. 478.
4. *Zeitschr. f. slaw. Phil.*, II (1925), 525. Further information on the subject is to be found in: *Arch. f. slav. Phil.*, XLI (1929), 40 ff., *Zeit. f. Ortsnamenforsch.*, III, 42, and IX, 84, 97; *Zeitschr. f. slaw. Phil.* (1932), X, 42–43; *The Slavonic and East European Review*, XVIII (1932), 145.
5. N. Iorga, *Documentele dela Bistriţa*, I, 1–2.
6. W. Pol, *Hidrografia Polska; Polski słownik geograficzny*, VI, 802; XIII, 331.
7. *Bull. de l'Acad. des Sciences de St. Petersburg* (1914), pp. 815–40.
8. M. Vassmer, "Beiträge zur slawischen Altertumskunde," *Zeitschr. f. slaw. Phil.*, X (1933), 422–43.
9. Cf. W. J. Sedgefield's statement: "It is to be noted that while the place-name student is mainly concerned with the original meaning of a name, he may in some cases be concerned with the meaning, whether true or false, that a later generation may have attached to the name, leading thereby to a change of form which may not be in accord with strict phonological law," in A. Mawer and F. M. Stenton, *Introduction to the Study of English Place-names*, I (Cambridge, 1924), 5.
10. Cf. J. Rozwadowski, "Uwagi o nazwie Warszawy," in his *Wýbor pism*, I, Warsaw (1959), 328; K. Kozierowski, "Nazwy rzeczne w Lechii przybałtyckiej i w przyległych częściach Słowianszczyzny północno-zachodniej, II: Nazwy na -awa i -ew/wa', *Slavia occidentalis*, X (1931), 160–243; M. Vasmer, *Russisches etymologisches Wörterbuch*, II (1955), s.v. *Moldavija*.
11. A. Stender-Pedersen, *Slawisch-Germanische Lehnwortkunde* (Gothenburg, 1927), p. 346.
12. T. Lehr-Spławiński, *O pochodzeniu i praojczyznie Słowian* (Poznan,

1946), p.80; J. Rozwadowski, "Kilka uwag do przedhistorycznych stosunków wschodniej Europy i praojczyzny indoeuropejskiej na podstawie nazw wód," *Wybór pism*, II (Warsaw, 1961), 88.

13. V. Pârvan, *Getica* (Cambridge: 1926), pp. 564–65; *idem, Dacia* (Cambridge, 1928), p. 130.

14. J. J. Mikkola, "Samo und sein Reich," *Arch. f. slaw. Phil.*, XLII (1928); *id.*, "Południowa granica Słowian u Jordanes," *Symbolae Gram. J. Rozwadowski*, II (Kraków 1928), 114.

15. Of the Mommsen (*MHG*) edition (Berlin, 1882) of Jordanes' *Getica*, 33, where it is identified with the river *Aluta*. Later scholars, e.g., V. Bogrea (*Anuarul Institutului de Istorie Naţională*, III [Cluj, 1926], 518–19) accept the identification.

16. Carol Aug. Closs, *Iordanes de Getarum sive Gothorum origine et rebus gestis* (Stuttgart, 1861).

17. *MHG, op. cit.* fn 15, p. 75.

18. *Pat. lat.*, LXIX, 1255.

19. Cf. P. Kretschmer, *Einleitung in die Geschichte der Griechischen Sprache* (Göttingen, 1896), pp. 236f.

20. A. Holder, *Altkeltischer Sprachschatz*, II (Leipzig 1904), p. 1713. This view is considered by Professor J. Lloyd-Jones, Dublin, to be "not so probable" (from a letter of February, 1942).

21. H. Pedersen, *Vergleichende Grammatik der keltischen Sprachen*, I (Göttingen, 1908), 55.

22. A. Macbain, *Etymology of the principal Gaelic National Names* (Stirling, 1911), p. 28.

23. A. Holder, *op. cit.*, p. 1713.

24. These Welsh names of rivers have been kindly communicated to me by Professor D. W. T. Jenkins of the University of Wales (Bangor).

25. Cf. *The Concise Oxford Dictionary of English Place-names* (1936); A. Holder, *op. cit.*, p. 1774.

26. J. Rozwadowski, "Stosunki leksykalne między jezykami słowiańskimi a irańskimi," *Wybór pism*, (Warsaw, 1961) II, 123; A. Rosetti, *Istoria limbii romîne*, II (Bucharest, 1943), 123.

27. J. Rozwadowski, "Kilka uwag do przedhistorycznych stosunków wschodniej Europy i praojczyzny Indoeuropejskiej na podstawie nazw wód," *Wybór piśm*, II (Warsaw, 1961), 88.

28. M. Vasmer, "Die Urheimat der Slawen," *Der Ostdeutsche Volksboden* (Breslau, 1926), p. 128.

29. M. Vasmer, *Russisches etymologisches Wörterbuch*, I (1953), 116.

30. A. Brückner, *Zasady etymologii słowiańskiej* (Warsaw, 1917), p. 65.

31. *Mélange Vendryès*, p. 210.

32. M. Vasmer, *REWb, op. cit.*, 322; A. Belić in *Rocznik slawistyczny*, XII (1921), 15.

33. Jordanes, *Getica* (ed. Mommsen), p. 33, see n. 15, above.

34. V. Pârvan, *Dacia, op. cit.*, p. 112.

Some High-Style Elements in Seventeenth-Century Russian

ANNE E. PENNINGTON

On more than one occasion, the lack of studies of late Church Slavonic has been deplored.[1] A knowledge of the Church Slavonic current in sixteenth- and seventeenth-century Muscovy is, among other things, a necessary preliminary to the elucidation of the eighteenth-century fusion of Church Slavonic and Russian. The analysis of the usage of good literary stylists of the seventeenth century is an essential part of the study of Church Slavonic. Perhaps a small contribution to a part of this preparatory work may be made by the analysis of the usage of a good non-literary stylist, an expert in administrative Russian, and by a brief account of some of the linguistic features he considered to be "high style."

It seems useful to make a tentative distinction between a) Church Slavonic—the liturgical language of the Russian church; b) "literary Church Slavonic"—the Russianised but basically Church Slavonic language of works with literary pretensions; and c) "high style," which here refers to the temporary raising of tone in a Russian work. It is sometimes denied that there is such a thing as style in Russian before the eighteenth century. But in works such as the *Poètičeskaja povest' ob Azovskom sidenii*, the author's occasional departure from his basic administrative Russian into Church Slavonic on the one hand and prose with elements of folk poetry on the other, shows literary awareness. It is not possible to call the language of the *Povest'* "literary Church Slavonic" in the same sense as, for example, the language of the *Skazanie* of Avraamij Palicyn, but it seems possible to call it "Russian, with high-style passages." This "high style" does not usually consist of passages of consistently written literary Church Slavonic, but it contains enough distinctly non-administrative, non-colloquial features to make it clear to the reader or listener that an elevated subject is under discussion.

A classic example of non-literary Russian, more precisely of the administrative Russian used in the *Posol'skij Prikaz*, where the author worked most of his life, is Grigorij Kotošixin's *Account of Russia* (1666–1667). It is an important source for this type of language, being, as is well known, a work of considerable extent and originality, but remarkably free from Church Slavonic. However, in the first of the thirteen chapters of the work (pp. 1–22, fols. 1–32),[2] an account of the Tsars since Ivan IV and of official ceremonies, Kotošixin makes an obvious effort to write high style. The first chapter is not written on a consistently exalted level e.g., the account of the career of the Pretender, *Vor Griška Otrep'ev* (3. 15–38), shows fewer high-style features than the histories of the genuine Tsars. Nevertheless, the chapter can be contrasted as a whole to the rest of the work, where high style occurs only in well-defined phrases or ecclesiastical contexts.

This clear limitation of high style, together with Kotošixin's expertise in administrative Russian, makes his work an excellent source for the definition of some high-style features of seventeenth-century Russian.

There is no space to list all the lexical, morphological, and syntactic features which are regarded as high style by Kotošixin, but a few examples will be given, especially of those which are not Church Slavonic in origin, or which, if they are, are used in a way that would not be normal in Church Slavonic.

VOCABULARY

Vocabulary is most easily adopted into a foreign language, and before it is assimilated, it most obviously lends colour to a style. There are a number of words, mostly of Church Slavonic origin, which Kotošixin used in high style passages only, while their Russian counterparts are used freely, in the first chapter and elsewhere, e.g., *ašče* 5.26 (Russian: *budet* 6.30, 44.4, etc. and *eželi* 53.28, 155.6, etc.); *jadi* 5.35 (Russian: *ěstva* 66.17, 158.24, etc.); *zrjaxu* 15.9 (Russian: *videl* 57.17, 101.15, etc.); *velija* 4.17 (Russian: *velikaja* 98.14, 99.32, etc. and *bol'šaja* 36.9, 9.20, etc.); *zělo* 2.8, 2.13, 4.23, and *velmi* 2.25, 2.27, etc. (Russian: *gorazdo* 52.22, 57.29, etc.); *vo svojasi* 21.1 (Russian: *domov* 153.17, 152.41, etc.); *na glavě* 154.21, 154.24 (in the marriage service) (Russian: *golova* 46.27, 116.9); *pomoščiju Božieju* 54.26, 54.27, 127.8 (Russian: *pomoč'* 103.28, 126.27 'human help'); *tščeri* 4.33, 15.8, 8.40 (Russian: *dočeri* 5.27, 34.16, etc.).

Phonological oppositions naturally form the basis of the stylistic differentiation in a number of these words, but are confined to a few words only. There is no example of a phonological feature used as an independent stylistic element. As G. Y. Shevelov has shown, this tendency develops further, so that in Modern Russian, no stylistic pairs based on phonological oppositions are found.[3]

Like most educated Muscovites of his day, Kotošixin knew some Polish, and a number of Polish words occur in the work. Only one seems to be high style: *edinu mněišuju doč'* (6. 3). The Church Slavonic form of the comparative adjective would be identical with the Russian, while the Polish form, which echoes the Church Slavonic ending = *ějšij*, is distinctive. It might be regarded as a "hyper-Slavonicism."

MORPHOLOGY

The morphological systems of Old Church Slavonic and of tenth- to eleventh-century Russian were very similar; it is obvious that many of the forms felt to be Church Slavonic in the seventeenth century were originally common to both languages, but had been eliminated by Russian, with its comparatively rapid development. The forms of the vocative, aorist, pluperfect, the dative sg. of masculine substantives in *-ovi*, the nominal forms of the attributive adjective—these were current in early Old Russian, but persist in Church Slavonic. Some of the original morphological distinctions are indeed scarcely felt as stylistic alternatives; as with the phonological features, Church Slavonic forms may be restricted to set phrases—so the pronominalized adjectival ending of the feminine genitive sg. *-yja* and the accusative pl. of pronouns in *-ja* (*vsja, naša*). In such phrases, in titles and quotations, Church Slavonic features, original or recently developed, are used consistently. e.g., *Velikii knjaz' vseja Rusii* 2. 7, sim. 4. 8 etc.; *vseja Velikija i Malyja i Belyja Rosii samoderžec* 126. 9, sim. 126. 1; *Velikii Novgorod* 124. 6, 109. 6 (the regular combination of Church Slavonic adjective ending with Russian substantive is additional evidence that neither is a free stylistic element); *gorod Ustjug Velikii* 108.17; *Prikaz Bolšago Dvorca* 76. 21, 168. 2, etc. (but cf. *Prikaz Bolšogo Prixodu* 92. 9, sim. 87. 7, etc.); *Miloserdija radi milosti Boga našego, vo ježe posěti nas vostok svyše i napraviti nogi naša na put' miren, sego ubo Boga našego v Troicě slavimago milostiju my, velikii gosudar' car'* 36. 4–7; *po vsja gody* 22. 18; *po vsja dni* 20. 2, 29. 27, 86. 32 (temporal phrases are a traditional sphere of Church Slavonic influence).[4]

It is the morphological features used outside these phrases, when Kotošixin is composing, not quoting, that are of greater interest in the present context. In several cases, it seems that the distinctions caused by quite recent developments in Russian have greater stylistic value than traditional differences. Some examples follow.

1. The forms of the past active participles and later, of the gerund (the function is discussed below, with other points of syntax), were originally identical in Church Slavonic and Russian. By the sixteenth century, distinct suffixes had been developed for the gerund: the suffixes -*vše* and -*vši* were regarded as the endings of the Church Slavonic gerunds; they were apparently still used as such by Avvakum.[5]

By the seventeenth century, a further stylistic distinction is made in the form of the past gerund of *i*-type verbs. The older form of the participle from verbs of this class, with *jod*-palatalisation of the stem consonant, was often replaced by the form with suffix -*iv* even in Old Church Slavonic. It is found in modern Church Slavonic, but in well-known phrases and often side by side with the newer form. e.g., *i voplotivšagosja ot Duxa Svjata i Marii Děvy i vočelověčšasja* (Creed). It is the newer form, in -*iv*, which is used in Russian for the past gerund from the first, and it is still so used in the sixteenth century.[6] During the seventeenth century, however, this gerund in -*iv* becomes stylistically limited. It is apparently absent from the *Uloženie* of 1649 —in his description, Černyx gives no examples of -*iv* forms, although he does not comment on their absence.[7] Cocron mentions that these forms appear only in the literary texts of his selection.[8]

Kotošixin's usage is clear. Forms in -*iv* appear only in the first chapter: in one nominal declined participle and in three gerunds with the Church Slavonic suffix -*vše*: *pravivše* 2.12, 1.16, 4.19: *usmotrivše* 4.29; *otloživše* 6.9; *uspokoivšusja* 4.19. Elsewhere, the function of the past gerund of *i*-type verbs is fulfilled by the present gerund, formed from both perfective and imperfective verbs. There are many examples. A few are: *činja im nakazanija, rozoslali* 104.1; *myslja o tom mnogie dni, ukazal* 6.18; *čtob oni, pomyslja, dali sposob* 24.29; *pokradči i pograbja bojar svoix, uxodjat* 135.8–11. The subsequent fate of this gerund presents some interest as an example of a Church Slavonic form becoming established as the literary norm.

In the eighteenth century, the perfective present gerunds from verbs of the *i*-type are regarded as alternatives to the past forms, but with a clear stylistic distinction. Tredjakovskij thought them vulgar, saying of Sumarokov: "*Nastojaščie deepričastija za prošedšie pišet po-ploščad-nomu, kak-to: premenja vmesto premeniv i premenivši, uvidja za uvidevši, usladjas' za usladivšis', utomja za utomivši i pročie*" and Sumarokov, replying, acknowledges that these forms are "*malye vol'nosti.*"[9] Lomonosov in his *Grammar* does not even mention the forms in -*ja*.[10]

At the end of the eighteenth and in the early nineteenth centuries, the use of the perfective present gerunds for past gerunds is extended to some verbs with present stems in -*e* and -*je*, e.g., *Počuja serogo tak blizko zabijaku, Psy zalilis'* (Krylov); *Grušču i plaču gor'ko Počuvstvuja, kak malo Talantov ja imeju* (Karamzin) II; *zavezja ženu domoj* (Fonvizin, *Pis'ma*).[12] Obnorskij, who gives many similar examples, calls these forms "*razgovornye formy literaturnogo jazyka.*"

Toward the middle of the nineteenth century, there is a movement away from these Russian forms, back to the past gerund. In 1840, the grammarian N. I. Greč, admitting the present perfective forms in verse for reasons of euphony, condemned their use in careful speech and writing.[13] It is at this time also that the Russian forms of the present gerund in *-uči, -juči* begin to be eliminated from the literary language.[14] During the second half of the century, the past perfective gerund replaces the present with increasing frequency. The aspectual and morphological basis for this development can be argued.[15] Yet the stylistic factor—both in the process and the result of the development —cannot be ignored. The expressions in which the perfective gerunds survive in modern Russian tend to be colloquial—*bežat' slomja golovu, slušat' razinja rot, rabotat' spustja rukava,* etc. Moreover, among twentieth-century writers it is, according to A. V. Isačenko, Gor'kij who uses this form most freely.[16] Isačenko finds, however, that in recent years it is more common "bei guten Stilisten."

2. A stylistic distinction may be seen in the declension forms of certain substantives.

The second half of the seventeenth century is the period of the generalisation of *a*-type flexions in the dative, locative, and instrumental pl. of other types. This process takes place at different speeds in different classes. In Kotošixin's text, the *a*-endings are regular in the dative pl. of feminine *i*-type substantives, with the exception of two words, both of which form part of the ecclesiastical vocabulary and are Church Slavonic in derivation: *vlastem* 13.30, 18.23, etc. (12 examples) 'Church authorities'; *moščem* 7.40 'relics' (cf. *močam* 52.1 'diplomatic powers'). These forms must be seen as high style—the *a*-type endings penetrate Church Slavonic very gradually and irregularly.[17]

In a comparable example, the older ending, retained in a single expression, is not Church Slavonic, but archaic Russian: the *a*-endings are generalised in the three relevant cases of the neuter hard *o*-type substantives, except in the phrase: *sadjatsja po městom* 9.10, sim. 9.3—a fixed expression of protocol.

In other classes and cases, the new endings are not so well established that the old can be used stylistically, as they are in the eighteenth and nineteenth centuries.[18]

3. A few examples of morphological features present special interest, since they suggest that not only archaic, but also new—even

colloquial—Russian forms might be acceptable in high style, if only because they were not administrative Russian.

In sixteenth- and seventeenth-century administrative Russian, *den'* is regularly declined as an *i*-type substantive, with genitive sg. *dni*.[19] In Kotošixin's work, there are forty-eight examples of *dni* to two of *dnja*. Of these two, one occurs in the first chapter: *v navečerii togo dnja* (7.29), and the other in a phrase with a Church Slavonic ending to the adjective: *včerašnjago dnja* 103.2. The conclusion—that the newer form is high style—is supported by the examples of *dnja* in literary, but not in administrative, texts found by Cocron and Bergman in their examination of other works of the century.[20] It is true that the literary texts chosen belong mostly to the latter part of the century; nevertheless, it is interesting that the sole example of *dnja* in a non-literary text (the Xovanskij correspondence) given by Cocron, is in an "ecclesiastical" phrase: *prežde dnja Nikolaja.*

4. Two case forms of the demonstrative pronoun *tot* show similar stylistic distinctions.

In the feminine genitive sg., the normal form in Kotošixin's work is *toě/toe* thirty-two examples), but the new form *toj*, identical with the dative-locative, occurs ten times. Four examples are in the first chapter, in which *toě* is found only once: *toj cerkvi* (10. 4, 22. 3); *toj polatu* (11. 20, 11. 25); but: *toě děvicy smotril* (6. 5).

It seems certain that although the genitive sg. *toj* must have been generally known in the sixteenth and seventeenth centuries, it was carefully avoided by Muscovite official language.[21] It was not, apparently, avoided by literary Church Slavonic. A check on thirty-five pages of Avraamij Palicyn's *Skazanie* shows not a single example of *toě/toe*, but three of *toj*, and two of the Church Slavonic *toja*.[22] These are also the forms mentioned by Lomonosov in his *Grammar*, § 436, while he ignores the old administrative form.

One might compare the forms of the feminine genitive sg. of the pronominalized adjective. Kotošixin, in his whole work, uses *-ye* 105 times, the newer *-oj* only 50 times; but in the first chapter, besides the Church Slavonic *-yja*, there are 8 examples of *-oj* to only 6 of *-ye*. Again Lomonosov mentions only *-yja* and *-oj*, ignoring the old Russian form.[23]

5. The distribution of the masculine nominative sg. forms *tot, toj* is interesting. From the fourteenth century in Moscow, *toj* seems to be regarded as Church Slavonic, *tot* as Russian. In modern Church Slavonic *toj* is the regular form. In sixteenth-century administrative Russian, its use in the one phrase *v toj že den'*, noted by Unbegaun, may be due to the influence of Church Slavonic in expressions of time. In some regions other than Moscow, *toj* had a wider extension and was

probably normal in the spoken language. It is the only form given by Ludolf, and its regular use by Avvakum is probably a colloquial rather than a Church Slavonic feature.[24]

The high-style value of *toj* for Kotošixin is quite clear. It is found only in the first chapter, and there only for persons of exalted rank, while *tot* is used for humbler objects, e.g., *toj car'* (3.9, 4.5, etc.); *toj velikij knjaz'* (1.15); *toj bojarin* (3.12, 2.12); but: *tot čelověk* (16.20); *tot xlěb* (9.20); *tot den'* (12.3). The sole exception might even be construed as a pejorative use of the Russian form, counterbalancing the Church Slavonic adjective: *tot zloumyšlennyi bojarin* (2.38)!

In this case, the colloquial and the Church Slavonic forms coincide and are distinct from the administrative form. But it is the administrative form which is established as literary in the eighteenth century.

SYNTAX

The absence of studies of late Church Slavonic makes comparisons of points of syntax particularly unsatisfactory, but certain features stand out.

1. A striking syntactic development in Russian is the system of indeclinable gerunds, contrasted to the Old Church Slavonic declinable participles. For a Russian of the Muscovite period, the Church Slavonic participle forms were fairly simple to adopt, but the whole system of usage was more complex. Declined participle forms do occur, but it happens also that in high style, Church Slavonic participle forms—pronominal and nominal, but not agreeing with the subject—are used as gerunds, e.g., Sestry že carskie . . . imějaj svoi osobye ž pokoi raznye i živušče jako pustynnicy, malo zrjaxu ljudej (15.8–10); Ljudie že . . . mysljaše o nem, čto ešče v mladyx sušče lětex zla tvorit mnogo . . . usmotrivše vremjani čas, upoiša ego otravami (4/26–30). In the latter example, probably not only *sušče* but also *mysljaše* are gerunds. From the construction this seems more likely, and there are other cases of Kotošixin confusing *š* with *šč*. Confusion of imperfect and participle forms is found in the sixteenth century also.[25]

2. If a Church Slavonic form in a Russian construction is high style, so also is a Russian form in a Church Slavonic construction. In the first chapter, there are two examples of a declined Russian participle: *inym pri tom buduçim ženam* (15.27); *Gore togda ljudem, buduçim pri tom pogrebenii* (21.22). Elsewhere, *buduçi* is used as an indeclinable form. Cf. in a comparable construction: *čto im, buduçi u carskogo děla, ne vorovat'* 98.22.

3. A further fusion of the two traditions is found in the dative absolute construction. This, a striking feature of old and new Church

Slavonic which is not found in Russian, is affected by most Muscovite writers of high style. The participle may fail to agree and the "subject" of the absolute construction may govern the main verb, producing in effect a Russian gerund construction. Nevertheless, the "subject" is in the dative, the "gerund" has a "Church Slavonic" form, and the result is undoubtedly high style: *Carju že otloživše vsjakie gosudarstvennye i zemskie děla praviti... počal.... mysliti* (6.9–11). There are also more traditional examples: *Carju že na pogrebenie brata svoego s Moskvy ěxavšu, i byvšu u Troicy... i tot zloumyšlennyi boljarin velěl* (2.35–36); *Carju ž... ot krovorazlitija xristianskogo uspokoivšusja praviše gosudarstvo svoe tixo* (4. 17–19).

4. One syntactic high-style feature is apparently a polonism. In one completive clause, a statement of fact depends on a negated verb of thinking: *nikto že o tom domyslisja, jakoby prišel emu čas smerti* (4.31). Such a suppositional use of the conjunction *jako + by* is found in Polish from the fifteenth century, but it is not commonly used in Russian until the eighteenth century, when it may well be a Gallicism.[26]

5. Finally, one syntactic feature, used as high style, seems to be Kotošixin's own invention. In the exclamation *Blagorazumnyi čitatelju! čtuči sego pisanija, ne udivljajsja!* (53.10), the genitive of the direct object after *čtuči* is neither Church Slavonic nor Polish. Sreznevskij's examples show no such construction.[27] Possibly a vague awareness of other case usage in Church Slavonic—e.g., the genitive of direct object after the supine—caused Kotošixin to introduce the case here. A comparable confusion is found in his letter to the King of Sweden, in which he uses a number of polonisms, among them, apparently, the following curiosity: *velěl menja učit' svějskogo jazyku studentu, a ja togo studenta budu učit' po ruski*[28] Here Kotošixin has made an unhappy compromise between Polish *uczyć kogoś czegoś* and Russian *ucit' kogo-nibud' čemu-nibud'*.

It will be seen that for Kotošixin, high style embraces Church Slavonic, Polish, archaic Russian, and probably also new Russian elements. Stylistic oppositions are often based on new distinctions, formed by recent developments in Russian, while many Church Slavonic forms of long standing are not free stylistic elements, but are confined to certain words or phrases.

In the recurring task of disentangling elements which are historically Church Slavonic from those which are stylistically Church Slavonic (or high style), the examination of texts which are basically Russian, but which show a facultative use of high style may complement the examination of literary texts.

Oxford

NOTES

1. Cf. B. O. Unbegaun, "L'héritage Cyrillo-Méthodien en Russie," *Cyrillo-Methodiana* (Köln-Graz, 1964), pp. 470–82; "Le russe littéraire est-il d'origine russe?" *Revue des Études slaves*, 44 (1965), 19–28; A. Šaxmatov and G. Y. Shevelov, *Die kirchenslavischen Elemente in der modernen russischen Literatursprache* (*Slavistische Studienbücher*, [Wiesbaden, 1960]), pp. 45–106.

2. Page and line references are to: A. Barsukov (ed.), *G. Kotošixin, O Rossii v carstvovanie Alekséja Mixajloviča* (4th ed., St. Petersburg, 1906). The text has been compared with a microfilm of the autograph MS (kindly provided by Uppsala University Library), and fully excerpted from the point of view of morphology. Quotations are from the printed text, but final hard *jer* has been consistently omitted.

3. A. Šaxmatov and G. Y. Shevelov, *op. cit.*, pp. 91–105.

4. Cf. B. O. Unbegaun, *La langue russe au XVIe siècle (1500–1550), I. La flexion des noms* (*Bibliothèque russe de l'Institut d'études slaves, XVI* [Paris, 1935]), pp. 391, 446.

5. S. D. Nikiforov, *Glagol, ego kategorii i formy v russkoj pis'mennosti vtoroj poloviny XVI veka* (Moscow, 1952), pp. 272–274; P. Ja. Černyx, *Očerki po istorii i dialektologii severno-velikorusskogo narečija* I–II (Irkutsk, 1927; hereafter Černyx, 1927), 6.

6. Cf. examples in D. Kudrjavskij, *K istorii russkix déepričastij* (Jur'jev 1916), pp. 8–9; Nikiforov, *op. cit.*, pp. 272–80.

7. P. Ja. Černyx, *Jazyk Uloženija 1649 goda* (Moscow, 1953; hereafter Černyx, *Uloženie*), pp. 358–59.

8. F. Cocron, *La langue russe dans la seconde moitié du XVIIe siècle* (Paris, 1962), p. 220.

9. Cited from V. V. Vinogradov and N. Ju. Švedova (ed.), *Očerki po istoričeskoj grammatike russkogo literaturnogo jazyka XIX v.* (Moscow, 1964; hereafter *Očerki*), II, 178–79.

10. M. V. Lomonosov, *Rossijskaja grammatika* (St. Petersburg, 1755), §§ 359–427. Akademija Nauk SSSR, *M.V. Lomonosov, Polnoe sobranie sočinenij* (Moscow-Leningrad, 1952), VII, 499–539.

11. Cited from *Očerki* II, 178.

12. Cited from S. P. Obnorskij, *Očerki po morfologii russkogo glagola* (Moscow, 1953), p. 222.

13. N. I. Greč, *Čtenija o russkom jazyke* (St. Petersburg, 1840), p. 45, Cited from *Očerki*, II, 181.

14. Cf. V. V. Vinogradov, *Očerki po istorii russkogo literaturnogo jazyka XVII–XIX vv.* (Reprint, Leiden, 1949), pp. 341–42.

15. Cf. *Očerki*, II, 181–85.

16. A. V. Isačenko, *Die russische Sprache der Gegenwart. I. Formenlehre* (Halle, 1962), p. 329.

17. M. Smotrickij, *Grammatiki slavenskija pravil'noe sintagma* (Ev'je, 1619 and Moscow, 1648), gives a certain number of *a*-type endings, mostly in the instrumental and as alternatives to the older flexions. His paradigms are imitated by many grammarians of Church Slavonic in the nineteenth century; some, however, show alternative *a*-type forms more frequently. Cf. V. Klassovskij, *Grammatika Slavjano-cerkovnago jazyka novago perioda* (4th ed., St. Petersburg-Moscow, 1881); S. Mirovol'skij, *Kratkaja grammatika Cerkovno-slav-*

janskago jazyka novago perioda.
Kurs èlementarnyj (St. Petersburg,
1901). Even in these textbooks, the
dative is the most conservative case,
and the *i*-type the most conservative
class. Cf. also the very conservative
paradigms in the latest printed
manual: Ieromonax Alipij (Gama-
novič), *Grammatika cerkovonoslav-
janskago jazyka* (Jordanville, N.Y.,
1964).

18. *Očerki*, I, 265–66; Černyx, *Uloženie*, p. 267.

19. Unbegaun, *op. cit.*, p. 72; Černyx,
Uloženie, p. 267.

20. Cocron, *op. cit.*, p. 52; G. Bergman,
The Melusina Saga (Uppsala, 1964),
p. 159.

21. Cf. Unbegaun, *op. cit.*, p. 375;
E. N. Petuxova, "Sklonenie uka-
zatel'nogo mestoimenija tъ ta to v
pamjatnikax XIV–XVI vv." (Ir-
kutskij Gosudarstvennyj Pedago-
gičeskij Institut) *Učenye zapiski
kafedry russkogo jazyka*, XIV (Irkutsk, 1958), 67–91.

22. L. V. Čerepnin (ed.), *Skazanie
Avraamija Palicyna* (Moscow-Leningrad, 1955), pp. 113–48.

23. Lomonosov, *op. cit.*, § 161.

24. The distribution of *tot*, *toj* is discussed by Petuxova, *loc. cit.*, pp.
71–73; cf. also Unbegaun, *op. cit.*,
p. 372; Cocron, *op. cit.*, p. 139; H.
W. Ludolfus, *Grammatica russica*
(Oxford, 1696), ed. B. O. Unbegaun
(Oxford, 1959), p. 24; Černyx
(1927), p. 46.

25. Nikiforov, *op. cit.*, p. 264.

26. Cf. Z. Klemensiewicz, T. Lehr-
Spławiński, and S. Urbańczyk,
*Gramatyka historyczna języka
polskiego* (Warsaw, 1955), pp. 454–
55; L. A. Bulaxovskij, *Istoričeskij
kommentarij k russkomu literatur-
nomu jazyku* (5th ed.; Kiev, 1958),
p. 368.

27. I. I. Sreznevskij, *Materialy dlja
slovarja drevnerusskogo jazyka* III
St. Petersburg, 1903, (photomecha-
nical reprint; Moscow, 1958), cols.
1526–27.

28. Ja. K. Grot, "Novyja svěděnija o
Kotošixině po švedskim istočni-
kam," *Sbornik otdelenija russkago
jazyka i slovesnosti*, XXIX/3 (1882),
13.

On the Textual Criticism of Xrabr's Treatise

RICCARDO PICCHIO

THE NUMBER and character of the textual variants in the more than thirty codices of the monk Xrabr's *Apology* can raise doubts on the possibility of establishing, through a complete collation, a text that might reflect the original one with sufficient precision. The very concept of an "original text" here, as well as in many other items of medieval Slavic literature, is seriously questionable. It is difficult, in fact, to postulate an autograph where one does not know for certain whether the pages that have come into our hands ever had one single author or, if they had, where and when this author composed his work. The "monk Xrabr" is actually just a name written by some copyists in front of late recensions of a short treatise known with the conventional title of *Apology of the Slavic letters*. In spite of the authoritative hypotheses so far advanced, this name—which sounds like a pseudonym—has not yet found a certain historical frame.

These who want to identify the author with an important personage of tenth-century Bulgaria cannot produce the indisputable evidence that Hrabr himself had drawn up—at that very time—the first text of the composition in defence of Slavic writings, a composition widely spread all over orthodox Slavdom as it is evidenced by the various manuscripts both of Eastern Slavic and Balkan Slavic origin. None of these MSS. goes farther back than the thirteenth or fourteenth centuries, but the tradition of the *Apology* seems older: this is shown by the obvious linguistic archaisms of passages concordantly preserved by different manuscripts. But the documented ancient origin of single passages does not necessarily constitute absolute evidence for the ancient origin either of the whole textual material which has reached us or of the text handed down through a single manuscript.

The technique of writing transmission used in the orthodox Slavic Middle Ages—where the copyist very often performed also the functions of a rewriter—does not give the critic the possibility of determining absolutely the beginning of a textual tradition on the basis of linguistic considerations. If we were to attribute to the word "text" the exact meaning it usually has in philological studies, we should very often give up speaking of "textual tradition" for a wide sector of Slavic studies. In fact, when a composition is not just faithfully copied, but rather adapted to new rhetorical usages and often to new conceptual necessities, it is clear that tradition does not record a proper handing down of the text but the evolution of composition patterns, namely a succession of "versions" or recensions, each of which constitutes a new text. This particular situation explains the uncertainties of many scholars in medieval Slavic Literature as well as the well-known suggestions by Professor Lixačev, who wishes to substitute for the actual textual criticism a special "textology" of his own, based on the concept that history of the text must not be restricted to the phase of its composition by the author since—as, for example, in the Old Russian literature—"the work continues being created even after coming out of its first author's pen."[1] This is a historical-collective conception based on facts known to every Slavic scholar which, however, deprives of all foundations not only the notion of "text" but the very notion of "literary work." In the specific case of Xrabr's *Apology*, if we were to accept the validity of such criteria for the whole literature of the orthodox Slavic Middle Ages, we could but study the single MSS. or, at most, the single recensions, following their history from the thirteenth to fourteenth centuries onward. We would no longer speak of the monk Xrabr's *Apology* (so much the less if we identified him with a writer of the tenth century), but of various *Apologies* created anew from time to time according to the formal uses of a certain milieu and of a certain time.

It seems to me, though, that such a critical attitude, with regard to the work connected with the name of the monk Xrabr, should be discouraged. Against such a philological skepticism one could oppose not only considerations of a general character, but also specific exigencies connected with the whole of the studies so far produced on the *Apology of the Slavic letters*. The question to be asked is this: Would it be legitimate to deny Xrabr's composition any reliability as a historical source regarding Slavic cultural origins only because we cannot deduce a fully reliable original text? Would it not be more accurate to try and see how much of the material we have received reflects or at least continues, even if not reproducing it faithfully, a hypothetical primitive text whose existence might be confirmed by research carried out according to the general principles of philological criticism? To be exact, it is not a question of aiming at a *"constitutio textus"* but of collating all the MSS. in order to see how much of them can be brought back to a *common textual patrimony*.

The orthographic, phonetic, and morphologic variety of the single textual variants does not allow us to postulate real "archetypes" otherwise than within the families of MSS. of the same origin (Bulgarian, Russian, Serbian, etc.), but, beyond the formal variants, the structural and lexical correspondences may allow us to go back to a primitive *common textual source*. The examination of variants, neatly distinguishing between formal variants and variants concerning the intrinsic structure of the text, should bring us to a real *svodnyj* text, expunging interpolations and glosses: the problem of a chronological collocation of a possible *Urtext*, and consequently the evaluation of the historical reliability of our textual material, founded on the basis of its relationship with the common textual source, would then become more concrete.

At the present stage of studies these considerations of mine can only have general programmatic value. The comparative examination of the whole textual material of Xrabr's *Apology* still has to be carried out. The scholar who had felt its need most, Lavrov, could not even start a systematic *"recensio"*—i.e., a complete census—of the MSS.[2] Other historians and philologists have limited themselves to comparisons of few manuscripts or have relied upon the choice of one MS. which they have, with inevitable arbitrariness, elected as "the best," implicitly attributing to it the dignity of "the source."

This alleged better MS. is usually identified with the oldest one that has reached us, which is preserved in a Leningrad miscellany dated 1348. In various handbooks, as well as in scholarly dissertations, the text of this manuscript is quoted as a sort of official edition of Xrabr's *Apology*. The routine of Slavic studies has sanctioned an implicit reasoning according to which, having taken for granted that the monk Xrabr belonged to tenth-century Bulgarian culture and having acknowledged the reliability of the *1348 MS.* as if it were a direct apograph, it seems legitimate to discuss single passages or single words of this text considering them as a contemporary testimony of the situation of the Balkan Slavs soon after their conversion to Christianity. Even when one does not confine oneself to the 1348 MS., one always uses it as a sort of fundamental text for the examination of the other codices. Add to this the fact, that even when the criticism of the work which goes under Xrabr's name is carried out on a philological comparative basis, the codices which are then examined are but a small part of the existing textual patrimony: the arbitrary criterion of a "better text" is also supplemented in cases equally questionable by the discrimination between "good" and "bad" texts. This method is, in my opinion, arbitrary and questionable, both because such judgment would require an accurate comparison that has not yet been accomplished, and because—in the absence of a unitary author and textual tradition from a linguistic and structural point of view—we cannot possibly believe *a priori* that one codex gives a better text than another. Under the circumstances, what we can conceive as a traditional "text," may possibly not be found in any specific document, but only result from the census and collation of the available documents.

The manuscripts of the *Apology of the Slavic letters* (the generally accepted Slavic title being *O pis'menex*) are usually divided into two groups: the first including the MSS. which contain the versions of what is supposed to be the original text of the work; the second, on the contrary, including indiscriminately those manuscripts which—just because they differ from the tradition set by the first group—are considered "re-workings," compendia, or incomplete documents.[3] As a result, this distinction corresponds to the one I mentioned beforehand, between "good" and "bad" texts.

A famous instance of such procedure is given by Kul'bakin's article "Beleške o Hrabrovoj apologiji," published in 1935 in the "Glas" of the Serbian Academy.[4] Xrabr's work is examined here on the basis of only eight codices with further division between "better" and "worse" codices grounded not on the careful evaluation of the textual material of each MS., but on the formal correctness of the text, with the risk of considering a "better" text one which was revised and adapted in a later time and refuting instead, as obscure and incorrect, a more ancient one, may be only so characterized because of the copyist's errors, which are more easily emendable than the corrections of a scholarly rewriter.

It is not necessary to dwell on the damages that can be caused to the study of the textual transmission by such impressionistic *eliminatio*. One cannot prove, in fact, that the codices of the first group should document an autonomous tradition of their own. Rather, in several cases, it will be possible to prove a common textual tradition for a codex of the first group and another one of the second, in opposition to other readings of the first group itself: readings that might ultimately reveal a more marked corruption of the supposedly "better" codex.

The highly appreciated codex of 1348 (hereafter, *1348 MS.*) for example, does not carry the enumeration of the letters of the Slavic alphabet created by Cyril and of the letter taken over from Greek: in this regard, the *1348 MS.* is not only opposed to the codices of the first group, such as the Muscovite MS. of the fifteenth century, the first Hilandarian, the Wrocław, and the Savinskij codices, but even to some texts of the second group (the majority of which, however, do not record this passage) among which is, first of all, the so-called *"Late Russian recension"* is found.

This last text can be taken as an example of the very questionable way a document is often devaluated. Jagić had already published in his *Rassuždenija*[5] the *"Late Russian recension,"* typographically stressing its supposed difference from other texts of the *Apology* which he considered "better" ones. Kul'bakin, after nearly half a century, summarized the now widespread diffidence of Slavic philologists, stating that it was a corrupt text, full of lacunae and interpolations. The touchstone for the definition of "interpolation" was, of course, the *1348 MS.* and others of the same level. But the idea that, in a MS. so heavily "interpolated," the passage about the relationship of the Slavic and Greek alphabets might be an addition, was decidedly refuted. Now, if we compare the beginning of the *"Late Russian recension"* with the beginning of the *1348 MS.*, we immediately remark that whereas the *1348 MS.* bears the classical title *O pismenex čr'norizca Hrabra*, the former refers more vaguely to *kako sostavi Kirilъ filosofъ azbuku*, etc. This reference explains the *ubo* (*prežde ubo slověne...*) which opens the narration. This kind of title is well-represented in "secondary" texts, among which, besides the well-known *Bolgarskaja peredel'ka* (*Bolg. per.*) of the thirteenth–fourteenth centuries published by Jagić, is the noteworthy MS. of *Marča* recently made known by Biljana Stipčević in the journal *Slovo*.[6] The form *sostavi...azbuku*, of the *"Late Russian recension"* is connected with a textual tradition which is no longer resumed in the rest of the same MS., but documented both by *Bolgarskaja peredel'ka* and by *Marča*: this might infer a "textual koine" of the *"late Russian recension"* also for the other passages decidely defined by Kul'bakin as "interpolations."

Another common source of the *Marča* text, the *Bolg. per.*, and the *"Late Russian recension"* is represented by *togo radi*, where the supposed fundamental text of the 1348 MS. has *tembže...*[7] In this case, Kul'bakin does not hesitate to consider correct the formulation of the "late Russian recensions" *togo radi...nesutъ*, spotting an evident misreading in the formulation *togo radi...sut* (without *ne*). A more accurate examination of the various texts could conversely prove that both formulations are supported by an authoritative manuscript tradition. Just as in the *Bolg. per.*, we find *togo radi...sut* also in the *Marča* codex. At least as far as the internal logic of the text is concerned, the absence of the negative particle is perfectly justified: the textual formulation in the *"Late Russian recension"* refers *něsut* (*slovenьskye knigi*) to the polemic speech of the opponents of Slavic letters, whereas in *Marča* and in *Bolg. per.* the same verbal material refers to the speech of the apologist confuting his opponent's objections.[8] Which of the two versions is to be preferred? At this stage of the research, this question cannot be answered. We can only say that in neither case can we speak of an "error." We are confronted with two different readings whose legitimacy from the point of view of textual tradition can be validated only by the complete collation of all the MSS. that have reached us. Until this indispensable work has been done, all judgments about the "good" or "bad" quality of single textual fragments will necessarily be insufficiently documented and arbitrary.

To clarify the reasons for this critical attitude of mine—which might be viewed by some scholars as too self-assured, since the text is so widely known and the critics so accustomed to arguing over passages belonging to the "better" text of 1348 and to the codices nearest to it—I will give a couple of examples of how a codex can be too lightly condemned, as well as how some readings are accepted without sufficient critical discrimination.

Once again with regard to the *Bolg. per.*, Kul'bakin affirms that "we must admit that it is a rather queer elaboration,"[9] quoting as evidence the passage where the text states *sъstavilъ edinъ madukarina*. These words have no meaning whatsoever and Kul'bakin is quite justified, since he reads them like this, in adding a "sic" followed by a shocked exclamation mark. It is quite evident that this passage has undergone a "copyist's earthquake." This is not a good reason, however, for attributing the distortion of the meaning to its "elaboration," much less to judge as unquestionably unreliable the textual tradition which might be concealed under the clumsy misreading of the scribe. Before ever judging the quality of the text, the critic must try to emend, namely try to understand where the error of the copyist actually lies. Let us take the passage of the *Bolg. per.* in Jagić's edition (p. 304): *A slovenьskya knigi sъstavi Konstantinъ sъmatrae gramotu vъ nemixъ dnexъ a ošegra sostavil edin malu aky rina. Temьže sъstavi pismena*... A first and simpler correction—*nemix = nemnogix* (omission of an above-the-line abbreviation)—had escaped Lavrov's attention, whereas Kul'bakin had the merit of noticing it. Let us see now how we can put together the verbal fragments which make this passage so incomprehensible. What is the meaning of *ošegra...malu ...aky...rina*? If we compare the text with other codices (*Marča, Late Russ. recension, 1348 MS., Muscovite*), we can immediately see that Constantine's name is followed by Cyril's name (*Konstantin naricaemyi Kiril*: the late Russian recension adds *vo mnišeskom činu*, which incidentally confirms that the pas-

sage has been subjected to reelaborations beyond the evironmental
limits of one MS. family). Thus the first correction to be done is to
emend *aky rina* to *a Kiril* (paleographically the confusion between лъ
and на is quite admissible, especially in a southern Slavic area where
copyists were accustomed to graphic rules already influenced by the
vocalization of *jers*: лъ > ла > на). The other corrections, always
supported by a collation of the readings of other codices, mainly of the
Marča codex, will be: *ošegra* changed to *ošte* separated from *gra*, which
instead will bring about the correction of *gra-malu* into *gramatu*. The
textual scraps that shocked Kul'bakin, once they are put together,
will give us then: *a Kirilъ edinъ sostavilъ ošte gramatu...* ("and Cyril
alone composed the letters also," cf. *Marča*: *a Kyrilъ edanъ stvori
gramatu...*). Once the correction has been effected, the text of the
Bolg. per. finds its place within a serious textual tradition.

The second example I give, to underline how necessary it is to have
a more accurate textual criticism based on the complete collation of the
codices, is the famous passage—the object of so many elaborate critical
hypotheses and of dutiful quotations in many handbooks—where the
"monk Xrabr" states that the Slavs, before being christianized, used to
"read and interpret with marks and notches": "... *no črътami i režami
čъtěxǫ i gataaxǫ*" (1348). The *Marča* codex has: "... *Po slovinъskomъ
oučъrtania i rezania rezaxou*," whereas the *Bolg. per.* reads: "*no crъtaniemъ
crъtaxǫ i rězъmi rěžaxǫ togda....*" The last formulation is easily ex-
plicable as a stylistic feature falling within the usual technique of the
tautologic alliteration, or "*pletenie sloves*," which was particularly
developed from the end of the fifteenth century, within the so-called
Second South Slavic Influence. The richer stylistic formulation of the
Bolg. per. implies then the creation of two new verb forms: *črъtaxǫ* and
rěžaxǫ. Even in the 1348 text we find two verbs, which might belong
to the stylistic sphere of the same feeling of *cursus*: *čъtexǫ and
gataaxǫ*. As is known, these same two verbs from the *1348 MS*. have
stimulated the interpretative imaginations of philologists for genera-
tions. As for me, I do not want to commit myself with a definite answer
to the question raised by these two verbs. First, I insist we must
complete the *recensio* and the full collation of MSS.

I wish to suggest, however, a rather interesting hypothesis on the
basis of the limited comparison of the codices quoted above. If the position of the texts of *Marča*, of the *Bolg. per.*, and of the 1348 one
within the general textual tradition does not offer arguments to the
contrary, one is allowed to consider the hypothesis that the form
čъtexǫ derives from a form *črъtexǫ*, of which the *črъtaxǫ* of the *Bolg. per.* is
a clear witness. If that were true, the whole discussion about the value
and the meaning attributed by Xrabr to this verb would have no sense.

We still have to solve *gataaxo*: this form, being so exceptional, has tormented many critics, even more than *čъtexǫ*. I will advance my hypothesis again with reservations, waiting for the result of the complete collation of the codices. If we were to think of a form arising from misreading, the transformation into *gataaxǫ* might have taken place from *togda* (тогда) recorded by the *Bolg. per.*, Paleographically the reading of т⟨да⟩г abbreviated as if it were г⟨да⟩т (with the inversion of т an г united in a graphic nexus) is quite possible. A copyist confronted by the abbreviated form *gdat* is easily induced to believe it to be a verbal form stylistically coupled with the previous *čгъ taxǫ*. The addition of the ending -*xǫ*, which is read *g* [*a*]—(*a* for д)—*t*—[*a*] (> *a* of the abbreviations)—*xǫ* namely *gataxǫ* (of which *gataaxǫ* is an orthographic variant) would be quite explainable in this case The conjecture seems to me well grounded. If we had a confirmation of it, the two verbs *čъtěxǫ* and *gataaxǫ* would be the result of a late textual evolution, and they should no longer torment the Slavic philologists and historians.

These are, I want to make clear, just examples indicative of the work we face with regard to the text of Hrabr's *Apology*. Beyond my special argumentations, it seems to me that at least the application of the principle of critical examination of the manuscript tradition before arguing about the reliability of Xrabr's work as a historical source, an application which is dictated by an elementary scientific correctness, cannot be questioned.

Yale University

NOTES

1. Cf. D. S. Lixačev, *Tekstologija-kratkij očerk* (Moscow-Leningrad, 1964), p. 5. See also, D. S. Lixačev, *Tekstologija, na materiale russkoj literatury X–XVII vv.* (Moscow-Leningrad 1964), pp. 20 ff.

2. Cf. P. A. Lavrov, *Materialy po istorii vozniknovenija drevnerusskoj slavjanskoj pis'mennosti* (Leningrad, 1930), pp. 40 ff.

3. A division of the MSS., according to these traditional criteria, can be found, for example, in P. Dinekov, K. Kuev, and D. Petkanova, *Xristomatija po starobэlgarskata literatura* (Sofia, 1961), pp. 76–77.

4. *Glas Srpske Kraljevske Akademije*, CLXVIII, drugi razred, 86 (Belgrade, 1935), 43–77.

5. V. Jagič, "Rassuždenija južnoslavjanskoj i russkoj stariny o cerkovnoslavjanskom jazyke," *Issledovanija po russkomu jazyku*, I (St. Petersburg, 1885–1895), 297 ff.

6. B. Stipčević, "Marčanska varijanta Skazanija o sloveseh Crnorisca Hrabra," in *Slovo*, 14 (Zagreb, 1964), 52–58.

7. I am referring to the passage of the *Apology* where Xrabr begins to present his arguments against the "heresies of the three languages." I

give below, the readings of *Marča*,
Bolg. per., *Late Russian recension*,
1348 MS., and *Moscovite*:

Marča

... Raspeti daska napisana židovsky,
a slovinьskije ne be tou. *Da togo radi*
slovinьskije knigi o(tъ) B(og)a soutъ,
jako x(ri)s(ti)janska na posledak, tako
i kniga slovinьska s(ve)ta jes(tь)...

Bolg. per.

...Vь raspjatie bě dьska napisana
židovski i latinsky i grъčskyi, a slovenskyjǫ ne bě tu. *Togo radi sǫtь* otъ B(og)a
slovenskyjǫ knigьii: jako věra krsti-
janska bi na poslědok tako i kniga
blь garska sta jestь...

Late Russ. rec.

... rěša jakože i vo Evgli gletsja eže
bě titla napisana na krstě g(o)s(jo)dni
evrejski, grečesky i latinьski, a slovenьs-
ky nestь tu. *I togo radi* gljutь něsutь
slovenьskija knigi ot Bga...

1348 MS.

... Jakože vo Evgli pišetь i bě dъska
napisana židovьsky rimsky i ellinsky
a slověnьsky ne(stь)tu, *těmьn* nesǫtь
slověnskyjǫ ot B(og)a...

Muscovite

...jako vъ Evalii pišet : i bě dъska
napisana židovsky, rymsky, ellinsky,

a slověnsky něstь tu. *Těm že* ne sǫtь
slověnsky knigy ot Ba...

8. The way in which the *Late Russian recension* reproduces this passage, by adding here an explanatory
"they say," could be the result of a
kind of *lectio facilior* due to the
equivocal *"togo radi"* ("The reason
why..."). Both in *Marča* and
Bolg. per., if we interpret the whole
passage as belonging to the argumentation of the apologist, the basic
sense would be: "The reason why
the Slavic letters derive from God is
that they came to us in a later age,
as in a later age came to us the
Christian Faith." This "the reason
why" (*togo radi*) announces the
argumentation which follows and
therefore does not refer to the preceding passage (i.e., to the argumentation of the "Pilatians' adversa-
ries" who are quoting the writing on
the Cross). One recalls here the great
popularity among the Slavs of the
Pauline polemic theme according to
which the "recent" world is superior
to the "ancient," be it pagan or
biblical (see for example, the *Slovo
o Zakoně i Blagodati* by Ilarion of
Kiev).

9. Kul'bakin, *op. cit.*, p. 45: "...
treba konstatirovati da je to malo
nastrana prerada."

Un cas de bilinguisme Regional:

Le bilinguisme anglo-ukrainien au Canada

J. B. RUDNYČKYJ

> "Qui dit en effet *bilinguisme* (au Canada) ne dit pas forcément *bilinguisme franco anglais*... Il y a d'autres bilinguismes, en général orientés dans le même sens, l'anglais exerçant presque partout sa force d'attraction. Ces bilinguismes posent plusieurs problèmes particuliers."
>
> J. P. Vinay, *Problèmes de bilinguisme au Canada*, communication au colloque international de l'Unesco sur le bilinguisme, Université de Moncton, juin 1967 pp. 18–19.

SELON UNE CLASSIFICATION généralement reconnue les langues du Canada se divisent en trois categories:

(1) langues indigènes (amérindiennes),
(2) langues coloniales et
(3) langues d'immigrants.[1]

Celles du premier groupe sont parlées par une grande varieté de familles linguistiques, dites esquimaudes et indiennes (amérindiennes), établies depuis longtemps sur ce continent avant l'arrivée des Européens. Certaines vivaient dans l'isolement et d'autres pratiquaient le nomadisme. Enfin, quelques-unes avaient imposé leur domination sur les autres.

Les langues coloniales se sont implantées au Canada du fait de peuples qui ont réussi à y prendre pied et à y assurer leur domination. Deux de ces langues de colonisation, le français et l'anglais, ont pu s'imposer comme langues officielles au Canada.

Les langues de la troisième catégorie, celles des immigrants, comprennent l'islandais, l'allemand, l'ukrainien, le polonais, le yiddish, l'italien, etc. Des colons les ont introduites dans des régions où régnaient l'unilinguisme officiel ou le régime du bilinguisme.

Parmi elles, des langues ont déjà appartenu à la catégorie précédents, celle des langues coloniales mais sont devenues langues d'immigrants par suite de circonstances historiques particulières. Le russe et l'ukrainien sont de ce nombre. Au XVIIIe siècle les Slaves orientaux s'établirent fermement en Amérique du Nord, sur la côte du Pacifique. Le rayonnement du russe et de l'ukrainien se rattachait à la création de la Compagnie russe d'Amérique (1799). Leur expansion a été enrayée d'abord en 1825, puis une deuxième fois en 1867. De nos jours le russe et l'ukrainien appartiennent au groupe des langues d'immigrants, et non à celui des langues coloniales au Canada.

Les langues régionales du Canada appartiennent manifestement à la première ou à la troisième catégorie. Parmi les langues indigènes et les langues d'immigrants, certaines sont peu importantes, et même négligeables numériquement; d'autres, au contraire, jouent un grand rôle et occupent de vastes zones. Au nombre de ces dernières figurent les langues esquimaudes et indiennes dans les Territoires du Nord-Ouest, une langue slave (l'ukrainien), et l'allemand dans la Prairie, de même que l'italien dans les régions de Montréal et de Toronto.

Trois grandes branches de l'indo-européen se sont répandues dans le monde au moyen âge et à l'epoque moderne:

1) la *branche germanique*, avec l'anglais en Europe, en Afrique, en Amérique du Nord, en Australie et en Nouvelle-Zélande;

2) la *branche romane*, avec le français en Europe, en Afrique et en Amérique du Nord, puis l'espagnol et le portugais dans les Amériques centrale et du Sud;

3) la *branche slave*, avec le russe et l'ukrainien en Europe orientale, en Asie septentrionale et en Amérique du Nord.

Aucune autre branche de la souche indo-européenne n'a connu pareil prestige, pareille expansion.

Au Canada, les effectifs des trois branches se répartissent ainsi: branche germanique, 11 607 890 personnes; branche romane, 5 472 942; branche slave, 666 533.

L'anglais et le français ont statut officiel. Quant aux langues régionales, les suivantes se détachent par le nombre: l'allemand, l'italien et l'ukrainien, qui représentent respectivement les groupes germanique, roman et slave.

Parmi les idiomes du groupe esquimau-indien, parlés par 166 531 personnes, aucun ne prédomine. C'est le cas aussi du reste des langues régionales qui se partagent 406 798 sujets.

Aussi l'allemand, l'italien et l'ukrainien devraient ils être considérés non seulement comme grandes langues régionales, mais aussi comme langues des principales familles linguistiques d'imigrants.

* * *

Pour permettre de mieux apprécier l'aire de l'une des grandes langues régionales du Canada, nous avons inséré à la page 152 une carte montrante la diffusion de l'ukrainien dans les provinces de la Prairie (i.e. Manitoba, Saskatchewan et Alberta) en 1961.

D'après le recensement de cette année-là, l'ukrainien est parlé par 10% ou plus de la population dans une zone allant du sud-est du Manitoba aux régions d'Edmonton et de Rivière-de-la-Paix en Alberta. La zone est étayée de secteurs intermédiaires où moins de 10% parlent l'ukrainien. Il existe en outre un couloir entre la Saskatchewan et l'Alberta où 5% ou moins de la population parlent cette langue. La carte suivante (p. 153) est consacrée à la répartition du groupe ethnique ukrainien. De façon générale elle couvre le même territoire, mais il arrive qu'elle le déborde çà et là. A quelques exceptions près, la répartition selon la langue est la même que selon l'origine. Comme on peut le constater par la deuxième carte, la zone de l'ethnie ukrainienne dans la Prairie est bordée elle aussi de secteurs intermédiaires où ceux qui se réclament de cette origine s'élèvent à moins de 10%.

Voici quelques constatations applicables à l'ukrainien comme une langue regionale du Canada:

1) Cette langue couvre de larges secteurs de recensement contigus, qui forment comme deux rubans rapprochés; c'est là une disposition qui la distingue des petites enclaves urbaines et rurales, ainsi d'ailleurs que sa continuité géographique relative et quelques pointes dans les autres domaines linguistiques;

2) Elle est usitée par les particuliers et les groupes de façon ininterrompue depuis 50, 75 ans ou plus, sans déplacement marqué de sa axe régional;

3) Elle a suscité une riche tradition orale et écrite s'exprimant par le folklore ainsi que par des oeuvres artistiques et littéraires, qui sont à peu près inconnues des Canadiens de langue anglaise et de langue française;

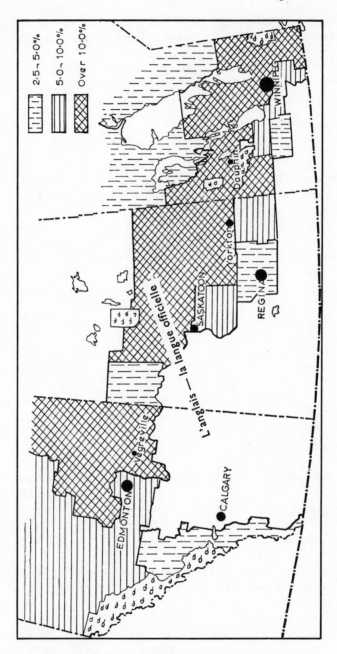

La langue ukrainienne dans les provinces de la Prairie comme la langue regionale vs.:
L'anglais-la langue officielle au Canada de l'Ouest (1961).

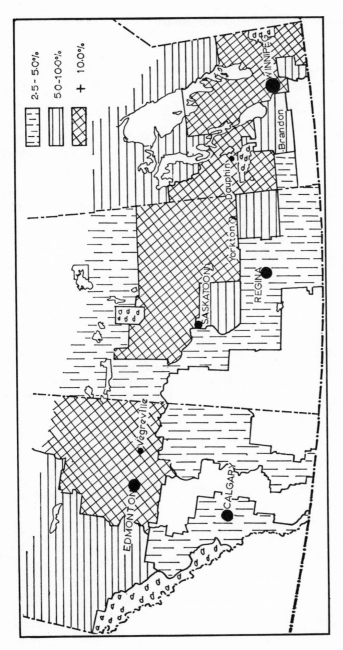

Les Ukrainiens au Canada de l'Ouest (1961) : Manitoba, Saskatchewan et Alberta.

4) Elle demeure usuelle dans la vie des particuliers, des familles et des collectivités.

Ces considérations m'ont amené à conclure qu'objectivement il y a lieu de reconnaitre deux types principaux de bilinguisme Canadien:

1. *Le bilinguisme officiel* anglais-français ou français-anglais (au Québec surtout) et
2. *Le bilinguisme regional,* qui associe à la langue maternelle la connaissance et l'emploi de l'une des deux langues officielles (le français ou l'anglais).

Le bilinguisme regional de genre anglo-ukrainien, presenté au-dessus, est le plus individualisé et le plus clair type de bilinguisme regional au Canada.

University of Manitoba

NOTES

1. E. Haugen, *Bilingualism in the Americas: A Bibliography and Research Guide* ("Publications of the American Dialect Society," No. 26 [University of Alabama Press, 1956]); J. A. Fishman et al., *Language* *Loyalty in the United States*: The Maintenance and Perpetuation of Non-English Mother Tongues by American Ethnic and Religious Groups (Mouton & Co., London-The Hague-Paris, 1966), pp. 22–25.

Some Observations on the History of the Astrolabe and of Two Russian Words: *astroljabija* and *matka*

W. F. RYAN

IN AN ARTICLE written in 1957,[1] Professor B. O. Unbegaun made the imaginative suggestion that the late Old Russian term *matka* for (magnetic) compass might be derived from the name of the outer container of an astrolabe, in Arabic *umm*, in Latin *mater*. In the course of work on the history of scientific terminology I have had occasion to examine the historical circumstances in which this development might have taken place.

The scientific instrument known in English as the astrolabe, and by cognate words in most other European languages, has a history and a name, which, despite the considerable amount of research that has been devoted to them, have yet to be fully elucidated.

Ptolemy in his *Almagest* (*c.* A.D. 150) used the adjective ástrólabos to describe his observational armillary sphere, the ástrólabon órganon. He also used the noun ástrólabos (still the form used in modern Greek) from which the Byzantine ástrolabion is formed.[2] It is the commonly held view that knowledge of the astrolabe came to Europe probably about the tenth century by way of Islam (and certainly the earliest European texts, that mention the instrument were translations from Arabic). However, a number of Latin manuscripts of the same period contain a certain amount of technical vocabulary of Greek origin.[3] As Byzantium was at a higher cultural level than was Western Europe at this time, it may well be that both craftsmen and artefacts were finding their way from East to West. Certainly *astrolabium* is more likely to be a Latinized form of ástrolabion than a reconstruction from the Arabic *asṭurlāb* (or *aṣṭurlāb*) which it is usually held to be. The possibility that knowledge of the astrolabe existed in Europe independently of the Islamic tradition is supported by the existence of a European astrolabe, ascribed to the Carolingian period, inscribed with numerals according to the Byzantine system but using Latin letters.[4] Further evidence for this possibility may be found when the question of the survival in Europe of the anaphoric clock described by Hero and Vitruvius is finally elucidated. This clock was similar to an astrolabe in that its dial bore a stereographic star map with a framework representing the circles of altitude in stereographic projection rotating above it in place of hands.[5]

The word *astrolapsūs* found in the very earliest translations of treatises on the astrolabe is probably a reconstruction based on the Arabic word and influenced by popular etymology.[6] That it was superseded is surely due to the fact that the original Greek term became known.

An alternative form appears at the time of the Renaissance—*astrolabum*. One book, the *De expetendis et fugiendis rebus opus* (Venice, 1501) by Georgius Valla Placentinus, uses this form in a chapter heading, "De astrolabi fabrica usuque" (lib. XVII, cap. V). The best-known example of its use is in the title of a book by Gemma Frisius, *De astrolabo catholico* (Antwerp, 1556). This is no mere misprint, for the book was printed again in 1583 by a different printer who retained the spelling. This is probably an attempt at classical "purity," for one of Gemma's students, Juan de Rojas, specifically stated that he wished to free Latin from its Arabic accretions and use only classical Latin and Greek words.[7] To a man ignorant or scornful of late Greek, *astrolabum* may well have seemed a more "correct" form.

All three Latin forms were used, like the Arabic, to denote a planispheric (or more rarely, spherical) astrolabe. The most usual form of planispheric astrolabe consists of a series of plates for various latitudes engraved with lines representing the horizon, circles of altitude, etc. in stereographic projection. The plates are covered by a rotating pierced star map, also in stereographic projection (the *rete*), which (like the plates) is placed in a shallow case (the *mater*). The instrument is engraved with various scales and is furnished with an alidade and sights. It probably derives from Ptolemy's work on the stereographic projection known as the *Planispherium* (the Greek original is not extant). Some later types of planispheric astrolabe use an orthographic projection.

In modern Russian the term *astroljabija* has acquired a rather wider meaning than it possesses in medieval Latin and other European languages.[8] A recent book, *Pamjatniki russkoj kul'tury pervoj četverti XVIII veka* (Moscow-Leningrad, 1966), consistently uses the term to denote any early angle-measuring instrument with alidades and a graduated circle or segment of a circle. The *Bol'šaja sovetskaja ènciklopedija* (2nd edition, 1949) in its entry on the astrolabe (III, 291) shows a picture of an instrument which appears to be a circumferentor (an early surveying instrument with two sighting rules moving on a graduated circle in the center of which is a compass). Moreover, the description of the instrument, although mentioning ancient astronomy, certainly does not correspond to the appearance of a planispheric astrolabe.

A glance at the better-known dictionaries of Europe (excluding Russia) shows that since the eighteenth century at least, encyclopedists and lexicographers have agreed (with due allowance made for minor variations in knowledge and competence) that the term *astrolabium* and its vernacular derivatives may be applied to four things: (1) Ptolemy's observational armillary sphere; (2) a planispheric astrolabe; (3) a mariner's astrolabe (a suspended graduated ring but with no *rete* and involving no stereographic projection); or (4) a modern prismatic astrolabe. The *Encyclopaedia Britannica* (1947) also mentions the possible secondary uses of the planispheric astrolabe, including surveying, and several English encyclopedic dictionaries of the eighteenth century use the term to describe the two basic types of projection of the sphere, stereographic and orthographic, used on planispheric astrolabes.

The only modern encyclopedias to dissent from this comparative unanimity, apart from the Russian, are the Polish and the Czech. The Polish Academy encyclopedia (*Wielka encyclopedia powszechna PWN*, [Warsaw, 1962]) has an entry for *astrolabium* (I, 425) which appears to be based on the entry for *astroljabija* in the *Bol'šaja sovetskaja ènciklopedija*, and has an identical illustration. However, in the entry for astronomical instruments (I, 429) the astrolabe is described and illustrated as a normal planispheric astrolabe, as it is in the older *Wielka ilustrowana encyclopedja powszechna* ([Cracow, 1929], II, 8). The *Ilustrowana encyclopedja Trzaski, Everta i Michalskiego* ([Warsaw, 1927], I, 194) describes the astrolabe as an angle-measuring instrument chiefly used in geodesy and illustrates it with a sketch of a mariner's astrolabe! The *Ottův slovník naučný* ([Prague, 1889], II, 926) has an entry for *astrolabium* which describes accurately the Ptolemaic and planispheric astrolabes. This definition seems to be supported by other Czechoslovak reference works with the exception of the *Ottův slovník naučný nové doby* ([Prague, 1930], I, 302) which contains an entry for *astroláb* clearly describing a circumferentor. I am unable to discover whether any distinction of meaning can be read into the two forms quoted, or from the three forms *astrolab*, *astrolabja*, and *astrolabjum* found in Polish.

Russian dictionaries and encyclopedias are less unanimous in their definitions of what is meant by *astroljabija*. The Academy dictionary of 1867 (*Slovar' cerkovnoslavjanskogo i russkogo jazyka*, I, 30) defines it as a surveying instrument with sights, or a mariner's astrolabe. The Brockhaus-Efron *Ènciklopedičeskij slovar'* ([St. Petersburg, 1890], II, 373–4) gives a fairly full description of Ptolemy's armillary sphere and of the mariner's astrolabe which it considers a simplification of the former instrument. It further states that with the replacement of the alidade and sights by a sighting telescope, the instrument became a theodolite, and that the astrolabe is still in use as a surveying instrument. Later in the same encyclopedia, in the entry for *semka* (LXIII, 200), the three instruments to be used for angular measurement in surveying are listed as *bussol'*, *astroljabija*, *teodolit*.[9] The second edition of the encyclopedia (*Novyj ènciklopedičeskij slovar'* [St. Petersburg, 1911], IV, 140) attempts to describe a planispheric astrolabe but quite misunderstands the terms *mater* and *rete* and provides as an illustration a drawing of an instrument which has neither. The Granat *Ènciklopedičeskij slovar'* (7th ed. [1909], IV, 140) thought that an astrolabe could be two things: In its first meaning it could be a modern surveying instrument, and in its second, Ptolemy's armillary sphere. More detail is given in the entry *geodesičeskie instrumenty* ([1912], XIII) where it is stated that theodolites were then replacing astrolabes, which were instruments of the same type used for the same purpose. It goes on to say that the astrolabe became known in its present form in the eighteenth century. The accompanying illustration is of a circumferentor, and it appears to be the common source from which the illustrations in the Soviet and Polish Academy encyclopedias are taken. All the other modern Russian non-encyclopedic dictionaries give "surveying instrument" as the first or only meaning of *astroljabija*.

Reference to *astroljabija* in Russian literature other than specialized works on the history of science, where the term also has its international meaning, tend to confirm this.

The "astrolabe," in the use of which, according to the *Encyclopaedia Britannica* (13th ed.; XXI [1926], 289), Peter the Great was instructed by Franz Timmerman, and which he asked Prince Jakov Dolgorukij to bring back from France in 1687, seems from Peter's description in the preface to his *Morskoj ustav* (1720) ("instrument, kotorym možno bylo brat' distancii ili rasstojanija, ne doxodja do togo mesta") also to have been a surveying instrument.[10] K. I. Bylinskij and N. N. Nikol'skij, *Spravočnik po orfografii i punktuacii dlja rabotnikov pečati* ([Moscow, 1957], p. 88) give the following quotation to illustrate a point of punctuation: "odin rabočij neset astroljabiju, drugoj – trenogu." For such a sober book this would appear to be a rather fanciful, not to say obscure, example if the word *astroljabija* were to be taken as possessing the meaning "planispheric astrolabe." Even more fanciful, if less surprising, would be the passage at the beginning of the fourth chapter of the famous satirical novel by I. Il'f and E. Petrov, *Dvenadcat' stul'ev* (Moscow-Leningrad, 1925) in which the hero, Ostap Bender, "Vtisnulsja v šerengu prodavcov, torgovavšix na razvale, vystavil vpered astroljabiju i ser'eznym golosom stal kričat', 'Komu astroljabiju? Dlja delegacij i ženotdelov skidka!'... K obedu astroljabija byla prodana intelligentnomu slesarju za tri rublja. 'Sama merjaet', skazal molodoj čelovek, peredavaja astroljabiju pokupatelju, 'bylo by čto merit'."

Ostap's cryptic parting shot, that the astrolabe "Measures on its own, if you've got anything to measure," makes better sense in a country that had just abolished private ownership of land if the "astrolabe" is a surveying instrument rather than a medieval astronomical instrument.

A not irrelevant consideration is, of course, what a Russian surveyor thinks an *astroljabija* is: for example, V. Vitkovskij's *Topografija* (St. Petersburg, 1904) devotes a whole chapter to surveying with the *astroljabija*, which is illustrated by a sketch of a circumferentor.

It is indeed quite clear that although Russian dictionaries and encyclopedias are not very precise, or even in agreement, about what exactly an astrolabe was or when it was used, they all share the opinion that *one* of its uses, if not its main use, was in the field of surveying, an opinion evidently shared by Russian surveyors. Equally clear is the fact that, despite minor differences of detail or emphasis, dictionaries and encyclopedias of all other countries, with the partial exception of Poland and Czechoslovakia, are agreed that an astrolabe is an astronomical instrument.

I would suggest the following explanation both of the modern meaning of the word *astroljabija* in Russian and of the origin of the term *matka* used in the sense of "compass."

In Europe the astrolabe was used (if the published literature is an accurate guide) primarily for astronomical and horological purposes. However, it could also be used (and was so used even in its Islamic form) for surveying purposes.[11] R. T. Gunther in his *Astrolabes of the World* ([Oxford, 1932], p. 380) states that toward the middle of the sixteenth century the astrolabe, probably at the suggestion of Gemma Frisius of Louvain, came to be used extensively in the Low Countries as a triangulation instrument for land surveying.

As a result, versions of the astrolabe designed specifically for the more limited uses of surveying and navigation (the so-called mariner's

astrolabe) were developed, in particular in the sixteenth century when
the surveying of land was a matter of some importance both in
Russia and in the rest of Europe.[12] The earliest surveying instruments
which can be looked upon as the precursors of the theodolite were
very similar to astrolabes.[13] They were simplified, retaining only the
graduated circle and alidade but with the important addition of a
compass.[14] These compasses were already to be found on some true
astrolabes mounted in the *kursi* or 'throne' (the projection to which
the suspension ring was attached). The omission of the plates and
rete made it possible to move the compass into the body of the instrument and finally it came to be placed in the centre so that the
whole instrument became in fact a compass with a graduated outer
circle and alidade. With the addition of a second alidade—(and
possibly telescopic sights) the instrument became a basic theodolite.[15]
Thus the compass—from being a minor adjunct to the astronomical
astrolabe—becomes the central part of a geodetic instrument.

Although in most European languages derivatives of the astrolabe
soon acquired special names, it seems that as late as the seventeenth
and eighteenth centuries the term *astrolabium* could still be applied to a
surveying instrument of the kind described above.[16] In Benedictus
Hedraeus, *Nova et accurata astrolabii geometrici structura* (Leiden, 1643),
although the instrument described is not illustrated, there is no mention
of any projection of the sphere or star map, and almost the whole of
the book is concerned with surveying. In the eighteenth century the
usage persists: Tobias Mayer, *Mathematische Atlas* (Augsburg, 1744)
has an illustration (Tab. XI) of an "astrolabium" which is in effect
a circumferentor. A similar instrument is referred to as an "astrolabium" in C. L. Reinhold. *Geometria Forensis, oder die aufs Recht ange-
wandte Messkunst* (Münster, 1781). Reinhold's work has been referred
to in connection with confusion of nomenclature by Benjamin Smith
Lyman in his "Notes on Mine-surveying Instruments, with Special
Reference to Mr. Dunbar D. Scott's Paper on their Evolution, and its
Discussion" in the *Transactions of the American Institute of Mining
Engineers* for 1901. In a discussion of the names and history of
mining instruments Lyman writes:

> In some cases a new name has been devised without any
> radically important change in the instrument, but more often
> the same name has been applied to different instruments, one
> form having been derived from another by repeated gradual
> improvements before a change of name was considered neces-
> sary. For example, the name "astrolabe," given, as appears
> from Reinhold, in 1781 to a mere semicircle with two fixed

sights and a moveable alidade bearing sights, and 150 years
earlier applied to a copper disk for astronomical observations,
hung vertically, with such an alidade, but with no fixed
sights, was still used by Reinhold, after the addition of
various improvements, for an instrument that is essentially
a theodolite . . . . It seems clear that instead of calling a theodolite an astrolabe, even though it be plainly developed from
an astrolabe, the word "astrolabe" should at the present day
be used only for the simpler forms, forms to which it belonged before the invention of special names for the improved
and essentially altered forms.

One example of a derivative of the circumferentor (and thus of the
astrolabe), a late version of the "graphomètre" or surveyor's semicircle,
of Philippe Danfrie,[17] is to be seen in the Hermitage in Leningrad. It is
labelled *astrolabija*. Since Russian contact with Western Europe to any
significant degree developed only after the astrolabe had lost its use as
a serious astronomical instrument and survived mostly as a scientific
toy or instrument for astrologers, or in various mutations, as a
surveying instrument,[18] it seems reasonable to suppose that to a Russian an astrolabe was (and, to judge from a number of the books
quoted above, still is) a surveying instrument built round a compass.[19]
The *mater* of the astrolabe had become, in fact, the case containing
the compass needle. In these circumstances it must have seemed quite
reasonable to call the compass *matka*.[20]

Museum of the History of Science, Oxford

NOTES

1. B. O. Unbegaun, "Le Nom de la boussole en russe," *Slavistična revija*, X (1957), 179–84
2. The term is found in the works of Synesius of Cyrene (4th–5th cen-tury) and Johannes Philiponus of Alexandria (6th century). See Willy Hartner, "The Principle and Use of the Astrolabe," *Survey of Persian Art*, III (New York and London, 1939), pp. 2530–54.
3. I am indebted to Professor M. Schramm of Tübingen University for this information.
4. Described in M. Destombes, "Un Astrolabe carolingien et l'origine de nos chiffres arabes," *Archives Internationales d'Histoire des Sciences*, Nos. 58–59 (1962).
5. See Derek J. de Solla Price, "On the Origin of Clockwork, Perpetual Motion Devices and the Compass," *Contributions from the Museum of History and Technology* (United States National Museum Bulletin 218 [Washington, D. C., 1959]), pp. 90–92.
6. See J. Millàs Vallicrosa, *Assaig*

d'història de les idees físiques i matemàtiques a la Catalunya medieval (Estudis universitaris catalans. Serie monogràfica I [Barcelona, 1931]). Also A. Van de Vyver, "Les Premières traductions latines de traités arabes sur l'astrolabe," *Mémoires du Ier Congrès International de Géographie Historique*, t. II (Brussels, 1931), 3–27.

By the fourteenth century the word *astrolabium* was accepted as being of Greek origin by at least one writer. A mid-fourteenth-century manuscript in the Bodleian library, Ashmole 1796, f. 40v., contains the passage: "Sciendum quod astrolabium sit nomen grecum cuius interpretacio est acceptio stellarum." Other, more strange forms and etymologies may be found both for the Latin *astrolabium* and the English *astrolabe*. H. Kurath, *Middle English Dictionary* (Ann Arbor, 1956) gives among other forms: *astrelabre, aristable, astroby, astrolaboure, ars table*. An elaborate example in Latin is found in the *Granarium* of John of Whetehamstede, a fifteenth-century abbot of St. Albans and one of the first English humanists. He writes: "Secundum Haly ['Alī b. Riḍwān] super *Quadripartitum* Ptholomei, inventor primevus instrumenti istius fuit insignis astronomus Abrachis [Hipparchus], temporibus regis Salomonis, vel, ut volunt alii, vir nomine Lab, a quo Astot, quod dicitur linea, est vocatum. Unde astrolabium, quasi linea Lab, dicitur per interpretationem" (Br. Mus. M. S. Cotton Nero C VI, f. 149r.). I am grateful to Dr. J. D. North of Merton College, Oxford, for drawing my attention to this passage.

7. *Illustris viri D. Ioannis de Roias Commentariorum in Astrolabium, quod Planisphaerium vocant, libri sex nunc primum in lucem editi* (Paris, 1550), sig. b. ii. Plainly Rojas did not go as far as his master in linguistic purity, at least insofar as the spelling of *astrolabium* is concerned.

8. The modern form of the word is found first in the *Geografija general'naja* (1718). See N. M. Šanskij, *Ėtimologičeskij slovar' russkogo jazyka*, I (Moscow, 1963), 166. Other forms include *astroljabium* ([1688], Šanskij, *loc. cit.*), *astroljabiov* (*g. pl.*) in an early 18th (?)-century translation from Italian (see A. I. Sobolevskij, "Iz perevodnoj literatury petrovskoj epoxi," *Sbornik Otdělenija russkago jazyka i slovesnosti Imperatorskoj Akademii nauk*, LXXXIV, No. 3 [1908], 21), and *astrolavija* (*g. sing*) in a translation from Latin (1722). See Gerta Hüttl Worth, *Foreign Words in Russian* (Berkeley and Los Angeles, 1963), p. 60. The spelling of these various forms is discussed in Gerta Hüttl Worth, *op. cit.*, pp. 38, 40. The adaptation of Latin nouns in -ium by replacing the ending with the alternative Russian endings -ij and -ija is described by L. L. Kutina (*Formirovanie terminologii fiziki v Rossii* [Moscow-Leningrad, 1966], p. 248) as "traditional." In fact the Russian treatment of loanwords of this type was, and is, by no means consistent, as the modern forms *laboratorija, sanatorij, akvarium, uran* demonstrate.

9. *Bussol'* too has acquired a rather more specialized sense in Russian than it has in its native French. It is usually described in Russian encyclopedias as a compass fitted with two sighting pieces for use in

surveying or artillery. V. Vitkovskij, *Topografija* (St. Petersburg, 1904), devotes Chapter 8 to surveying with a *bussol'*, which he specifically distinguishes from any other kind of compass. From the description and illustrations, it is clear that the term is to be applied to a surveyor's compass (also sometimes called a circumferentor) or a prismatic compass.

10. See M. M. Bogoslovskij, *Petr I*, I (Leningrad, 1940), 62–63.

11. The Museum of the History of Science, Oxford, possesses a seventeenth-century Flemish astrolabe (Billmeir Coll. 57-84/18) which has an extra pair of sights so that the astrolabe could be used as a circumferentor. Most books about the astrolabe have illustrations showing astrolabes in use for surveying.

12. The first book to be translated from English into Russian was part of A. Rathborne, *The Surveyor* (London, 1616). See W. F. Ryan, "Rathborne's *Surveyor* (1616–1625): the first Russian translation from English?" *Oxford Slavonic Papers*, XI (1964), 1–7.

13. Such instruments are described in Petrus Apianus, *Cosmographia* (Ingolstadt, 1524), and William Cunningham, *The Cosmographical Glass* (London, 1559).

14. For example the "Theodelitus" of Leonard Digges (1571).

15. For example, the "Holland circle" of Jan Dou, described in *Traktat vant maken ende gebruycken eens nien gheordenneerden matematischen instruments* (Amsterdam, 1612).

16. See F. Schmidt, *Geschichte der geodätischen Instrumente und Verfahren im Altertum und Mittelalter* (Veröffentlichungen der Pfälzischen Gesellschaft zur Förderung der Wissenschaften [Neustadt an der Haardt, 1935]), pp. 273–77.

17. Described in Philippe Danfrie, *Declaration de l'usage du graphomètre* (Paris, 1597).

18. This is not to suggest that astrolabes were not still being made. Indeed it seems that "presentation models" were still being made by instrument makers as examples of their craftsmanship as late as the eighteenth century. It is of interest that Russia's southeastern neighbor, Armenia, which had a distinguished history in astronomy, was still making purely astronomical astrolabes in the seventeenth century: one such is described in B. E. T'umanyan, *Haykakan norahayt astłagitakan gorcik'* (Erevan, 1958). Although the Armenian astronomical tradition was derived primarily from Islam and Byzantium, Western scientific literature seems to have penetrated Armenia before it arrived in Russia. The *Cosmographia* of Petrus Apianus for example (see above, note 13) was translated into Armenian in 1611. The first Armenian printed maps (both geographical and celestial) were produced in Amsterdam in 1695, some years before the first Russian maps were printed there. It is perhaps surprising that none of this activity should have affected Russia. See B. E. T'umanyan, *Hay astłagitowt'yan patmowt'yown* (Erevan, 1964), p. 399.

19. There is, however, some evidence of the use of planispheric astrolabes for finding latitudes in Russia. Herberstein, who was in Russia in 1517 and 1526, was the first to determine the latitude of Moscow—with an astrolabe. Olearius, who was in Russia between 1633 and 1643 also used

an astrolabe for this purpose. Although an astrolabe at this date was hardly the most accurate instrument for the job, it was presumably the most convenient for travellers, and for this purpose, in the simplified form of the mariners astrolabe, it survived until the eighteenth century. See M. K. Vencel', "Kratkij očerk istorii praktičeskoj astronomii," *Istoriko-astronomičeskie issledovanija*, No. 2 (1956), p. 33. R. T. Gunther, *op. cit.*, p. 444, notes that miniature astrolabes were much used in the sixteenth century in Central Europe. They usually formed part of the ingenious pocket astronomical *compendia* which were being made for travellers at this time, notably by Christopher Schissler of Augsburg. These instruments would often combine a compass, perpetual calendar, sundial, lunar volvelle, and astrolabe. A notable late use of the astrolabe was the determination of the latitude of Rhodes in 1638 by John Greaves, Professor of Geometry at Gresham College, London, and later Savilian Professor of Astronomy at Oxford. He recorded that "By my observa-tions under the walls of the city of Rhodes, with a fair brass astrolabe of Gemma Frisius, containing 14 inches in the diameter, I found the Latitude to be 37° and 50'. A larger instrument I durst not adventure to carry on shore in a place of so much jealosy" (Thomas Birch [ed.], *Miscellaneous Works of Mr. John Greaves, Professor of Astronomy in the University of Oxford* II [London, 1737], 371). I have to thank Mr. F. R. Maddison, Curator of the Museum of the History of Science, Oxford, for this last reference and for his invaluable help in the collection of material for this paper.

20. *Matka* did not necessarily mean a magnetic compass as an instrument. It could also mean a compass rose. A number of seventeenth-century Russian manuscripts of navigational instructions contain the following passage and an illustration which makes this clear: "sia matka ukazuet skolko nemeckix milei v vsjakom" grade na kotoroj stroke skolko ot severa do vostoka (MS. Bibl. Akad. nauk 17–6–24, f. 162v.). Here of course *matka* cannot mean a magnetic compass.

Образ рассказчика в повести Солженицына «Один день Ивана Денисовича»

Л. РЖЕВСКИЙ

1.

«Один день Ивана Денисовича» отнюдь не пример целостного по форме сказа, где устность повествования и выраженность речевого облика рассказчика (сказителя) оказываются главными структурными координатами.

Сказовое единство повести Солженицына нарушается прежде всего стилями литературно-письменного сообщения, принадлежащего самому автору как повествователю. Возникают они обычно тогда, когда тема этого сообщения отдалена от главного персонажа как субъекта или комментатора действия. Так, например, в рассказе о фельдшере Вдовушкине:

> ... А Вдовушкин писал своё. Он вправду занимался работой «левой,» но для Шухова непостижимой. Он переписывал новое длинное стихотворение, которое вчера отделал, а сегодня хотел показать Степану Григорьевичу, тому самому врачу, поборнику трудотерапии. (19)[1]

Или — о кавторанге (капитане второго ранга) Буйновском, — здесь и обобщения, и эмоциональность повествовательной манеры отчетливо авторские:

> Такие минуты, как сейчас, были (он сам не знал этого) особо важными для него минутами, превращавшими его из властного морского офицера в малоподвижного осмотрительного зэка, только этой малоподвижностью и могущего

перемочь отверстанные ему двадцать пять лет тюрьмы ...
... Виноватая улыбка раздвинула истресканные губы ка-
питана, ходившего вокруг Европы и Великим северным
путем. И он наклонился, счастливый, над неполным черпа-
ком жидкой овсяной каши, безжирной вовсе, над овсом и
водой. (61–62).

Суверенны по отношению к сказовым стилям и диалоги (в отличие
от диалогов лесковского сказа, сказово унифицированных). Например:

— Нет, батенька, — мягко этак, попуская, говорит Цезарь,
— объективность требует признать, что Эйзенштейн ге-
ниален. «Иоанн Грозный» — разве это не гениально? Пляска
опричников с личиной! Сцена в соборе! (63)

И все же стилеобразующе в повести именно устное ведение
речи, сказывание.
Структурные корни этого сказывания уходят в историко-бытовые
и диалектные слои народного языка — просторечна лексика и
фразеология, просторечно-народны синтаксические конструкции,
ритмы, приемы словесного живописания и выражения экспрессии.
Фиксирующая просторечный словоотбор картотека по повести
содержит свыше 250 выписок; из них около полусотни отмечают
просторечные словообразовательные (иногда и произносительные)
формы.
Характер словарного просторечия по природе своей причудливо
разнообразен. Особое место в языке рассказчика занимает просторе-
чие локальное, относящееся непосредственно к бытовому словоу-
потреблению лагерников. Это нейтрально-номинативные опер (опе-
ративный работник), халабуда («Производственная кухня — это
халабуда маленькая, из лесу сколоченная вокруг печи». 55) и др.;
это и множество речений экспрессивного типа от бранных до таких,
в которых выраженность эмоций отталкивания или вражды едва
улавливается. Вот ряд примеров, расположенных в порядке затуха-
ния экспрессии: падло, попки (часовые на вышках), полканы (о
работающих при столовой), придурки (и собирательное «при-
дурня» — об устроившихся на легкую или никакую работу),
дежурняк (дежурный надзиратель), шмон (личный обыск),
шмонять и т.д.
Целеустремленнее (в смысле творческой функции создания речевого облика) просторечные элементы, принадлежащие личному сло-
воупотреблению рассказчика. Здесь и общераспространенные:
загнуть (сказать неправдоподобное), вкалывать (интенсивно

работать), подначивать (подзадоривать), матернуть, гвозда-
нуть, недотыка, житуха и пр.; здесь и стилевые группы таких
простонародных речений, которые иногда трудно представить себе в
живом звучании какого-либо одного, индивидуального, языка.

Первую группу таких речений составляют заимствования из
словаря Даля вроде: внимчиво, ежедён, закалелый, затёмка,
заторить, издобыть, кесь, лють, обневолю, осторожка,
поменеть, прозор, терпельник и многое другое. Взятое у Даля
используется иногда с некоторыми изменениями словосостава и
значения: добычник у Даля, недобычник — у Солженицына,
буркотать (Д.) — буркотеть (С.); горготать приведено у Даля
в значении «гоготать» (кричать, громко смеяться), в языке рассказчика — «болтать на непонятном слушателю языке» («Лежит латыш
на нижних нарах ... и с соседом по-латышски горгочет», 114);
захрястка по Далю — «удар по шее, по голове», в повести захря-
сток — обозначение места удара («И по захрястку его кулаком!» 90).
Размещены эти собранные в языке рассказчика диалектизмы на
диалектологической карте весьма разноместно — «захрястье», например, относится к тверским говорам, заторить (о дороге) — к
псковским; к словечку кесь (кажется), встречающемуся в языке
рассказчика много раз, Даль делает пометку: «влд., мск., ряз.,
тмб.» и т.п.

Другая группа лексического просторечия носит еще более внятный
след авторских поисков в процессе просторечной стилизации языка
рассказчика.

В своей работе по исследованию лесковского сказа академик
А. С. Орлов писал: «Трудно сказать ... какие из речений действительно подслушаны автором и какие им сочинены в стиле, соот-
ветственном действительно существующему образцу.»[2]

Это очень справедливо и в отношении Солженицына. Вот ряд
подслушанных либо сочиненных им находок в области народно-
разговорной лексики: гахнуть (о неожиданном выкрике, руга-
тельстве), залупаться («закидываться», противоречить), подсо-
саться (пристроиться: «Тут же и Фетюков, шакал, подсосался». 25),
пригребаться (придираться, привязываться), прокликаться
(окликая, проталкиваться вперед: «Прокликаясь через тесноту ...
работяги ... носили на деревянных подносах миски с баландой» ...
13), протяжно (в значении «долго», «много времени»: «До обеда —
пять часов, протяжно». 38), разморчивый (размаривающий),
сумутиться (мудрить, выдумывать разное, беспокойное для себя
и других) и т.п.

Иной раз очевидность стилизаторского замысла (авторской «за-
думки» можно было бы сказать, следуя стилю Солженицына) сооб-

щает таким находкам оттенок искусственности. Таковы, например: довидеть в значении «заметить,» «углядеть»; доспеть и обоспеть в значении «успеть»; наоткрыте (в открытом месте), неуладка, рассмеркивалось (рассветало), сочнуть (сосчитать: «. . . еще успел сочнуть, что все на месте». 59), улупить в значении 1. «побежать» и 2. «съесть» и т.п.

То же и в части отклонений от морфологических и произносительных норм. Здесь и традиционно-просторечные окунумши, набраты, ляжь (ляг), убег, потяжельше, поспокойней (с самим автором поставленным ударением на последнем слоге), деревеньских (с опять-таки самим автором подчеркнутым мягким «н»); здесь и вполне неожиданные диалектно-архаические ихим (ихним, их), ихьего («Ихьего объекта зона здорова» . . . 43), лёду («Взял с собой для лёду топорик». 69); деепричастные образования типа пролья («. . . поди вынеси не пролья.» 6), стережа, ждя и многое другое.

Столь же обильна в языке рассказчика и просторечно-народная фразеология:

а) Местная, лагерная: паять срок, совать новую десятку (о штрафных дополнительных приговорах), качать права (требовать положенного по закону), ходить стучать к куму (доносить), залечить в деревянный бушлат («уморить» — о лагерных врачах), доходить на общих (гибнуть постепенно на тяжелой физической работе), от пуза (в значении «вволю»: «ешь от пуза», «свободы здесь от пуза») и пр.

б) Своя, также отражающая немалые поиски автора в области сказовой стилизации. Традиционное, типа «горше смерти», «надоесть хуже серы горючей» и т.п. перемежается здесь с находками вроде «И в больничке отлёжу нет» или «Он ему и дых по морозу не погонит» (т.е. «не заговорит»). Среди пословично-поговорочных выражений можно различить: 1) заимствования из Даля же: «Кряхти да гнись. А упрешься — переломишься» (как формула практической философии лагерника), «Брюхо — злодей, старого добра не помнит» . . . (как обозначение повседневной голодной тревоги)[3]; 2) семантико-стилевые параллели к известным образцам; например:

> «Испыток не убыток» (ср. «Попытка не пытка»)
> «Битой собаке только плеть покажи»
> «Кто кого сможет, тот того и гложет»
> «Теплый зяблого разве когда поймет»
> «Гретому зяблого не понять»

3) образования оригинальные и по внутренне, локально, обусловленной теме, и по внешнему разговорно-афористическому обличью:

«Двести грамм жизнью правят» (47)
«Не выкусишь — не выпросишь» (42)
«Миски нести — не рукавом трясти» (110)
«Волочи день до вечера, а ночь наша» (46)
«Для людей делаешь — качество дай, для дурака делаешь —
дай показуху» (13)

Разнообразны просторечные отклонения в области синтаксической структуры речи. От норм управления, например:

... а не обновишь номера впору — тебе же и кондей: зачем
за н о м е р о м не заботишься? (24)

От обычной последовательности частей сложного предложения:

Который бригадир умный — тот на процентовку налегает.
С ей кормимся. (47)

От литературности синтаксических конструкций вообще, которые определяются здесь динамикой разговорного сообщения, его экс-прессивно-интонационными акцентами, выдыхами и перебоями:

Видит Шухов — заметался Цезарь, тык-мык, да поздно.
(124)
Восемнадцатым и Шухов втиснулся. Да бегом к своей ва-
гонке, да на поднапорочку ногу закинул — шасть! — и уж
наверху. (132)
Дошла каша — сейчас санинструктору: ешь от пуза.
И сам — от пуза. Тут дежурный бригадир приходит,
меняются они ежедён — пробу снимать, проверять будто,
можно ли такой кашей работяг кормить. (56)

Интонации сказывания создаются также инверсией:

А вот пришла 104-я. И в чем ее души держатся? — брюхи
пустые поясами брезентовыми затянуты; морозяка трещит,
ни обогревалки, ни огня искорки. А все же пришла 104-я —
и опять жизнь начинается. (45)

Возникают типично сказовые интонационные членения, ритмы, повторы, отражающие черты устного речеведения, само «дыхание» рассказчика:

А было вот как: в феврале сорок второго года на северо-
западном окружили их армию всю, и с самолетов им ничего

жрать не бросали, а и самолетов тех не было. Дошло до того,
что строгали копыта с лошадей околевших, размачивали ту
роговицу в воде и ели ... (52)
Так он и ждал, и все ждали так: если пять воскресений в
месяце, то три дают, а два на работу гонят. Так он и ждал,
а услышал — повело всю душу, перекривило: воскресень-
ице-то кровное кому не жалко? (102)

В речевую ткань повествования вводятся стилевые элементы
фольклорного типа:

Диво дивное: вот время за работой идет! (50)
Стежь, стежь, стежь — вот и дырочку за пайкой сцрятан-
ной прихватил. (22)
Долго ли, коротко ли — вот все три окна толем зашили. (49)

Народно-сказового типа и живописание словом. Характер пей-
зажа, например:

Напересек через ворота проволочные, и через всю строи-
тельную зону, и через дальнюю проволоку, что по тот бок, —
солнце встает большое, красное, как бы во мгле. (35)
Солнце взошло красное, мглистое над зоной пустой: где
щиты сборных домов снегом занесены, где кладка каменная
начатая ... (37)

Сравнения:

... кожа на лице, как кора дубовая. (36)
Окружили ту печку, как бабу, все обнимать лезут (54)
... черпак ... пустых щей для него сейчас, что дождь в
сухмень. (100)
... сидят один к одному, как семечки в подсолнухе ... (108)
... с верхних коек прыгают медведями (123)

Из всех — вкупе — рассмотренных выше особенностей и приемов
авторского творческого отбора в представлении читателя сама собою
складывается языковая маска рассказывающего, с чертами
одного из простых, умудренных лишь тяжким жизненным опытом,
лагерных «работяг». Синтетический характер этой маски делает тем
не менее весьма интересной более точную идентификацию лица,
которому она принадлежит.

2.

> Вот хлеба четыреста, да двести, да в матрасе не меньше
> двести. И хватит. Двести сейчас нажать, завтра утром
> пятьсот пятьдесят улупить, четыреста взять на работу —
> житуха! А те, в матрасе, пусть еще полежат ... (117)

Говорит Шухов (внутренний монолог). Это его, зэка из бывших
колхозников, словоотбор («нажать», «улупить» в значении «съесть»),
его, довольного малым, экспрессия («Житуха!»), — словом, его
говорок, к которому прислушивается читатель на протяжении всей
повести.

Но если продолжить цитату, то за словами «еще полежат» следует:

> Хорошо, что Шухов обоспел, зашил — из тумбочки, вон, в
> 75-й уперли — жалуйся теперь куда хочешь. (117)

Это « ... Шухов обоспел, зашил» и т. д. выдвигает перед читателем
«я» собственно рассказчика, говорящего о Шухове в третьем лице.
Рассказчика с к а з о в о г о, чья речевая манера отлична от письменно-
литературных стилей от-авторской речи в повести, с шуховским же
говорком совпадает вполне.

Совпадение это[4] особенно полно в части «комментариев к действию», относимых то к «я» рассказчика, то к «я» самого Шухова и
имеющих часто форму внутреннего монолога. Эти «комментарии к
действию» — уточнения, афоризмы, оценки — составляют стилевой
стержень сказового повествования. Их отнесенность к тому или
другому сказовому «я» кажется, однако, иной раз случайной: в том
же, например, приведенном выше продлении рассказчиком шу-
ховских размышлений («Хорошо, что Шухов обоспел, зашил» ...)
сто́ит только выпустить имя (Шухов) — и фраза органически
примкнет к шуховскому внутреннему монологу:

> ... четыреста взять на работу — житуха! А те, в матрасе,
> пусть еще полежат ... Хорошо, что ... обоспел, зашил, —
> из тумбочки, вон, в 75-й уперли — жалуйся теперь куда
> хочешь.

Иногда, если связь комментариев-монологов с субъектом текущего
действия выражена неотчетливо, отнесенность эту вообще трудно
определить. Вот, например, автор вводит читателя вместе с Шуховым
в лагерную столовую:

> Внутри стоял пар, как в бане, — напуски мороза от две-
> рей и пар от баланды. Бригады сидели за столами или тол-

кались в проходах, ждали, когда места освободятся.
Прокликаясь через тесноту, от каждой бригады работяги
по два, по три носили на деревянных подносах миски с
баландой и кашей и искали для них места на столах.
И всё равно не слышит, обалдуй, спина еловая, на
тебе, толкнул поднос. Плесь, плесь! Рукой его
свободной — по шее, по шее! Правильно! Не стой
на дороге, не высматривай, где подлизать. (13)

Первые пять строк этого описания (если не считать придуманного
словечка «прокликаясь») выдержаны в нейтральном стиле авторского
письменно-литературного повествования. Затем следует резкий
переход к устности — сказово-просторечный «комментарий», тоже в
пять строк. Кому он принадлежит? Шухову? Или тому, кто рас-
сказывает о нем, как бы стоя с ним где-то рядом, плечо к плечу, и
передавая нам этот комментарий от его имени?
И дальше:

Там, за столом, еще ложку не окунумши, парень молодой
крестится. Значит, украинец западный, и то новичок. А
русские — и какой рукой креститься забыли. (14)

Кто видит это: Шухов? рассказчик? оба одновременно?
Это двуединство облика сказового рассказчика нигде не рас-
членяется грамматическим «я»; синтетическая его природа, напро-
тив, отчасти подчеркивается прорывающимся кое-где «мы»:

1. И попрятались все. Только шесть человек стоят на вышках, да
   около конторы суета. Вот этот-то наш миг и есть! Старший прораб
   сколько, говорят, грозился разнарядку всем бригадам давать с
   вечера — а никак не наладят. ... А миг наш! (37)
2. Вспомнил Шухов, что хотел обновить номерок на телогрейке,
   протискался через линейку на тот бок. Там к художнику два-три
   зэка в очереди стояли. И Шухов стал. Номер нашему брату —
   один вред ... (24)
3. Тридцать восьмая, конечно, чужих никого к печке не допускает,
   сама обсела, портянки сушит. Ладно, мы и тут, в уголку, ничего. (37)
4. — Раство-ор! — перенимает Шухов. Всё подровняли в третьем
   ряду, а на четвертом и развернуться. Надо бы шнур на рядок
   вверх перетянуть, да живет и так, рядок без шнура прогоним. (79)

В первых двух примерах эти размышления от первого лица («наш»,
«нашему брату») могут, как и в ряде других случаев, принадлежать

и сказовому рассказчику, и Шухову самому; «мы» здесь — «зэки» вообще.

В примере третьем «мы» более персонализовано: — в нем сливаются, по-видимому, о б а сказовых «я»; оно здесь может означать и только о д н о лицо.

Так же и в последнем примере, взятом из описания кладки Шуховым стены на строительстве ТЭЦ (одного из самых ярких эпизодов в повести), «мы» в п р о г о н и м имеет уже конкретно-личностное значение — оно соотнесено с «я» самого Шухова.

Это раскрывающееся наконец «я» главного персонажа невольно отводит читателя к автобиографической природе повести: в каторжном лагере Караганды Солженицын, по собственному признанию, сделанном им одному из интервьюеров, «работал каменщиком и там же задумал повесть об Иване Денисовиче». ... «заключенные носили свои номера на лбу, на груди, на спине и на коленях. У Солженицына был номер 232»[5]

* * *

Образ рассказчика в сказе отчетливее всего проясняется сопоставлением его с речевым обликом самого автора. Соотношение этих двух обликов обычно определяет структурные формы сказа и интенсивность сказовой стилизации.

Композиционно-стилевую структуру повести «Один день Ивана Денисовича» создает д в и ж е н и е от письменно-литературных стилей, принадлежащих автору, к устным, принадлежащим сказовому рассказчику.

Как и у Лескова, первичным приемом сказового «остраннения» оказывается введение элементов несобственно прямой речи. В приводимом ниже отрывке выделенное разрядкой принадлежит речевой сфере Шухова:

> Всегда Шухов по подъему вставал, а сегодня не встал. Еще с вечера ему было не по себе, не то знобило, не то ломало. И ночью не угрелся. Сквозь сон чудилось, то вроде совсем заболел, то отходил маленько. (6)

Черты несобственно прямой речи могут перерастать в семантико-стилевое целое — внутреннюю реплику, например, сказового типа:

> Потом, глядя на беленький-беленький чепчик Вдовушкина, Шухов вспомнил медсанбат на реке Ловать, как он пришел туда с поврежденной челюстью и недотыка ж хренова! Доброю волею в строй вернулся. А мог бы пяток дней полежать. (19)

Структурно-стилевой «эталон» речевой ткани повести Солженицына вообще, как правило, представляет собой д в у ч л е н, первая часть которого — констатация сюжетно-коммуникативного характера, вторая же — комментарии типа внутреннего монолога, уже упоминавшиеся выше. Часть п е р в а я по своему стилевому облику может принадлежать: автору (1); автору и сказовому рассказчику вместе, то есть содержать разнородные по стилю элементы (2); сказовому рассказчику одному (3) — «движение к устности» в последнем случае особенно наглядно. Часть в т о р а я всегда выдержана в форме сказовой, устно-речевой импровизации. Примеры:

1. Было все так же темно в небе, с которого лагерные фонари согнали звезды. И все так же широкими струями два прожектора резали лагерную зону. К а к э т о т л а г е р ь, о с о б ы й, з а ч и н а л и, — еще ф р о н т о в ы х р а к е т о с в е т и т е л ь н ы х м н о г о б ы л о у о х р а н ы, ч у т ь п о г а с н е т с в е т — с ы п я т р а к е т а м и н а д з о н о й, б е л ы м и, з е л е н ы м и, к р а с н ы м и, война настоящая. П о т о м н е с т а л и р а к е т к и д а т ь. И л и д о р о г о о б х о д я т с я? (15–16)

2. Потом Шухов снял шапку с бритой головы — как ни холодно, но не мог он себя допустить есть в шапке и, взмучивая отстоявшуюся баланду, быстро проверил, что там попало в миску. П о п а л о т а к, с р е д н е. Н е с н а ч а л а б а к а н а л и в а л и, н о и н е д о б о л т к и. С Ф е т ю к о в а с т а н е т, ч т о о н, м и с к у с т е р е ж а, и з н е е к а р т о ш к у в ы л о в и л. (14)

3. Отпыхался Шухов пока, оглянулся — а месяц-то, батюшка, нахмурился багрово, уж на небо весь вылез. И у щ е р б л я т ь- с я, к е с ь, ч у т ь н а ч а л. В ч е р а о б э т у п о р у в ы ш е м н о г о о н с т о я л. (85)

Это целеустремленное движение к устности помогает идентификации образа рассказчика в «Одном дне Ивана Денисовича»: карагандинский зэка № 233, задумав писать повесть из жизни каторжного лагеря, р а с т в о р и л себя в сказовом просторечии зэка № Щ-854.

3.

Тягу к устности речевого отбора, отчасти и к сказово-интонационной напевности речевого строя, находим во всех позднейших (из числа опубликованных) вещах Солженицына[6]. В рассказе «Матренин двор», например:

И шли года, как плыла вода ... В сорок первом не взяли на
войну Фаддея из-за слепоты. (216)
И попросила она у той второй забитой Матрены чрева
ее урывочек (или кровиночку Фаддея) — младшую их
девочку Киру (216)

Автор как бы следует своей героине в словоотборе и речевой интонации:

Так одной утельной козе собрать было сена для Матрены —
труд великий. Брала она с утра мешок и серп и уходила в
места, которые помнила, где трава росла по обмежкам,
по задороге, по островкам среди болота. (206)

И в других рассказах:

И теперь, когда со станции, где холодный ветер нес пере-
месь дождя и снега, где изнывали эшелоны, безутолку
толпошились днем и на черных полах распологом
спали ночью люди, — как было поверить, что и сейчас есть
на свете этот садик, эта девочка, это платье? («Случай на
станции Кречетовка», 179)
Тогда народ наш в седьмую ли долю был так люден, как
сейчас, и эту силищу вообразить невозможно — двести
тысяч! («Захар-Калита», 304)
Лютый князь, злодей косоглазый, захватил озеро: вон дача
его, купальня его. Злоденята ловят рыбу, бьют уток с
лодки. Сперва синий дымок над озером, а погодя — выстрел.
(«Озеро Сегден», 292).

Подчеркнуто разговорен синтаксис («А выглядел Зотов себе еще
работу такую». ... 149–50). Просторечный словоотбор в духе выде-
ленного выше разрядкой представлен обилием заимствований из
Даля: клешнить, ослониться, доброжилой, навыпередки,
обмышку, прихотник и пр. Здесь и находки самого автора —
встречавшиеся уже в «Одном дне» запышенные (запыхавшиеся),
расстарываться (стараться); и новые: лив («... стоял в шинели
под лив, хлест, толчки ветра» 140), вразнокап («шапки были только
слегка примочены, вразнокап», 160), на досветьи (на рассвете),
утыкалка для ручек», увышать («Долгая голова еще увышала его»,
281), угрозить («... угрозила ему пальцем»), «безлукавая память»,
отрубисто ответить», «злонаходчивый забор», «чудомудрый
пиджаю» и др. Встречающееся в рассказе «Для пользы дела» утверж-

дение по поводу некоторых военных слов и выражений: «Русский язык
расчудесно обможется и без них» (278) можно отнести и к иным
словообразованиям самого автора, но, кажется, и его собственное
отношение к ним критично — в упомянутом выше интервью он
признается, что довольно часто ошибался в своем эксперимен-
тальном словоотборе.

Наиболее полно взгляды Солженицына на обиход современного
русского литературного языка отражены в его статье «Не обычай
дегтем щи белить, на то сметана», напечатанной в «Литературной
газете» № 131 1964 года. Этой статьей Солженицын включился в
дискуссию о стилистике современной советской литературы, начатую
в той же газете академиком В. В. Виноградовым, которая, в части
собственно языка, велась между поборниками просторечия и сторон-
никами нормативного лексического отбора.[7] По мнению Солженицына, словарь и склад устной народной речи «дает нам еще не
оскудевший источник напоить, освежить и воскресить наши строки».
Солженицын приводит множество примеров просторечной лексики
и словообразований в духе использованных им в «Одном дне» и в
стиле избранного им для статьи заголовка.

В свете таких рассуждений отмеченные выше примеры столкно-
вения просторечных и книжных элементов в сюжетно-коммуни-
кативных стилях расказчика (типа: «...мог он себя допустить
есть в шапке — и, взмучивая отстоявшуюся баланду,...
проверил, что там попало в миску», 14) получают дополнительное
объяснение, которое впрочем еще более подчеркивает динамику
«движения к устности».

* * *

«Саморастворение» автора в речевом облике колхозника-сказителя
немыслимо, однако, объяснить одной лишь приверженностью к
словарю и складу устной народной речи — контраст между семан-
тико-стилевыми основами обоих языков слишком велик.

Это саморастворение есть несомненно замысел автора, генезис и
природа творческого его процесса, скованного в свободном своем
течении «методом» социалистического реализма.

В интервью 1890 года с одним журналистом[8]. Лев Толстой высказал
такую внешне парадоксальную мысль: «Вредно и нехорошо, —
сказал он, — когда произведения печатаются при жизни их автора:
он, когда пишет, не свободен, он непременно будет думать, что
скажут о его труде, как его встретят и пр. и пр.»

«Непременно думать», взявшись за перо, должен был и Солженицын, думать о том, как встретят его повесть партийные редакторы

и что и как сделать, чтобы ее не постигла судьба «Доктора Живаго». Запретительность несравненно в большей мере, чем программность, составляет существо социалистического реализма в литературе: автору предписывается отказ от традиции критицизма, отказ от попытки наделить своего положительного героя мировоззрением и суждениями, сколько-нибудь отличными от обязательной в СССР идеологии.

Проблему «автора и героя», поистине головоломную в свете этой запретительности и автобиографичности повествовательной темы, Солженицын решил прежде всего средствами языка: растворение автора в облике сказового рассказчика обеспечило такое изображение «человека за проволокой», которое, как выразился в предисловии к «Одному дню» Твардовский, «ограничено ... кругозором главного героя повести».

Какие-либо обобщения, устанавливающие связь жестокой лагерной действительности с природой господствующей в СССР системы, были этому кругозору не по плечу. Во спасение повести кругозорг этот занят был «хлебом единым».

«Не хлебом единым» сказалось лишь в символике некоторых эпизодов и картин. Например — в описании кладки лагерной ТЭЦ, лучшем в советской литературе, по богатству и подлинности живописной экспрессии, изображении трудового «порыва». Объяснение этому порыву надо, однако, искать в «Записках из Мертвого дома» Достоевского, но никак не в современных программных его толкованиях: при всем желании немыслимо ведь приписать лагерным заключенным «энтузиазм социалистического строительства».

А то, как об этом порыве рассказано, раскрывает за маской сказового рассказчика образ большого и самобытного мастера творческого слова.

New York University

NOTES

1. Цитаты здесь и дальше приводятся по изданию: Александр Солженицын. Сочинения. «Посев», 1966.
2. Академик А.С. Орлов. Язык русских писателей. Изд-во АН СССР. М.-Л. 1948, стр. 77.
3. В. Даль. Пословицы русского народа. ГИХЛ. М. 1957, стр-цы 208 и 806.
4. Сравнение речи рассказчика и реплик, принадлежащих непосредственно Шухову в диалогической речи, устанавливает совершенную общность словаря, фразеологических и фразовых особенностей и конструкций.
5. Цитируется по статье Марка Слонима «Интервью с Солженицыным» в

Новом Русском Слове (Нью-Йорк) от 21 мая 1967 г.

6. Напевности нет в рассказе «Для пользы дела», где обилие диалогов почти полностью вытесняет стили от-авторского сообщения.

7. Среди первых особенно воинствующую позицию занимал А. Югов (см. его статью «Эпоха и языковой пя-тачок» в Литерат. газете от 15 и 17 января 1959 года); противники его, учитывая послеоктябрьские социальные сдвиги и потрясения, приведшие к стихийной демократизации языка, отстаивали необходимость традиционной нормализации литературной речи.

8. Журнал Новый мир № 3, 1963.

Kartavoe R in Russian

MICHAEL SAMILOV

Šepeljavyj s kartavym sošlis' (Dal')

Služit', tak ne kartavit'; a kartavit', tak ne služit' (Suvorov, in Dal', II, 94).

... elle avait un seul défaut: elle grasseyait.
«Quel dommage, madame, que la pointe de votre langue ne puisse pas prononcer la lettre canine.»
(Casanova, X (Chapter X), 265).

THE MODERN meaning of *kartávit'* is '*proiznosit' nečisto, neverno zvuki russkogo jazyka r ili l.*'[1] Vasmer (*s.v.*) reconstructs *kartavyj* as **kortavyj* (**kъrtavъ*), though *kortavyj* is attested in several sixteenth-century grammatical studies,[2] and connects it with Church Slavonic *krъtěnije* (*grunnitus, gryllismós* in Miklosich), Polish *karcić* 'scold, punish.'[3] This originally onomatopoeic word apparently did not denote an "abnormal" pronunciation of either liquid, because in the sixteenth-century Russian grammatical treatises the following "acoustic" descriptions are given: '*k, r* kortavye.'[4] Another treatise disassociates *r* from the velars: '*l r* glasъ kortavъ.'[5] Taken at face value, the following OR description of *r* implies a cacuminal trill, possibly with a simultaneous uvular vibration: "r'cý kor'távo, no jako by jazyka zagnutiem koncá, v' nébo gortani udaritь."[6] *Kortav-* is not listed among the speech impediments in the fourteenth (?)-century Russian translation of Philip the Hermit's *Dioptra*:

> Ov že travlivъ, inъ že flekavъ, gougnivъ
> že paky drougyj, k sim že inъ zajaklivъ, boblivъ
> že estь drougyj, i fofletъ drougy, i momletъ paky inъ.[7]

179

None of the above terms seems to portray *kartavlen'e* as an onoma-topoeia. Only *travlivъ* contains an *r* but goes back to Gr. *traulós* 'lisping, twittering,' possibly misinterpreted by the translator as pertaining to *r*. The quotation linking *k* and *r* suggests that *kortavyj* could denote velar and possibly uvular articulations, and the one pairing off *l* and *r* implies that *kortavyj* could also refer to the post-dental liquids.

With time, *kortavyj/kartavyj* was applied more narrowly to the non-apical variants of *r*, a deviation from the adult norm of Russian peas-ant speech. Examples in Dal''s dictionary show the more recent folk connotations of the term *kartávit'*: '*falšivit'*, *krivit'*, *delat' delo lenivo'*; *skartávil* = *solgal*. The older meaning is still seen in *ètogo ne vykarta-viš'* = *ne vygovoriš'*. Examples in Dal' seem directed against fellow villagers rather than the upper-class *gallomanes* with their affected Pari-sian *R. Kartavye* peasants are not unknown in Russian literature. Akim's peers mock his strong burr.[9] Even though many instances of *kartavlen'e* were due to affectation,[10] we must carefully search for its roots in Russia.[11] Russian writers report many instances of burring among the upper classes.[12] Not only society girls or fashionable officers were guilty of voluntary or involuntary *kartavlen'e*,[13] it could be observed even among university professors, such as N. S. Trubetzkoy's father and uncle:[14]

> Tonom uprašivanija, gluxovatymi aristokratičesko-kartavymi, kljančaščimi golosami čitali svoi zamečatel'nye kursy.

Yet already N. S. Trubetzkoy himself stated that the uvular *r* was considered a pathological deviation or a sign of affectation and snobbery.[15]

The Russian stage sanctions only the apical trill, no doubt because its sound carries farther, and after 1917 the partly upper-class uvular *R* has been deemed socially undesirable. The present Russian orthoepy admits only the lingual trill.[16]

Further research is necessary to shed light on the extent to which *kartavoe r* may be widespread among the Russian preschool children and on whether it might not be integrated into the Russian phonemic pattern better than the lingual *r*. The task is made more difficult by the great variety of the *r*-sounds possible and observed. Even apart from such substitutions as *w*, *j*, or *l*, the term *kartavoe r* covers a multitude of sins, referring to any *r*-variant other than the apical or cacuminal *r* (which will be denoted by *r* in our tables and their discussion). Numbers designate optional variants observed, reported or merely conjectured.[17]

r	apical or cacuminal vibrant
2	apical or cacuminal fricative
3	uvular fricative[18]
4	glottal fricative [ɦ]
5	dorso-uvular fricative, the Parisian *R*.[18]
6	voiced velar spirant [ɣ][18]
7	uvular trill
8	glottal trill
9	glottal stop

The palatalized phoneme is indicated by ' (e.g., *r'*, *3'*). In some speakers the plain *r* or 2 and 9 replaces *r'* or 2' and 9', while other individuals may use *j* for *r'* or 2' and 9'.[19] Even more complex situations have been observed. A Russian uses 3/3', 3/*j* and 7/7' as optional variants, depending on his rate of speech, emphasis, and expression: *Amé*[i]*ka, Amé*[ji]*ka, Amé*[3'i]*ka, govo*[j]*ú, govo*[3']*ú,* [7]*az,* [7']*ad.* I have not observed or heard reports of 8 or 8'. The double trill or the simultaneous *r* and 7 of some French dialects is not reported for any Russian speaker.[20]

r, 2–9 are very different articulations, but most of them (4, 6, and 9 apart) are remarkably close acoustically.[21] As articulations, 4 and 6 are close to 3 and 5.

Inasmuch as the various types of the uvular *R* (our types 3, 5, 7, and, possibly, others) are easier articulations than the apical or cacuminal *r*,[22] and the children are guided by their auditory impressions,[23] one is hardly surprised that children are often reported to acquire the non-apical (or non-cacuminal) variants and may go uncorrected even later.[22]

The uvular R has been observed by Rūķe-Draviņa and A. Grégoire at the babbling stage, when the apical (or cacuminal) trill is as yet impossible. This is not yet the definitive acquisition of a phoneme. Jakobson and others have shown that the second liquid phoneme is the last phoneme a child acquires.[24]

Pending more systematic and extensive studies, we may presume that children find it easier to articulate the "uvular *R*" than the apical (or cacuminal) *r* during the definitive acquisition of the liquid phoneme(s).

If *kartavlen'e* is at least partly a native phenomenon, what bearing could it have on the Russian diachronic phonemics? As N. S. Trubetzkoy pointed out, in Russian and many other languages *r* is outside the series of localizations, or, as Martinet put it, such languages do not economize a distinctive articulation.[25] Therefore, the optional variants of the Russian *r* are not limited by the structure of the consonantal system and it is phonemically irrelevant whether *r* is apical or uvular; while Gilyak with its fifth (uvular) order can admit only a dental *r*, as the position of the uvular *R* is already occupied by [γ] (our 6).[26] Structure provides the "green light" for most types of *kartavlen'e* in Russian. But the active reasons for such a change have not been as potent in Russian as in French. Haden, Juilland and Haudricourt, Wolff and Martinet have studied the structural implications of the French *r* > *R* change.[27] In French, according to Martinet:[28]

> ...des réalisations uvulaires de la forte, lapsus ou pronon-
> ciations individuelles défectueuses, ont été favorisées comme
> offrant un moyen d'éviter des confusions ou des hésitations
> à comprendre dues à des prononciations insuffisamment
> énergiques de /-*rr*-/.

In regional or social[29] dialects, the single French *r* tended (presumably via our 2) to *z* (chaise, bésicle) or to *h*, or spirant δ, as well as to zero.[30] But this tendency was counteracted by the substitution of the uvular *R*. Russian, on the other hand, has lacked the geminate *r* which could have played such a catalytic role. Moreover, Russian has lacked nasal vowels or [ŋ], phenomena which some scholars associate with the French, Portuguese, and (possibly) Romanian tendency to change the apical *r* into the uvular *R*.[31]

Yet some of the variants of *kartavoe R* may be better integrated into the Russian consonantal system and thus represent an articulatory economy. The following table contains the various instances of *kartavoe R* superimposed onto the Russian consonantal pattern.[32]

	LABIAL	APICAL	ALVEO-PALATAL	VELAR	DORSO-UVULAR	UVULAR	GLOTTAL
stops	p/p'	t/t'		k/k'			ʕ/ʕ
	b/b'	d/d'		g/g'			
affricates		c	č'				
fricatives	f/f'	s/s'	š/š'	x/x'			(h/h')
	v/v'	z/z'	ž/ž'	6/6'	5/5'	3/3'	4/4'
nasals	m/m'	n/n'					
laterals		l/l'					
vibrants		r/r'	r (cacuminal)			7/7'	8/8'
semi-vowels	(w)		j				

r/*r*' are, as we have seen, difficult to acquire and represent an isolated articulation which safeguards their identity. Because it may be either apical or cacuminal, *r* has been entered here twice.

2/2' occupy the positions of r/r' but are continuant and not intermittent. Hence a greater possibility of confusion with *l/l'*, or with the acoustically close *ž*.[34]

7/7' avoid the pitfalls of 2/2' and are easily acquired. Especially 7' seems easier to learn than *r*' or 2'.

8/8' have been neither observed nor reported for Russian; yet 8 has been noted in some Slovak children.[35]

6/6' would seem ideal as they would fill a Standard Russian (though not South Russian) *case vide*.[36] Yet the box is not entirely empty, as it contains a positional variant of *x* (when it is voiced by assimilation) and an optional variant of *g* (as in *Boga*).

Therefore, 5/5' and 3/3' are often chosen instead; though not as well integrated as 6/6', they are acquired more easily than *r/r'*, 2/2', 8/8', or even 7/7'. 5/5' and 3/3' are better integrated into the pattern than 7/7', 8/8', and, possibly, *r/r'*, because 5/5' and 3/3' avoid the potential confusion with the other (and usually older) liquid, i.e., l/l'.

More studies are needed to ascertain the frequency of 4 4' (4 being the "voiced" glottal [ɦ], similar to the English *h* in "ahead" or to the Czech *h* in *noha*).[37] Perhaps some reports of the hiatus instead of *r* might conceal 4. It may be that some instances of *r* > *h* (in Brazil, in some French dialects, and in the speech of a Czech child)[38] would turn out to have been "voiced" [ɦ], i.e., our 4, on closer inspection. Since the Russian *x/x'* are reportedly drifting towards the voiceless (*h/h'*),[39] they might become the voiceless partners of 4/4', if the latter are the ultimate destination of *kartavoe* R. N. S. Trubetzkoy observed that the liquids and *h* were "opposed" to all the other consonantal phonemes.[40] The *r/r'* > 4/4' and *x/x'* > **h/*h'* might be prompted by a tendency to associate phonemes that are now alike in being less well integrated than others. Yet 4 may inherit the drawbacks of 6 (see above).

9/9' [ʔ/ʔ'] also deserve to be investigated as replacements of *r/r'*. Since the glottal stop is non-phonemic in Russian it may escape detection and be reported as hiatus. It seems equally plausible that 9' could be perceived as *j*. Was Tolstoj's *čog't* intended for *čogt*?

l, w, v, j, even *y* may serve as substitutes of *r* (and *l*), yet this brings about mergers of phonemes and is uneconomical on the distinctive level. Hence such substitutes are eliminated faster than *kartavoe r* in the narrower sense of the word.[41]

"Defects of speech" may structurally "improve" phonemic patterns of individuals or social groups and hence are to be reckoned with in linguistic change.[42]

University of London

NOTES

1. A.N.S.S.S.R., *Slovar' sovremennogo russkogo literaturnogo jazyka* (17 vols.; Moscow, 1950 ff.), *s.v. kartavit', grassirovat', kosnojazyčie.*
2. I. V. Jagič, *Rassuždenija južnoslavjanskoj i russkoj stariny o cerkovno-slavjanskom jazyke*, "Issledovanija po russkomu jazyku O.R. Ja. S.A.N.," I (St. Petersburg, 1885–1895), 685, 808, 921, 985, 1108. I. I. Sreznevskij (*Materialy dlja slovarja drevnerusskogo jazyka po pis'mennym pamjatnikam* [Moscow, 1958]) did not list *kortavyj* in any form.
3. F. Sławski, *Słownik etymologiczny języka polskiego*, II, 69–70. Possibly this word goes back to the Indo-European zero-grade *$k\bar{r}t$*, cf. Julius Pokorny, *Indogermanisches etymologisches Wörterbuch*, I (Bern, 1959), 531.
4. Jagič, pp. 658, 808, along with such remarks as "*ě gibokъ*," "*Rousia radi jatь*," "*jusъ gugnivъ . . . radi Polęcъ*," *ibid.*, pp. 636, 655, 807–808.
7. *Ibid.*, p. 925, alongside with "*ě glasъ xrabrъ . . . y gibokъ . . . ě glasъ smirenъ*," p. 920.
6. 'stands here for paerčikъ. *Ibid.*, p. 1008. Cf. "*g mjagkoe slovo s gougnaniem, jazykъ málo iz zubъ vyxodit . . . onъ gugnivoe*," *loc. cit.* The double-trill *r* of some French dialects in Anjou is described by A. Dauzat, *Histoire de la langue française* (Paris, 1939), par. 122.
7. Sreznevskij, *s.v. bobletъ*; see his translation of each word and the (inexact) Latin version of this passage in Book IV, Chapter III of "Philippi Solitarii Dioptra," ed. Migne, *Patrologia Graeca*, Vol. 172, col. 825A, as well as I. U. Budovnic,

Slovar' russkoj, ukrainskoj, belorusskoj pis'mennosti i literatury (Moscow, 1962), pp. 62, 356, and M. V. Bezobrazova, "Zametka o Dioptre," *Žurnal Ministerstva Narodnogo Prosveščenija* (November, 1893), pp. 27–47.
8. Vladimir Dal', *Tolkovyj slovar' živogo velikorusskogo jazyka*, II (St. Petersburg, 1880–1882), 94. Our first epigraph *ibid.*, IV, 628. V. Dal', in his *Poslovicy russkogo naroda* (Moscow, 1957), pp. 976–77 also cites the folk *skorogovorki* or *čistogovorki* surely intended for children with *kartavost'*. Other interesting words for speech defects include the R. dial. (*a*)*lalyka*(*t'*), cf. F. P. Filin, *Slovar' russkix narodnyx govorov*, I (Moscow, 1965), 230, V. Dal', I, 10, 'to mumble, use *l* for *r*, speak nonsense.' This is connected with *alalá, alalój, alalúja* 'nonsense, chatter' and possibly derives from the *djačok*'s rapid *allilújja*. Note also *gugnívyj = kartavyj, osobenno gnuslivyj, kto govorit v nos, v něbo; gugn(j)avit', gundosit' = govorit' nevnjatno, v nos ili gorlom*, V. Dal', I, 405.
9. I. A. Bunin, "Derevnja," *Sobranie sočinenij v 5 tomax*, II (Moscow, 1956), 69–73: *baggčuk, so skggipom, doxtogga, daggom*. It is not clear what *gg* portrayed, 7/7' or 3/3' (see our table) or even the double trill (cf. our note 6). *gg* was hardly 4/4'.
10. "Kartavlen'ja niskol'ko uže bylo ne slyxat' v proiznošenii polkovnika" (Pisemskij), cited in the seventeen-volume *Slovar' sovr. r. lit. jaz.*, V, 830.
11. Despite V. Vondrák's exclusive dictum of *Nachahmungssucht*, in *Vergl. Gramm. d. slavischen Sprachen*, 2, I

(Göttingen, 1924), 381, and O. Broch's hesitation, *Slavische Phonetik* (Heidelberg, 1911), p. 52. A. V. Isačenko, *Fonetika spisovnej ruštiny* (Bratislava, 1947), p. 137, confirms *kartavoe r* in Russian village speech.

12. See the quotations in the A.N.-S.S.S.R. seventeen-volume *Slovar'* under *kartav-* ("... s kakoj-to osobenno miloj detskoj kartavost'-ju," Mamin-Sibirjak), *kosnojazýčie, grassírovat'* ("... s prijatnym grassirovaniem ...," L. Tolstoy). Isačenko, *loc. cit.* quotes from *War and Peace*, V. Denisov's speech: "Junkeg' Mig'onov, nexog'ošo, na menja smotg'ite."

13. See our note 12 and A. I. Kuprin, "Poedinok," *Sobranie sočinenij v 6 tomax*, III (Moscow, 1957), 385, 513: "Baryšni raznoobrazno kartavili ... djuzej ... zjoj ... plixodili, zvoj, nexolosyj, pejvuju kadjil'."

14. Boris Pasternak, "O sebe," *Proza 1915–1958* (Ann Arbor, 1961), p. 30. Cf. also Jurij's enjoyment of his father-in-law's "... staromoskovsk[aja] reč' naraspev s mjagkim, poxožim na murlykan'e, gromekovskim podkartavlivan'em," *Doktor Živago* (Ann Arbor, 1958), p. 183.

15. N. S. Troubetzkoy, *Principes de phonologie* (Paris, 1949), p. 48.

16. The hard *r* can be apical or cacuminal, the palatalized *r'* is apical. See L. R. Zinder and L. V. Bondarko, "Akustičeskaja xarakteristika različija tvërdyx i mjagkix soglasnyx v russkom jazyke," *Voprosy fonetiki* (Uč. zap. Leningr. un-ta, No. 325 [1964]), pp. 40–41; L. G. Skalozub, *Palatogrammy i rentgenogrammy soglasnyx fonem russkogo lit. jazyka* (Kiev, 1963), pp. 46–48; V. V. Vinogradov (ed.),

Grammatika russkogo jazyka, I (Moscow, 1960), 68; R. I. Avanesov, *Fonetika sovremennogo russkogo literaturnogo jazyka* (Moscow, 1956), p. 155; G. P. Torsuev, *Obučenie anglijskomu proiznošeniju* (Moscow, 1956), pp. 87–88, compares the British and the Russian *r*; cf. also Pierre Delattre, *Comparing the phonetic features of English, French, German and Spanish* (London, 1965), pp. 72–74, 77–80, 82–83, 91–92, 94, 98–99. The first three studies describe the number of flaps in various positions and the partial devoicing of the trill in final position. The non-final *r* consists of one or two flaps, the final of three or four. Too many flaps are a dialectal trait called "raskatistoe *r*," R. I. Avanesov, *Očerki russkoj dialektologii* (Moscow, 1949), p. 139. D. B. Èl'konin, *Razvitie reči v doškol'nom vozraste* (Moscow, 1958), p. 98, considers "*r* odnoudarnyj" a speech defect, but does not specify its position.

17. Unaware of a systematic study of *kartavoe R* in Russian, I had to rely on personal observation and the following: Gladys Wolff, *French R: a study in historical phonetics and phonemics* (Ann Arbor, Mich.: University Microfilm, 1958), pp. 22–37 (articulatory and spectrographic study of the *r*-sounds in Europe, with extensive literature), P. Delattre, "A contribution to the history of R grasseyé," *Modern Language Notes*, LIX (December, 1944), 562–64; Jozef Liška, *Rotacizmus, foneticko-logopedická štúdia o chybnej výslovnosti hlásky r a jej náprave* (Vlastivedný sborník I, Práce vedeckých ústavov ... východn. Slovenska, ed. Ondrej Halaga [1956]), reviewed by Š. Pečiar, *Slovenská*

reč (SAV), XXII, 5 (1957), 313–15. D. B. Èl'konin (*op. cit.*, 85 ff.) deals with Russian, but rather sketchily.

18. A. A. Reformatskij, *Vvedenie v jazykoznanie* (Moscow, 1955), p. 139, observes that in (our) 3 the uvula approaches the dorsum, while in (our) 6 the converse takes place. In (our) 5 both organs are active, see Maurice Grammont, *Traité de phonétique* (Paris, 1933), p. 73. However, A. Martinet, *A functional view of language* (Oxford, 1962), describes the Parisian *R* as a "weak dorsal continuant."

19. On the difficult articulation of *r'*, see Isačenko, p. 137. *r'* > *r* is typical of Belorussian and some adjacent Russian dialects, see R. I. Avanesov (ed.), *Russkaja dialektologija* (2nd ed.; Moscow, 1965), p. 92. *r'* is also relatively difficult to perceive. More errors are reported in the identification of *r'* and *l'*, than *r* and *l*, especially in final position, see N. A. Ljubimova, "O gruppovyx i individual'nyx priznakax sonantov v zav. ot ix fonet. polož.," *Voprosy fonetiki* (Uč. zap. Lengr. un-ta, No. 325 [1964]), pp. 75, 81. In these experiments *r'* was often perceived as *l'*, *j*, *l*, *r*; and *r* as plosive *g* and *ž*. Position and environment played a great role in these errors.

20. Dauzat, par. 122. Could some instances of the "raskatistoe *r*" (cf. our note 16) be of this type?

21. Wolff, pp. 33–37. P. Delattre (*Comparing*, pp. 78–80) shows that the three formants are similar in the French, German and Spanish *r* (similar to the Russian *r*), while the American *r* differs considerably in its third formant.

22. V. Rūķe-Draviņa, "The process of acquisition of apical /r/ and uvular /R/ in the speech of children,"

Linguistics, XVII (October, 1965), 58–68 (in Latvian and Czech): The uvular /R/ ... gives cause for less difficulties and is acquired by the little child earlier than /r/. ... /R/ can be said to be an easier sound and to have a greater power of expansion," pp. 66–67; E. F. Haden, "The uvular R in French," *Language*, XXXI, 4 (1955), 507 (in European Portuguese and Spanish, possibly Italian). Èl'konin's statistics (pp. 97–98) imply the expansion of the uvular *R* at the cost of the hiatus at the ages five to seven; and later, at eight and nine, the expansion of the apical trill at the cost of the uvular R and other substitutes of *r*. I. S. Turgenev seems to allude to that process: "... očen' skoro perestala kartavit' i uže na četvertom godu govorila soveršenno jasno." (17-volume *Slovar'*, *s.v. kartavit'*).

23. Èl'konin, p. 91.

24. Roman Jakobson, *Selected Writings*, I (The Hague, 1962), 321, 366, 368 (he notes that in early aphasia *l* and *r* [or uvular *R*] are interchanged), Rūķe-Draviņa, Èl'konin, pp. 89–90, and Antoine Grégoire, "L'apprentissage du langage," *Readings in linguistics*, II, ed., Eric P. Hamp (Chicago, 1966), 201–202. The difficulty of the 2nd liquid for Italian children is illustrated by the Italian translation of A. A. Milne, *Winny-Puh l'orsetto*, trans. M. C. Gaetani (Rome, 1967), p. 89: "*Aiuto! Polcellino (io).*"

25. Trubetzkoy, *Principes*, pp. 74–76; "La plupart du temps les liquides et *h* font partie des ... phonèmes consonantiques en dehors des séries de localisation," p. 156. Cf. A. Martinet, *Économie des changements phonétiques* (Berne, 1955), pp. 79–80, 103;

and R. Jakobson, I, 278–79, 331–32, 366, 368.

26. N. S. Troubetzkoy, pp. 74–76.

27. Haden, *op. cit.*, A. G. Juilland and A. G. Haudricourt, *Essai pour une histoire structurale du phonétisme français* (Paris, 1949), Wolff, *op. cit.*, A. Martinet, *loc. cit.*, and "*R*, du latin au français d'aujourd'hui," *Phonetica*, VIII, 4 (1962), pp. 193–202. Cf.also Rebecca Posner, *The Romance languages, A Linguistic Introduction* (Garden City, 1966), pp. 120–24.

28. "R...," p. 201, Wolff (p. 13) reports that children in a French dialect with apical *r* start out with the uvular *R*; thereupon boys acquire *r* earlier and more consistently than girls. If Dauzat, par. 122 (cf. our note 20) rightly posited *-rr-* > (more or less simultaneous *-rR-*) > *-R-*, we could speak of simultaneous gemination.

29. "Jeru" and "Mazia" of the *Parisinae mulierculae delicatulae* in 1531, Haden, p. 505.

30. Haudricourt et Juilland, pp. 57–59.

31. Cf. Posner, pp. 120–24. The ties between nasality and the uvular *R* are responsible for the semantics of *gugnivyj* (our note 8). Did perhaps Common Slavonic with its nasal vowels have a uvular *R*, later replaced by the apical trill? The *R* > *r* change is not implausible, see William Cowan, rev. of Haim Blanc, *Communal dialects in Baghdad*, *Language*, 42, 3 (1966), p. 696. Wives from partly assimilated foreign tribes could help the *R* > *r* change. A Common Slavonic or Old Russian *kartavoe r* would not be inconsistent with the apparent absence of a term for *kartavlen'e*. Burring could have been normal.

32. Cf. the tables in L. R. Zinder, *Obščaja fonetika* (Leningrad, 1960),

pp. 150–51; Reformatskij, pp. 140–42, H. A. Gleason, Jr., *An Introduction to Descriptive Linguistics* (New York, 1956), p. 200.

33. See our note 16. Avanesov, *Fonetika*, p. 155, notes the *š*-like noises of *r*, in keeping with the cacuminal character of *r*.

34. Cf. Ljubimova, p. 81 (our note 19) and our note 33.

35. But see Liška and Pečiar, cited in our note 17.

36. "Les locuteurs auront fait l'économie d'une articulation distinctive," Martinet, *Économie*, p. 103 (cf. pp. 79–80).

37. On the "voiced" ɦ, see Gleason, p. 189 and Reformatskij, p. 141.

38. E. M. Vol'f and B. A. Nikonov, *Portugal'skij jazyk* (Moscow, 1965), p. 18; Haudricourt et Juilland, p. 57; Rūķe-Draviņa, *op. cit.* English has some instances of *r* > *h*: Hodge, Hob, Hick derive from Roger, Robin/Robert and Richard; Hobgoblin is also known as Robin Goodfellow. See Wolff, p. 16 and Walter W. Skeat, *A Concise Etymological Dictionary of the English Language* (Oxford, 1911), p. 243.

39. Broch, *Slav. Phonetik*, p. 67; Paul Diels, "Velarer Reibelaut und Kehlkopfreibelaut," *Die Welt der Slaven*, I, 1 (1956), pp. 11–17. Isačenko, *Fonetika*, p. 151, places the Russian /x/ between [x] and [h].

40. *Principes*, p. 156.

41. Èl'konin, pp. 95, 97–98: *K[w]andaš, tli*. Cf. Kuprin in our note 12.

42. See R. Jakobson, I, 331–32: "Ein gewisser Sprachstil im allgemeinen oder eine Gruppenmundart, z.B. die Frauensprache im allgemeinen, kann sich infantile Züge aneignen, und die Mode kann ihren Gebrauch wiederum erweitern und auf die ganze Sprache ausdehnen."

Labialization in Old Prussian

WILLIAM R. SCHMALSTIEG

THE PURPOSE of this paper is to propose that unpalatalized consonants in Old Prussian were labialized by following non-front vowels. Following Endzelin I have supposed the existence of palatalized consonants in Old Prussian.[1] I assume also that this palatalization was phonemic as in Lithuanian and Russian.[2] An interesting feature of languages which have phonemic palatalization is that such languages frequently have non-phonemic labialization also. One can compare, for example, the Russian situation where labial consonants followed by certain vocalic phonemes are labialized, cf. Russ. *myt'* 'to wash,' *most* 'bridge,' etc. This phonetic labialization carries no phonemic burden, but it is nevertheless noted by non-native speakers. Thus André Martinet says, "...un Français qui entend les mots *byl* et *most* pourrait être tenté de transcrire *bwil* et *mwost.*"[3]

This phonetic labialization of consonants was misinterpreted by various German-speaking scribes who tried to mark it in a rather haphazard fashion by writing *-u-, -ua-, -wa-,* or *-o-* where one might not expect these letters otherwise.

The following vacillations in orthography are to be explained in this way: (The words given below are in the Enchiridion unless they are marked with I or II which denote the first and second Catechisms respectively.)

	LABIALIZATION UNMARKED	LABIALIZATION MARKED
Nom. Sg. Masc.	*kawijds* (interrogative and relative pronoun)	*kuwijds*
Nom. Sg. Fem.	*aucktimmisikai* 'Obrigkeit'	*aucktimmiskū*
Acc. Sg. Fem.	*mērgan* 'Magt'	*mergwan* (I & II)[4]
Acc. Sg. Fem.	*prābutskan* 'ewige'	*prabusquan* (II) *prabitscun* (I)

Acc. Sg. Fem.	*crixtianiskan* 'christlich'	*crixtiāniskun*
		krichstianisquan (II)
Acc. Sg. Fem.	*perōniskan* 'Gemeinde'	*perronisquan* (II)
	(in this example the last	
	syllables are to be com-	*perroniscon* (I)[5]
	pared; the *ō* may denote	
	a labialized /ā/)	
Acc. Sg. Fem.	*sallaubiskan* 'Ehestand'	*salobisquan* (II)
Acc. Sg. Masc.	*malnijkikan* 'Kindlein'	*malnijkikun*
Gen. Pl. Masc.	*grīkan* 'Sünde'	*griquan* (II)
		grecon (I)
		grekun (I)
Adverbs	*deineniskai* 'täglich'	*deinenisku*
	perarwiskai 'gewißlich'	*perarwisku*
	laimiskai 'reichlich'	*laimisku*
	etnīwingiskai 'gnädichlich'	*etnīwingisku*
Prefix *pa-*	*pagauts* 'empfangen' (II)	*pogauts*
	pakūnst 'behüten'	*pokūnst*
Verbs	*asmai* 'bin'	*asmu, asmau*
	polīnka 'bleibt'	*polijnku*
	(The form *polijnku* is not	
	a "conjunctive"; it is	
	doubtful that a "conjunctive"	
	ever existed in Old Prussian.)	

Sometimes the testimony of related forms in Old Prussian or other languages suggests that we are encountering an attempt to record the labialization of a velar or a labial. Thus we find a nom. pl. masc. *malnijkiku* "Kinder" but also a nom. pl. masc. *malnijkai* 'id.' The masc. voc. pl. *waikai* 'Knechte' probably reflects the same form as the nom. pl. *waikui* 'id.' Old Prussian *kurwan* 'dem Ochsen' which occurs once in the Enchiridion (beside *curwis* 'ochze' in the Elbing vocabulary) is apparently cognate with Lith. *kárvė* 'cow.' The -*u*- here is probably the rendering of /a/ after a velar.

If *quāits* 'Wille' is to be related to Lith. *kviēsti* 'to invite,' then the related word (3 sg. pres.) *quoitē* 'will,' etc. may have been written with -*o*- to denote labialization. (There was no phonemic contrast between short [o] and [a] in Old Prussian, although there was possibly a phonemic distinction between /ā/ and /ō/. The initial element of a diphthong must have been a phonemically short vowel so that a contrast of the type */ai/ *vs.* */oi/ was impossible.)

The relative pronoun has a masculine form *kas* 'der,' but a feminine form represented by *quai* or *quoi*.

In all three Catechisms we find *asmus* 'Das Achte' in the nom. sg. masc. but *asman* in the acc. sg. The form can be compared to Lith. *ašmas* 'eighth.'

In the first Catechism we find a form *pirmas* 'Das Erste' which seems to be the nom. sg. masc. indefinite adjective as opposed to the definite form *pirmois* (II).

The comparative adverb *muisieson* 'grösser' occurs just once in the Enchiridion, but it is usually considered cognate with Latin *māior*, Goth. *mais*, etc. According to Trautmann, "*muis-* aus **mā-is-*."[6] But Trautmann's assumption is completely unnecessary. The *-ui-* is merely the orthographic representative of /ai/ after a labial consonant.

It should also be noted that in the Slavic languages the excrescence of a /v/ from a back rounded vowel in word initial position is a phenomenon related to the labialization of consonants by the same vowels. In other words, if there was no consonant to be labialized preceding the vowel, then a /v/ or /w/ was created. The Slavic examples are well known, e.g., *vy-* < **ū-*, *vŭ* < **ŭ-* and (specifically Russian) *vosem'* 'eight,' etc.

Now it seems that there may have been a sporadic excrescent /v/ or /w/ in Old Prussian also, although the only example I have noted in the Catechisms is *wuschts* "Das Sechste" (I) which is attested without the initial orthographic *w* elsewhere, e.g., *usts* 'id.' (II). On the other hand the Elbing vocabulary (in the Pomeranian dialect) seems to have many examples of words with an initial orthographic *w-* which seems to represent some kind of excrescent labial, e.g., *woasis* 'Esche' (cf. Lith. *úosis* 'ash'), *wosee* 'Czege' (cf. Lith. *ožkà* 'she-goat'), *woble* 'Appel' (cf. Lith. *obuolỹs* 'apple'), etc. There are also words with an initial *w-* in the Elbing vocabulary, and without this *w-* in the Catechisms, e.g., *wormyan* 'Rot,' *wundan* 'Wasser,' but in the Enchiridion *urminan* 'Roten' and *undan* 'Wasser.' Could Gerullis be right in assuming that at one time in all Old Prussian dialects there was before every *u* a *w* which later disappeared in some of the dialects?[7] One might note the fact that in Slavic an etymological *v-* was sometimes lost in initial position, cf. Russ. *osa*, but Lith. *vapsvà* 'wasp.'

Kazlauskas has stated that following velars and labials the original contrast between etymological /ā/ and /ō/ is neutralized.[8] One can certainly agree that the orthographic evidence favors this view, and one may go even further and suggest that perhaps the contrast between etymological /ā/ and /ō/ was lost completely in Old Prussian. Spellings with *ō* as in the words *perōni* 'Gemeinde,' *tickrōmien* 'die Rechte' may merely denote the labialization of the preceding consonant. Such labialization, which was particularly noticeable after velar and labial consonants gave rise to such spellings as *mūti* 'Mutter' probably to be phonemicized either as /mōťi/ or /māťi/; *wissemokin* or *wissemukin* 'allmächtig' the second element of which is to be phonemicized either as /mōkin/ or /mākin/; *laikūts* 'gehalten' to be phonemicized either as /laikōts/ or /laikāts/. It is curious to note that since Trautmann believes that *ā* passed to *ū* after labials and velars (*op. cit.*, p. 126) he is obliged to correct certain readings in the Catechisms. Thus the actual reading of the 3rd person *islāika* 'erhielt' he corrects to *islāiku* (p. 347), *popaikā* 'betrüge' he corrects to *popaikū* (p. 405). And Trautmann also quotes de Saussure's statement: "Nulle part un *ā* après *p b m k g*" (p. 126), although the evidence of *popaikā* obviously controverts it. Additional evidence that an /ā/ after labials can be rendered by orthographic *u* is seen in such variants as the 3rd past *līmauts, limatz* vs. *lymuczt* 'brachs' all to be phonemicized as /līmāts/.

In conclusion then, it seems likely that in Old Prussian consonants were labialized by following non-front vowels. This was marked more often with labial and velar consonants, but also elsewhere by spellings with *o* and *u* for expected *a*.

The Pennsylvania State University

NOTES

1. *Altpreussische Grammatik* (Riga, 1944), p. 25, and "Prūšu tekstu grafika," *Filologu biedrības raksti*, XV (1935), 96.
2. William R. Schmalstieg, "The Phonemes of the Old Prussian Enchiridion," *Word*, XX (1964), 212.
3. *Économie des changements phonétiques* (Berne, 1955), p. 356.
4. Chr. S. Stang, "Altpreussisch *quai, quei, quendau*," *Norsk tidsskrift for sprogvidenskap*, IV (1930), 146–55, points out that the accusative singular of *ā*-stems for words with a root final velar always ends in *-quan*, or *-gwan* in the second Catechism, whereas the accusative singular of *o*-stems always ends in *-kan* or *-gan*. There are not enough examples to draw any particular conclusions. From the second Catechism there is also an example of an

o-stem genitive plural with the same ending, cf. *griquan* (2×) 'der sünden.' It merely seems that the scribe who prepared the second Catechism was more impressed by the phonetic labialization than those who prepared the other two Catechisms.
5. I should remark here that I do not believe that the Old Prussian orthographic sequence *-on* represents phonemic */ōn/ in word final or tautosyllabic position. Any final or tautosyllabic */ōn/ would either have been shortened to */on/ and fallen together with /an/ or else the final /n/ would have been lost in Common Baltic or Common Balto-Slavic. Three more syllables were lost in Balto-Slavic (provided that they ever existed). Only Old Prussian gives the false impression of retaining these. No other Baltic or Slavic language re-

tains from Indo-European a contrast of three syllabic lengths, *viz.* short *vs.* long *vs.* super-long. The Balto-Slavic situation cannot be compared to Sanskrit where we find a *guṇa vs.* a *vṛddhi* lengthening. Thus the orthographic testimony of such forms as (gen. pl.) *menschon* 'des fleysches' and (acc. pl.) *tūsimtons* 'tausent' is not to be counted as evidence for */ōn/. Old Prussian is like Lithuanian in that the *o-* and *ā-*stem accusatives singular are the same and like Slavic in that the *o-* and *ā-*stem genitives plural are the same. Apparently all of these cases were the same (i.e., **-an*) in Balto-Slavic and were differentiated in the various Baltic and Slavic languages (except for Old Prussian which seems to retain the original distribution). See my article, "Slavic *o-* and *ā-*Stem Accusatives," XXI, *Word*, 238–43. It is interesting to note a similar phenomenon in Hittite where the *a-*stems (representing Indo-European *o-* and *ā-*stems) have an acc. sing. and a gen. pl. in *-an*, see Heinz Kronasser, *Vergleichende Laut- und Formenlehre des Hethitischen* (Heidelberg, 1956), pp. 99–105.

6. *Die altpreussischen Sprachdenkmäler* (Göttingen, 1910), p. 380.
7. *Die altpreussischen Ortsnamen* (Berlin, 1922), p. 270.
8. "K razvitiju obščebaltijskoj sistemy glasnyx," *Voprosy jazykoznanija* (1964), no. 2, p. 22.

On the Lexical Make-Up of the Galician-Volhynian Chronicle

An Experiment in the Comprehensive Study of Vocabulary
followed by a Few Remarks on the Literary Language of Old Rus'

GEORGE Y. SHEVELOV

I. PRELIMINARIES

The best answer to B. O. Unbegaun's question, "le russe littéraire
est-il d'origine russe?"[1] can be provided by a comprehensive analysis of the vocabulary of the extant texts written in OR and MR.[2]
This has never been made so far, not even for a single text. Instead,
scholars either single out impressionistically "interesting" words, or
rely on phonetic, partly morphological criteria such as pleophonic
forms *vs.* non-pleophonic (*gorod* ~ *grad*) or the use of certain prefixes and suffixes, etc. The first approach may be exemplified by
Nikol'skij's study on the language of Hyp[3] and is characteristic of
the pre-Šaxmatov period in research on OR texts. A typical example
of the other approach is found in a more recent study of the same
text by Hens'ors'kyj.[4] The latter approach goes back to Šaxmatov and
his school.[5]

But if phonetic and morphological criteria are attractive in their
simplicity and apparent precision, they are still insufficient, if only for
the simple reason that they permit genetic identification of less than
half the vocabulary.[6] Other methods have been proposed, based on
word derivation, semantics, and synonymy, especially in studies by
Vinogradov, Unbegaun, and Obnorskij.[7] I have proposed what can be
called a linguo-geographic method.[8] But, again, none of these methods
has ever been applied to an exhaustive treatment of OR vocabulary
as a whole or as represented in a particular text.

195

This article does not claim to find an answer to Unbegaun's provocative question. To begin with, the text selected for examination is of too late a date. Edited and at least partly written after the Tartar invasion, the GV is, strictly speaking, not precisely an OR text but a text on the boundary line between OR and MU, though tenaciously rooted in the tradition of OR. Then, no single manuscript is sufficient for the solution of the problem. In addition, I have chosen here not even the entire text of GV but two small samples taken from it: the entry of 1259 (6767), the next to the last of the Galician part of the Chronicle (ll. 1–65) and the entry of 1262 (6770), the second of the Volhynian part (ll. 1–67),[9] thus, two entries separated from each other by no more than three years. Although this article heavily relies on factual data and would even possibly permit a passing glance at the make-up of the literary language vocabulary of the time (see section 5), its main intent is to find whether an exhaustive genetic inquiry into OR vocabulary is possible and what kind of results it might yield.

I have tried to classify virtually *every* word of the texts under scrutiny, from a genetic viewpoint, by applying all the criteria available. Anticipating the conclusions that follow, I may state that this method may indeed have a certain validity, in spite of the fact that in this preliminary case the method as applied is far from subtle enough. Although other sources have been taken into account, emphasis has been laid on the data of three standard dictionaries, with full awareness of their shortcomings and/or incompleteness: Sreznevskij, the Prague dictionary, and Sadnik-Aitzetmüller.[10] From Sadn. evidence was traced back farther to OCS texts where this was necessary and made possible by the availability of word indexes to these particular texts (especially Ma, Ps, Su).[11] With Sr, however, mere reference without screening his data would be nonsensical. As is well known, Sr lumps together everything found in texts written or copied in the ESl area from the eleventh through the fourteenth centuries without any discrimination of what is ChSl and what is OR. It has been necessary to break down all Sreznevskij's data according to the character of sources for each specific quotation: those taken from church books have invariably been considered genetically ChSl. The converse principle would, however, be wrong: the secular character of a text by no means guarantees a genetically pure ESl vocabulary. Contrary to the widespread anachronistic view transferred uncritically from the eighteenth century to the eleventh through fourteenth centuries, the distribution of Church Slavonicisms *vs.* native words was determined not by genre directly but by subject. The thematic key of a passage is crucial for the selection of lexical units in a given passage, often contaminating the segment(s) immediately following, even if these are essentially in a different thematic key. Examples can easily be drawn from various secular genres starting with the chronicles or Vladimir Monomax's testament and coming down to charters and even private letters. Hence when we deal with a quotation from a secular text, the fact of its secularity does not suffice per se; it is necessary to go farther, to look at the text itself and establish in what thematic key the passage in question is composed. With the mosaic-like character of texts of the time, passages tuned to a religious key inserted into secular texts are often unmarked quotations from some church text in the strict sense of the word; but even when they are not (or where this is not established) they function, in a stylistic sense, as if they were quotations from a different text, having more or less a cliché character. For linguistic analysis the distinction between quotations in the textual sense and in a purely stylistic sense is of secondary importance and has largely been disregarded here.

Thus if a word does not occur in any text compiled in the ESl area but is represented in OCS sources or their ESl copies, it is likely to be ChSl; if it occurs in texts which arose in Rus' but which are of church character, there are strong reasons to assume its ChSl provenance; finally, if it occurs in secular texts as well but only in passages attuned to a religious key, there also are reasons to assign it to the ChSl layer of vocabulary. No doubt, in many specific instances such an attribution may be inadequate. There are several reasons for this. Our knowledge of OCS and OR vocabulary is arbitrarily limited by the haphazard preservation of some texts and the loss of others. Even for the extant texts there are no exhaustive thesauri. Establishment of the genre and, within the genre, of the stylistic key of a given passage is more or less subjective. It is hoped, however, that while the attribution of many specific words may be erroneous, still, the percentage of improper labelings will not be exceedingly high and through the cancellation of errors working in opposite directions, the general picture will be roughly adequate.

2. Scope of the Material and the Problem of Frequency and Synonymy

In both fragments selected for examination, certain types of words have been excluded from word count and analysis: proper names (except the loan-translated ones) non-adverbial prepositions, conjunctions, particles, and pronouns shared by OCS and OR. Of these, conjunctions are very characteristic for the general coloration of a text due to the high frequency of their use, their status as the principal device of cohesion, and rather important differences in their inventory in the two languages. It was felt, however, that they are too strongly connected with the syntactic structures and that their analysis would therefore imperil the intended purely lexicological character of the experiment.

With the exclusion of these words, the total number of lexical items in G is 218, in V 217. The total number of words used is much smaller because many words repeat: these figures respectively are 132 and 129, figures which, incidentally, do not confirm the widespread view that the vocabulary of the Galician Chronicle is substantially richer than that of the Volhynian Chronicle. In G, 21 words are used twice, 11 words three times each, 7 words four times each (*grad*[12] [+ *gorod* 3×], *ljudie, město, pole, sozdati* 'construct, build,' *stvoriti, viděti*), 1 word five times (*sbirati*), 2 words six times each (*ěxati, iti*),[13] 1 word seven times (*bog*), and 1 word eleven times (*byti*). In V, 16 words are used 2× each, 13 words 3× each, 6 words 4× each (*brat, gnati, načati, okolo, rat', voevati*), 1 word 5× (*iti*), 2 words 7× each (*knjaz', korol'*), 1 word 8× (*ěxati*), and 1 word 11× (*byti*).[14] Repetitions of words in both fragments occur in most cases at a close distance and are motivated situationally, not stylistically.

While there is thus no difference between the two fragments in their treatment of word repetition as such, there is the distinction that G has, among the words with high frequency, several obvious Church Slavonicisms (*grad, sozdati, stvoriti*), while V has none (ignoring for the time being the choice of prefixes with some verbs).

Another distinction may be noticed in the use of synonyms which may be employed as a device to eschew repetition. G is richer in synonyms: *bitisja* 9, 13[15]—*borotisja* 11; *dějati* 56—*tvoriti* 36, 43, 64; *metati* 47—*vergati* 45; *pečal'* 27—*želja* 26; *ratnye* 7—*voi* 8; *viděti* 19, 20, 22, 57—*zrěti* 20; it does not use synonyms in a cumulative way and prefers to scatter them through the text. In V the number of scattered synonyms is somewhat lower: *běg* 33—*uteči* 33; *nadějatisja* 13—*upovanie* 25; *povědati* 55—*skazati* 65; *veselitisja* 40—*radost'* 57. Characteristically, it is in most cases synonymy of roots, not words, i.e., it occurs in different parts of speech within a pair (three out of four examples cited). It is primarily this lack of special care in the use of synonyms and not necessarily the smaller number of words used which makes an impression of greater paucity in the vocabulary of V. Instead, V is more ready to indulge in cumulative (emphatic) use of synonyms in pairs, as if applying the well-known folklore stylistic device: *okannyi i bezakonnyi* 3; *slavja i xvalja boga* 46; *xvalu vozdav bogu reče slava tobě, gospodi* 58.

3. GENETIC BREAKDOWN: *Church Slavonicisms in G*

Thirty-two words in G may be qualified as ChSl. The ChSl character of nine of these is evidenced by their phonetic peculiarities (see reservations in note 6): *grad* 10, 16, 23, 54; *gradec'* 62, 65; *gražane* 8, 11, 41; *oběščatisja* 62; *obraščati* 46; *plamja* 18, 21; *preiti* 41; *vratitisja* 49; *Zlatoust* 63. Meaning warrants ChSl provenance of two words (whether by this time they have become part and parcel of the colloquial vocabulary is immaterial for the purposes of our analysis; this problem is disregarded through the entire essay): *cerkov'* 17, 65; *poganskyi* 26.

For most words involved, however, ChSl origin is established through the examination of contexts in which they occur and comparison with their OR synonyms: *drevle* 'before' 50 (Sr: RT, RK);[16] *imenovati(sja)* 'name' 59 (vs. *nazyvati*; other synonyms in Hens. 76; the most outspokenly ChSl among them is of course *naricati*); *izbaviti* 31 (cf. R synonym in Sr *s.v.*: "Ože ny bog izbavit, *oslobodit* ot ordy" Dog. gr. Dm. Iv. 1388, where *izbavit* occurs in RK, *oslobodit* in SK); *iziiti* 8 (Cf. OR *vyěxati* 7); *našestvie* 30 (*vs. naxoženie*);[17] *obrěsti* 34 (RT; Sr's citation from the Primary Chronicle 6488 is actually from Proverbs 31, 13; the citation from the Novgorod Chronicle 6712 comes in the interpolation on the fall of Constantinople drawn from SSl sources; yet cf. there OR *naidoxa* (40 *kadii čistago zlata*[18]); *okannyi* 15 (OCS typical *okajanъ ~ okaanъ*, but *okanъ* also occurs, e.g., Su 107, 14; in Rus' the word is often applied to locally known persons as *Svjatopolk, polovci*, but this does not prejudge the origin of the word as ChSl); *okrug* 58; *pečal'* 27 (Sr has it also in ST; but the fact that the word is used only in OCS and R testifies to its OCS provenance. Vasmer, *REW s.v.* refers also to Br, U, Sn but in none of these is the word native, nor does it belong to the spoken language); *pogibel'* 17 (Sr: RT, the only secular example in Sr is in RK[19]); *rekše* 'or; i.e.', 50 (Sr: RT, RK, except one late text, of 1408); *sice* 14, 18, 52 (Sr has 3 × in ST; of these one in RK, all three rather mannerisms. Negligibly low frequency compared to synonymous *tako* also bespeaks the artificial character of *sice*. Novgorod birch bark texts have only *tako*, 4×[20]); *sozdanie* 'construction,' *sozdati* 'construct' 52, 54, 61 (OR synonyms *rubiti, staviti*, see Kov. 77f; O. Trubačev, *Remeslennaja terminologija v slavjanskix jazykax* [Moscow 1966], p. 149); *stvoriti* 'perform' (*čjudo* 36, 43); 'construct' (*cerkov'* 64, *gradec'* 64) (both meanings have models in OCS: *čjudesa . . . sъtvori*, Ma, Mat. 21, 15; Su 6, 25, etc.; *sъtvoritъ mi xyzinǫ* Su 204, 1[21]); *těšiti* 25 (Sr: only 1× in ST, from our fragment; this is however in RK); *tozeměc'* 59 (? Not attested in OCS, but typically occurs in the Bible and RChSl text plus 2× in Hyp

and Daniel Abbot); *velen'e* 53 (typically in a cliché *božie velěnie*; Sr 1 ×
in ST, but this is the interpolation on the fall of Constantinople in the
Novgorod Chronicle. But *velěti* is rather RS); *voi* 8 (? Sr: only RT.
Cf. Hens., 57); *voprašati* 58 (Sr: low frequency; in ST only 1 × ; more
typical of OR is *pytati*, cf. Kov. 161); *vozljubiti* 61. One is inclined to
add to this list *odinako* 'anyway,' in spite of its ESl phonetic shape
(*o-*): it seems to be built on typically OCS *edinako* (Rila fragment;
cf. also K. Horálek, *Evangeliáře a čtveroevangelia* [Prague 1954], p. 90)
~ *edinače*. Not counting the latter word, one arrives at 21 ChSl
words not identified phonetically or semantically. The total percentage
of ChSl words, then, is 24 per cent.

OR, and supposedly not ChSl words, are the following: *baba* 'woman'
15 (OCS 'grandmother' and 'midwife'); *borotisja* 11 (pleophony); *dějati*
56 (generally RS; but *lovy dějati* as here is specifically R. Cf. Bräuer
130); *družina* 'retinue' 29, 32 (ChSl rather 'comitatus, socii.' See PD
s.v.); *gorod* 8, 51, 52 (pleophony); *ispovědati* 'tell, narrate' 11 (in OCS
'confess'; but there is contradictory evidence in Mikl *s.v.* in the
meaning 'enunciare'); *knjažiti* 54 (not in OCS; but Mikl cites SChSl
examples); *kolodnik* 34; *perešedšu* 6; *pěšec'* 9 (not in OCS; Mikl 2 ×
in SChSl); *poěxati* 5; *porok* 42, 45; *urjažen* 37; *utveržen* 37; *věst'*
'warning' 2 (but 'news' not only R); *vyběžati* 10; *vyěxati* 7, 33;
zagorětisja 14 (ChSl *vъzgorěti sę*; the form in *za-* only in Christ. Ap.,
a ChSl text but copied in the Ukrainian regions. See PD *s.v.*). One
is tempted to add *prak* 48 which is an *ad hoc* Slavonicization of
porok.[22] Not counting it, the number of non-ChSl words amounts to 18
or 14 per cent.

The bulk of the vocabulary (62 per cent) is constituted by words
which OR shared with ChSl: *běda* 26; *biti* 34; *bitisja* 9, 13; *bog* 25, 27,
30, 31, 36, 43, 63; *božii* 48, 53; *brat* 25; *byti* 18, 23, 25, 28, 31, 37, 39, 45,
52, 60; *čudo* 36, 43; *ěxati* 28; *ězditi* 56; *gora* 57; *gorěnie* 21; *grěx* 14
(not only in RT: see e.g., in *Gramota rižan* ab. 1300 in Sr); *imati* 35;
iměti 26; *imja* 60, 64; *iti* 10; *izlomitisja* 47;[23] *kamen'* 46; *krasn-* 57;
krěpcě ~ *krěpko* 9, 11, 47; *lěsn-* 23, 57 (in OCS *lěsъ* only is attested);
ljudie 6, 22, 33, 38; *lovy* 56 (OCS usually sg); *mal* ~ *malo* 29, 62, 65;
mečuščii 47 (phonetically of course with ChSl suffix); *město* 23, 57, 59,
61; *mnog* 17, 38; *molitisja* 30; *most* 41, 42; *moči* 24, 31, 40; *nadějatisja* 27;
obxoditi 'surround' 58 (in this meaning not OCS; but Mikl. cites it in
RChSl. Hens. 105 unconvincingly seeks Polish influence); *onamo* 32
(as cited in Sr not in RT; but the word has low frequency and
occurs chiefly in the phrase *sěmo i onamo*, words which would rhyme
in OCS but not in R. Much more widespread synonyms are *tu(da)*,
tamo ~ *tam*. The word may be ChSl, in which case it would belong
to the first listing[24]); *onyi* 17, 39; *otgnati* 43; *otsěk* 42 (only ChSl in

Sr but not in this context); *paky* 46; *pisati* 50; *piskup* 55 (for OCS see Sadn. *s.v. episkupъ*; the form is better represented apparently in Northern R. On its use in GV see Hens. 101); *poiti* 1; *pole* 20, 50, 56, 58; *pomysliti* 61 ('intend'; 'think' seems to be ChSl); *poslati* 4, 6; *postaviti* 'place' 43, 'appoint, nominate' 55 (for OCS cf. Su 197, 1: "postavi imъ cĕsarja"); *potom* 15, 28, 35; *priĕxati* 2; *priiti* 40; *prijati* 'seize, capture' (cf. in the same meaning Ps 36b12: "prijęti dšǫ mojǫ sъvĕštašję"); *rat'* 51 (more typical for OCS is *branь*, for OR *voina* which as evidence of Sr shows characterizes ST while in general *rat'* is more frequent. See also Kov. 318, Hens. 62); *ratnyi* 7; *reči* 60; *sbĕžatisja* 38; *sbiratisja* 3, 13, 24; *sĕmo* 32; *sila* 48; *sil'nyi* 21; *slati* 32; *snjatisja* 25; *sobrati* 29, 32; *spisati* 16; *stan* 49; *stojati* 35; *svjatyi* 44, 63; *sžalitisja* 'grieve' 18; *ukrašenie* 16 (Possibly ChSl: Sr 2×, both RT); *uspĕti* 48; *vbĕžati* 23; *velik* 36, 39; *verg(ati)* 45; *vĕtr* 44, 46; *vidĕti* 19, 20, 22, 57; *voda* 39; *vozložiti* 27; *xotĕti* 13, 41, 43; *zarja* 19; *zažžen*, *zažženie* 22, 51; *zemlja* 19; *zima* 39; *zrĕti* 20; *želja* 26 (Possibly ChSl. Sr has one ST, Hyp, but in RK: "Gsь ... navede na ny ... vo veselьe mĕsto želju" 1185, p. 643).

A comprehensive analysis of the vocabulary of OR texts could possibly shed light also on the connection of OR with specific recensions of OCS: Mor, Mac, and Bg. In the small fragment scrutinized here, the number of coincidences with the Bg recension is truly striking. Of words in common with a single recension of OCS, eleven are shared with the Bg recension alone, and only two with the Mac.

4. GENETIC BREAKDOWN: *Church Slavonicisms in V*

In the Volhynian Chronicle fragment examined, the number of ChSl words is lower. By phonetic peculiarities *prečist* 25, *predivnyi* 47 (not in Sadn), *vozvratišasja* 9 qualify as ChSl; by meaning, in connection with etymological considerations, the following may be added: *bezakonyi* 3,[25] *gospod'* 'Lord' 59 (as opposed to *gospodin* common in OR proper as well), *kanun* 5 (not in canonical OCS texts but well attested in both S, Bg, and RChSl), *xrest* 'Christ' 26 (see Sadn *s.v. chrьstъ*). A greater number of what may be supposed to be ChSl is discovered by criteria of context and synonymy: *lĕto* 'year' 1 (? The word in this meaning is represented well in OCS, relatively meagerly in OR, where *god* prevails. Cf. 4× *god* in Novgorod birch bark texts but not a single time *lĕto*, Kur. 96); *nĕkto* 54 (Sr has it once in the Novgorod Chronicle in ST); *okannyi* 3 (see commentary in section 3); *pečalovati* 'grieve' 52 (OR rather 'care, intercede.' See besides Sr Kur. 49, also the commentary above, sec. 3 on *pečal'*); *pobĕda* 45 (? Apparent absence of an OR equivalent as seen from Kov. 330 may be explained by the character of the notion. The derivation seems to have proceeded from *běda* ~ *běditi* to *poběditi* and from there to *poběda*. Further derivation is clearly ChSl: *poběditel'*, *pobědonosec*, even *pobědьnikъ* employed in Su.); *pokoriti* 47 (but *pokoritisja* may be RS); *sice* 55 (See commentary in sec. 3. In the Volhynian Chronicle *sice* is rather exceptional, see Hens. 148.); *slaviti* 'glorify' 46 (Sr: 1× in ST but RK); *stvoriti* 'create' 46; *svojasi* 9, 44 (the word is based on the use of nom. pl. of adjective as device of substantivization in abstract meaning, characteristic of loan translations from Greek; cf. τὰ ὑμέτερα αὐτῶν (*tokmo*) 41 (? Sr has 2× in ST); *upovanie* 25 (though 1× in ST in Sr[26]); *voskočiti* 58 (*vs.* OR *skočiti*); *vozdati* 58; *vozděti* 58; *vozložiti* 24; *vprašati* 63 (see commentary in sec. 3); *vspomjanuti* 9. The total number of Church Slavonicisms in V is 24, or 19 per cent of the whole vocabulary *vs.* 24 per cent in G. Moreover, some of the Church Slavonicisms in V are less outspokenly ChSl in their character or even dubious.

OR non-ChSl words in V are the following: *bogatyr'* 10; *bojare* 24 (OCS *boljar-*. PD has *bojar-* only from CzChSl texts extant in R copies); *družina* 41 (see commentary in sec. 3); *gorod* 27; *izgnati* 'take unawares' 5 (in this meaning only OR or even local), *izrjaditi* 'form up' 28, 30 (military term); *korol'* 49, 50, 52, 57, 61, 63, 66 (Western OR); *kupal'ja* 6; *molod* 54; *norov* 30; *odin* 37, 42; *okolo* 12, 20, 34, 35; *ol'no* 16; *ozero* 28, 34; *poěxati* 23, 44, 45, 50 (Cf. Novgorod birch bark texts 19, 69 in Kur. But Mikl. cites the word from SChSl.); *polon* 8, 17, 22; *povodnyi* 57; *sajgat* 48, 61; *srazitisja* 31 (? Not in canonical OCS texts; Sr has it from Hyp and texts of the fifteenth century. The word seems to have come from, or be in common with, WSl. It is attested in Sn, Cz, Sk, Polish, U, Br. See Vasmer, *REW s.v. razit'*. The contradicting fact is its presence in Svajatoslav's *Izbornik* of 1073, p. 18b. Although the passage seems to be corrupted, the word may be ChSl.); *sulica* 56, 62 (Not in OCS; but Mikl. has it from SChSl. Possibly also a word of WSl area.); *synovec* 53, 64, 66 (not in OCS; but attested in SChSl, see Mikl. *s.v.* O. Trubačev, *Istorija slavjanskix terminov rodstva* [Moscow, 1959], does not mention it); *šelom* 62; *tot'* 59(?); *ugoniti* 'catch up' 16, 26, 51 (SChSl examples in Mikl. mean 'successu uti, coniicere.' More examples from GV in Hens. 77); *uiti* 18 (but 1× in SChSl in Mikl.); *uteči* 33; *vorog* 40, 47, 67; *zaběči* 4; *zdorov'e* 63, 64, 66. The total is 30 words or 23 per cent *vs.* 14 per cent in G.

The main body of the vocabulary of V (58 per cent, *vs.* 62 per cent in G) consists of words common to ChSl and OR: *běg* (not in OCS where *běžanie* is attested, but in *Izbornik* of 1073); *bog* 25, 46, 59; *borzo* 19 (Su; for popular usage in OR cf. Kur., text 32); *brat* 49, 52, 63, 66; *byti* 4, 17, 18, 20, 22, 33, 34, 50, 52, 54, 65; *cěl* 41;

čest' 46; *čestnyi* 26; *den'* 6; *drugyi* 14, 19, 35; *ěxati* 13, 56; *goniti* 15; *gospodin* 55; *isto(p)nuti* 35; *iti* 1; *izbiti* 36, 40, 67;[27] *jati* 8; *knjaz'* 7, 10, 12, 22, 37, 44, 48; *kon'* 56, 61; *ljudie* 55; *lzě* 33; *mal* 17; *mater'* 25; *mnogo* 9, 22; *načati* 34, 39, 54, 63; *nadějatisja* 13; *nedělja* 20; *noga* 47; *obiti* 31; *oboi* 32, 65; *ostati* 'remain' 36; *pit'e* 39; *poběditi* 60 (contrary to *poběda*, see above); *poiti* 31; *polk* 'army' 28, 30, 42; *posem* 43 (cf. Kur. 59); *poslati* 11, 14, 48; *povědati* 55, 64; *priěxati* 39, 60; *privesti* 60; *radost'* 57, 65; *rat'* 11, 14, 17, 19; *reči* 59; *rjad* 29; *ruka* 58; *samyi* 6; *sbytisja* 65; *sěči* 34; *sěsti* 28; *sila* 26; *skazati* 65; *slava* 59 (contrary to *slaviti*? See above.); *sluga* 24, 54; *stati* 27; *sterpěti* 32; *syn* 7, 23, 43; *ščit* 29, 56, 62; *tako* 34, 35; *těm že* 18 (Cf. En 28a13); *tri* 27; *tu* 6; *ubiti* 7, 42; *uslyšati* 37; *ustremitisja* 32; *velik* 46, 52, 66; *veselitisja* 40; *viděti* 28, 40; *voevati* 2, 10, 12, 19; *voevoda* 21; *voiti (všed-)* 54; *vzjati* 18, 21; *xvala* 58; *xvaliti* 46; *zemlja* 11.

As for the sources of ChSl components, V shows the same predilection for the Bg recension as G. At least six words are shared here with the Bg recension alone, and none with Mor or Mac alone. If this observation is confirmed in more OR tects, it can be connected with the Bg (and not Mac or Mor) source of Christianity and written literature among the Eastern Slavs.[28]

5. INFERENCE AND SIDE GLANCES

The comprehensive, nonselective analysis of the vocabulary of two samples of GV does not bring any surprises in what concerns the difference between the language of the G and that of the V parts of the Chronicle. It only confirms what we have known (adding a few observations of detail): that the Galician part is richer in ChSl, the Volhynian part in OR lexical items. As usual, comprehensiveness and count do not change the essentials of our knowledge. What was already known is only presented in a different, more precise manner.

It may be hoped, however, that with the application of this method (refined in the process of its use) we may one day get an adequate dictionary of OR, not only "materialy dlja slovarja" of diverse value and validity, a dictionary that will tell us not only which words are found in OR texts and what were their meanings, but also where these words came from and how they functioned. It is then that a definitive and nonintuitive answer to the question of the genuine nature of OR literary language will become possible. As long as we do not possess such a dictionary and such knowledge, we are bound, by necessity, to mere suppositions. One such supposition may be introduced for discussion at this point. Like other suppositions, e.g., by Šaxmatov, Jakubinskij, Obnorskij, Vinogradov, Unbegaun,[29] *et al.*, it is subject to verification before it can eventually be accepted or refuted.

We all speak customarily of the literary language of Kievan Rus'. Could we not question whether such a thing as a "literary language" existed then at all, i.e., a normalized language generally accepted by, and compulsory for, the educated? Or, to make such an idea more palatable, perhaps the acceptable range of deviations within the written language (from, say, *Russkaja pravda* to *Slovo o zakoně i blagodati*) was then much wider than we are ready to assume, with our education of the twentieth century and the academy-perpetuated tradition of the nineteenth century?

Perhaps the beginning of literary Russian was ChSl simply in that elementary sense that, since writing, reading, and literature came to the Eastern Slavs in their OCS form, every *knižnik* tried to be as ChSl in his language as his education, his ability and the thematic key of the text permitted, but all degrees of attainment from a theoretical 100 per cent of mastery and consistency to 0 per cent were admitted, and the whole scope, if not from 0 per cent to 100 per cent then at least from, say, 5 per cent to 95 per cent was represented and all was "literary," not in our sense (we are no longer broad-minded enough to accept so much liberty), but in the view of the time.

The unity of this language in this case was more ideal than material: it rested on the acceptance of ChSl as the ultimate frontier of perfection. It was not yet the specific "bilinguality" of the Muscovite (MR) period.[30] It was ideally one language, yet materialized not in two, but in innumerable personal and local variations.

If this was the case, the question of the origin of modern literary Russian will have to be divorced from studies of OR writings and relegated to the later (MR) choice of a narrower tradition which evidently derived from some manifestations in the wide compass of the permitted variations of OR.

Leaving this speculative digression at this point, let us remember that this is, as stated above, not a study of the character of the literary language of Old Rus' but of the methods for collecting evidence for such a study. In this respect the present small-scale experiment seems to show, hopefully, that the comprehensive analysis of the texts of the time, based on the genetic identification of every word, is capable of yielding essentially reliable characterizations of various texts in all their diversity. The very fact that, in using this method, we arrived at positive and reliable results known from previous studies confirms the validity of the method. If this can be done fairly convincingly for the Galician Chronicle *vs.* the Volhynian Chronicle, with a very limited stretch of text and with a simplified approach far from any requisite, feasible, or desired subtlety, it certainly can be applied fruitfully to other and larger texts. (In our case, a more subtle analysis may result in shifting some words from one group to another. The classification of some words will probably always remain uncertain. But within the framework of attainable precision, the suggested method is justified.) This method is to be perfected by more handmade (like this one) studies by various scholars, of various texts. Then machines can come to cover the entire scope of the texts extant.

It is then and only then that we shall know with all possible precision (after so many losses of texts caused by lapse of time and the vicissitudes of eastern European history) what was "literary Russian" of the oldest period and if such a language existed in general. As stated at the beginning of this study and restated at the end, the author had neither the intention nor the ambition to solve the problem.

Columbia University

NOTES

1. *Revue des études slaves*, 44 (1965), 19.

2. The following abbreviations are used in this essay: Bg—Bulgarian, Br—Belorussian, ChSl—Church Slavonic, Cz—Czech, En—Acts and Epistles of Enina, ESl—Eastern Slavic, G—the fragment of Galician Chronicle examined in this essay, GV—the Galician-Volhynian Chronicle, Hyp—Hypatian Chronicle (all three used from *Polnoe Sobranie russkix letopisej*, 2 [Moscow, 1962]), Ma—Codex Marianus, Mac—Macedonian, Mor—Moravian, MR—Middle Russian (14th–17th centuries), MU—Middle Ukrainian (same period), OCS—Old Church Slavonic, OR—Old Rus' language (11th–14th centuries), Ps—the Psalter of Sinai, R—Russian, RChSl—Russian Church Slavonic, RS—common Russian (or old Rus') and Church Slavonic, S—Serbian, SChSl—Serbian Ch Slavonic, Sn—Slovenian, Su—Codex Suprasliensis, U—Ukrainian, V—the fragment of the Volhynian Chronicle examined in this essay (from Hyp). Other abbreviations are explained in the text.

3. "Otmetim bolee ili menee zamečatel'nye slova." A. Nikol'skij, "O jazyke Ipatskoj letopisi," *Russkij filologičeskij vestnik*, 42 (1895), pp. 100f.

4. A. Hens'ors'kyj, *Halyc'ko-volyns'kyj litopys* (*Leksyčni, frazeolohični ta stylistyčni osoblyvosti* [Kiev, 1961]), pp. 9–46 (Further references to Hens.) Characteristically, even when Hens'ors'kyj presents synonyms of GV, such as *reči, věščati, molviti, skazyvati* (p. 73), he does not try to classify them genetically. But Hens'ors'kyj also has in his book a section on what he calls "ridkisni slova" proceeding thus in the footsteps of Nikol'skij.

5. Although Šaxmatov proposed these rather for the identification of ChSl components in modern Russian.

6. Besides that, if applied straightforwardly they may often prove to be anachronistic. To take as an

example the feature of pleophony: it is usually said that *grad* is ChSl, *gorod* OR. But OR texts show so many optional cases in the choice of, say, *ra~oro* forms, and so many free substitutions that one can ask the question if these really were two *words* or two forms of the same word. Thus neither would be a ChSl word or an OR word but rather a common RS word which appears now in ChSl mounting (*grad*), now in OR (*gorod*). In this essay, however, this consideration will be ignored and the traditional approach followed.

7. A survey of these methods may be found in my "Die kirchenslavischen Elemente in der russischen Literatursprache und die Rolle A. Šachmatovs bei ihrer Erforschung." A. Šachmatov and G. Y. Shevelov, *Die kirchenslavischen Elemente in der modernen russischen Literatursprache* (Wiesbaden, 1960), pp. 58 ff.

8. *Ibid.*, pp. 64 ff.

9. On the border between G and V, see D. S. Worth, "Linguistics and historiography. A problem of dating in the Galician-Volhynian Chronicle," *Indiana Slavic Studies*, 3 (1964), 183 ff.

10. I. Sreznevskij, *Materialy dlja slovarja drevnerusskogo jazyka po pis'mennym pamjatnikam* (St. Petersburg, 1893–1912); Československá Akademie Věd, Slovanský ústav. *Slovník jazyka staroslověnského* (Prague 1958–1966 [*a-i*]); L. Sadnik and R. Aitzetmüller, *Handwörterbuch zu den altkirchenslavischen Texten* (The Hague, 1955). Referred to, respectively, as Sr, PD, Sadn.

11. The evidence of later ChSl texts such as George Amartolus, Joseph

Flavius, etc. has been largely ignored except for the data of F. Miklosich's *Lexicon palaeoslovenico-graeco-latinum* (Vienna 1862–1865 [further referred to as Mikl]), no doubt, to the great disadvantage of this study. But this material would need special methods of analysis and make this tentative inquiry into method exceedingly long.

12. Since in this study, phonetics and spelling are of no greater bearing, the examples from GV are given in a normalized form; weak *jers* are omitted.

13. For this count but not for that in the following sections, verbs which differ in aspect and/or in prefix of aspectual or spatial function are considered one word. Hence *iti* comprises also *iziiti, pereiti, preiti, priiti, poiti*, etc.

14. Some work on word frequency in OR was done by L. Vjalkina and G. Lukina, see their articles in *Issledovanija po istoričeskoj leksikologii drevne-russkogo jazyka* (Moscow, 1964), pp. 298 ff, and *Leksikologija i slovoobrazovanie drevne-russkogo jazyka* (Moscow, 1966), pp. 263 ff. They did not include GV in their sources, neither did they treat conjunctions, prepositions, or particles separately. Their count is not designed specifically for genetic classification of OR vocabulary although indirectly it can be used for that purpose.

15. Numbers after examples refer here and farther on to the lines of G and V.

16. Abbreviations used in characterization of the environments in which words are employed: RT—religious text; ST—secular (nonreligious) text; RK—used in a secular text, but in a passage attuned to a

religious key; SK—used in a passage attuned to a secular key.

17. For this and other synonyms in OR, see P. Kovaliv, *Leksyčnyj fond literaturnoji movy kyjivs'koho periodu X—XIV st.*, I (New York, 1962), 324. Further referred to as Kov.

18. Akad. Nauk SSSR, Institut istorii. *Novgorodskaja pervaja letopis' staršego i mladšego izvodov* (Moscow-Leningrad, 1950), p. 245.

19. Laurentian Chronicle. *Polnoe sobranie russkix letopisej*, I (Moscow, 1962), 398.

20. W. Kuraszkiewicz, *Gramoty nowogrodzkie na brzozowej korze* (Warsaw, 1957), pp. 102 f. Further references to Kur. cf. also F. Filin as retold by Pan'kevyč, *Slavia* 25 (1956), 85 (Filin's *Leksika russkogo literaturnogo jazyka drevne-kievskoj èpoxi po materialam letopisej* [Leningrad, 1949], is not available to me and is quoted here from Pan'kevyč's extensive exposition).

21. H. Bräuer, " 'Tun' und 'machen' im Altkirchenslavischen und Altrussischen," *Orbis scriptus, Dmitrij Tschiżewskij zum 70. Geburtstag* (Munich, 1966), p. 126, observed that *stvoriti* was losing terrain in OR while *dějati* gained it. This, as well as its stable connection with *čudo*, points to its ChSl provenance. (Bräuer has no quotations with *čudo*.)

22. GV broadly uses *porok*. This is the sole instance when the author takes it into his head to Slavonicize this positively non-ChSl word. See the data collected in Hens. 16.

23. On *izlomiti*, see G. Belozercev, "Sootnošenie glagol'nyx obrazovanij s pristavkami *vy*- i *iz*- vydelitel'nogo značenija v drevnerusskix pamjatnikax XI–XIV vv," *Issledovanija po istoričeskoj leksikologii*

drevne-russkogo jazyka (Moscow, 1964), p. 173.

24. This was also Filin's assumption. See Pan'kevyč, p. 85.

25. On the meaning 'God's law' in *zakon* up till the eighteenth century, see B. O. Unbegaun, "Jazyk russkogo prava," *Na temy obščie i russkie* (Festschrift N. Timašev [New York, 1965]), p. 183.

26. Cf. also A. L'vov, *Očerki po leksike pamjatnikov staroslavjanskoj pis'mennosti* (Moscow, 1966), pp. 252 ff.

27. On *izbiti*, see Belozercev, p. 173.

28. These tentative conclusions must be taken, however with great caution. Nearly all the material on coincidences in vocabulary comes from Su, and the affinity may be caused by different thematic range and consequently by the different vocabulary of this manuscript compared to other OCS texts.

29. Unbegaun quite appropriately advanced his concept of literary (Old) Russian in a question form, as quoted in the introductory sentence of this essay.

30. As anachronistically posited, for example, by M. Panov: "V X–XI vv. i pozdnee v Drevnej Rusi bylo dva literaturnyx jazyka, blizkix po svoej grammatičeskoj sisteme i po leksičeskim formam (? G. S.): vostočnoslavjanskij i staroslavjanskij ... Ėti jazyki vzaimodejstvovali i vzaimno obogaščali drug druga, no ostavalis' protivopostavlennymi drug drugu" ("Russkij jazyk," in *Jazyki narodov SSSR*, I [Moscow, 1966], 57). If the thesis of bilinguality is assumed, the next step should logically be the statement that chronicles and many literary works of the time were macaronic, a rather unattractive idea.

Homage Volumes in Slavic Linguistics:
A Tentative List

JOHN S. G. SIMMONS

THE EMOTIONS that stir a scholar's "colleagues, friends, and pupils" to mark a milestone in his career by presenting him with a volume of specially commissioned studies are undoubtedly pious and laudable; and the resultant homage or memorial volumes (*Festschriften*) contain numerous contributions of importance, together with many others that do not fall into the category of mere *ad hoc* compositions. But the volumes themselves are denizens of the limbo that lies between the monograph and the periodical, and they consequently tend to be bibliographical Cinderellas which are rarely accorded the detailed analysis that they preeminently deserve. We attempt to take the first steps toward purging our bibliographical conscience by offering in the pages that follow a tentative list of 106 homage volumes in the field of Slavic linguistics. We draw encouragement for our somewhat unusual contribution from two facts in particular: the first, that though the Unbegaun homage volume must of its very nature be a recruit to the ranks of the bibliographical Cinderellas, it will at least go out into the world with a kind of built-in bibliographical Prince Charming; the second, that the distinguished recipient of the volume—like Šafařík and Šaxmatov before him (to say nothing of Leibniz and Lessing)— at one time adorned the profession of librarianship and is, indeed, a practiced and practicing bibliographer.

* * *

A few lines must be devoted to technical aspects of our admittedly tentative and partial list. In the first place it is restricted to homage volumes offered to scholars who are—or were—Slavic philologists in the technical sense, i.e., whose interests lay essentially in the field of the study of the Slavic languages (including metrics and stylistics)—either exclusively or together with other branches of Slavistics or linguistics. It therefore excludes the many *Festschriften* offered to other scholars (whether Slavists or not) which include *some* articles on Slavic linguistics. Secondly, we include only volumes presented to individual scholars, published during their lifetime (or shortly after their death), and containing articles of a miscellaneous nature. This ruling cuts out volumes that concentrate on the work of a single scholar, e.g., the Dobrovský and Karadžić volumes, one of the Šaxmatov volumes (the other includes miscellaneous articles in addition to those devoted to Šaxmatov's work), and also institutional *Festschriften*.

Titles are listed in order of dedicatees' names, no attention being paid to diacritics, e.g., s, ś, and š are treated as one letter. Joint volumes are entered under both names, and in cases in which there are widely variant forms of names, entries are similarly duplicated.

* * *

The special bibliographical problems raised by the homage volume have already been faced in certain other fields. Dorothy Rounds and Sterling Dow in an Appendix to the former's exemplary *Articles on antiquity in Festschriften* (Harvard University Press, 1962; [736])[1] give particulars of published bibliographical indexes covering the contents of homage volumes in Italian [19], Jewish [53], medieval Romanic [498], New Testament [640], economic history [519], modern French [309], modern Iberian [424], and modern Italian [474] studies. To this list can be added volumes covering history [2624], theology [196], law (in part) [145], and art history [ca. 1350].[2] All these works, though they of course include lists of the homage volumes themselves, are essentially classified or subject indexes to their contents. It is our hope that our modest list may stimulate the production of a similar comprehensive reference work covering the whole field of Slavic studies. The task is a not inconsiderable one, but there is a good deal of experience in other fields which can now be drawn on; moreover, if the work were subdivided on a national basis it could be rapidly accomplished. Surely here is an admirable opportunity for the coordinating hand of the Bibliographical Commission of the International Committee of Slavists.

A LIST OF HOMAGE VOLUMES IN SLAVIC LINGUISTICS

Prace lingwistyczne, ofiarowane Janowi **Baudouinowi de Courtenay** dla uczczenia jego działalności naukowej, 1868–1921. Cracow, 1921. Pp. xvi, 263.

Zbornik filoloških i lingvističkih studija A. **Beliću** povodum 25–go-dišnjice njegova naučnog rada.... Belgrade, 1921. Pp. xviii, 264.

Zbornik lingvističkih i filoloških rasprava A. **Beliću** o četrdeseto-godišnjici njegova naučnog rada posvećuju njegovi prijatelji i učenici. Belgrade, 1937. Pp. xxxvi, 472.

Zbornik Filozofskog fakulteta (Beogradski univerzitet), 2 [for A. **Belić**]. Belgrade, 1952. Pp. xii, 428.

Pamjati V. A. **Bogorodickogo**: sbornik statej k stoletiju so dnja roždenija, 1857–1957 (= *Učenye zapiski Kazanskogo gos. un-ta*, 119 No. 5). Kazan, 1961. Pp. 390.

Mélanges publiés en l'honneur de M. Paul **Boyer** (= *Travaux publiés par l'Institut d'Études slaves*, 2). Paris, 1925. Pp. vi, 376.

Festskrift til Professor Olaf **Broch** på hans 80-årsdag. Oslo, 1947. Pp. [viii], 296.

Scando-slavica, 3 [for Olaf **Broch**]. Copenhagen, 1957. Pp. iv, 260.

Studja staropolskie: księga ku czci Aleksandra **Brücknera**. Cracow, 1928. Pp. x, 793.

Voprosy stilistiki: sbornik statej k 70-letiju so dnja roždenija pro-fessora K. I. **Bylinskogo**. Moscow, 1966. P. 268.

Festschrift für Dmytro **Čyževśkyj** zum 60. Geburtstag am 23. März 1954 (= *Veröffentlichungen der Abteilung für slavische Sprachen und Literaturen des Osteuropa-Instituts* (*Slavisches Seminar*) *an der Freien Universität Berlin*, 6). Wiesbaden, 1954. Pp. [viii], 306. See also Tschižewskij.

Münchener Beiträge zur Slavenkunde: Festgabe für Paul **Diels** (= *Veröffentlichungen des Osteuropa-Institutes München*, 4). Munich, 1953. P. 330.

Profesorowi Doktorowi Witoldowi **Doroszewskiemu** w trzydzie-stolecie jego pracy naukowej tom ten składają w hołdzie przyjaciele, koledzy, uczniowie (= *Prace filologiczne*, 18, i–iv). Warsaw, 1963–1965.

Prof. Dr. Ant. **Dostálovi** k 60. narozeninám (= *Bulletin Ústavu ruského jazyka a literatury*, 10). Prague, 1966. P. 186.

Počest': sbornik statej po slavjanovedeniju, posvjaššennych pro-fessoru Marinu Stepanoviču **Drinovu** ego učenikami i počitateljami (= *Sbornik istoriko-filologičeskogo obščestva, sostojaščego pri Imp. Char'kovskom universitetu*, 15). Char'kov, 1908. Pp. xxiv, 304, 83.

Scando-slavica, 1 [for R. **Ekblom**]. Copenhagen, 1954. Pp. iv, 134.

Rakstu krājums veltījums Akadēmiķim Profesoram Dr. Jānim **Endzelīnam** viņa 85 dzīves un 65 darba gadu atcerei: sbornik statej, posvjaščennyj akad. professoru doktoru Janu Endzelinu v svjazi s 85-letiem so dnja roždenija i 65-letiem naučnoj dejatel'nosti. Riga, 1959. Pp. 736.

Izbornik kievskij: Timofeju Dmitrieviču **Florinskomu** posvjaščajut druz'ja i učeniki. Kiev, 1904. Pp. iv, 356.

Sbornik statej, posvjaščennyx učenikami i počitateljami akademiku i zaslužennomu ordinarnomu professoru Filippu Fedoroviču **Fortunatovu** po slučaju tridcatipjatiletija ego učenoj i prepodavatel'skoj dejatel'nosti v Imp. Moskovskom universitete, 1872–1902 (= *Russkij filologičeskij vestnik*, 48 (1902), 1–468; 49 (1903), 1–249). Warsaw, 1902. P. 720.

Slavica Pragensia, 1 (*Acta Univ. Carolinae*, 1959, *Philologica Supplementum*) [for A. **Frinta**]. Prague, 1959. P. 296.

V čest na Vladimir **Georgiev** po slučaj šejsetgodišninata mu (= *Izvestija na Instituta na b''lgarski ezik*, 16). Sofia, 1968. P. 757.

Studia slavica Gunnaro **Gunnarsson** sexagenario dedicata (= *Acta Universitatis Upsaliensis, Studia slavica Upsaliensia*, 1). Stockholm, 1960. P. 198.

K šedesátým narozeninám akad. Bohuslava **Havránka** (= *Studie a práce lingvistické*, 1). Prague, 1954. P. 556.

Problémy marxistické jazykovědy: akademiku Bohuslavu **Havránkovi** . . . k sedmdesátým narozeninám. Prague, 1962. P. 426.

Slavika Pragensia, 4 (*Acta Univ. Carolinae*, 1962, *Philologica*, 3) [for B. **Havránek**]. Prague, 1963. P. 784.

Oldřichu **Hujerovik** šedesátým narozeninám (= *Listy filologické*, 67). Prague, 1940. Pp. 129–407.

Zbornik u čast Stjepana **Ivšića**. Zagreb, 1963. Pp. xxii, 424.

Jagić-Festschrift: zbornik u slavu Vatroslava Jagića. Berlin, 1908. P. 726.

For Roman **Jakobson**: essays on the occasion of his sixtieth birthday. The Hague, 1956. Pp. xii, 682.

To honor Roman **Jakobson**: essays on the occasion of his seventieth birthday, 11 October 1966 (*Janua linguarum*, series major, 31–33). 3 vols. The Hague, Paris, 1967. Pp. xxxiii, 832; xii, 833–1668; ix, 1669–2664.

Xenia Pragensia: Ernesto Kraus septuagenario et Josepho **Janko** sexagenario ab amicis collegis discipulis oblata. Prague, 1929. Pp. viii, 472.

Adolfu **Kellneroví**: sborník jazykovědných studií. Opava, 1954. P. 196.

Lingua viget: commentationes Slavicae in honorem V. **Kiparsky**. Helsinki, 1964. P. 192.

Studia slavica, 12 [for S. **Kniesza**]. Budapest, 1966. P. 484.

Rusko-české studie věnováno prof. L. V. **Kopeckému** (= *Sborník Vysoké školy pedagogické v Praze, Jazyk a literatura*, 2). Prague, 1960. P. 488.

Recueil linguistique de Bratislava, 1 [for J. M. **Kořínek**]. Bratislava, 1948. P. 212.

Festschrift für Erwin **Koschmieder** (= *Südost-Forschungen*, 17, 1. Halbband). Munich, 1958. P. 232.

Festgabe für Erwin **Koschmieder** (= *Welt der Slaven*, 10, iii-iv). Munich, 1965. Pp. 225–456.

Aus der Geisteswelt der Slaven: Dankesgabe an Erwin **Koschmieder**. Munich, 1967. Pp. xi, 327.

Symbolae linguisticae in honorem Georgii **Kuryłowicz** (= *Prace Komisji Językoznawstwa* (PAN, Odzział w Krakowie), 5). Cracow, 1965. Pp. viii, 394.

Zbirnyk na pošanu Zenona **Kuzeli** (=*Zapysky Naukovoho Tovarystva im. Ševčenka*, CLXIX. Praci filolohičnoji ta istoryčno-filosofičnoji sekcij za redakcijeju Volodymyra Janeva). Paris-New York-Munich-Toronto-Sydney, 1962. Pp. vii, 583.

Voprosy teorii i istorii jazyka: sbornik v čest' professora B. A. **Larina**. Leningrad, 1963. P. 342.

Przegląd zachodni, 7, v–viii [for T. **Lehr-Spławiński**]. Poznań, 1951. Pp. viii, 734.

Studia linguistica in honorem Thaddaei **Lehr-Spławiński**. Warsaw, 1963. P. 512.

V čest na Ivan **Lekov** po slučaj šejsetgodišninata mu (= *Izvestija na Instituta za b"lgarski ezik*, 11). Sofia, 1964. P. 494.

Sprachlicher Ausdruck und Sinngehalt: Festschrift zum 65. Geburtstag von Prof. Dr. Dr. h. c. Ferdinand **Liewehr** (= *Wissenschaftliche Zeitschrift der Ernst-Moritz-Arndt Universität Greifswald, Gesellschafts- und Sprachwissenschaftliche Reihe*, 13, v–vi). Greifswald, 1964. Pp. [iv], 385–508.

Slavica Pragensia, 5 (*Acta Univ. Carolinae*, 1963, *Philologica*, 1) [for B. **Mathesius**]. Prague, 1963. P. 360.

Studi in onore di Ettore Lo Gatto e Giovanni **Maver**. Florence-Rome, 1962. Pp. xxxii, 738.

Mélanges André **Mazon** (= *Revue des études slaves*, 27). Paris, 1951. P. 338.

Mélanges de philologie offerts à M. J. J. **Mikkola** à l'occasion de son soixante-cinquième anniversaire le 6 juillet 1931 par ses amis et ses élèves (= *Annales Academiae Scientiarum Fennicae*, Ser. B, 27). Helsinki, 1931 [wrapper, 1932]. Pp. ii, 432.

Sbornik v čest na profesor L. **Miletič** po slučaj na 25–godišnata mu knižovna dejnost, 1886–1911, ot učenicite mu. Sofia, 1912. P. 416.

Sbornik v čest na prof. L. **Miletič** za sedemdesetgodišninata ot roždenieto mu (1863–1933). Sofia, 1933. Pp. xxx, 688.

214 JOHN S. G. SIMMONS

V čest na Kiril **Mirčev** po slučaj šejsetgodišninata mu (= *Izvestija na Instituta za b"lgarski ezik*, 8). Sofia, 1962. P. 616.

Ezikovedski izsledvanija v čest na akademik Stefan **Mladenov**. Sofia, 1957. Pp. iv, 654.

Janu **Mukařovskému** k šedesátce. Prague, 1952. P. 96.

O literárnej avantgarde: k 75. vyročiu narodenia akad. Jana **Mukařovského** (= *Litteraria—studie a dokumenty*, 9). Bratislava, 1966. P. 228.

Česká literatura, 14, v–vi [for J. **Mukařovský**]. Prague, 1966. Pp. 365–528.

Struktura a smysl literárního díla [for J. **Mukařovský**]. Prague, 1966. P. 232.

... Akademiku Dr. Rajku **Nahtigalu**... za sedemdesetletnico... (= *Slavistična revija*, 1). Ljubljana, 1948. Pp. viii, 320.

Rajku **Nahtigalu** za osemdesetletnico (= *Slavistična revija*, 10). Ljubljana, 1957. Pp. [viii], 334.

Slavia occidentalis, 12 [for K. **Nitsch**]. Poznań, 1933. Pp. iv, 436.

Inter-Arma: zbiór prac ofiarowanych prof. Kazimierzowi **Nitschowi** w siedemdziesiątą rocznicę urodzin... (*Uniw. Jagielloński, Studium słowiańskie, Biblioteka*, Ser. A1). Cracow, 1946. Pp. xx, 130.

Naukovyj zbirnyk prof. dr. Ivanovi **Ohijenkovi** v trydcjatu ričnycju joho naukovoji ta hromads'koji praci. Warsaw, 1937. P. 224.

Slovanský sborník věnovaný J. M. prof. Fr. **Pastrnkovi** k sedmdesátým narozeninám. Prague, 1923. Pp. xxxii, 378.

Symbolae philologicae in honorem prof. Mil. **Pavlović** septuagenarii obtulerunt amici collegae discipuli (= *Zbornik za filologiju i lingvistiku*, 4). Novi Sad, 1961–1962. P. 390.

Mélanges linguistiques offerts à M. Holger **Pedersen** à l'occasion de son soixante-dixième anniversaire 7 avril 1937 (= *Acta Jutlandica. Aarsskrift for Aarhus Universitet*, IX, 1). Copenhagen, 1937. Pp. xxvii, 549, [4].

Mélanges linguistiques offerts à Emil **Petrovici** par ses amis étrangers à l'occasion de son soixantième anniversaire (= *Cercetări de lingvistică* (Cluj), 3 (1958), supliment). Bucharest [? 1962]. P. 572.

Franu **Ramovšu** za šestdesetletnico (= *Slavistična revija*, 3, iii–iv). Ljubljana, 1950. Pp. 221–476.

Zbornik iz dubrovačke prošlosti Milanu **Rešetaru** o 70-oj godišnjici života... (= *Dubrovnik*, 2). Dubrovnik, 1931. P. 500.

Ezikovedsko-etnografski izsledvanija v pamet na akad. Stojan **Romanski**. Sofia, 1960. P. 982.

Omagiu lui Alexandra **Rosetti** la 70 de ani. Bucharest, 1965. Pp. viii, 1050.

Romanoslavica, 12 [for A. **Rosetti**]. Bucharest, 1965. Pp. 426.

Studia językoznawcze poświęcone profesorowi Stanisławowi **Rospondowi**. Breslau-Warsaw-Cracow, 1966. P. 464.

Symbolae grammaticae in honorem Ioannis **Rozwadowski**. T. 1–2. Cracow, 1927–1928. Pp. xxiv, 336, 562.

Księga pamiątkowa ku czci profesora Mikołaja **Rudnickiego** (= *Slavia occidentalis*, 20, ii). Poznań, 1960. Pp. 274.

Izvestija Otdelenija russkogo jazyka i slovesnosti Rossijskoj Akademii Nauk, 25 (1920) [for A. A. **Šaxmatov**]. Petrograd, 1922. Pp. viii, 488.

A. A. **Šaxmatov**, 1864–1920: sbornik statej i materialov (= *Trudy Komissii po istorii Akademii nauk SSSR*, 3).Moscow-Leningrad, 1947.P.476.

Pamjati akad. L'va Vladimiroviča **Ščerby** (1880–1944): sbornik statej. Leningrad, 1951. P. 320.

Sborník na počest' Jozefa **Škultétyho**. Turčiansky sv. Martin, 1933. P. 668.

Onomastické práce: sborník rozprav k sedmdesátým narozeninám univ. prof. dr. Vladimíra **Šmilauera** DrSc. Prague, 1966. P. 136.

Slavica Pragensia, 8 (*Acta Univ. Carolinae*, 1966, *Philologica*, 1–3) [for V. **Šmilauer**]. Prague, 1966. P. 424.

Sbornik statej v čest' Alekseja Ivanoviča **Sobolevskogo**, izdannyj ko dnju 70-letija so dnja ego roždenija... (= *Sbornik Otdelenija russkogo jazyka i slovesnosti AN SSSR*, 101, iii). Leningrad, 1928. Pp. viii, 508.

Slavistische Studien Franz **Spina** zum sechzigsten Geburtstag von seinen Schülern (= *Veröffentlichungen der Slavistischen Arbeitsgemeinschaft an der Deutschen Universität in Prag*, I Reihe: *Untersuchungen*, 5). Reichenberg, 1929. P. 202.

Istoriko-literaturnyj sbornik. Posvjaščaetsja Vsevolodu Izmailoviču **Sreznevskomu** (1891–1916 gg.). Leningrad, 1924. Pp. vi, 426.

Sborník filozofickej fakulty Univerzity Komenského, Philologica, A16 [for J. **Stanislav**]. Bratislava, 1966. P. 208.

Rozprawy Komisji Językowej (Łódźkie Tow. Naukowe), 8 [for Z. **Stieber**]. Lodz, 1962. P. 280.

Studia z filologii polskiej i słowiańskiej, 5 [for Z. **Stieber**]. Warsaw, 1965. P. 464.

Sbornik v čest na akad. Aleksand"r **Teodorov-Balan** po slučaj devetdeset i petata mu godišnina. Sofia, 1955. P. 438.

Pocta Fr. **Trávníčkovi** a F. Wollmanovi. Brno, 1948. P. 548.

Studie ze slovanské jazykovědy: sborník k 70. narozeninám akad. Františka **Trávníčka**. Prague, 1958. P. 494.

Études phonologiques dédiées à la mémoire de M. le prince N. A. **Trubetzkoy** (= *Travaux du Cercle linguistique de Prague*, 8). Leipzig, 1939. P. 346.

Zum Todestag von N. S. **Trubetzkoy** (= *Wiener slavistisches Jahrbuch*, 11). Vienna, 1964. P. 218.

Orbis scriptus: Dmitrij **Tschiżewskij** zum 70. Geburtstag. Munich, 1966. P. 988. See also Čyževśkyj.

Polono-slavica, ofiarowane prof. dr. H. **Ułaszynowi** przez Koło Slawistów studentów Uniwersytetu Poznańskiego. Poznań, 1939. P. 134.

Henrykowi **Ułaszynowi** . . . z okazji osiemdziesiątej rocznicy urodzin. . . (= *Rozprawy Komisji Językowej* (Łódźkie Tow. Naukowe), 2). Lodz, 1955. P. 252.

Annuaire de l'Institut de Philologie et d'Histoire Orientales et Slaves, 18 (1966–1967)–19 (1968) [for B. O. **Unbegaun**]. Brussels, 1968. Pp. xxi, 514; xix, 515–799.

Melbourne Slavonic Studies, 2 [for B. O. **Unbegaun**]. Melbourne, 1968. P. 79.

Studies in Slavic Linguistics and Poetics in Honor of Boris O. Unbegaun. New York, 1968.

Mélanges André **Vaillant** (= *Revue des études slaves,* 40). Paris, 1964. P. 254.

Slovanské studie: sbírka statí věnovaných prelátu univ. profesoru dr. Josefu **Vajsovi** k uctění jeho životního díla. Prague, 1948. P. 266.

Zbornik posvećen Josipu **Vajsu** prilikom 60-te godišnjice njegova dolaska u Hrvatsku (= *Slovo,* 6–7). Zagreb, 1957. P. 422.

Festschrift für Max **Vasmer** zum 70. Geburtstag, 28. Februar 1956 (= *Veröffentlichungen der Abteilung für slavische Sprachen und Literaturen des Osteuropa-Institutes (Slavisches Seminar) an der Freien Universität Berlin,* 9). Wiesbaden, 1956. Pp. viii, 576.

Akademiku V. V. **Vinogradovu** k ego šestidesjatiletiju. Moscow, 1956. P. 312.

Sbornik statej po jazykoznaniju prof. akad. V. V. **Vinogradovu** v den' ego 60–letija. Moscow, 1958. P. 372.

Problemy sovremennoj filologii: sbornik statej k semidesjatiletiju akad. V. V. **Vinogradovu**. Moscow, 1965. P. 476.

Festschrift für Margarete **Woltner** zum 70. Geburtstag am 4. Dezember 1967. Hrsg. von P. Brang in Verbindung mit H. Bräuer und H. Jablonowski. Heidelberg, 1967. P. 318.

Prace ofiarowane Kazimierzowi **Wóycickiemu** (= *Z zagadnień poetyki,* 6). Vilnius, 1937. P. 496.

Problemy sravnitel'noj filologii: sbornik statej k 70-letiju členakorrespondenta AN SSSR V. M. **Žirmunskogo**. Moscow-Leningrad, 1964. P. 496.

Μνῆμα: sborník vydaný na pamět' čtyřicíletého učitelského působení prof. Josefa **Zubatého** na universitě Karlově, 1885–1925. Prague, 1926. P. 498.

Oxford

NOTES

1. The Appendix reprints with corrections and additions an article which originally appeared in *Harvard Library Bulletin*, 8 (1954), 283–98. Figures in square brackets indicate the number of homage volumes indexed in each list.
2. Respectively, M. Rothbarth & U. Helfenstein, *Bibliographie internationale des travaux historiques publiés dans les volumes de mélanges, 1880–1939* (Paris, 1955) and T. Baumstark, *Bibliographie . . . , 1940–1950, avec compléments au tome 1er, 1880–1939* (Paris, 1965); G. Thils, *Theologica e miscellaneis* (Louvain, 1960); H. Dau, *Bibliographie juristischer Festschriften und Festschriftenbeiträge, 1945–1961: Deutschland-Schweiz-Österreich* (Karlsruhe, 1962); and P. O. Rave & B. Stein, *Kunstgeschichte in Festschriften* (Berlin, 1962). To these can now be added a recent contribution covering 415 music *Festschriften*: W. Gerboth, "Index of Festschriften and some similar publications," in: *Aspects of Medieval and Renaissance Music: a Birthday Offering to Gustave Reese*, ed. J. Larue, (New York, 1967), pp. 183–307.

The Etymology of Common Slavic *skot'ъ* 'cattle' and Related Terms

EDWARD STANKIEWICZ

COMMON SLAVIC *skot'ъ* 'cattle,' and its modern Slavic correspondences Russ. *skot*, SCr. *skòt*, Cz. *skot*, Pol. *skot*, UpSorb. *skót*, L. Sorb. *skot* have no satisfactory and agreed-upon etymology. In addition to 'cattle, livestock,' the word may mean also 'possessions' and 'money.'[1] The Slovenian *skòt*, *skóta* 'the young of an animal' ("Tierjunges") is mistakenly listed by Vasmer together with the above words. As we shall see, it is rather to be connected with Slov. *kòt*, *kóta* and SCr. *kôt*, *kòta* 'offspring.'

In his *Dictionary of Selected Synonyms of the Indo-European Languages*, C. D. Buck cites what may be considered the standard etymology of the word: "Ch. Sl. *skotъ* (Boh. *skot* now of bovine species) loanword from Germanic; Goth, *skatts* 'money'; OHG. *skaz* 'money, riches'; NHG *Schatz* 'treasure'; O. Fris. *sket* 'money' and 'cattle.' Root connection dubious; but 'property' probably the earlier meaning."[2] The assumption that C. Sl. *skot'ъ* is a loanword from Germanic raises several problems, some of which were recently pointed out by Trubačev.[3] Etymologically the word is "unclear" also from the point of view of Germanic, since it cannot be correlated with any other Germanic word. The semantic development from "treasure" or "property" to "cattle" seems questionable, as the expected development would be from a concrete to an abstract term, as attested, at least, by Latin *pecunia* 'money' from *pecus* 'cattle.' And, finally, of the Germanic languages only Old Frisian *sket* has the meaning of both 'cattle' and 'money,' whereas the Slavs could have borrowed the word only from Gothic where *skatts* meant 'money.' Despite these reservations Trubačev accepts the hypothesis of a Germanic loanword into Slavic, allegedly on the grounds that it explains best the phonetic and accentual facts of C. Sl. *skot'ъ*, i.e., the simplification of the cluster *tt* into *t*, and the final (oxytonic) stress. Trubačev rejects the various attempts at an internal Slavic explanation of the word; e.g., the connection of *skot'ъ* with *kotiti sę* (posited by Martynov); with **skok-to* and *skakati* (assumed by M. Rudnicki), and with *ščetina* (posited by G. A. Il'inskij).

The formal considerations in favor of the Germanic hypothesis are not, however, as compelling as they would seem. In casting doubts on this hypothesis, Jakobson writes: "*Skot* is obviously an alternant of *ščet'*, *ščetina* 'animal hair.'" Vasmer denies Schrader's, Brückner's, and Jagić's hypothesis of the Slavic origin of such forms as the Gothic *skatts*, '*weil auf diese weise das germ. tt völlig unerklärt bleibt.*' The geminate of this word, however, remains unexplainable within the Germanic sound development; cf. A. Martinet, *La gémination conso-nantique d'origine expressive dans les langues germaniques* (Copenhagen-Paris, 1937), pp. 150–200. Perhaps the Germanic geminate was but a means of rendering the Slavic voiceless stop without aspiration."[4]

The most recent attempt by Martynov to derive *skot'ъ* from **sъkotъ* (which is, presumably, connected with Greek κτάομαι 'to acquire, possess,' κτῆμα 'treasure,' κτῆνος 'cattle') has little advantages over the older etymologies, leaving, in addition, unexplained the lack of the first *jer* in OCSl and OR *skotъ*. Martynov himself reaches the con-clusion that "sleduet, po-vidimomu, ocenivat' dannyj primer liš' kak obladajuščij srednej otnositel'noj nadežnost'ju."[5]

Before proceeding with our own explanation of the origin of CSl. *skot'ъ*, it would be useful to start with some general remarks on the lexical classification of domestic animals.

The names of domestic animals can be viewed as a dichotomous scale which in its fullest form involves the following oppositions:

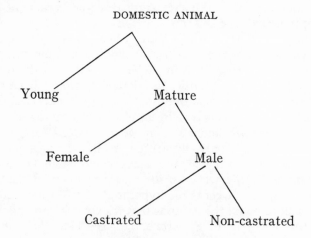

DOMESTIC ANIMAL

The male *vs.* female, and young *vs.* mature oppositions are rendered also in the domain of non-domesticated animals. In most cases, these are expressed, however, by means of derivational suffixes; e.g., Russ. *lev: l'víca: l'vënok, orël: orlíca: orlënok*. In the case of domestic animals, these oppositions are expressed predominantly by means of "suppletion", i.e., through different lexical items, e.g., Russ. *koróva* 'cow': *byk* 'bull': *telënok* 'calf'; *barán* 'ram': *ovcá* 'ewe': *jagnënok* 'lamb'; *petúx* 'rooster': *kúrica* 'hen': *cyplënok* 'chick'; *kobél'* 'male-dog': *súka* 'bitch': *ščenók* 'puppy.' (Compare the similar treatment of distant *vs.* close relatives in kinship systems.) But even in the case of close and economically important domestic animals the "suppletive" scheme admits several variations. Thus the name may function as the generic (or unmarked) term (as in Russ. *ovcá* 'ewe'; sheep': *baran* 'ram', pl. *óvcy* 'sheep'; *kúrica* 'hen': *petúx* 'rooster,' pl. *kúry* 'chickens'; *svin'já* 'sow,' 'pig': *kabán* 'boar,' pl. *svín'i* 'pigs'), or the masculine name may be a derivative of the feminine, (as in Russ. *kozá* 'goat': *kozël* 'billy-goat'; SCr. *óvca* 'sheep': *òvan* 'ram'), or the generic term may be represented by a hyponym (such as Russ. *sobáka* or *pës* 'dog,' *lóšad'* or *kon'* 'horse').

The Slavic names for domestic animals contain a core vocabulary which is obviously a direct continuation of IE. or Balto-Slavic terms, e.g., CSl. **ovьca, *jagnę, *telę, *žrebę, *korva, *svinьja, *porsę, *gǫsь, *ǫty*.

None of the Slavic names for castrated animals belongs to this basic vocabulary. The diversity of these names which is encountered not only in Slavic, but also in other Indo-European languages, points up the fact that they are either late, internal language formations, or loanwords from other languages. Different manners of castration and factors of taboo must have contributed considerably to the variety and specialization of this vocabulary. "The castration of domestic animals," writes C. D. Buck, "is a practice that goes back to the earliest times among cattle-raising peoples, and so presumably to IE times, although the only evidence of any common term is the limited Skt. *vadhri-* and the rare Greek ἴθρις 'castrated.' It was effected by cutting or crushing the testicles, also by burning, cauterizing."[6] That the Slavs were particularly inventive in the methods of castration is amply documented by K. Moszyński.[7] The variety of methods finds its expression in an equally rich terminology designating the process. Even a small region of Poland (Warmia and Mazury) presents us with such an impressive array of descriptive and metaphoric verbs as *mnisić, krasać, wyrżnąć, czyscić, kastrować, trzebić, kleszczyé*.[8] The Slavic and other European languages exhibit also numerous loanwords for castrated animals and for castration, or terms that point to the foreign origin of the specialists in this *métier*; e.g., Russ. *mérin* (originally from Mongolian), *valáx* 'gelding' (based an the German place name *Walachei*), *kaplún* 'capon,' NHG *Schöps* 'wether' (from Slavic *skopьcь*), Fr. *mouton* originally 'wether' (from Celtic and Vulgar Latin), Fr. *hongre* 'gelding' (originally "Hungarian").

In the light of the above, the conclusion imposes itself that the origin of native words designating castrated animals is to be sought in verbs with the meaning 'to castrate.' The other question to be investigated is the possible shift of meaning from the marked term 'castrated animal' to an unmarked term designating the 'bull,' or the 'animal' in general.

Common Slavic *skot'ъ* can thus be assumed to be a nominal derivative of the CSl. verb *skop'iti* 'to castrate' with the suffix *-tъ*. The original meaning of **skop-tъ* would have been 'a castrated (bovine) animal; an ox.'

The posited etymology recommends itself, in the first place, in that it solves, some formal problems connected with CSl. *skot'ъ*, and with Gothic *skatts*, a loanword of the former.

As is known, Common Slavic has simplified the inherited IE. clusters *kt*, *pt* into a single stop; e.g., **plok-tъ* > *plotъ*, **pok-tъ* > *potъ*, **nekto-per-* > Russ. *netopýr'*, **dъlb-tъlъ* > *dętъlъ*, **nept-* > OR. *netii*. It is plausible, however, to assume that *kt* (except in position before *i*) and *pt* yielded a geminated stop *tt* before they changed into *t*. This change was obviously subsequent to the change of an inherited IE. sequence *tt* > *st*, which Slavic shared with a number of other IE. languages.[9] The clearest examples of the posited changes *kt*, *pt* > *tt* > *t* are, not surprisingly, provided by derivative forms which were relatively young, internal Slavic formations. Gothic **skatts* could have been borrowed from Slavic at a time when the latter still had the cluster *tt*.

The final (oxytonic) stress of **skot'ъ* corroborates, in turn, the derivational structure of this word. Though many nouns of Germanic origin exhibit a final stress (e.g., CSl. *pop'ъ*, *post'ъ*, *polk'ъ*, *kot'ъ*, *korlj'ь*), this stress was, primarily, characteristic of Slavic-derived stems. Most conspicuously it occurred in masculine derivatives formed with the suffix -j- (e.g., *ključ'ь*, *bič'ь konj'ь*, *ež'ъ*, *plašč'ь*), but it was common also in derivatives formed with other suffixes, including *-tъ-* (e.g., *byk'ъ*, *gvozd'ь*; *list'ъ*, *pěst'ъ*, *ščit'ъ*, *plast'ъ*, *čьrt'ь*).[10] Some derivatives of the latter type also carried, no doubt, an initial (circumflex) stress (e.g., *p'otъ*, *l'etъ*; *čīstъ*, *č'ęstъ*), though this type of stress was rather characteristic of derived stems without suffix (i.e., of stems with the so-called "métatonie douce"). Derived stems formed by means of a prefix were, on the other hand, marked by a non-initial (or acute) accent (e.g., *sǫs'edъ*, *nar'odъ*, *pot'okъ*, *sъr'okъ*, *sъn'osъ*, *sъb'orъ*). To the last category also belongs CSl *sъk'otъ* 'offspring,' the source of Slovenian *skòt, skóta*, quoted above. This noun is based on the CSl. *k'ot* 'offspring' (SCr. *kôt, kòta*) which carried a circumflex accent, and was, in turn, a derivative of the verb *kot'iti* 'throw' or *kot'iti sę* 'give birth,' a verb which is well attested in all modern Slavic languages (together with many derived cognate forms). The CSl nouns *k'otъ* and *sъk'otъ* 'offspring' (of animals) must, therefore, be sharply separated from the CSl *skot'ъ* 'cattle' (from *skop-t'ъ*), as well as from *kot'ъ* 'cat,' which was borrowed into Slavic from Germanic. The CSl verb *skop'iti* has in Slavic and in other IE languages a number of cognates which appear in different vowel-grades and with or without the "mobile *s*." The variant without *s*, *kopíti* 'to castrate,' appears in Slovenian. The various vowel grades *(s)kóp-/*(s)kep-/*(s)keip-/*(s)koip-* underly a number of Slavic verbal and nominal forms which can all be deduced from an original meaning 'to hit, to cut'; (e.g., Russ. *ščepít', ščepá* 'splinter,' Pol. *szczep* 'branch; tribe'; Russ . *ščipát* 'pinch,' *ščipcý* 'pincers'). Similar variants of form and meaning can be observed in such cognate Greek words as κόπτω 'to hit,' κοπάς 'castrated,' κοπίς 'ritual knife,' and σκέπαρνος 'axe.' It is possible that a verbal stem *ščep-t-* 'to cut,' also lies at the basis of the Slavic *ščetína*, *ščetь* 'animal hair, bristle' (especially of pigs), which cannot be connected with *skot'ъ* in any obvious or direct way. A base form meaning 'to cut,' however, could have given rise to two such different types of derivatives as *skot'ъ* and *ščet'ь*. The narrowing of meaning in the latter form can be compared with the similar change in *kosá* 'scythe; hair,' which is based on *česáti* and *kosíti* (cognates of the Latin *castrāre*).

The semantic change *skot'ъ* 'castrated bull; ox' > 'cattle' is easily understood when one considers the use of castrated animals for work or for consumption, "castration for fattening" . . . being "an old and almost universal practice."[11] Other IE. languages provide ample examples for a similar change from a specific to a generic meaning (e.g., Ital. *maiale* 'pig,' Fr. *mouton* 'mutton,' OHG *galt* 'boar,' English 'hog').

Let us now consider several other Slavic terms designating various castrated animals. Some of these terms are labelled "unclear" in etymological dictionaries, while others are treated apart from words with which they were, probably, closely connected.

The verb *skop'iti* which underlies *skot'ъ* is also the basis of CSl. *skop'ъ, skopьc'ь*, a term which designates mostly the 'wether' (cf. Russ. *skopéc* 'castrate, eunuch'; Slov. *skópǝc, škópǝc;* SCr. *škòpac* 'castrated billy-goat; wether,' Slk. *škop* 'wether; ram,' OCz. *škop*; Czech *skopec*; Pol. *skop, skopek* 'wether.' As indicated by the Lith. cognate *škãpas* which means both 'wether' and 'ox,' the specialized meaning 'wether' is a dialectal restriction of the original meaning which still adheres to the Russ. *skopéc*. In view of the common use of the castrated horse as a work animal, it may be assumed that *škapa* 'work horse,' which was of masculine gender in Czech and in Polish, had originally the meaning 'gelding.' The change of gender and meaning to (fem.) 'old nag' is in the West Slavic languages of late date (in Polish since the seventeenth century); Russ. *škápa* is probably justly considered a loanword from West Slavic.[12]

Ingenious etymologies have been advanced both for Russ. and Ukr. *knóroz*, BR *knóraz*, *knórez*, Pol. *kiernoz*, Kaš. *knórz*, Slk *kornaz* 'barrow,' and for CSl **volъ* 'ox.' The first is, according to E. Berne-ker,[13] derived from **kъrno-orzъ*, a compound of **kъrn-* 'cut' (cf. Russ. *kórnyj, kornát'*) and **orzъ* 'testicle' (cf. Greek ὄρχος 'testicle'; μόνορχος). The Bulg. *nerěz* 'non-castrated pig' is obviously a folk-etymological adaptation to *knóroz*. It is interesting that in most Slavic languages the word has also the meaning of a non-castrated pig.

Common Slavic **volъ* is, according to Trubačev,[14] derived from *valíti* 'to throw; to press,' Russ. *valját'* 'to castrate' (cf. *konovál*). In addition to *vol*, some Russian dialects have also the form *val*; *valušók* and *válux* refer, on the other hand, to a 'barrow' or 'wether.'

It is generally assumed (with Berneker[15]) that Pol. Russ. Ukr., and Br. *knur* 'barrow'; 'hog'; 'worthless pig' and Cz. *kňour* 'boar' is an abbreviation of **kъnorzъ* < **kъrnorzъ*. Only Brückner has expressed reservations about this etymology, without providing, however, an alternative.[16] The underlying form of *knur* is, most likely, the verb **knъv'ati*, *kъnujǫ*, Pol. *knuć*, Kaš. *knovac* which meant originally 'to cut, to split,' (cf. the Polish collective *knowie* 'something cut; the lower part of a sheaf').[17] The nominal stem contained, in addition to the root, the suffix *-ur-* (as in *koturъ, kosturъ*), or simply *-r-*.

The etymology of **konjь* 'horse; gelding' remains uncertain. While Moszyński and Trubačev derive it from **kop-njь*, the similarity of **konjь* and **komonjь* speaks rather in favor of an original **komnj'ъ*, a derivative of the verb *komíti* 'to press, to cut out,' and its variant *ščemíti* (Russ. *ščemít'*, OPol. *szczmić* 'to press').

Common Slavic *šutъ* 'truncated (hornless, tailless, earless); fool' and *košutъ* (with the prefix *ko-*) 'billy goat,' Russ. *košúta* 'hornless' are obviously related terms. While Pol. *szuta, siuta*, and Cz. *šuta* refer respectively to 'hornless sheep' and 'goat,' other Slavic languages ex-hibit a number of variants (SCr. *šŭka, šŭša* 'hornless goat,' *šŭvak* 'left-handed person') which point to the original meaning 'cut, castrat-ed.' SCr. *šŭtalj* means a 'special kind of knife.' Despite Vasmer's doubts, the words in question are clearly related to the IE. roots **kseu-/*ksu-* (cf. Gr. ξύω 'rub, press'; ξυρόν 'knife,' Skt. *kṣurás* 'knife,' Lith. *skùsti* 'shave'). This etymology explains, also the Russ.

ChSl. *ašut'*, *óšut'* 'in vain'; Cz. *ješut'* 'emptiness, vanity,' *ješitný* 'vain, empty'; OPol. *jeszutnosć* 'vanity,' and Slk. *jašo* 'windbag.'

In turn, the above forms throw light on the origin of CSl **porsę* and **porzъ*. The first term is a diminutive derivative designating the 'young pig,' and is related to Greek πόρκος, German *Ferkel* 'pig,' Lat. *porcus* 'tame pig.' The Lithuanian *paršas* 'barrow' reveals, however, the original meaning which is based on the IE verbal stem **perk̑-* 'to cut' (cf. Skt. *parśuḥ* 'curved knife,' Lat. *compesco* < *comparscō* 'to press together'). According to Walde,[18] the IE. **perk̑-* had a variant **perg̑-* which would correspond to the CSl. nominal stem **porz-*. The various meanings of its modern Slavic cognates (Russ. *póroz* (or *póros*) bull; non-castrated pig'; SCr. and Slov. *prâz* 'ram') must not obscure the original meaning of the word 'wether' which is attested in OR. *póroz*. As in the case of *šutъ*, the stems **pork̑-/*porg̑-* underlie two derivatives meaning 'empty, vain.' One is the ChSl. *naprasnъ* 'vain,' Russ. (Ch. Sl.) *naprásno* 'in vain,' and the other the SCr. *nàprázno* 'in vain,' SCr. *prázan*, Slov. *prázən*, Cz. *prázný* 'empty,' as well as OChSl. *prazdьnъ*, OR. *porozdьnъ*, Cz. *prázdný* 'empty' with enlarged stems (containing the suffix *-dь -nъ*).

We shall conclude this, by no means exhaustive, list with the CSl. **borvъ*, Russ. *b'orov* 'barrow,' SCr. *brâv* 'barrow, sheep,' Slk. *brav*, Pol. *browek* 'barrow'; Cz. *brav* 'sheep and goats; cattle.' According to Vasmer **borvъ* is an old collective *-u* stem. It seems, however, more convincing to view **borvъ* as a derivative from the verb **borti, borjǫ* 'to overwhelm, to fight' with the suffix *-vъ*. IE. cognates of this verb mean "to hit, press, pierce." Another type of derivative from the same stem, but with the suffix *-nь* is **bornь* 'weapon, fight, plowshare' (Russ. *bóron'*, Cz. *braň*, Pol. *broń*).

In addition to clarifying a number of Slavic etymologies the above list also testifies to the richness of vocabulary in one of the oldest domains of Slavic material culture.

University of Chicago

NOTES

1. Cf. I. I. Sreznevskij, *Materialy dla slovarja drevnerusskogo jazyka*, III (1903), 387–88.
2. § 3.15, p. 145.
3. O. N. Trubačev, *Proisxoždenie nazvanij domašnix životnyx v slavjanskix jazykax* (Moscow, 1960), pp. 101–102.

4. R. Jakobson, "Marginalia to Vasmer's Dictionary," *International Journal of Slavic Linguistics and Poetics*, ½ (1959), p. 271. Upon completion of this article Prof. K. Taranovsky, one of the editors of the present *Festschrift*, drew my attention to the most recent etymo-

logical explanation of Slavic *skot'ъ* offered by R. Jakobson (*Selected Writings*, IV, 605–606), which is the same as the one suggested in this paper.

5. V. V. Martynov, *Slavjano-germanskoe leksičeskoe vzaimodejstvie drevnejšej pory* (Minsk, 1963), p. 187.

6. *Op. cit.*, § 3.14, p. 140.

7. K. Moszyński, *Kultura ludowa Słowian*, I (*Kultura materialna* [Cracow, 1934]), 116 ff.

8. H. Horodyska, *Słownictwo Warmii i Mazur, Hodowla. Studia warmińsko-mazurskie* (Wrocław, 1958), p. 36.

9. For other examples and discussion of the simplification of Slavic clusters, cf. G. Shevelov, *A Prehistory of Slavic. The Historical Development of Common Slavic* (Heidelberg, 1965), Ch. 13, pp. 183 ff.

Shevelov follows Vasmer in the assumption that C. Sl. *skotъ* is a loanword from Germanic.

10. W. Vondrák, *Vergleichende Slavische Grammatik*, I (Göttingen, 1906), 440 ff.

11. C. D. Buck, *op. cit.*, p. 158.

12. Cf. M. Vasmer, *Russisches etymologisches Wörterbuch*, III (1958), 405.

13. *Jagić Festschrift. Zbornik u slavu Vatroslava Jagića* (Berlin, 1908), p. 601.

14. *Op. cit.*, pp. 43–44.

15. *Op. cit.*, p. 601.

16. Cf. F. Sławski, *Słownik etymologiczny języka polskiego*, II (Cracow, 1958–65), 290.

17. *Idem, op. cit.*, pp. 288 ff.

18. A. Walde, *Lateinisches etymologisches Wörterbuch* (Heidelberg, 1906), pp. 481–82.

Some Observations on Pasternak's Ternary Metres*

GLEB STRUVE

In his *Russian Versification* Professor Unbegaun writes:

> Unlike binary verse, the rhythmic pattern in ternary verse is
> much closer to the metrical scheme. As a general rule, the
> two notions are even identical, which is not hard to under-
> stand. The strong syllables, in these lines, are separated by
> two weak syllables and the omission of a stress would result
> in a sequence of five unstressed syllables, a hiatus which the
> rhythm would hardly tolerate. . . . Thus the stress in ternary
> verse may be weakened, but, as a rule, is not omitted. On the
> other hand certain weak syllables may receive a stress not
> demanded by the metre.[1]

And a little farther down, after a discussion and illustration of
specific ternary metres, we read:

> It has been shown that the rhythmic pattern of ternary
> lines is, generally, identical with the metrical scheme. That is
> true to the extent that, in this type of verse one word may
> even take two stresses if it is sufficiently long to spread over
> two feet. In such a case the metrical stress other than the
> usual stress is necessarily weakened, but is still perceptible.
> Examples of this are rare. . . [2]

---

* I have briefly touched upon this subject earlier in an article on Pasternak's
rhymes in *Vozdušnye Puti*, I (New York, 1959) and in a paper read at the
Liège Congress of FILLM in 1960 (see a short summary in its Proceedings).

Professor Unbegaun proceeds then to give some examples of omission of stresses in ternary lines. Three of them are taken from Vladislav Xodasevič's three-foot anapaestic poem "Pered zerkalom" and two from Marina Cvetaeva's three-foot amphibrachic poem "Petr i Puškin." Of this latter example it is said that the accumulation of such lines in a single stanza (three consecutive lines in one quatrain) "suggests that this is a deliberate device."[3]

After a discussion of non-metrical extra stresses in ternary metres Professor Unbegaun goes on to say:

> It has been explained above that the threat of a hiatus of five syllables ensures the preservation of stress in ternary verse. All the same, this threat does not hang over the first foot of a dactylic line. In fact, the removal of the initial stress would produce a sequence of only three unstressed syllables, which, as has been shown, is extremely frequent in binary metres. Accordingly, the first stress in a dactylic line is readily removable under the same conditions as apply to binary metres. These are: (1) if a line opens with a word incurring a fourth-syllable stress; (2) if the first syllable of the line consists of an unstressed word.[4]

As examples of this, Unbegaun gives two four-foot dactylic lines from Nekrasov's poem "Saša" and six three-foot dactylic lines from Gumilev's famous poem about Rasputin, i.e., "Mužik" (in *Koster*). À propos of the latter, noting that in six lines out of twelve we have the omission of the initial stress, he says: "In certain poems the removal of the initial stress is extended and becomes a regular feature of the rhythm."[5]

While Professor Unbegaun is undoubtedly right in what he says about the greater frequency of the omission of stress in the first foot of a dactylic line, it is my contention that the omission of stresses in Russian ternary metres is by no means such a rare phenomenon as is often thought. This is particularly true of some twentieth-century poets. Though I cannot claim to have made a detailed statistical analysis of the work of many such poets from this point of view, I have found in Gumilev, besides the above-mentioned examples from "Mužik," quite a number of ternary lines with omitted stresses, not all of them dactylic, and with the omission not always on the initial foot.[6] Probably many more examples than given by Unbegaun could be found in Cvetaeva. But the most striking illustration of frequent and conscious deviations from the metrical scheme in ternary metres is to be found in the poetry of Boris Pasternak, whom Professor Unbegaun does not mention at all in this connection. This is true both of Pasternak's early poetry and of much of his late poetry. Here are the total figures for Pasternak's ternary lines with omitted stresses: three-foot dactyls—6; four-foot dactyls—39; three-foot anapaests—50; four-foot anapaests—1; three-foot amphibrachs—76; four-foot amphibrachs—51. To begin with, these figures reveal that, contrary to the accepted assumption, Pasternak is much less prone to omit a stress in a dactylic line than he is in an anapaestic or, especially, an amphibrachic one. Irregular amphibrachic lines—irregular in the sense of omitting stresses, rather than "skipping" syllables, which results in a kind of *dol'nik* and is very common in other poets, e.g., Gumilev—might almost be said to be a hallmark of Pasternak's ternary verse, his title to originality.

Let us now look at the actual examples of Pasternak's omission of stresses. I shall begin with his dactyls and shall cite the examples more or less in the order in which they appear in the 1965, one-volume Soviet edition of his poetry; the page references are to that edition and the initials refer to the title of the section in it (which in some cases means the title of the original volume); for the poems from *Doctor Živago* the page references are to the Michigan edition of the novel.[7]

THREE-FOOT DACTYLS

There are only six cases in which Pasternak leaves out a stress in his three-foot dactylic lines, but in three of them, the omission is in the second foot, and not in the first as in all the examples from Gumilev given by Professor Unbegaun:

Надоминáет! Пеуёт (165; *TiV*)

Дымами Кассиопéю (168; *TiV*)

Самоубиййство не в суёт (166; *TiV*)

Бýдущего недостáточно (485; *KR*)

Гóлым и полуодéтым (486; *KR*)

Заночевáвшие гóсти (486; *KR*)

It will be readily seen that there is nothing unusual in the rhythmic figure of the first three lines: it is identical with what we get in trochaic tetrameter with two pyrrhic substitutions in the middle. Such lines are not very common in Russian trochaic verse but we do find them in Belyj, in Pasternak's own poetry, and in other poets. The point, however, is that here they are part of a clearly dactylic metre and therefore represent a distinct metrical deviation.

FOUR-FOOT DACTYLS

In four-foot dactyls the omission of the initial stress is quite usual in Pasternak. Here are seven lines, all taken from the same poem "Dvor" (74–75; *PB*):

> На недоéд, недосы́п, недобóр
>
> На недопóй и на бóль в заты́лке
>
> И зарывáются в кóнские гри́вы
>
> Что со всегó околóтка с налёту
>
> О наложéнии зи́мнего и́га
>
> Огороди́тесь от вьюги в стихáх
>
> От дуновéнья надéжд впопыхáх

In the short poem "Zimnee nebo" (83; *PB*) there are four lines in which the initial stress is omitted:

> Что, как глазá со змеи́ным разрéзом
>
> Что языкóм обомлéвшей легáвой
>
> На поворóте созвéздьем врéжется
>
> О конькобéжцы! Там — всё равнó

In the last two lines above, the omission of the initial stress is combined with syllable recession, something by no means uncommon, as we shall see below, in Pasternak's ternary metres.

Such syllable recession in one line is combined with an omitted syllable in the same foot (in this case, the second):

> Чóкается со звóнкою нóчью катóк

In line 15 of the same poem, if we take the initial *kak* to be unstressed and do not look upon the word *fal'šivomonetčikov* as necessarily having two stresses (and I do not see why we should), we have two stresses omitted:

> Как у фальшивомонéтчиков — лáвой

In two lines in this poem there is a syllable recession without omission of stress, and in one line there is an extra foot, but the first two are one syllable short, thus creating very skillfully the effect of a deliberate slowing down of tempo in the appeal to the skater:

Ре́-же — ре́-же — ре́-же ступа́й, конькобе́жец

Therefore, this poem may perhaps be seen as departing too much from the metrical scheme to serve as a good example. Nevertheless, its general dactylic lilt is unquestionable, and the omission of stresses in several lines represents an important modification of the metre.

Here are some more examples:

И огурца́ми — барка́сов кора́ (80; *PB*)

Не добира́й меня со́тым до со́тни (208; *SRL*)

За высоту́ ж этой зво́нкой разлу́ки (*ibid.*)

Благодарю́ и целу́ю вас, ру́ки (*ibid.*)

In the poem from which the last three lines are taken, there is also a line in which two stresses are omitted, but in one case the omission is combined with a dropped syllable:

О, пренебре́гнутые мой

(it is, of course, possible to see here the initial exclamatory "O" as carrying at least a secondary stress).

In the charming poem "Val's s čertovščinoj" (402–403; *NRP*), basically a four-footed dactyl, there are many lines which represent *dol'niki* (with one syllable missing), but there are also lines in which the stress is simply omitted, as in the following:

И возника́ющий в фо́рточной ра́ме

or omitted in combination with the recession of one or even two syllables, as in the following lines:

Великоле́пие вы́ше / си́л

Ту́ши и се́пии / и бели́л

И догора́ет дотла́. // Мгла́.

Го́сти выхо́дят / из-за стола́

Вре́мя пред тре́тьими / петуха́ми

The poem ends very effectively in a line of four stressed mono-syllables, which suggest the going-out of the candles on the Christmas tree:

Фук. Фук. Фук. Фук.

This poem is followed immediately by another charming poem about Christmas, called "Val's so slezoj" (403–404; *NRP*), in which there are nine lines with a stress missing, the omission being now in the first, now in the second, now in the third foot, thus contributing to a great rhythmic variety (in one line there is also a syllable dropped):

Ве́тки нело́вкости не одоле́ли

Ни́тки лени́вые, без суетни́

Ме́дленно перелива́я на те́ле

Ви́снут сере́бряною каните́лью

Озолоти́те её, осчастли́вьте

И не смигнёт. Но стыдли́вая скро́мница

Шти́фтики гри́ма, / а не огни́

Э́то волну́ющаяся актри́са

Э́то — отме́ченная избра́нница

The last line in this poem is also a complete break with the metre:

Когда́ о ёлке то́лки одни́!

In the poem "Opjat' vesna" (405; *NRP*), in which there are many *dol'niki* lines, we find one dactylic line with two stresses omitted:

Неузнава́емая сторона́

and three lines in which the omission of a stress is coupled with the dropping of a syllable:

Бе́столочь, ку́мушек / пересу́ды

Ла́мпой вися́чего / водопа́да

К кру́че с шипе́ньем / пригвождена́

and one line in which two stresses are omitted and a syllable dropped:

Полубезу́много / болтуна́

FOUR-FOOT ANAPAEST

The one and only example here is a somewhat dubious one. It occurs in the last line of the poem "Spasskoe" (183; *TiV*), in which the first foot, instead of the regular metrical stress on the third syllable, has a stress on the initial syllable; however, the effect is somewhat similar to that of an omitted stress, inasmuch as we have here an accumulation of four unstressed syllables after the first stress:

Ви́дит, галлюцини́руя, та́ же тоска́

THREE-FOOT ANAPAEST

Of the following seven lines, the first six are from one poem of Pasternak's early period, "Zima" (71; *NP*), in which they constitute 25 per cent of the total number of lines; and the last, from another poem of the same period (68; *NP*):

Завива́ющуюся жгуто́м

Сме́хе, су́толоке, беготне́

Это ра́ковины ли гуде́нье

И осма́триваются — и в пла́ч

И невы́полотые зано́сы

За стака́нчиками купоро́са

Затума́нившегося напи́тка[8]

In the second and third lines above, there is an additional non-metrical stress (or half-a-stress) in the first foot. In the earlier version of "Zima" (the dates under the final version are: "1913, 1928"), there were only four lines with a stress omitted, one of which was later eliminated:

И назре́вшие невдалеке́ (582; *RR*)

In "Poems of Different Years," which formed part of the 1929 edition of *Poverx bar'erov*, there are only a few examples of omitted stresses in three-foot anapaestic lines, three of them in the multimetrical poem "Gorod" (in two cases here the omission of a syllable accompanies that of a stress):

Той же пье́сою неповтори́мой (202; *SRL*)

Растека́ющихся по стеклу́ (214; *SRL*)

О страда́лице / бельэта́жей (216; *SRL*)

О рассро́ченном / платеже́ (*ibid.*)

In *Vtoroe roždenie*, which was seen by many people as a turning point in Pasternak's poetic development—a turn toward more traditional forms—there are two characteristic anapaestic lines, with the second stress omitted, and in one case a hypermetrical stress on the initial syllable. The original rhythmical effect of these lines is, however, due to the omission of the stress, as a result of which we get five unstressed syllables. It is my firm conviction that it is not impossible, as is often said, to articulate them as unstressed, and that this is what the poet means us to do: these lines have a deliberate *panting* effect. I shall come back to this point later, in connection with Pasternak's amphibrachic verse. In the meantime, below are the examples from *VR*:

Ве́рой в бу́дущее не бою́сь (358)

Перепи́сывало мертвецо́в (369)

There are quite a number of stress omissions in Pasternak's later collections, in *NRP* and *KR*:

В тёмном те́реме стихотворе́нья (449; *NRP*)

Посмотри́, как преображена́ (*ibid.*)

Е́сли хо́чешь, переимену́ю (*ibid.*)

Я прислу́шиваюсь на досу́ге (473; *KR*)

Без неро́вностей и без угло́в (*ibid.*)

По́сле угомони́вшейся вью́ги (*ibid.*)

Вы́сунешься, быва́ло, в окно́ (484; *KR*)

В переу́лке, как в каменоло́мне (*ibid.*)

Разбрани́вшись без обиняко́в (485)

Мне протя́гивает бандеро́ль (487)

Переше́йки и материки́ (*ibid.*)

Не выка́зывали быума́ (*ibid.*)

In the poem from which come the last three lines, there is also a line with the initial syllable stressed and the stress in the second foot omitted:

Дéти, ю́ноши и старикѝ (ibid.)

Here are some more examples taken from poems belonging to different periods, the first of them from an early poem, written in 1913:

Раскатѝвшеюся эспланадóй (498; Var.)

Заколдóванное числó (558; Var.)

И опя́ть, двадцатипятилéтье (ibid.)

Я оцéниваю твой прихóд (ibid.)

Из Елáбуги перенестѝ (567; Var.)

Finally, below are some examples from anapaestic poems in *Doctor Živago*:

Как раскѝнувшийся панорáмою (536)

Слéд подслу́шанного разговóра (ibid.)

Вéтви я́блоновые и вѝшенные (ibid.)

Лес забрáсывает как насмéшник (541)

И теря́ется в березнякé (542)

The third of the above examples, with its hyperdactylic rhyme, can be even seen as a line of *four*-footed anapaests, with two stresses left out.

The long poem "Devjat'sot pjatyj god" represents a somewhat special case. The short introduction to it is written in regular three-foot anapaests. In its seven quatrains we find two lines in which a stress is skipped:

Ты из су́мерек, социалѝстка (245; 1905)

Озарѝв нас и оледенѝв (ibid.)

In the remaining six sections, entitled "Otcy," "Detstvo," "Mužiki i fabričnye," "Morskoj mjatež," "Studenty," and "Moskva v dekabre," we have lines of different length grouped into strophes also of varying length (their length varies between nine and thirteen lines). But, as Mr. Vejdle (Weidlé) has rightly pointed out in his introductory article to the first volume of the Michigan edition of Pasternak's Collected Works, this narrative part of the poem is actually written in *five*-foot anapaests: each strophe—whether it be 9, 10, 11, 12, or 13 lines long—represents two quatrains of five-foot anapaests, with alternating feminine and masculine rhymes (although there are also many internal rhymes: the sound structure of this poem is highly intricate and would repay a close study in its own right).

If we approach the poem as a specimen of five-foot anapaests, disregarding its wayward graphic appearance, we shall see that there are in it twenty-nine lines in which a stress is omitted (there are also a number of extra stresses, especially on the first foot, but this is a problem we are not concerned with here). Here are those twenty-nine lines (the initials after the page number stand for the title of the section):

Эта ночь — Наше детство И молодость учителей (246; *O*)
Динамитчиков, Дагерротипов, Горенья души (*ibid.*)
Это — народовольцы, Перовская, Первое марта (247; *O*)
Да и ближе нельзя: Двадцатипятилетье — в подпольи (*ibid.*)
Клад — в земле. На земле — Обездушенный калейдоскоп (*ibid.*)
Средь мерцанья реторт Мы нашли бы, Что те лаборантши (248; *O*)
Наши матери Или Приятельницы матерей (*ibid.*)
Облетевшим листом И кладбищенским чертополохом (*ibid.*)
Подзовёт нас к окну. Мы одухотворим наугад (249; *O*)
Телеграфных сетей, Открывающихся с чердака (*ibid.*)
Точно Лаокоон Будет дым На трескучем морозе (*ibid.*)
Смотрят сумерки, Краски, Палитры, И профессора (250; *D*)
Сзади — лес, Впереди — Передаточная колея (252; *D*)
На Каменноостровском Стеченье народа повсюду (*ibid.*)
Ошибает На стуже Стоградусною нищетой (254-55; 1905: *MiF*)
Забастовка лишь шастает По мостовым городов (255; *MiF*)
Оголённый, Без качеств, И каменный, как никогда (256; *MiF*)
Взвыло: — Братцы! Да что ж это! — И волоса шевеля (260; *MM*)
Скрыли хлопья. Одёрнув Передники на животе (263; *S*)
Соревнуя студенчеству В первенстве и правоте (*ibid.*)
Пляшут книжные лавки, Манеж И университет (*ibid.*)
Эхом в ночь: «Третий курс! В реактивную, на перевязку!» (264; *S*)
Озарённая даль, Как на сыплющееся пшено (265; *MvD*)
И купается в просе, И просится На полотно (*ibid.*)
Солнце смотрит в бинокль И прислушивается К орудьям (*ibid.*)
Ночью, стужей трескучей, С винчестерами, вшестером (268; *MvD*)
И сдавала Смирителям Браунинги на простынях (270; *MvD*)
«Протестую. Долой». Двери вздрагивают, упрямясь 265; *S*)
В свете зарева Наспех У Прохорова на кухне (269; *MvD*)

In the last two examples, the omission of a stress is combined with syllable recession in the last foot. Out of the twenty-nine cases of omitted stresses, twenty-one are in the fourth foot, four in the third, three in the first, and only one in the second. The omitted stress in the first foot is often compensated by a hypermetrical stress on the first syllable.

FOUR-FOOT AMPHIBRACH

Разби́ться им не обо что́, и зано́сы

Пол я́ми по черезполо́сице, в по́езде

Поля́ми, по во́здуху, сквозь околёсицу

Присни́вшуюся небе́сному по́стнику

Всё вы́шиблено, ни еди́ного в це́лости

Как ко́локол на перекла́дине да́ли

Нет, косноязы́чный, гундо́сый и си́плый

Он на́ руку вы́валится из рассе́лины

Расска́льзывающуюся артилле́рию

All these nine lines are from one poem, "Durnoj son" (75–76; *NP*), and are the first example of Pasternak's extensive use of this rhythmic *xod*. The last line, with two consecutive stresses omitted—or weakened, if one prefers it that way—is almost unpronounceable without some secondary stresses. But there are other similar examples in Pasternak:

О, вольноотпу́щенница, е́сли вспо́мнится (83; *NP*)

О, вне́дренная! Хлопоча́ об амни́стии (*ibid.*)

В садо́вую и́згородь календаре́й (*ibid.*)

Of course, most people will find it natural to provide at least a secondary stress in such compound words as *čerezpolosice, kosnojazyčnyj,* and *vol'nootpuščennica.* But does Pasternak mean us to do so?

Following are more examples, mostly from poems of the early period:

> Все в крéстиках двéри, как в Варфоломéеву (85, *PB*)
>
> Нóчь Варфоломéева. Зá город, зá город! (86; *PB*)
>
> Сначáла все óпрометью, вразноря́д (95; *PB*)
>
> В полы́ни и мя́те и перепелáх (104; *PB*)
>
> С лицóм пучеглáзого свечегáса (105; *PB*)
>
> Покáзывался на опýшке пастýх (*ibid.*)
>
> И располагáлся росóй на поля́х (*ibid.*)
>
> Всю жи́знь удаля́ется, а не дли́тся (*ibid.*)

In the same fragment from which the last five lines are taken, there is also the following line, with further "irregularities": it has only two stresses but one syllable is dropped and we have seven consecutive unstressed syllables, instead of eight:

> Выпáрхивало на архипелáг (104; *PB*)

What is important, however, is that it is embedded in regular amphibrachic metre, and the lines preceding and following it read:

> Из пáрка спускáлось в оврáг, и впотьмáх
>
> Поля́н, утопáвших в лохмáтом тумáне

In the famous poem "Marburg" (107–109; *PB*) there are seven lines in which one stress is omitted, and one with two stresses missing. The missing stresses are either in the first or in the second foot; where two stresses are omitted, they are in the first and third feet. In one case (the fourth example below) there is also a syllable recession:

> Их взгля́дов. Я не замечáл их привéтствий
>
> Был невыноси́м мне. Он крáлся бок ó бок
>
> Чрез дéвственный, непроходи́мый тростни́к
>
> Не смáргивая, на крóвли. / А в Мáрбурге
>
> Кровоостанáвливающей áрники
>
> Шатáлся по гóроду и репети́ровал
>
> Вокзáльная сýтолока не про нáс
>
> И с кни́жкою на оттомáнке помéстится

In an earlier version of the poem there were fewer omissions of stresses, but we find in it two in the lines discarded later:

> Берёзы и прóчие окаменéлости (544; *RR*)
> Сверши́ть замечáтельнейшую экскýрсию (*ibid.*)

Here are further examples from different volumes:

> Толпóю тесня́щихся на полотнé (113; *SMŽ*)
> Как общелягýшечью э́ту икрý (149; *SMŽ*)
> И пéсня — как пéна, и — наперерéз (182; *TiV*)
> Впивáешься как в помутнéлый флакóн (197; *TiV*)
> Захлёбывающийся локомоти́в (215; *SRL*)
> Окрéстности взя́ты / на буферá (*ibid.*)

In the Živago poems there is a whole sequence of such lines in the magnificent poem about the Christmas star (554–556; *DŽ*):

> А ря́дом, невéдомая перед тéм
> Всё великолéпье цветнóй / мишуры́
> Все я́блоки, все золоты́е шары́
> Топтáлись погóнщики и овцевóды
> Ругáлись со всáдниками пешехóды
> У вы́долбленной водопóйной колóды

Not only do these lines break the customary monotony of the amphibrachic metre (traditionally used in Russian in balladic poems), but even within these deviations, Pasternak plays changes by omitting the stress now in the first, now in the second, now in the third foot.

There are also eight lines with omitted stresses in the poem "Čudo" (558–559; *DŽ*):

> Он шёл из Вифáнии в Ерусали́м
> Шёл в гóрод на сбóрище ученикóв
> Всё перемешáлось: теплы́нь и пусты́ня
> И я́щерицы, и ключи́ и ручьи́
> Смокóвница вы́силась невдалекé
> О кáк ты оби́дна и недарови́та
> Как мóлнии и́скра по громоотвóду
> Смокóвницу испепели́ло дотлá

Three-foot amphibrach

Pasternak's three-foot amphibrachs are particularly rich in metrical
deviations. This is equally true of the early poems, of wartime poems
and of *Kogda razguljaetsja*. In several poems there is an accumulation
of lines with omitted stresses:

Чтоб под буфера́ не попа́л (70; *NP*)

И ви́деть, как в единобо́рстве (84; *PB*)

Столи́ственное торжество́ (91; *PB*)

Там заштемпелёван тепло́м (*ibid.*)

Бушу́ющего обожа́нья (*ibid.*)

Моля́щихся / вышине́ (*ibid.*)

Безво́згласно великоле́пье (92; *PB*)

Милиционе́ром зажа́т (124; *SMZ*)

Трепе́щущего серебра́ (*ibid.*)

Пронзи́тельная / горо́шина (*ibid.*)

Уто́пленникам и седы́м (162; *TiV*)

С невы́дохшимися духа́ми (197; *TiV*)

Осы́павшихся папиро́с (*ibid.*)

Заде́рживается по зна́ку (203; *SRL*)

Выве́шивает свой би́сер (*ibid.*)

Пятни́стые / пятаки́ (*ibid.*)

И не попада́ет зуб на́ зуб (*ibid.*)

Железнодоро́жная на́сыпь (*ibid.*)

Как пло́шкою иллюмино́ван (*ibid.*)

Исто́рию как стеари́н (*ibid.*)

Отстро́ившейся красоты́ (210; *SRL*)

Examples 14–20 above are all from one and the same poem, and four
of them represent the concluding line of a stanza. There are also
eleven such lines, all in one poem ("K Oktjabr'skoj godovščine: 1,"
228–229, *SRL*), which is thirty-two lines long:

> Растя́гивались эшело́ны
> Бессро́чно и тысячевёрстно
> Их вы́рвавшееся упо́рство
> Их дви́гало на города́
> Что тре́бовали полномо́чий
> В их а́вгустовское убра́нство
> Могло́ ли им вообрази́ться
> Что по́д боком, невдалеке́
> Окли́кнутые / с пози́ций
> Ни в сто́йке их сторожево́й
> Не чу́вствовалось ничего́

Taken in themselves, those lines in which the omission of stress is in the second foot are, of course, identical with those in iambic tetrameter in which the second and the third stresses are omitted (this is described by Andrej Belyj, and those who adopted his approach, as a combination of the second paeon with the fourth). But if we consider the line as the real unit of the verse (as does Professor Unbegaun in his *Russian Versification*), the essential point here is that those lines occur within a regular amphibrachic pattern. The general amphibrachic cadence of the poem cannot be questioned: the omission of stresses just gives it rhythmical spice and variety.[9]

In *Vtoroe roždenie*, the following ten lines, all from one poem, are the only example of a lavish and consistent use of omission of stresses. The poem (373–75) recalls the death of M. Blumenfeld, a musician and a relative of Heinrich Nejgauz (Neuhaus), Mme. Pasternak's first husband:

> Ую́та и авторите́та
> И консервато́рский порта́л
> Кати́вшийся из-за полми́ра
> Укра́шенная орга́ном
> И освобожда́ясь от брёвен
> Но пу́щенный из заточе́нья
> Воспо́льзовавшись темното́й
> Напра́вилась на кремато́рий
> Как на рубежа́х у Варша́вы
> Озя́бнувшие москвичи́

There are also many examples to be gleaned from Pasternak's late poetry, from *Na rannix poezdax* and from *Kogda razguljaetsja*. Here they are:

Расстра́иваться не на́до (399; *NRP*)

Всё обледене́ло с разма́ху (400; *NRP*)

И кра́дущейся росома́хой (*ibid.*)

Подсма́триваем с ветве́й (*ibid.*)

Торже́ственное зати́шье (*ibid.*)

Опра́вленное в резьбу́ (*ibid.*)

Похо́же на четверости́шье (*ibid.*)

В прови́нции или дере́вне (414; *NRP*)

И бе́лая как рукоде́лье (415; *NRP*)

Бле́ск за́морозков оловя́нный (*ibid.*)

Чайко́вского и Левита́на (*ibid.*)

Геро́ев и богатыре́й (456; *KB*)

Средь круговраще́нья земно́го (457; *KR*)

С действи́тельностью иллю́зию (461; *KR*)

Им ми́лости возвещены́ (*ibid.*)

Разва́линами старины́ (*ibid.*)

Сходя́щейся над голово́й (*ibid.*)

И бу́дущего красоту́ (462; *KR*)

Осы́павшихся крепосте́й (*ibid.*)

Нас не принима́л в сыновья́ (464: *KR*)

Просла́вленный не по програ́мме (*ibid.*)

Он не изгото́влен рука́ми (*ibid.*)

Загля́дываться недосу́г (465; *KR*)

В дере́вне или на селе́ (466; *KR*)

Пока́чивалась фельдшери́ца (467; *KR*)

Стоя́ли как перед витри́ной (*ibid.*)

Со скля́нкою нашатыря́ (*ibid.*)

Присма́тривался новичо́к (468; *KR*)

Пока́чивавшей головой (*ibid.*)

Он по́нял, что из переде́лки (*ibid.*)

Из го́рода озарена́ (*ibid.*)

Чуть па́дающем на крова́ть (*ibid.*)

The last eight lines come from the poem "V bol'nice," which, prior to the 1965 edition, had not been printed in the Soviet Union. There is a recording of it in Pasternak's own reading, and his reading quite clearly and convincingly confirms that he means us to treat the unstressed syllables as unstressed, avoiding, if possible, even secondary stresses.

In the Živago poems we find only two three-foot amphibrachs with omitted stresses, both of them in the poem "Durnye dni" (560–561). In the first example, the word "Ierusalim" should be read as a *five*-syllable word, as distinct from "Erusalim" in the poem "Čudo" (see above, p. 240); Pasternak himself took care to indicate this by the spelling:

Входи́л он в Иерусали́м
Загля́дывала из воро́т

Were we to add to these examples from Pasternak's original poetry similar ones from his translations, the total number of lines with omitted stresses would be greatly increased. For instance, in Pasternak's translation of the famous Georgian poem "Zmeeed" (The Snake-Eater) by Važa Pšavela (pseudonym of Luka Razikašvili, 1861–1915), which he did in three-foot amphibrachs, there are ninety-six lines in which a stress is omitted.[10]

The very fact that Pasternak chose this medium for translating the poem is significant: a later translation of it by Zabolockij was done in iambic metre. There are many omitted stresses in ternary metres in Pasternak's translations of other Georgian poets, such as Tabidze, Leonidze, Baratašvili, Jašvili, and others.[11] There seems to be no doubt that Pasternak should be regarded as an outstanding renovator of Russian ternary verse, even though more examples of omission of stresses than is usually suspected can be found in other poets, too.

University of California, Berkeley

NOTES

1. B. O. Unbegaun, *Russian Versification* (Oxford: The Clarendon Press, 1956), p. 46.
2. *Ibid.*, pp. 50–51.
3. *Ibid.*, p. 51. Here are the examples:

Nekrasov:

Где с полугосуда́рства дохо́ды
Cvetaeva:

За непринуждённый покло́н
Разжа́лованный — Никола́ем,
Пожа́лованный бы — Петром.
Xodasevic:

Желтосе́рого, полуседо́го
И всезна́ющего как змея́?

4. *Ibid.*, p. 53.
5. *Ibid.* Prof. Unbegaun quotes only twelve lines, taken out of the middle of the poem. Actually, in the remaining thirty-two lines there are six more omissions of the first stress. Here are the six lines:

У оловя́нной реки́

Где разбежа́лся ковы́ль

С остановившимся взгля́дом

Но озорно́й, озорно́й

Над потрясённой столи́цей

Обороня́ющей львя́т

Out of the eleven stanzas of the poem, only three are without an omitted stress.
6. According to a preliminary estimate, based on the three volumes of Gumilev's *Collected Works*, edited by Boris Filippov and the present writer, there are in Gumilev forty-six dactylic lines with omitted syllables, seventeen anapaestic (all three-footed), and only one amphibrachic.
7. The following abbreviations are used henceforth to designate these volumes or sections: *NP—Načal'-naja pora* (1912–1914); *PB—Poverx bar'erov* (1914–1916); *SMŽ—Sestra moja žizn'* (1917); *TiV—Temy i variacii* (1916–1922); *SRL—Stixi raznyx let* (1918–1931); *1905—Devjat'sot pjatyj god* (1925–26); *VR—Vtoroe roždenie* (1930–31); *NRP—Na rannix poezdax* (1936–1944); *KR—Kogda razguljaetsja* (1956–59); *DŽ—Doctor Živago* (1946–1953); *Var*—those poems which in the Soviet *odnotomnik* are printed under the heading "Stixotvorenija, ne vošedšie v osnovnoe sobranie"; *RR*—early variants.
8. It will be seen from these examples, as well as from some of the earlier and later ones, what an important part in such lines is played by participles, especially reflexive ones (and other forms of reflexive verbs), the prerequisite being a combination of long and fairly long words.
9. In Part Two of the same poem (229–30) there are seven lines in ternary metres with omitted stresses (some of them also with recession of syllables), but I have disregarded them as a somewhat special case because the poem itself is polymetric.
10. See Važa Pšavela, *Sočinenija v dvux tomax*. Perevod s gruzinskogo. Tom vtoroj: Poèmy (Moscow, 1958), pp. 267–97.
11. See *Antologija gruzinskoj poèzii* (Moscow, 1958), *passim*.

Some Problems of Belorussian Vocabulary

V. SWOBODA

BELORUSSIAN VOCABULARY contains much that has not yet been investigated from the etymological and historical points of view; this applies particularly to those words that have no near cognates in the neighboring Slavic languages. The aim of these notes is to examine some of these words, chiefly nouns, and to consider certain etymological problems which they offer.

Ljámec 'felt, felting; matted hair; felt horse-collar pad'; *ljámcavy* 'of felt'; *ljamcaváty* 'matted'; *ljamcowka* 'felt hat'; *ljámčyc'*, *ljámčycca* 'to felt, mat together,' pfve *zljámčyc'*, etc.; *zljamcowvacca* 'to felt'; *zljamcowvanne* 'felting';[1] U (H.)[2] *ljámec'* 'felt' (Poltava); *ljámci, ljamcevi čoboty* 'felt boots' (Volynia); *ljámčytysja* 'to mat (of hair)' [Hajsyn] (none of these U examples are in *URS*); R (D.) *ljámec*, (South) *ljámcy* 'felt horse-collar pad'; P dial. (<BR) (K.) *lamiec 'idem*; matted hair.' V. derives R, BR *ljámec*, U *ljámec'*, all in the meaning 'felt horse-collar pad,' from P *lemiec*, Old Cz *lémec*, Cz *límec* 'collar.' Yet it may be better to separate the group with the root meaning 'felt' from the one with the meaning 'hem, edging, border'; this latter group, apart from the three last quoted words, is also represented by Cz *lem* 'hem, edging,' *lemovati* 'to hem,' *lemovka* 'hemming, ribbon,' P *lamować*, *lamówka*, BR *ljamavác'*, *abljamowvac'*, *(ab)ljamowka*, *ljamavánne*, *abljamowvanne*, U *ljamuváty*, *(ob)ljamívka*, all with analogous meanings. The two groups may seem to have a semantic link in Old Cz *lémec*, etc. 'collar,' and BR, R *ljámec* 'horse-collar pad,' but it is rather tenuous. What is more, both in WR and in U the two groups are well defined and self-contained but apparently have no links between them. Thus, the movement of the "hem" group suggests itself in the direction Cz > P > BR, U, with the word for "collar" (semantically < "hem") not going beyond P. The "felt" group, on the other hand, is strongest in

245

BR, less so in U, and marginal in R; it would seem that it originated, as far as the Slavic ground goes, in the BR area.

Adlíha, adléha 'thaw,' U *vidlýha,* Ž. *vídliž 'idem'.* J. Rudnyc'kyj[3] quotes also *vidléha* and connects the U word with the root *-l'g-* (as in U *píl'ha,* R *l'góta* 'easement,' *nel'zjá,* BR *nél'ha* 'must not'). Should it not be associated with the root *liti* 'to pour'? Cf. BR *ablìváxa* 'glazed frost, slippery ice,' *ablivácca, ablícca* 'to become covered with ice.'

Snowdacca, snowdac' 'to ramble about' is obviously ultimately connected with *snovati* (S.), cf. BR *snavác'* 'to weave; to roam about,' R *snovát',* U (*URS*) *snuvaty 'idem.'* The *-d-* form must be related to U (H.) *snovydáty* 'to ramble about,' itself a doublet of *snovygáty 'idem'* (apparently also *snovyháty*: H.). The *-g-* (*-yg-*) infix is a typical emotionally charged formative element. (It has often been noted that interjections, pejorative and other emotionally charged words frequently stand outside the phonological system of a language. Cz, for instance, is another language with *h* < Common Slavic *g* which uses *g* in words of this type.[4]) Again, it would seem that, once created, a *g*-form in U is liable to decay either in the direction of its usual fricative counterpart, *h,* or of another voiced plosive, *d.* This latter change must have been facilitated by popular etymology in *snovýga/ snovýha* 'one who rambles about' > *snovýda* 'sleep-walker' (*URS*; H.: Loxvycja), also *snovýdnyj 'idem'* (H.: *ibid.*) (cf. R [D.] *snobród* 'sleep-walker,' *snovídec* 'one who has had a dream, who dreams often,' U [*URS*] *snovýdec',* P *snowidz 'idem'*). The meaning 'to somnambulate' has not reached the verbs discussed, though Ž. interprets *snovydáty/snovygáty* as 'to wander about like a sleep-walker.'

Mjantáška 'emery hone for scythes,' *mjancíc'* 'to whet a scythe' (with a *mjantaška*), U *mantáčka* 'hone for scythes (piece of wood covered with pitch and sand),' *mantáčyty* 'to whet a scythe.' This group seems to have no relatives in the neighboring languages; borrowing from Turkic may be suspected (cf. Turkish *taş* 'stone,' *bileğitaşı* 'hone,' *mehénk* 'touchstone' > Daco-Rumanian *meng;*[5] or Arabic *minğal* 'sickle, butcher's knife'[6]).

Vadýr 'blister,' obviously connected with *vadá* 'water'; cf. P *wodunka* 'blister.' Perhaps R *voldýr' 'idem'* which V. had to leave as 'unclear' may be explained from the BR form contaminated with R (cf. V.) *buldýr'.*

Harapášny 'wretched, miserable,' *harapášnik* 'poor wretch,' U *horopášnyj, horopáxa* resp. *'idem,'* Ž also *horopášnyk* 'greedy person,' *horopášlyvyj, horopášnyj* 'miserable; greedy,' P dial. (K.) *harapasznik, horopasznik* 'person working painfully and awkwardly; simpleton.' In P < BR; also obviously in U < BR, since an independent U form would have had *hore-* as in, say, *horezvísnyj* 'notorious' (*URS*) or *horécvit* 'helleborus niger' (H.). The formation is with two suffixes, *-pa-* + *-xa* (assuming [an earlier?] BR **harapáxa*), both of them emotionally charged and occurring separately, but hardly ever used together elsewhere in the formation of one word. (Cf. R [D.] *začupáxa* 'untidy, dirty person.')

Skljud 'adze,' *skljudaváć* 'to adze,' *skljudavánne* 'adzing'; Lithuanian *skliùtas* 'adze,' *skliutúoti* 'to adze,' P dial. (K.) *schlud, sklut,* U *skljut* (Kobryn) 'adze.'[7] This is one of the words originating in Lithuanian and spreading in BR, as well as to a greater or lesser extent in the other languages of the old Grand Duchy of Lithuania.

Prýmxi 'superstitions, omens,' *prýmxlivy* 'superstitious'; U *prýmxa* 'whim, caprice,' H. also 'superstition, omen' (Lubny); *prymxlývyj* 'whimsical, capricious,' H. also *prýmxlyvyj, prymxuvátyj*; *prýmxaty* 'to be capricious'; *prymxlývist'* 'capriciousness, whimsicality' (*URS*). This is an example of an original Slavic word common to BR and U alone; the $x < s$ (if the root is related to that of *mysl'*) is a testimony of antiquity; cf. S. *primyšlenije* 'artfulness, cunning, contrivance, wile.'

There are very many other exclusively BR words whose origins are still to be clarified, e.g., *abzá* 'edge of a board' (hardly connected with P dial. [K.] *obza* 'tether'), but they fall beyond the scope of this brief note.

University of London

NOTES

1. The source of Belorussian vocabulary is K. Krapiva (ed.), *Belaruska-ruski slownik* (Moscow, 1962). Stress over *o* is not indicated. (I. Nosovič's *Slovar'* unfortunately remained inaccessible.)

2. Abbreviations: BR—Belorussian; Cz—Czech; P—Polish; R—Russian; U—Ukrainian. D.—V. Dal', *Tolko-vyj slovar' živogo velikorusskogo jazyka* (St. Petersburg-Moscow, 1880); H.—B. Hrinčenko, *Slovar ukrajins'koji movy* (Kiev, 1907–1909); K.—J. Karłowicz, *Słownik gwar polskich* (Kraków, 1900–1907); S.—I. Sreznevskij, *Materialy dlja slovarja drevnerusskogo jazyka* (St. Petersburg, 1893–1903); *URS—Ukrajins'ko-rosijs'kyj slovnyk* (Kiev, 1953–1963); V.—M. Vasmer, *Russisches etymologisches Wörterbuch* (Heidelberg, 1950–1958); Ž.—Je. Želexovs'kyj, *Malorus'konimec'kyj slovar* (L'viv, 1886).

3. *An Etymological Dictionary of the Ukrainian Language*, Part 5 (Winnipeg, 1966), p. 415.

4. V. Machek, "O hlásce *š* v slovan-štině," *Charisteria Guilelmo Mathesio quinquagenario a discipulis et Circuli linguistici Pragensis sodalibus oblata* (Prague, 1932), pp. 42–44.

5. F. Miklosich, "Die türkischen Elemente in den südost- und ost-

europäischen Sprachen," *Denk-
schriften der k. Akademie der Wissenschaften, philosophisch-historische
Klasse*, XXXV (Vienna, 1884), 125.
6. K. Lokotsch, *Etymologisches Wörterbuch der europäischen . . . Wörter*

orientalischen Ursprungs (Heidelberg, 1927), p. 118.
7. Professor O. Horbatsch was kind
enough to draw my attention to
the existence of this word in the
area of Kobryn.

Certain Aspects of Blok's Symbolism

KIRIL TARANOVSKY

In the poem composed in 1902 and entitled *Religio*, Blok wrote:

Любил я нежные слова,
Искал таинственных соцветий.

Color symbolism, and visual images in general, were indeed a fundamental feature of the poetic model of the world created by him. But Blok not only sought mysterious correspondences in color; he also gave ear to the mysterious sound correspondences of the surrounding world. This is what he wrote in 1919 in the foreword to his long poem *Vozmezdie*: "Ja privyk sopostavljat' fakty iz vsex oblastej žizni, dostupnyx moemu zreniju v dannoe vremja, i uveren, čto vse oni vmeste sozdajut edinyj muzykal'nyj napor." The musical sense of phenomena is expressed in Blok's poetry both by means of recurrent images, which act in his lyrical cycles and long poems as musical leitmotifs, and through the sound texture and rhythmical diversity of his verse. In his poetry, the rhythm and the sound often carry quite definite information, which is usually perceived by the reader synaesthetically, beyond the cognitive level.

Contemporary literary scholars have asserted on numerous occasions that Blok gradually evolved in his poetic practice from symbolism to realism. It seems to me that this assertion is based on a misunderstanding. There were changes in the subject matter of his poetry, some poetic images were replaced by others, but none of the images of his poetry, whether early or late, ever lost its symbolic value. Of all Russian Symbolists, Blok is, perhaps, the most consistent in his symbolism.

The poetic images of Blok are not to be interpreted as simple reflections of real objects, or as ordinary metaphors and metonymies

which are merely endowed with some abstract sense. His images always
retain both the concrete and the abstract meaning, i.e., are symbols.
The pale-blue vistas, the rosy horizons, and the white church over the
river in his early poetry, and the yellow St. Petersburg sunset, the
violet dusk ("lilovyj sumrak"), the night, the street, the lamp-post, and
the pharmacy of his later poems equally resist interpretation at a single
level of meaning, being charged as they are, with complex, polysemous
information.

The central image of Blok's early lyrics (1901–1902), the image of the
Beautiful Lady (*Prekrasnaja Dama*), appears, at times, to incorporate
the actual features of the poet's future bride and wife, Ljubov' Men-
deleeva, but much more often it is a sublime symbol of the Eternal
Feminine (*das ewig Weibliche* of German Romanticists), or of the Platon-
ic ideal of eternal beauty. Under the influence of the philosophy and
poetry of Vladimir Solov'ev, this image is identified also with the image
of Sophia, the Divine Wisdom. At the same time, certain attributes of
the Holy Virgin are bestowed upon it: "Ty v polja otošla bez vozvrata,
/ Da svjatitsja imja Tvoe," exclaims the poet in the ecstasy of prayer.
On one occasion, it even becomes the Russian Venus (*Rossijskaja Ve-
nera*), the precursor of the feminine image of Russia in Blok's later
poetry.

The very name of the Beautiful Lady—*Prekrasnaja Dama*—contains
in stressed syllables, two compact *a*-sounds. The distinctive feature of
compactness is usually associated with emotions of vastness, completeness, greatness, balance, strength, and power. All these, and similar
emotions may be characterized by the concept of *stability*.[1] It is no
wonder, therefore, that in some poems dealing with the theme of the
Beautiful Lady, stressed *a* dominates already in the first line: Oná
molodá i prekrásna bylá.../ Oná roslá za dál'nimi gorámi.../ Oná
strojná i vysoká.../ Ty v poljá otošlá bez vozvráta. ...

The worship of the Eternal Feminine would remain a major theme
of Blok's poetry. When the image of the Beautiful Lady was eventually
replaced by that of the Incognita (*Neznakomka*), the Fallen Star, her
appearance would nevertheless evoke in the poet the same feeling of
greatness (note nine stressed *a*'s in the following stanza):

> И медленно пройдя меж пьяными,
> Всегда без спутников, одна,
> Дыша духами и туманами,
> Она садится у окна.

The alluring rosy and pale-blue vistas, the road receding in the
distance, the scarlet dawn, all this landscape of Blok's early poetry

creates an impression of an illusory world of "visions and dreams."
Nevertheless, it is not difficult to distinguish in it the actual landscape
of Šaxmatovo, the country estate of Blok's maternal grandfather, in
which the poet met his future bride:

> Я, отрок, зажигаю свечи,
> Огонь кадильный берегу.
> Она без мысли и без речи
> На том смеется берегу.
>
> Люблю вечернее моленье
> У белой церкви над рекой,
> Передзакатное селенье
> И сумрак мутно-голубой.
>
> Покорный ласковому взгляду,
> Любуюсь тайной красоты,
> И за церковную ограду
> Бросаю белые цветы.
>
> Падет туманная завеса.
> Жених сойдет из алтаря.
> И от вершин зубчатых леса
> Забрезжит брачная заря.

In this poem everything is real, and everything is symbolic. According to Brjusov's observation, for example, the river is not merely a
river, but also a symbol of the boundary separating the poet from his
ideal.[2] The imagery of the last stanza is based on the familiar symbolism of the New Testament (Christ, the Bridegroom; Christ's Church,
His Bride), which goes back to the "nuptial character of the nexus
between Yahweh and Israel, the Choosing God and the Chosen
People."[3] However, this symbolism is already revealed in the epigraph
to the poem, from St. John (III, 29): "He that hath the Bride is the
Bridegroom: but the Friend of the Bridegroom, which standeth and
heareth Him, rejoiceth because of the Bridegroom's voice." Thus, the
youth who lights the candles and cherishes the fire in the censer is
identified with St. John the Baptist, who prepares "the way for spiritual marriage of the Messiah with Israel."[4] The mystical expectation of
the "nuptial dawn" reflects also the idea of the "Third Testament,"
the highest, more spiritual life of mankind on Earth, which was such a
prominent topic of Religio-Philosophical Meetings even as early as
November, 1901. On December 13, 1910, Blok wrote in his article
Rycar'-monax, dedicated to the memory of Vladimir Solov'ev: "Te iz
nas, kogo ne smyla i ne iskalečila strašnaja volna istekšego desjatiletija,

—s polnym pravom i s jasnoj nadeždoj ždut novogo sveta ot novogo veka." And further: "Naši duši—pričastry Mirovoj. Segodnja mnogie iz nas prebyvajut v ustalosti i samoubijstvennom otčajanii; novyj mir uže stoit pri dverjax..."

It will be recalled that in 1905 Blok wrote:

> Мы все, как дети, слепнем от света,
> И сердце встало в избытке счастья,
> О нет, не темница наша планета:
> Она, как солнце, горит от страсти!
>
> И Дева-Свобода в дали несказанной
> Открылась всем — не одним пророкам!

The theme of revolution, however, is already present in the cycle *Stixi o Prekrasnoj Dame*, in the poem dated July 4, 1901:

> Предчувствую Тебя. Года проходят мимо —
> Все в облике одном предчувствую Тебя.
> Весь горизонт в огне — и ясен нестерпимо,
> И молча жду, — тоскуя и любя.
>
> Весь горизонт в огне, и близко появленье,
> Но страшно мне: изменишь облик Ты ...

It was probably this stanza that Blok's father had in mind when he said: "Vy ne ponimaete: Prekrasnaja Dama—èto revoljucija."[5] In 1910, in the article *O sovremennom sostojanii russkogo simvolizma*, written already after the death of his father, Blok provided his own commentary to the lines quoted above: My perežili bezumie inyx mirov, preždevremenno potrebovav čuda: to že proizošlo i s narodnoj dušoj: ona prežde sroka potrebovala čuda, i ee ispepelili lilovye miry revoljucii ... O narodnoj duše i o našej, vmeste s nej ispepelennoj, nado skazat' prostym i mužestvennym golosom: «Da voskresnet». Možet byt', my sami i pogibnem, no ostanetsja zarja toj *pervoj* ljubvi."

In Blok's later poetry, the entire model of his poetic world undergoes radical changes. The landscape of the Russian countryside is replaced by a vision of the "Northern Venice," the spectral city of Peter the Great, hymned by Puškin, Gogol', and Dostoevskij. The color symbolism of Blok's poetry changes, too:

> В эти желтые дни меж домами
> Мы встречаемся только на миг.
> Ты меня обжигаешь глазами
> И скрываешься в темный тупик ...
>
> (October 6, 1909)

> В черных сучьях дерев обнаженных
> Желтый зимний закат за окном.
> (К эшафоту на казнь обреченных
> Поведут на закате таком ...)
> (December 6, 1911)

It should be noted, however, that as early as 1904 Blok wrote:

> Фиолетовый запад гнетет,
> Как пожатье десницы свинцовой.

After 1904, all of Blok's colors become increasingly dark. The lighter shades of blue (*goluboj* and *lazurnyj*) and red (*rozovyj*) gradually vanish. While in the first volume the color azure formed 9.6 per cent of the total range of hues (in *Stixi o Prekrasnoj Dame* alone, its percentage reaches 13.3), after 1904 its share becomes quite negligible. The frequency of occurrence of the color black increases in subsequent volumes, but the percentage share of white remains relatively stable, somewhat diminishing only in the third volume.[6] This is understandable: the symbolic value of the color white has changed. It is no longer the color of the flowers the poet used to cast over the church fence; it is the color of death (*belaja smert'*, *belyj savan*) and the snowstorm, the blizzard, in which the black masks are whirling. The symbol of the blizzard, a polysemous symbol, occupies the central position in the lyrics written by Blok in 1907–1908. As a leitmotif, it runs through his long poem *Vozmezdie* and gains full motivation in *Dvenadcat'*.

Another significant symbol of Blok's poetry of the 1910's is the image of the imminent nightfall. The following poem, written on October 10, 1912, is characteristic of that period. It is taken from the cycle entitled *Pljaski smerti*.

> Ночь, улица, фонарь, аптека,
> Бессмысленный и тусклый свет.
> Живи еще хоть четверть века —
> Все будет так. Исхода нет.
>
> Умрешь — начнешь опять сначала,
> И повторится все, как встарь:
> Ночь, ледяная рябь канала,
> Аптека, улица, фонарь.

While the first stanza of this poem can be understood as a realistic description of a city at night, in the second stanza all the objects mentioned before acquire a symbolic meaning. On October 14, Blok read this poem to Vasilij Hippius. "I was struck by the gloomy irony of the poem," wrote Hippius. "This pharmacy, which at first sight may appear accidental in the series of night, street, and lamp, immediately impressed me as a remarkable poetic achievement. I said so to Blok, and added half in jest that the poem would remain especially memorable to me because there was a pharmacy near our house, too. But Blok somehow became very serious and said: "There is a pharmacy near every house.""[7] More than thirty years later, Axmatova began one of her poems with the following lines:

> Он прав — опять фонарь, аптека,
> Нева, безмолвие, гранит.

On February 27, 1914, Blok wrote his gloomiest poem, *Golos iz xora*:

> Как часто плачем — вы и я —
> Над жалкой жизнию своей!
> О, если б знали вы, друзья,
> Холод и мрак грядущих дней!

The third stanza of the poem leaves a definite impression that the poet deals here with the death of the Universe, as the material level of the imagery is a cosmic one:

> Все будет чернее страшный свет,
> И все безумней вихрь планет
> *Еще века, века!*

In the fourth stanza, however, the image of the Last Age is suddenly presented at a different angle. It appears that "both you and I will see" this age, that the metaphoric level of this symbol signifies a concrete historical instant—the nearest future. Thus, we have here a twofold time gauge, as it were:

> И век последний, ужасней всех,
> *Увидим и вы и я.*
> Все небо скроет гнусный грех,
> На всех устах застынет смех,
> Тоска небытия.

The image of the Sun which "is never to return from the approaching dark" already occurred in Blok's lyrics of 1902 ("Sny bezotčetny, jarki kraski"). But the sunset was not yet tinted with the apocalyptic terror: it signified reconciliation with the "calm coldness of the pale stars." In *Golos iz xora*, this theme rings quite differently:

> Весны, дитя, ты будешь ждать —
> Весна обманет.
> Ты будешь солнце на небо звать —
> Солнце не встанет.
> И крик, когда ты начнешь кричать,
> Как камень канет.[8]

In Blok's earlier poetry, the motif of despair never sounded so distinctly.

The sound texture of Blok's later poetry undergoes changes together with the color imagery. Notably, there is a frequent occurrence of the assonances with diffuse *u*, *y*, and *i*. It will be recalled that diffuseness is synaesthetically associated with incompleteness, loss of inner balance, weakness, and even distress, i.e., with the emotions which may be summed up by the common term *instability*.

> И вот уже ветром *разбиты, убиты*
> *Кусты* облетелой *ракиты.*
> И прахом дорожным
> *Угрюмая* старость легла на *ланитах,*
> Но в темных *орбитах*
> *Взглянули, сверкнули* глаза невозможным ...
>
> И *снится*, и *снится*, и *снится*:
> Бывалое солнце!
>
> (October 3, 1907)

In the first poem of the lyrical cycle *Na pole Kulikovom*, dated 1908, the image of the galloping mare of the steppe symbolizes the unbridled elements;[9] the frightened clouds that are drawing nearer are a symbol of the approaching catastrophe. In order better to understand these images, one should bear in mind the apocalyptic mood of certain circles of the Russian intelligentsia following the Russo-Japanese war and the revolution of 1905. There is nothing surprising in the fact that both the images just mentioned involve assonances with diffuse vowels. In the following two stanzas, in the rhymes, i.e., in especially conspicuous positions, all the stressed vowels are diffuse:

> И вечный бой! Покой нам только *снится*
> Сквозь кровь и *пыль* ...
> *Летит, летит* степная *кобылица*
> И мнет *ковыль* ...

И нет конца! Мелькают версты, *кру́чи* ...
    Останови́!
Иду́т, иду́т испу́ганные ту́чи
    Закат в *крови́!*

All the diffuse vowels are concentrated in the next to the last line of this fragment: four stressed *u*'s are supported by five unstressed *i*'s and one *y*.

On January 3, 1918, Blok wrote in his notebook: "*K večeru—uragan (neizmennyj sputnik perevorotov)*." Under January 7 and 8 there are two laconic entries: "*Vie de Jésus*" and "*Ves' den'—Dvenadcat*." The wind is mentioned also in the entries dated January 13 and 14: "*Bušuet veter (opjat' ciklon?)*." On January 28, the draft of *Dvenadcat'* was ready. The wind, in its black-and-white setting, was the opening theme of the poem:

Черный вечер,
Белый снег.
Ветер, ветер!
На ногах не стоит человек.
Ветер, ветер —
На всем божьем свете.

After the Second World War, Pasternak would recall this wind:

Тот ветер повсюду. Он — дома,
В деревьях, в деревне, в дожде,
В поэзии третьего тома,
В «Двенадцати», в смерти, везде.

In Blok's diary, under January 7, there is another notable, and very seldom mentioned, entry. We shall quote it in part: "Durak Simon s otvissej guboj udit . . . Vxodit Iisus (ne mužčina, ne ženščina). Grešnyj Iisus. Andrej (Pervozvannyj)—slonjaetsja (ne siditsja na meste): byl v Rossii (iskal neobyknovennogo). Apostoly vorovali dlja Iisusa (višni, pšenicu). Ix stydili . . . Tut že prostitutki." And in the middle of this plan: "*Čitat' Renana*." For Blok, Jesus Christ was, first and foremost, the "Son of Man."

The analogy between these fragments and the atmosphere of *Dvenadcat'* is self-evident. In January, 1918, Blok's creative imagination obviously worked on two projects: to destroy the old myth and to found a new one. The fact that the Red Guards of *Dvenadcat'* bear symbolic names—Andrjuxa and Petruxa—is beyond doubt. The murderer received the name of the only apostle who "drew the sword." The fragment from Blok's diary quoted above explains why the name of another Red Guard is Andrej.

Kornej Čukovskij affirmed that Blok started to write the poem from the middle, from the words "Už ja nožičkom polosnu, polosnu," because, as Blok said himself, he found those two ž-sounds highly expressive. Evidently, Blok felt that the distinctive feature of stridency, with its characteristic *Schneidenton*, corresponded very well to the theme of the knife. Accordingly, Blok saturated the whole fragment with strident consonants—*ž*, *š*, *č*, *šč*, *s*, and *z*—combining these with stressed *o* and *u*. The dark *o*, and dark and diffuse *u* emphasize the gloomy mood of the fragment.

> Ох ты, горе-горькое,
>   Скука скучная,
>   Смертная!
> Уж я времячко
>   Проведу, проведу.
> Уж я темячко
>   Почешу, почешу ...
> Уж я семячки
>   Полущу, полущу.
> Уж я ножичком
>   Полосну, полосну! ...
> Ты лети, буржуй, воробышком.
>   Выпью кровушку
>   За зазнобушку,
>   Чернобровушку.

This dissolute song, based on folklore elements, passes into a dirge: "Upokoj, gospodi, dušu raby svoeja," and merges with it, as it were. The short last line of the fragment—"Skučno"—completes its circular composition.

As early as December, 1908, in the article *Stixija i kul'tura*, Blok juxtaposed religious verses of Russian sectarians, who won over "the hearts of the lost by mellifluous singing": "Ty ljubov', ty ljubov'/ Ty ljubov' svjataja,/ Ot načala ty gonima,/ Krov'ju politaja," with the *častuški* "of the Orthodox people, lulled to sleep by the state monopoly vodka, with vodka in church cellars, with drunken priests": "U nas nožiki litye,/ Giri kovanye,/ My rebjata xolostye,/ Praktikovan-nye...// Pust' nas žarjat i kaljat,/ Razmazurikov-rebjat—// My načal'-stva ne uvažim,/ Lučše sjadem v kazemat.../ Ax ty, knižka-skladenec,/ V katorgu dorožka,/ Postradaet molodec/ Za tebja nemnožko..."

It is easy to recognize in the first of these *častuški* (which Blok received from Kljuev) the prototype of Blok's "nožiček." But this is of minor importance. Much more significant is what Blok had to say about the blending of these two songs: "V dni približenija grozy slivajutsja obe èti pesni: jasno do užasa, čto te, kto poet pro 'litye nožiki,' i te, kto poet pro 'svjatuju ljubov',—*ne prodadut drug druga*, potomu čto—stixija s nimi, oni—deti odnoj grozy. ..." Ever since 1905 Blok did not cease listening to the "music of revolution."

The color imagery of *Dvenadcat'* is rather simple. The prevailing color is black. It either appears simply as a color spot (black rifle slings, black moustache, "zaznobuška-černobrovuška"), or acquires a symbolic meaning: black evening; black, black sky; black anger—holy anger. The red color is the second most frequent. It is used twice metaphorically (Red Guard), and three times in the revolutionary symbol of the red flag. At the end of the poem, the red flag becomes blood-tinted, i.e., assumes a new quality. However, there is also another red spot in the poem, which reveals a different symbolic aspect of the red hue: it is the "ace of diamonds," "*bubnovyj tuz*," the mark of penal servitude, which the twelve apostles of revolution should be wearing. Here belongs also a naturalistic detail, Kat'ka's crimson birthmark, "puncovaja rodinka vozle pravogo pleča," which so fatally affected Petruxa that he killed her. The gray gaiters of Kat'ka provide another realistic detail. The golden color occurs in the poem only once, in an ironic context: "Ot čego tebja upas/ Zolotoj ikonostas?" The entire poem is framed in white, as it were: the white snow ("*belyj sneg*," "*belyj snežok*") appears in the beginning of the poem; the white crown of roses, "*belyj venčik iz roz*," marks its end. The latter image is linked, of course, with the white flower symbolism of Blok's early lyrical poems. The reader cannot help asking whether this crown is not made of the white flowers which the young poet cast over the church fence.

APPENDIX

A Comparative Table of Principal Colors in Blok's Poetry (based on *Sobranie sočinenij*, 1960, and covering all texts, except comic verses and translations)

I intend to give an extensive analysis of this table in a special article, and shall therefore limit myself here to some preliminary notes. Five colors, in a different sequence, play a decisive role in Blok's poetry. Volume I shows the following sequence: (1) all shades of blue (26.1%); (2) all shades of red (20.3%); (3) white (18.0%); (4) golden (11.2%); and (5) black (8.9%). In Volume II, red and white, as well as golden and black, switch places: (1) blue (20.6%); (2) white (19.3%); (3) red (17.7%); (4) black (10.5%), and (5) golden (10.3%). Finally, in Volume III, black moves to the first place: (1) black (21.8%); (2) red (18.1%); (3) white (15.8%); (4) blue (14.4%), and golden (10.6%). While the golden color mostly forms a positive semantic field /+/, and the black, a negative one /–/, the white shows considerable fluctuation between these two fields. In Volume I, the percentage ratio is as follows: /+/ 58%: /–/ 21%; the remaining 21% forms a neutral field /o/. In Volumes II and III, the ratio is completely different: /o/ 46.9%; /+/ 28.7%; and /–/ 24.4%. A description and analysis of the semantic fields of all shades of red and blue, and of green and yellow, should be of paramount importance. Let us also note that the color violet (*fioletovyj* and *lilovyj*) is not as significant in Blok's poetry as it is in his prose. In his poetry, Blok creates the image of the "violet worlds" by combining the negative fields of the darker shades of red and blue. This blending of colors is mentioned by Blok in his article *O lirike* (1907).

VOLUMES	I (1897–1904)	II (1904–1908)	III (1907–1921)
belyj	18.0%	19.3%	15.8%
černyj	8.9	10.5	21.8
zolotoj	11.2	10.3	10.6
krasnyj	8.2	9.9	8.9
alyj	3.8	3.1	5.7
rozovyj	5.0	2.2	2.3
other shades of red	3.3	2.4	2.0
sinij	9.1	12.5	8.9
goluboj	7.4	6.3	4.3
lazurnyj	9.6	1.8	1.4
lilovyj	—	1.3	0.9
zelenyj	4.5	6.1	4.3
želtyj	3.6	2.9	5.2
serebrjanyj	4.3	5.7	2.6
seryj	3.1	3.9	3.7

Harvard University

NOTES

1. See my article "The Sound Texture of Russian Verse in the Light of Phonemic Distinctive Features," IX, *IJSLP* (1965).

2. In his article "Aleksandr Blok," II, *Izbrannye sočinenija* (1955), 284.

3. Claude Chavasse, *The Bride of Christ* (London, 1939), 28.

4. *Ibid.*, 51. Later, in August, 1909, Blok would return to the same image: "V teni dvorcovoj gallerei, / Čut' ozarennaja lunoj, / Tajas', proxodit Salomeja / S mojej krovavoj golovoj. // Vsë spit—dvorcy, kanaly, ljudi, / Liš' prizraka skol'zjaščij šag, / Liš' golova na černom bljude / Gljadit s toskoj v okrestnyj mrak" ("Venecija," II).

5. E. V. Spektorskij, a disciple and friend of A. L. Blok, affirmed this to me on several occasions.

6. See *Appendix*, p. 258.

7. V. V. Gippius, *Ot Puškina do Bloka* (Moscow-Leningrad, 1966), p. 337.

8. The last two lines are particularly expressive because of the alliterating dark and compact *k*-sounds.

9. The image of the galloping mare can legitimately be juxtaposed with Gogol's racing troika. Blok's article *Narod i intellige..ija* (November, 1908), "dealing with the same subject" as *Na pole Kulikovom*, ends with this Gogolian symbol.

Toward a Contrastive Study of Word-Usage: Mickiewicz and Puškin

LAWRENCE L. THOMAS

A VAST AMOUNT of study has been devoted to Puškin's use of language—one need only mention V. V. Vinogradov's monumental contributions.[1] The appearance of the Puškin dictionary, under Vinogradov's editorship, will make possible even more extensive, and more accurate, investigations.[2] Rather less has been done on the language of Mickiewicz.[3] Only recently have more extensive studies been published on Mickiewicz' language, and they owe their origins largely to preliminary work on the Mickiewicz dictionary.[4] Mickiewicz studies will be greatly facilitated when the dictionary of his language,[5] under the editorship of K. Górski and S. Hrabec, reaches completion.

But the Mickiewicz and Puškin dictionaries should make another type of study possible as well—a contrastive study of their poetic language. Those who have read both Puškin and Mickiewicz can, of course, make contrastive statements without recourse to dictionaries of any kind. But their statements, unbuttressed by the truly formidable amount of preliminary data gathering which would be necessary, would inevitably suffer from impressionism. It may well be that the use of the dictionaries for contrastive studies will only confirm what is more-or-less subjectively known already and will not lead to any basic revision of such opinions. But at least one goal will have been gained, that a relatively objective basis for judgment will have been provided.

There are a number of reasons why a contrastive study of Mickiewicz and Puškin would be quite appropriate. They spoke and did their creative writing in closely related languages; they were contemporaries; they underwent, at least in part, the same experiences. They shared Neo-Classical influences (e.g., Voltaire), and Romantic ones (e.g., Byron, Scott). They shared Romanticism's folklore interests, and they both had an interest in the language of the folk (and, for both of them, that interest was highly reserved and selective). Finally, they both wrote, very roughly speaking, in the same genres: lyric poetry, *poèmy*, literary epic (if one may be allowed to apply that term to *Evgenij Onegin* and *Pan Tadeusz*), innovative drama, and historical, critical, "journalistic," epistolary, and artistic prose.

However, in contrasting the language of Puškin and Mickiewicz, there are also important qualifications to be made and distinctions to be kept in mind. The languages they used are indeed closely related; but, for any given word, one must make certain that the semantic range was approximately the same in the *general* Polish and Russian literary languages. Furthermore, although Puškin and Mickiewicz were contemporaries and shared a number of experiences, there were also considerable differences: Puškin never really left a Russian milieu; Mickiewicz left his native land at the end of 1824 and never returned to it (although he had access to, and participated in, the communal life of other Polish émigrés). Mickiewicz underwent more German literary influences than did Puškin; conversely, it would be safe to say that the Gallic influence (both literary and linguistic) on Puškin was much more profound than it was on the early Mickiewicz. The genres in which they wrote are not as strictly comparable as would appear at first glance. Mickiewicz's lyric poetry is not of the extent of Puškin's; although he wrote some poetry influenced by "folk" themes, he has no *skazki*; his artistic prose, when compared to Puškin's, is negligible in quantity; he wrote fewer *poèmy*; his main effort at drama, *Dziady*, has connections with the medieval mystery play. On the other hand, Mickiewicz' non-artistic prose is of far greater bulk and variety than is Puškin's: there are the youthful Philomath writings, the Biblical prose of *Księgi narodu . . . i pielgrzymstwa polskiego*, the political writings of *Pielgrzym polski* and *Trybuna ludów*, the religious-philosophical and Towianistic writings, and a somewhat greater number of letters. Furthermore, contrastive study would have to be watchful of any lexical item that might have acquired a special meaning during Mickiewicz' mystical period (e.g., *brat* was a technical term in Towianism). Last but not least, the problems the two poets faced in dealing with the Polish and Russian literary languages of their time were very different: for example, Mickiewicz did not have to contend with the problems of the Church Slavonic component in the literary language.

Despite these qualifications, a study comparing the two poets' usage of words is possible, and its results, used with caution, can be illuminating. Their differences are many, but Puškin and Mickiewicz *did* live in the same kind of literary atmosphere—they could influence it and be influenced by it, and they could also influence each other.[6]

The word selected for this preliminary study is *dar*. The reasons are practical: it is available in the completed portion of the Mickiewicz dictionary, and it is a word which, since it can mean the gift of poetry itself, has a strongly poetic, inspirational aureole. The standard Polish and Russian dictionaries are in substantial agreement concerning its semantics (the following dictionaries were consulted—for Polish: the new Academy dictionary, the so-called "Słownik warszawski," and Linde; for Russian: the new seventeen-volume Academy dictionary, Ušakov, and the second and third editions of Dal'). In addition, the Mickiewicz and Puškin dictionaries agree concerning its basic range of meaning. For both of them, its range is as follows: 1) simple gift; 2) gifts of nature, fate, supernatural powers (the Mickiewicz dictionary restricts this rubric to *material* gifts; the Puškin dictionary does not); 3) talent, capability. The frequency with which the two poets used the word in these different meanings is roughly comparable. The Puškin dictionary breakdown is as follows: of a total of eighty-seven occurrences of the word (three of which, in effect, are self-quotations and will therefore be omitted in this paper), Puškin used it forty-eight times in the first meaning, fifteen times in the second, and twenty times in the third. (The Puškin dictionary also isolates four usages in set phrases;[7] the Mickiewicz dictionary distributes various set phrases among the basic meanings.) The Mickiewicz dictionary gives a usage total of seventy-two, subdivided as follows: forty-eight in the first meaning, seven in the second, and seventeen in the third. One more point should be made: usage of the word does not significantly increase or decrease during the lives of the poets; increased usage in certain years seems, rather, to be connected with increased creativity in general or the publication of certain specific works.

The method applied in this investigation was the following: the dictionaries were used as concordances to the actual texts, which were then excerpted in sufficient detail to allow for unambiguous judgments concerning the following categories: accompanying qualifiers (adjectives, demonstratives, possessives), rhyming words, the actual nature of the gift, the actual giver of the gift, and the distribution of usage of the word between poetic and prose genres. The reporting of the results of the investigation will be largely statistical and for the most part, confined to the categories above. Extensive discussion in contextual depth would expand a short paper into a small monograph, without a corresponding gain in insight. A schematic presentation will, I think, prove to be of some interest in itself. References will not, normally, be given to the poets' works; they are recoverable through the respective dictionaries. Frequency counts will be placed in square brackets; if no frequency is given, the term, or concept, was used only once.

In one sense, this study, even in its present form, is seriously limited. As long as investigation is being made of the uses of a word that can refer to the sphere of poetic creativity, it would be interesting to apply the same methodology to other Russo-Polish pairs or near-pairs in the same general semantic range: for example, дарование— zdolność, вдохновение—natchnienie, талант—talent. Unfortunately, comparative investigation of these pairs will have to await the completion of the Mickiewicz dictionary.

In Puškin's and Mickiewicz' works, the word *dar* is accompanied by the following qualifiers (presented here, for the most part, in their dictionary form). Puškin used forty-four different qualifiers, for a total of sixty-seven occurrences. Mickiewicz used twenty-seven different qualifiers, for a total of forty occurrences.[8]

PUŠKIN

свой [7], бесценный [4], божий [3], все [3], мой [3], твой [3], блестящий [2], его [2], минутный [2], священный [2], слабый [2], тайный [2], благой, великий, веселый, грешный, грозный, дивный, добрый, заветный, их, княжеский, легкий, милый, мстящий, напрасный, неверный, не вечный, незапный, не приемный, не суетный, ни единый, первый, последний, прощальный, самый редкий, сей, скромный, скудный, сладостный, случайный, умственный, честный, чудесный.

MICKIEWICZ

ten [7], anielski [2], boży [2], jej [2], ślubny [2], wasz [2], wielki [2], wspaniały [2], cudowny, drogi, jaki, jego, miły, narodowy, niemiły, niewielki, ostatni, ów, pański, paryski, pierwszy, piękny, prosty, różny, smutny, swój, świeży.

Puškin rhymed fifteen different words with *dar*, for a total of thirty-one occurrences of *dar* in rhyming function; Mickiewicz rhymed *dar* eight times, with eight different words.

дар — жар [7], дары — пиры [7],
дар — удар [3], дар — стар [2],
дар(а) — пожар(а) [2], дары —
горы, даров — готов, дары —
добры, дары — ковры, дарами —
кунаками, дар — Лар, дарами —
мечтами, дарами — небесами,
даров — стихов, дар — угар.

dary—cary, darem—ciężarem,
dary—cytary, dary—czary, dary
—miary, darem—pożarem, dary
—sztandary, darów—talarów.

What the gift is and who the giver is, are also of interest in the two poets' uses of *dar*. In what follows, the gift and giver are presented even if the gift is only potential (refused or not, in fact, bestowed). The gift will be presented first, and the giver, if specified, will be placed in parentheses following the gift. More than one occurence will be grouped together, and assigned a frequency number, only if *both* the gift and the giver remain identical. The poets' own words will be used wherever possible (but, as a rule, put in the nominative case, singular or plural); if the gift is not specified, but inferable, an English adjective will be used to describe it. In accordance with the foregoing statements, the notation "лира [2] (Феб)" means that Apollo was the giver both times, the notation "poetic [7]" means that the gift is unspecified but safely inferable and that the giver, in all seven instances, is unspecified. If the giver is specified twice, metaphorically *and* explicitly, the two nouns will be separated by a dash, e.g., небо — Феб). Occasionally, additional information will be supplied in English (in Mickiewicz' case, gifts which are identified in the notes to the so-called "Wydanie narodowe" are put in quotation marks). Classification into larger classes (e.g., subsuming the "lyre," "the gift of song," etc. under "poetic") will not be attempted. Such classification would raise other problems which are not central to the aims of this paper—demonstration of the *range* of the poets' usage.

poetic (судьба); poetic [2] (Муза); poetic (Музы); poetic [7]—one of these instances has a broader meaning: Presumably all the virtues Lenskij possesses; лира (боги); лира (судьба); лира [2] (Феб); песни [2]; дух песен; проза, стихи (небо—Феб); поэзия

the Holy Ghost (Bóg [in "Veni Creator"; and, of course, the Holy Ghost is "siedmioraki w darach"]); miłość (Wszechmocny); not inferable (Opatrzność); not inferable (Przeznaczenie); not inferable (przyrodzenie); wielkość umysłu, zacność urodzenia; not inferable

трудолюбивая; дар пиитов (Аполлон); витийство (судьба); creative (жизнь); creative (небо); бессмертный гений; intellectual; мысль (God); дары вдохновения; охота (Феб); feminine charms (природа); erotic (Мария); erotic (любовь); erotic (любовница); огонь любви несчастной (Амур); стыдливость робкая (Хариты); святой залог любви, утеха грусти нежной (возлюбленная моя); обворожать сердца и взоры (судьба); все, что цены … не знает … чем жизнь мила бывает (бедняжка, Marija in *Poltava*); все—наслажденья, грусть, мученья, шум, бури, пиры (юность … моя); молитвы (Изабела); досуг, удел муз, наслажденья лени сонной, красы лаис, заветные пиры, клики радости безумной (природа); богатство, знатный род, возвышенный ум, простодушие с язвительной улыбкой (судьба); magical; шапка of invisibility (Черномор); жизнь [3]; счастье; здоровье; слава; дары мира 'peace' (мощная рука … из-за пределов мира); мир (Наполеон); дар слова; привлекать сердца; смотреть на вещи; нравиться (природа); дар(ы) свободы [2]; неволя (Alexander I); not inferable (вольность); веселость; две розы (Puškin); votive offering to the Holy Virgin (пловец); покров, упитанный язвительною кровью (кентавр); яд [3] (Изора [2]—любовь); перчатка as challenge (отец in *Skupoj rycar'*); сон (Морфей); праздник (Москва); книга (божий дар); старушка (бо-

(stworzenie); melancholia; działanie; modlitwa; przekonywanie; opowiadanie; pracowanie nad rodakami; not inferable (dary boże); strzała lotna (Apollo); Szczerbiec [2] (dar anielski); "a solemn letter and a ring depicting a lyre" (Polska [as represented by émigrés in France]); "a seal depicting the head of Goethe" (Niemcewicz); swój talent (każdy); the opportunity to marry and have children (Gerwazy); probably a poem (Mickiewicz); wiersze (Jan [Czeczot]); a medallion (młodzież [Polish]); listek (Mickiewicz); nitka z odzieży or zawiązka warkocza or kamyczek ze ścian wieży (Aldona); obrazek, relikwije (Zosia); kwiaty, koszyczki, ptasie gniazda, zauszniczki (Sak Dobrzyński); ślubne [3] (syn—Hassan); wdowi grosz (Danysz); niedźwiedź (Podkomorzy); miecz imperatorski (Witeliusz); princedom of Lida and Litawor's wife's patrimony (Witold); świeże snopki ziela (wieśniaczki); siła, wzrok ostry, dźwięki cytary; majątek rodziców (dar Boży); *Pamiętniki* Paska (Grabowska); Kralodworski rękopis, twoja gramatyka, *Pieśni* (Hanka); dykcjonarze (Januszkiewicz); grzyby (Wodziński); przysmaki (Onufry [Pietraszkiewicz]); food and drink (lato); kilkaset rubli (pewien książę [Czartoryski]); "money for the publication of a Paris edition of his work" [2] (Ostrowska); money (émigré Poles); sumka (Sędzia); talary (Gerwazy's masters); gotówka (Zaleski); kiesa ciężka dukatami

жий дар); конь (Олег); перстень (Самозванец); food (Ком); alcoholic beverage (Вакх); material (Гасуб); material; material (казанские татары); presumably worldly [2] (сеятель in "Podражanie Koranu"); not inferable (юность); not inferable (молодость).

(the people of Soplica); kufel kryształowy ... wódka to gdańska (Robak); material [conjoined with ziemie, ludzi, złoto] (nikt [can satisfy the Teutonic Knights with gifts]); material (Mickiewicz); material (kochanek); material (przyszła [żona Cichowskiego]); material (lud); material (Św. Otton); material [3] (Bolesław Chrobry).

Distribution of the word by genre in Puškin's works is as follows: lyric poetry [51], *poémy* [12], drama [7], *Evgenij Onegin* [4], artistic prose [1], epistolary prose [1], other nonartistic prose [8]. In sum, Puškin used the word only ten times in prose genres. He did not use' the word in his *skazki* (because their "folk" character and penchant for the colloquial language made them a "low" genre?). The distribution in Mickiewicz' work is as follows: lyric poetry [12], *poémy* [8], drama [1], *Pan Tadeusz* [11], artistic prose [1], epistolary prose [19], other nonartistic prose [16] (4 instances of *dar* remained in manuscript and do not appear in the final text). In sum, Mickiewicz' uses of the word were about evenly divided between prose and verse genres.

A survey of the material presented above will clearly show that, for Puškin, *dar* was a highly poetic word, whereas for Mickiewicz, it was decidedly prosaic (or, at least, neutral). The reason for this cannot be found in the Polish and Russian languages. Mickiewicz could, and did, use the word with poetic and symbolic tension when he was forced to; but normally he just preferred not to. The only usage that *may* have been dictated by their respective languages is that of applying the word to a gift from a friend. There is no example showing that Puškin would have called a gift to him from an equal a *dar*; Polish, clearly, imposed no such prohibition on Mickiewicz. The reason is to be sought, rather, in the poets' respective *attitudes* toward the use of the word. A vivid example of the difference in their outlook can be adduced from instances when they were both following a foreign model. In his *poéma, Giaur*, Mickiewicz uses *dar* extensively and with telling poetic effect. I will cite the relevant passages: "Nie przysłał darów ślubnych—czy się lenił? ... koń pewnie z ciężarem,/ Zapewne ślubnym objuczony darem ... W bramie zsiadł Tatar, od siodła odpina/ Juki niewielkie: czy to dary syna? ... Pilniejszy badacz odgadnie z wejrzenia/ Wielkość umysłu, zacność urodzenia,/ Dary, niestety, zbyt źle umie-

szczone,/ Skalane zbrodnią, smutkiem przetrawione./ Był to przybytek
nie podły, nie mały,/ Gdy w nim tak wielkie zalety mieszkały...
Zaiste, miłość jest świętym pożarem,/ Iskra zatlona w ogniach
nieśmiertelnych,/ Aniołów dobrem, Wszechmocnego darem,/ Balsamem
rajskim dla serc skazitelnych." *But every single one of these uses has its
justification in Byron*—"his promised gift," "the gift," "token," "be-
stow'd," and "given," respectively. Actually, Mickiewicz had one *more*
instance in his source which would have provided justification for using
the word—"lofty gifts"—toyed with it in manuscript, and rejected it in
favor of "wielkie zalety." A Puškinian parallel to this is Izabela's
speech to Andželo:

> ... Постой, постой!
> Послушай, воротись. Великими дарами
> Я задарю тебя ... прими мои дары,
> Они не суетны, но честны и добры,
> И будешь ими ты делиться с небесами:
> Я одарю тебя молитвами души
> Пред утренней зарей в полунощной тиши,
> Молитвами любви, смирения и мира,
> Молитвами святых, угодных небу дев,
> В уединении умерших уж для мира,
> Живых для господа.

In order to produce this dazzling display, Puškin even had recourse
to two derived verbs, one of which (задарить) occurs only four times in
all his work. But Puškin, unlike Mickiewicz, had only *one* justification
in his source for using *dar*: "Aye, with such gifts that Heaven shall
share with you."

Juliusz Kleiner repeatedly speaks of Mickiewicz' art in terms such as
"economy,"[9] "restraint,"[10] and "linking the imagination to concrete
elements."[11] More recent studies, working with autographs and the archives of the Mickiewicz dictionary, have provided concrete evidence
for such observations.[12] But the modern Polish poet, Jan Lechoń,
probably put the issue the most simply and directly: "One feels that
Mickiewicz always found the unique simple word and always combined
words in their indispensable quantity."[13] Mickiewicz' reserve in the use
of language is, therefore, well known. But only a comparative study
such as the one attempted here can show how *drastic* that reserve was.
After all, even if we disregard the numerous evaluations that have been
made concerning the language of Puškin's artistic prose, we have to
admit that Puškin criticism is *also* full of expressions such as "laconi-
cism," "everyday quality of images," "compressed and simple ex-

pressions," and "device [прием] of a niggardly, restrained, and even somewhat dry depiction of emotions."[14] But Puškin's simplicity and Mickiewicz' simplicity are of totally different orders even though their use of words is often superficially quite similar. Puškin's employment of words, not just for denotation but also for variously connotative, widely proliferating, stylistic coloration in varying contexts, was quite foreign to Mickiewicz.

The study of similar word pairs will probably yield only corroborating results. But then there is the saying, *quod autem potest esse totaliter aliter*. Only completion of the Mickiewicz dictionary and further research can tell us.

University of Wisconsin

NOTES

1. The most important of which are, of course, *Язык Пушкина: Пушкин и история русского литературного языка* (Moscow-Leningrad, 1935), and *Стиль Пушкина* (Moscow, 1941).
2. *Словарь языка Пушкина* (Moscow, 1956–1961).
3. See W. Weintraub, *The Poetry of Adam Mickiewicz* (The Hague, 1954), pp. 287–88.
4. E.g., Z. Klemensiewicz (ed.), *O języku Adama Mickiewicza: Studia* (Wrocław, 1959).
5. *Słownik języka Adama Mickiewicza* (Wrocław-Warsaw-Crakow, 1962). At the time of writing, three volumes were available to me: I (A–Ć), II (D–G), IV (L–M).
6. Cf. *Стиль Пушкина*, pp. 374–75.
7. One of these set phrases is божий дар. Both the second and the third editions of Dal' gloss it simply as "bread." Ušakov and the new Academy dictionary ignore the phrase. Puškin's two uses of it were "В тюрьме и в путешествии всякая книга есть божий дар, . . ."

and "На чужой сторонке и старушка божий дар."
8. One instance of *wielki* and one of *wspaniały* remained in manuscript and were rejected from the printed versions. It is also interesting that the adjective *cudowny* and both instances of *anielski* occur in prose and refer to the Polish nation's attitude toward Szczerbiec, the sword of Bolesław Chrobry.
9. *Mickiewicz*, I (Lublin, 1948), 553.
10. *Mickiewicz*, I, 547.
11. *Mickiewicz*, II, Part 2, 399.
12. See the collection of studies cited in note 4, above, but especially the article "Praca Mickiewicza nad językiem *Pana Tadeusza* na podstawie autografów," by H. Cieślakowa, H. Misz, and T. Skubalanka.
13. "Mickiewicz in Polish Poetry," in W. Lednicki (ed.), *Mickiewicz in World Literature* (Berkeley, 1956), p. 10.
14. *Стиль Пушкина*, pp. 222, 249, 255, 71, respectively.

Über Redewendungen und Figurative Bedeutungen im Russisch-Kirchenslawischen

GERTA H. WORTH

Professor Unbegaun, dem bedeutendsten Slawisten im Westen, der sich der geschichtlichen Erforschung des russischen Wortschatzes sowie der kirchenslawisch-russischen Beziehungen widmet, verdanken wir eine ganze Reihe von vorbildlichen lexikalischen Studien. Auf dem Gebiet der Lehnübersetzungen im Slawischen hat Professor Unbegaun ebenfalls Pionierarbeit geleistet[1] und die weitere Erforschung dieser gemeineuropäischen Art der Sprachbereicherung angeregt. Dieser kleine Beitrag zu Ehren meines Lehrers behandelt ein Thema aus demselben Problemkreise, nämlich phraseologische Lehnübersetzungen und figurative Bedeutungen, die bereits im Russisch-Kirchenslawischen der ältesten Periode belegt sind und bis in die Gegenwart erhalten blieben.

Als Quellen dienten die Psalterübersetzungen[2] und die Novgoroder *Služebnye Minei*[3]; damit ist durchaus nicht gesagt, daß diese Ausdrücke und sekundären Bedeutungen auf diese Übersetzungen beschränkt sind. Im Gegenteil, die Tatsache, daß diese erhalten blieben, deutet darauf hin, daß die meisten von ihnen in der religiösen Literatur sehr verbreitet waren, obwohl sie zum Teil von den Wörterbüchern ignoriert werden. Die Beispiele aus den russisch-kirchenslawischen Abschriften der Psalterübersetzungen sind ausnahmslos altkirchenslawischen Ursprungs, da sich dieselben bereits im Psalterium Sinaiticum[4] befinden. In den meisten Fällen handelt es sich um genaue Nachbildungen des griechischen Modells, also um phraseologische Lehnübersetzungen, beziehungsweise um semantische Entlehnungen. Für mehrere Beispiele aus den Novgoroder Menäen war es nicht möglich, die tatsächlichen Vorbilder anzuführen, da nur wenige Bruchstücke der griechischen Vorlage von Jagić gefunden und veröffentlicht wurden.[5]

Alle folgenden Wortverbindungen sind Verbalkonstruktionen. Eine
weitere Einteilung nach dem Grad ihrer syntaktischen und semantischen Unteilbarkeit, wie es seinerzeit Vinogradov vorschlug,[6] stößt auf
Schwierigkeiten, da der Übergang von festgefügten phraseologischen
Einheiten (frazeologičeskie edinicy) mit meist figurativer Bedeutung in
losere Verbindungen (frazeologičeskie sočetanija) mit auswechselbaren
Gliedern allmählich erfolgt, und so keine klare Abgrenzung erlaubt.
M. E. wären von dem angeführten Material nur *otkryt' komu glaza* und
zvat' na pomošč' zur ersteren Gruppe zu rechnen, da die anderen Ausdrücke leicht variiert werden können: z.B. *napravit' stopy — napravit'
šagi svoi*, oder *vložit' (čužie) slova komu-nibud' v usta — ... v rot*;
hier handelt es sich um den Ersatz archaischer, hochtrabender Wörter
durch neutrale, ohne den Sinn des ganzen Ausdruckes zu ändern, um sie
in "säkularisierter" Form der moderneren Literatursprache anzupassen.
Zu den loseren Verbindungen zählen weiter Verben mit sekundärer,
abstrakter Bedeutung, deren Objekt durch Synonyme oder Wörter mit
ähnlicher Bedeutung ersetzt werden kann, wie *počerpat' (počerpnut')
mudrost', znanie, svedenija, primery*.

Die stilistische Färbung der Redewendungen ist verschieden. Mit Ausnahme von *zvat' na pomošč'* gehören sie durchweg der Buchsprache an.
Zum Teil sind sie veraltet, doch haftet nur wenigen der Charakter eines
Zitates aus dem Kirchenslawischen an (wie *vzyvat' iz glubiny*), die eindeutig ihre Herkunft verraten. Die meisten Ausdrücke sind in zahlreichen europäischen Sprachen gebräuchlich (vgl. *sobljudat' zakon*, lat.
leges observare, franz. *observer une loi*, engl. *observe a law*, u.s.w.
'ein Gesetz beobachten'). Aus diesem Grund ist ihre Registrierung für
die älteste Periode wichtig, denn sonst läuft man in Gefahr, für sie
eine bedeutend spätere Entlehnung (etwa im 18. Jh.) durch die Vermittlung einer ganzen Reihe von europäischen Sprachen anzunehmen.
Die Wege, durch die Lehngut (Fremdwörter und alle Arten von Lehnübersetzungen) in das Russische gelangten, wechselten ja von Epoche
zu Epoche: für die älteste Zeit ist griech. > altksl. > russisch-
kirchenslawisch > altrussisch am wahrscheinlichsten, während z.B.
Ende des 18. Jh.s klassische Ausdrücke sicher durch französisch-
deutsche Vermittlung in das Russische übernommen wurden. Dies be-
trifft möglicherweise nicht nur einzelne Redewendungen, sondern einen
Typ, dessen Verbreitung man sonst erst für das 18. Jh. ansetzt. Es sind
dies analytische Konstruktionen, die durch ein Verbum ersetzt werden
können, wie *vozlagat' naoeždu na = nadejat' sja na, uvenčat' sja pobedoj =
pobedit', predat' ognju = sžeč'*. Vielleicht geht die Entstehung solcher,
für die Buchsprache typischer Konstruktionen auf das Kirchenslawische der ältesten Periode (und diese wieder auf das Griechische) zurück.
Diese Frage würde eine nähere Untersuchung verdienen. Es folgt nun

eine Aufzählung von Redewendungen aus den genannten Sprachdenkmälern, soweit diese erhalten blieben:

venčat'sja pobedami 'von Siegen gekrönt sein' побѣдами вѣньчаста
сѧ (*Služ.Min.*, 92)[7] = ταῖς νίκαις ἐστέϑφητε; aksl. (*Slovník*)[8]; in der
religiösen Literatur mehrmals im figurativen Sinn belegt (s. Sreznevskij
unter вѣньчати[9]); im modernen Russischen auch *uvenčat'sja pobedami*,
uspexami, u.ä.

vzyvat' iz glubiny (nur kirchlich)-'aus der Tiefe rufen' Из глоубины
възвахъ к тебе господи = ἐκ βαθέων ἐκέκραξὰ σοι κύριε (*Psal.* 129,1
II 431); *Sin.*; ein Übersetzer aus dem 17. Jh. fand es notwendig, diese
Stelle zu kommentieren: т.е. из глубокости срьдьца (Псалтирь
Фирсова, 1683)[10], doch hielt sich dieser Ausdruck, allerdings mit
stark religiösem Beigeschmack.

vložit' (čužie) slova komu-nibud' v usta 'jem. fremde Worte in den
Mund legen' И въложи въ оуста моя пѣснь новоу = καὶ ἐνέβαλεν εἰς
τὸ στόμα μου ᾆσμα καινόν (*Psal.* 39,4 I 258); *Sin.*; das Objekt kann
durch sinnverwandte Wörter ersetzt werden, ebenso das besonders
archaische оуста durch *rot*.

vozlagat' nadeždy na 'Hoffnungen auf jem. legen' надеждю бо на
тя възлагающе (*Služ.Min.* 280); die griechische Konstruktion weicht
ab: ἐλπίδας ἔχειν ἔν τινι aksl.; auch полагати н к (*ibid.* 424).

vooružat'sja terpeniem 'sich mit Geduld rüsten' Сама сѧ оружиемь,
вѣрьно въороужьши сѧ въздьрьжаниемь = ... πίστει καϑοπλίσασα
τῆς ἐγκρατείας (*Služ.Min.* 320); die genaue Entsprechung der russischen Redewendung ist seit dem XI. Jh. belegt: трьпѣниемь
въороужатьсѧ (Pand.Ant., s. Sreznevskij); aksl. въоржжатисѧ
милостьѭ. (*Slovník*).

zvat' na pomošč 'zu Hilfe rufen' на помощь вѣрно та зовоущиимъ
(*Služ.Min.* 0220, auch 0215, 0214) vgl. εἰς βοήϑειαν ἐπικαλεῖσϑαι
(*AT., Judith*, 6, 21) im Aksl. nicht belegt, in Sreznevskij nur dasselbe
Beispiel.

ispolnit' želanie 'einen Wunsch (oder ähnl.) erfüllen' Блаженъ
иже исполнить похоть свою ѡт нихъ = ...ὃς πληρώσει τὴν ἐπιθυμίαν.... (*Psal.* 126, 5 II 423); *Sin.*; vgl.: исполнити ся: Тогда
исполнишасѧ радости оуста наша = τότε ἐπλήσϑη χαρᾶς τὸ στόμα
ἡμῶν. (Psal. 125, 2 II 419 und 71, 19 I 498, *Služ.Min.* 9) *Sin.*; auch
dieser Ausdruck 'von einem Gefühl erfüllt werden' existiert noch im
Russischen, allerdings in Wörterbüchern mit dem Vermerk "kniž.
ustar." (Ušakov)[11].

napravit' stopy 'seine Schritte richten' Стопы моя направи по
словеси твоемоу — τὰ διαβήματα μου κατεύϑυνον κατὰ τὸ λογίον σοῦ.
(*Psal.* 118, 133 II 385); *Sin.*; weniger hochtrabend: *napravit' šagi
svoi*.

nasytiť sja strasti(-tiju) '(Gefühle) sättigen' Божьствьныя сладости
явѣ насыщьще ся (*Služ.Min.* 0193) = fig. κορέννυναι; kommt öfter
in figurativer Bedeutung vor (vgl. Sreznevskij). Vgl. auch: напитая ....
сладостью (*Služ.Min.* 80).

otkryť komu-nibuď glaza 'jem. die Augen öffnen' Отъкрыи
ѡчи мои и разоумѣю чюдеса от закона твоего = ἀποκάλυφον τοὺς
ὀφθαλμούς μου.... (*Psal.* 118, 18 II 345); *Sin.*; diese Redewendung
wird von Sreznevskij nicht zitiert, doch erscheint das Verbum mit
demselben griechischen Aequivalent oft in der Bedeutung 'eröffnen,
verständlich machen'.

popasť v seť fig. 'ins Netz gehen' въ сѣть да въпадеть въ ню =
ἐν τῇ παγίδι πεσεῖται ἐν αὐτῇ (*Psal.* 34, 8 II 207) vergleiche auch:
въпадоутьса въ мрежю свою грѣшници (*ibid.* 140, 10 II 491); *Sin.*;
Ausdrücke für 'Netz' werden oft figurativ in verschiedenen Bedeutungen gebraucht, (s. Sreznevskij); словесьныя мрѣжа (*Služ.Min.* 296);
auch *razložiť seti* (figurativ) ist in etwas veränderter Form bereits im
Psalter belegt: положиша грѣшници сѣть мнѣ — ἔθεντο ... παγίδα
μοι (*Psal.* 118. 110 II 376); *Sin.*

počerpať, počerpnuť fig. 'schöpfen' моудрость почьрыплъ еси
(*Služ.Min.* 0203); die im Griechischen entsprechende Form wäre:
ἔμπρακτον μηχανᾶν ἀντλεῖν vgl. къто не почьрьпеть ѿт источьника
спасенаго (*Služ.Min.* 0200).

predať ognju 'dem Feuer übergeben, verbrennen' огневи предана
(*Služ.Min.* 100); wird als Redewendung von Sreznevskij zitiert mit
einem Beleg aus der Pskover Chronik; vgl. смьрти не прѣдасть мене
= τῷ θανάτῳ οὐ παρέδωκὲν μέ (*Psal.* 117, 18 II 335); *Sin.* dasselbe;
sonst: въ смьрть прѣдати (Miklosich 13, Sreznevskij); предасть въ пленъ
крѣпость их = παρέδωκεν εἰς αἰχμαλωσίαν τὴν ἰσχὺν αὐτῶν (*Psal.* 77,
61 II 30); auch предасть глаголоу скотъ ихъ (*ibid.* 77, 48 II 23).

preterpeť bolezni 'Krankheiten erdulden' болѣзни претьрпѣвъше
(*Služ.Min.* 337) = πόνους ὑπομείναντες auch лютость претьрпѣваше
(*ibid.* 63).

prinesti žertvu 'ein Opfer bringen' всего себѣ господеви жьртвж
принесъ (*Služ.Min.* 392) = θυσίαν φέρειν (*Slovník* und viele ähnliche
Wendungen: жьртвж дати въздати, възносити etc.); häufig.

prinesti plody 'Früchte bringen' плоды принеслъ еси богоу оуче-
ниемь твоимь спасения (*Služ.Min.* 92) = καρποφορεῖν (Sreznevskij,
Zitat aus dem 11. Jh.); vgl. плоды добродѣтельныа (*Služ.Min.*
0195), плоды богоразоумия въздѣлавъ троуды своими (ibid. 90) —
καρποὺς θεογνωσίας..., auch im Lat., Franz., Engl., Tschech., Poln.,
u.a. gebräuchlich.

proliť krov' 'Blut vergießen' пролияша кръвь ихъ акы водоу =
ἐξέχεαν τὸ αἶμα αὐτῶν ὡσεὶ ὕδωρ (*Psal.* 78, 3 II 36); *Sin.*; ge-

bräuchlich im Altruss., Russisch-Ksl. (Sreznevskij), ebenso кръви
пролитие: пролитиемь прѣчистыя кръве (*Služ.Min.* 0215), кръви
прольяниемь (*ibid.* 91), стржями кръвьнами (*ibid.* 339), потоци
кръвьнии (*ibid.* 100).

prolit' slezy 'Tränen vergießen' vgl. слъзъ стькланицоу всьгда
проливающи (*Služ.Min.* 51) = δάκρυα ἐκχείσθαι vgl. пролѣи гнѣвъ
твои на языкы — ἔκχεον τὴν ὀργήν ... (*Psal.* 78, 6 II 38), im modernen Russischen: *izlit' gnev* 'seinen Zorn (oder andere Gefühle)
ausschütten.'

prosvetit' um 'den Geist erleuchten' всѣхъ просвѣщая оумъ (*Služ.
Min.* 9) vgl. φωτίζειν πνεῦμα; просвѣщати, просвѣтити, fig. sind
mehrmals im Russisch-Ksl. belegt. (Sreznevskij).

razgoret'sja fig. '(Leidenschaften u.ä.) entbrennen' яко разгорѣса
сьрдьце = ὅτι ἐξεκαύθη ἡ καρδία μου (*Psal.* 72, 21 I 508); *Sin.*;
mehrere ähnliche Ausdrücke, die konkret und figurativ 'anzünden,
entzünden, brennen' bedeuten, kommen in den Minei vor, doch sind
sie im modernen Russisch nicht mehr gebräuchlich: страстную
тишину попалила есть = ἔφλεξεν (52); любъвию христовою доушоу
си опаливъши разоумьнаго ѡгна (0208); für dieses Verbum gibt
Sreznevskij nur konkrete Beispiele; любъвию христовою распал-
аемъ = τῷ πόθῳ τοῦ Χριστοῦ φλεγόμενος (64), vgl. распалити яростию,
гнѣвомь (Miklosich), Sreznevskij nur in konkreten Bedeutungen; mod.
russ. *raspalit' serdce*.

svergnut' igo 'das Joch abwerfen' ѡтвьрземь ѡт нас иго ихъ =
ἀπορρίψομεν ἀφ' ἡμῶν τὸν ζυγὸν αὐτῶν (*Psal.* 2, 3 I 5); *Sin.*;
мытарьское иго ѡтвьрьгъ (*Služ.Min.* 382); vgl. ѡт себе мьртвость
ѡтвьрьгъша (*ibid.* 2) aksl.; vgl. im modernen Russischen auch:
sbrosit' jarmo.

sledovat' po stopam 'in den Spuren folgen' того бо стопамъ въсл-
ѣдовала еси (*Služ.Min.* 0197, derselbe Ausdruck *ibid.* 0218, 0223) =
ἀκολουθεῖν τοῖς ἴχνεσι (*NT*) vgl. aksl. вь слѣдъ тебе идомъ (Supras-
lensis); russisch-kirchenslawisch: в слѣдъ ходити, по стопам ходити
(Sreznevskij).

sobljudat' zakon 'ein Gesetz beobachten' законъ твои словъмь
съблюдающе (*Služ.Min.* 86) = νόμον τηρεῖν (*NT*) добрѣ вѣроу
съблюдьше (*ibid.* 380); auch im Sinn von 'bewahren': дѣвьство
съблюла еси (*ibid.* 12), wie heute: *sobljudat' nevinnost'* u.ä.

soxranit' fig. 'bewahren' вънегда съхранити словеса твоя — ἐν τῷ
φυλάσσεσθαι τοὺς λόγους σου (*Psal.* 118, 9 II 342 und 118, 17 II
345) хранахоу съвѣдѣния его — ἐφύλασσον τὰ μαρτύρια ἀυτοῦ
(*ibid.* 98, 7), auch 'das Gesetz bewahren': и схраню закон — καὶ
φυλάξω τὸν νόμον (*ibid.* 118, 44 II 354); *Sin.*; russisch-kirchenslawisch
oft, besonders im Psalter, dort fast ausschließlich für φυλάττειν;

'vor etwas bewahren': Господь съхранить та ѿ всакого зла — κύριος φυλάξεί σε ἀπὸ παντὸς κακοῦ (*Psal.* 120, 7 S. 405), съхранюса ѿ безакония (*ibid.* 17, 24 S. 91), съхрани ѿ сѣти (*ibid.* 140, 9 S. 491).

tajat' kak vosk 'wie Wachs zerschmelzen' бысть сьрдце мое яко воскъ тая посрѣде црѣва моего — ἐγενήθη ἡ καρδία μου ὡσεὶ κηρὸς τηκόμενος (*Psal.* 21, 15 I 121). Горы яко воскъ растаяша ѿ лица божия = τὰ ὄρη ὡσεὶ κηρὸς ἐτάκησαν ἀπὸ προσώπου κυдίου (*ibid.* 96, 5 II 196); яко таеть въскъ ѿ лица огню (*ibid.* 67, 3 I 442); *Sin.*

ugasit' fig. 'löschen' льстьное оугасилъ еси зъловѣрие (*Služ.Min.* 11), жадания не оугаси водами (*ibid.* 0201), оугли оугаси моихъ страстии (*ibid.* 291) Russisch-kirchenslawisch seit 11. Jh. (Sreznevskij); entspricht griech. σβέννυναι; russ. угасить страсти, желания u.ä. blieb erhalten, ist aber archaisch (Ušakov vermerkt: "kniž., retor., ustar").

ukrasit' fig. 'schmücken' оукрашенъ добротою (*Služ.Min.* 8), доушоу свою оукрасилъ еси пресвѣтьлыми чистыми лоучами (*ibid.* 9), украшена свѣтлостию (*ibid.* 12), кротостию оукрашенъ (*ibid.* 0221; die griechischen Vorlagen zu diesen Stellen fehlen; Miklosich und Sreznevskij führen verschiedene griechische Aequivalente an; am besten entspricht κοσμεῖν; das Abstraktum ist in der modernen Sprache meist im Nominativ z.B. *ljubov' ukrasila žizn'* (Ušakov).

ukrotit' fig. 'zähmen' оукротилъ еси всь гнѣвъ твои — κατέπαυσας πᾶσαν τὴν ὀργήν σου (*Psal.* 84, 4 II 76); καταπαύεσθαι 'aufhören' hat nicht die selbe Grundbedeutung wie *ukrotit'*; es handelt sich also hier nicht um eine Lehnübersetzung, doch vgl. griech. δαμάζειν 'zähmen' konkret und figurativ; страсти бо доушевьныя оукротивъши (*Služ. Min.* 0192); *Sin.*; russisch-ksl. (Sreznevskij).

upovat' na 'fest auf jem. hoffen' благо есть оуповати на господа, неже оупвати на кънаѕа — ἀγαθὸν ἐλπίζειν ἐπὶ κύριον, ἢ ἐλπίζειν ἐπ' ἄρχουσιν (*Psal.* 117, 9 II 331–332); *Sin.*; russisch-ksl.; im heutigen Russisch 'книжн. поэт.' (Ušakov); vgl. полагати на господа оупвание (*Psal.* 72, 28 I 511), das nicht erhalten blieb (vgl. aber *vozlagat' nadeždu*).

Beide Texte enthalten außerdem noch zahlreiche Ausdrücke, die keine Verbalkonstruktionen sind und ebenfalls Entlehnungen aus dem Griechischen darstellen, doch ist ihre Aufzahlung im Rahmen eines kurzen Artikels nicht möglich.

University of California, Los Angeles

NOTES

1. Unbegaun, B., "Le calque dans les langues slaves littéraires," *Revue des Études slaves*, XII, 1932, 19–48.

2. Древне-славянская псалтирь Симоновская до 1280 года, сличенная с рукописными Псалтырями XI, XII, XIII, XIV, XV, XVI, XVII в.... с Греческим текстом X в. ed. Archimandrit Amfilochij. I–II, Moscow 1880–81; zitiert Psal. Der griech. Paralleltext ist dieser Ausgabe entnommen.

3. Служебные Минеи за Сентабрь, Октабрь и Ноабрь в церковнославянском переводе по русским рукописям 1095–97 г. (Памятники русского языка I) ed. J. V. Jagić, SPb., 1886; zitiert Služ.Min.

4. Синайская псалтырь; глаголический памятник XI века, ed. S. Sever'-janov, Prague 1922; zitiert Sin., wenn die Ausdrücke in Psal. und Sin. identisch sind (mit Ausnahme der Orthographie, die oft abweicht).

5. *Služ.Min.* 517–605. Wenn bei den folgenden Zitaten die griechische Entsprechung vor der Quellenanga-be steht, so stammt sie aus der griechischen Vorlage. Andernfalls sind die griech. Entsprechungen Wörterbüchern entnommen.

6. V. V. Vinogradov, "Об основных типах фразеологических единиц в русском языке" in А. А. Шахматов 1864–1920, (Moscow-Leningrad, 1947), insbesondere S. 346–360.

7. Das Gleichheitszeichen bedeutet, daß der kirchenslawische und der griechische Ausdruck vollkommen übereinstimmen.

8. *Slovník jazyka staroslověnského*, ČSAV, Prague, 1959–, bisher erschienen 15 Lieferungen, А–крижма.

9. I. I. Sreznevskij, Материалы для словаря древнерусского языка I–III, St. Petersburg, 1893–1912.

10. Vgl. Psal. S. VIII.

11. Толковый словарь русского языка, под ред. Д. П. Ушакова, I–IV, Moscow 1935–1940.

12. F. Miklosich, *Lexicon palaeoslo-venico-graeco-latinum*, Vindobonae, 1862–65.

Notes on Russian Stress, 2:
любовь, вошь, etc.*

DEAN S. WORTH

THE MORPHOPHONEMIC analysis of accentual alternations in terms of overall patterns, i.e., in terms of hierarchally organized sets of stress oppositions, can permit the investigator to extract significant generalizations from what might otherwise seem intractible or even incoherently variant data.[1] Thus, for example, it is now generally recognized that the phonemically mobile stress of such words as стóл, столá or скачóк, скачкá arises from underlying morphophonemic forms with fixed ending stress: {stol+ǿ}, {stol+á} and {skač-#k+ǿ}, {skač#k+á};[2] this permits one to join this type of masculine to such neuters and feminines as веществó, питьё and клеветá, статья́ in a single class with fixed ending stress.[3] At the same time, however, concern with structural generalizations and the function of such abstract morphophonemic entities as stressed zero endings ({ǿ}) and alternating vowel-zero morphophonemes ({#}) must not lead the investigator too far away from the concrete material of the language(s) he is describing. It is only the phonetic surface ([skʌčók], [stʌt'éi̯], etc.) which is susceptible of objective verification; morphophonemic and even phonemic interpretations of these verifiable surface data are but hypotheses designed to account for the observed facts in some reasonable and efficient manner and to relate them to other observable facts of the linguistic system. Careful attention to observable detail can in some instances call attention to weaknesses in a given hypothesis or help to assign limits to the validity of the generalizations permitted by it. If our disobedience of Occam's

*Ed. note—Because the author is using transcription for both phonemic and morphophonemic representation, the specific examples are *not* transcribed but are intentionally set apart in the Cyrillic.

entia non sunt multiplicanda is at times rewarded by a view of some
deeper morphophonemic regularity beneath the confusing variety of
surface detail, we may at other times be punished by the discovery
that variety is not restricted to one level, that in some cases generali-
zation can be obtained only awkwardly, if at all, and that there is,
after all, a limit to the usefulness of clever abstractions. As a case in
point, I should like to examine the stress of a small group of Russian
words: вóшь, лóжь, любóвь, and рóжь.

The surface phonology of these words is generally well known, even
if all sources do not agree on exactly which words to include in the
brief.[4] Вóшь, лóжь, любóвь, and рóжь show a vowel-zero alternation
in their stems, with the so-called mobile vowel appearing in the nom.,
acc., and instr. and absent in the other forms of the paradigm:
вóшь, вши́, вши́, вóшь, вóшью, вши́, etc.[5] It is the stress of these
words that creates a problem in their morphophonemic interpretation:
the mobile {o} is accented whenever it appears, and when it is absent,
the stress falls on the ending. As a result, the bulk of the paradigm
seems to show the same stress as (C, below) the numerals 5–10, 20,
30,[6] whereas the instrumental appears to be stressed like the great
majority of third declension substantives (A), on the stem:

	(A)	(B)	(C)
Nom.	стéпь	любóвь	пя́ть
Gen.	стéпи	любви́	пяти́
Dat.	стéпи	любви́	пяти́
Acc.	стéпь	любóвь	пя́ть
Instr.	стéпью	любóвью	пятью́[7]
Prep.	стéпи	любви́	пяти́

The ambiguous accentual position of the group which concerns us here
becomes even more apparent if we extend this comparison to include disyllabic stems with initial (A), predesinential (A'), and mobile
initial-final stress (C), using wherever possible, stems with a vowel-
zero alternation as illustrations (A, C):

	(A)	(A')	(B)	(C)
N.	цéрковь	тетрáдь	любóвь	вóсемь
G.	цéркви	тетрáди	любви́	восьми́
D.	цéркви	тетрáди	любви́	восьми́
A.	цéрковь	тетрáдь	любóвь	вóсемь
I.	цéрковью	тетрáдью	любóвью	восемью́, восьмью́[8]
P.	цéркви	тетрáди	любви́	восьми́

So much for the surface facts. We shall come to grips with the problem of interpreting these facts morphophonemically after a brief survey of the way these words have been treated in the literature.

The grammar of the Soviet Academy of Sciences[9] gives лóжь, рóжь, and любóвь, together with цéрковь, as containing mobile {o}, but groups these words together with the numerals, глýшь, and marginally, óсь and Пéрмь as having fixed ending stress; the anomalous instr. sing. is not mentioned. A. V. Isačenko[10] devotes a special paragraph to вóшь, лóжь, любóвь, and рóжь, again together with цéрковь; the instr. forms are emphasized in boldface type, but the inclusion of цéрковь appears to indicate that the author's attention is concentrated on the mobile vowel rather than on the shifting stress. L. Ďurovič[11] also groups цéрковь with our four words in discussing the mobile vowel (as is, of course, appropriate), but in his paragraph on stress types in the third declension (p. 133) mentions only that the stress in любóвь and глýшь "moves to the ending -*i* in all cases," passing over the instr. in silence and implying that the underlying stress is on the stem. A number of studies of the past two decades dealing with noun stress, e.g., those by Kuryłowicz, Nikonov, Garde, Olechnowicz,[12] omit the class любóвь, вóшь, etc. altogether, and the same is true of the prospect for a new academic grammar in the Soviet Union.[13] One of the first authors to make a clear morphophonemic statement concerning the underlying stress of the words under discussion here was B. O. Unbegaun,[14] who states unambiguously that "fixed final stress occurs (in the third decl.—dsw) only in the numerals and in the word любóвь, gen. любви́," from which one may assume that the instr. любóвью is to be considered an individual aberration. In this, Unbegaun is followed (at least temporally, if not causally) by Zaliznjak[15] and Red'kin,[16] who list some or all of the words we are interested in here as variants, i.e., as irregularities within the fixed-ending-stress type (кишкá).

As is clear from this brief survey of some of the relevant literature, the stress peculiarities of the type любóвь, вóшь are either ignored entirely or considered an anomaly within the fixed-ending-stress type of third declension feminine and numeral substantives. The exception presented by the instr. sing. forms любóвью, вóшью, etc. present a challenge to the analyst: might it not be possible to discover some underlying morphophonemic order in this phonemic oddity? Could we not, by leaving Occam's razor folded, discover in the paradigm of любóвь the same sort of deeper regularity as has been generally accepted in the case of стóл, столá = {stol+ǿ}, {stol+á}? Such questions are of course designed to be answered in the affirmative, but as was hinted at the beginning of this note, the answer will not be entirely satisfactory.

Before turning to the stress itself, it may be useful to say a word about the morphophonemic abstractions that have already been used. The entity {#} is a morphophoneme which is rewritten as phonetic zero in some environments and as a full vowel in others (the environmental conditions determining the phonetic shape resulting from {#} are well known and need not be repeated here). The entity {ø} represents the phonetically zero "grade" of {#} at a point in the developing representation where the choice of vowel or zero has been made for the ending but not yet for the stem; i.e., {ø} = the usual "zero ending."[17] The need to introduce such entities as {#} and {ø} is not clear from the four words вошь, ложь, любовь, and рожь alone, since the mobile vowel could be introduced by purely phonetic rules in the "non-syllabic" stems[18] and also, though more clumsily, in the disyllabic любовь. However, it is clear from abundant other instances of vowel-zero alternations that the appearance of the mobile vowel cannot generally be predicted on phonetic criteria alone: the gen. plur. of сестра is сестёр, whereas the short form masc. of быстрый is not *быстёр but быстр; in morphologically parallel cases, one has смысл, смысла, but вымысел, вымысла; русло́, русл, but число́, чисел; игла́, игл, but ку́кла, ку́кол, etc.[19] It is clear, in other words, that stems manifesting a vowel-zero alternation have to be specifically marked as such, and the morphophoneme {#} is a convenient manner in which to so mark them.

We can assume, then, that the words вошь, ложь, любовь, and рожь have the underlying morphophonemic shapes {v#š-}, {l#ž-}, ľub#v'-}, and {r#ž-}. There are, therefore, three possible locations of the underlying stress: (1) on the first syllable of the stem, like {cérk#v'-}; (2) on the second "syllable" of the stem, like {tetrád'-} (i.e., on the {#'} in the case of our four words), and (3) on the ending, as in the case of the numerals, e.g., {p'at'-}, where end stress is represented by the absence of a stress mark on the stem. Not all possible underlying forms have distinct representations on the phonetic surface: monosyllabic forms like вошь, вши neutralize (1), (2), and (3), and disyllabic forms neutralize two of the three possible underlying forms, (1) and (2) in the case of вошью and (2) and (3) in that of любовь (whether любви neutralizes (2) and (3) cannot be determined at this point).[20] Let us examine each of the three possible underlying stresses in turn.

The first possibility, namely initial stress, can be eliminated at once, since initial stress would give *любовь, *любви like церковь, церкви. We must then choose between alternatives (2) and (3); i.e., in the case of the stem providing the maximum number of contrastive possibilities, we must choose between preterminally stressed {l'ub#ʹv'-} and end-stressed {l'ub#v'-}. As the second of these alternatives corresponds to the usual view (Academy Grammar, Unbegaun, Zaliznjak, Red'kin), we shall first examine the arguments that support this position.

The most immediate, although perhaps not the most compeling argument in favor of the interpretation {l'ub#v'-}—that is, in favor of morphophonemic end stress—is that nine of the twelve forms in the paradigm have the phonemic or "real" stress on the ending: вóшь, вшú, вшú, вóшь, вóшью, вшú; вшú, вшéй, вшáм, вшéй, вшáми, вшáх. Although one can obviously not determine the place of the morphophonemic stress by a kind of phonemic majority vote, it would be too simple merely to dismiss this sort of surface evidence as impressionistic and irrelevant: for one thing, a surface "impression" may well correspond to considerations of descriptive economy (the number of times some rule must be applied in the given paradigm, for example), and for another, surface phenomena can have a feedback effect on underlying forms, causing a structural reinterpretation on a deeper level.[21] However, the nine end-stressed forms like вшú will not help at all in the case of the instr. sing. вóшью, любóвью, etc. One can arrive at phonemically stem-stressed любóвью, etc. starting from morphophonemic end-stress only if this end stress is on the first syllable of disyllabic endings, i.e., on the {ø} of {øju}; this interpretation, though corresponding to the-óю, =-óй of the second declension (that is, in the decl. where the instr. fem. ending {#ju} → {oju} rather than {øju}), is contradicted by the numerals, where end stress falls on the last syllable (пятью́, десятью́, etc.). If we leave aside for the moment the counterevidence of the numerals, however, we can see {l'ub#v' +øju} → любóвью as simply one instance of a general rule to the effect that stressed {ø} loses its stress to the left whenever possible ({stol+ø}→/stól/, {klevet+ø} → /kl'iv'ét/, {naj#ʹm+a} → /nájma/, cf. below). The large number of words of the type стóл, клеветá renders irrelevant what would otherwise be an important objection to a rule about leftward shifts from {ø}, namely that it would here regularize four forms (вóшью, лóжью, любóвью, рóжью) at the expense of making the numerals (пятью́, шестью́, семью́, восемью́ or восьмю́, девятью́, десятью́, двадцатью́, тридцатью́—a larger class) irregular. Incidentally, we can note in passing that it will do no good to start from two different types of end stress in the instr., {l'ub#v'+øju} but {p'at'+øjú}, since this would not be a solution to, but merely a paraphrase of the problem.

None of the above arguments is really compelling. Much more serious is an argument not so much for end stress as against stem stress. If the underlying stress is on the {#′} of the stem, then we should expect the stress to move to the left, that is, onto the initial syllable, there where {#′} becomes zero: just as the underlying forms {naj#′m+ø}, {naj#′m+a}, and {zaj#′m+ø}, {zaj#′m+a} give us /najóm/, /nájma/, and /zajóm/, /zájma/, so should {l'ub#′v'+ø}, {l'ub#′v'+i} give us /l'ubóf'/, */l'úbv'i/ rather than the /l'ubóf'/, /l'ubv'í/ we actually find.[22] It is true that наём and заём are the only two words of their stress type in Russian, but on the other hand the class любовь itself contains but four words; taken together with {stol+ø} → /stól/ and {klevet+ø} → /kl'iv'ét/, the left shift in {naj#′m+a} → /nájma/ provides quite compelling evidence against an interpretation of любовь, etc. as containing stem stress.

There are several arguments in favor of an interpretation of любовь, etc. as containing underlying stem stress, but none can be considered really conclusive. First one has the fact that except for the numerals 5–10, 20, 30 (and marginally глушь, ось, and Пермь), all third declension substantives have fixed stem stress (степь, степи, степью, etc.). Furthermore, since the numerals have the additional peculiarity that (unlike любовь, etc.) they have grammatically motivated regressive stress shifts in the nom. and acc. (десять vs. десяти, десятью), to consider любовь, etc. as end-stressed would be to increase by one the number of stress classes within this declension type; one would then have the usual third declension feminines with fixed stem stress (степь, церковь), the numerals with underlying end stress but stem stress in nom.-acc., and a third class with underlying end-stress but no left shift in nom.-acc. (one has любовь, not *любовь). In addition, one notes that since /l'ubóv'ju/ can be derived only from {l'ub#v+øju}, not {l'ub#v'+øjú}, one cannot posit end-stress for the class любовь without adding a special rule to the grammar to account for the terminal stress of пятью, десятью, etc. The only apparent alternative would be to start from {l'ub#v'+øjú} and to consider /l'ubóv'ju/ a grammatically motivated (i.e., morphophonemic, not phonetic) stress shift marking the instrumental case; in this case, however, the class любовь, etc. would be doubly unique, first in marking the instr. by a stress shift (no other Russian noun does so), and secondly, in using a terminal → preterminal rather than a terminal → initial stress shift to mark case.[23] This cumbersome alternative is clearly to be rejected.

There are two other, minor items of evidence which speak in favor of stem rather than end stress. The proper name Любовь 'Amy' maintains the stressed /ó/ throughout the paradigm: gen. Любови, instr. Любовью, etc., which might tempt one to assume by analogy that the common noun любовь is likewise stem stressed. However, in spite of their common origin, these are two distinct stems in modern

Russian, and it is hard to see a formal reason for connecting them. The other minor bit of evidence is provided by the archaic instr. form любóвию, the disyllabic ending of which might be expected to retain the stress if the underlying form is {l'ub#v'+øju}. However, here again the evidence is only suggestive, since the form любóвию hardly ever occurs in modern Russian. The only real evidence in favor of stem stress in the class любóвь is that given by the end-stressed instr. numerals пятью́, десятью́, etc., which as we have seen force us either (1) to assume stem stress underlying любóвь, etc. or (2) to set up a special rule to account for end-stressed десятью́, etc.

The class любóвь, вóшь is thus seen to be caught between two contradictory sets of evidence. On the one hand, the end-stressed numerals argue for stem stress in the любóвь group; on the other hand, the evidence of наём, заём is compatible only with end stress in this same group. There is no way to reconcile these mutually contradictory sets of evidence, and the result is that whatever conclusion one comes to, it cannot be really satisfactory. The bulk of the evidence appears to favor the traditional solution (but at the price of adding a special rule for end-stressed десятью́, etc.), and we shall therefore conclude that B. O. Unbegaun was quite correct in stating that любóвь has fixed final stress. Our present contribution has tried to make two points. First, it has been shown that the instrumental singular forms вóшью, лóжью, любóвью, and рóжью need not be considered irregular; they can be derived by the same rule of regressive stress shift from {ø} that is needed to account for many other words in Russian, i.e. {l'ub#v'+øju} → /l'ubóv'ju/ and {l'ub#v'+ø} → /l'ubóf'/ by exactly the same rule as {stol+ø} → /stól/, {ruč#j+ø} → /ručéj/, {klevet+ø} → /kl'iv'ét/, {stat#j+ø} → /stat'éj/, {naj#'m+a} → /nájma/, etc. Secondly, it has become clear that such generalizations are attained only by putting aside a certain amount of contradictory evidence; in this case, the price that is paid for making любóвью, etc. regular has been to make десятью́, etc. irregular, and this solution, though not ideal, has been adopted for want of a better one. In other words, we hope to have contributed to demonstrating both the value and the limitations of this kind of linguistic research.

University of California, Los Angeles

NOTES

1. This approach has been evident in many works by J. Kuryłowicz, e.g., *L'accentuation des langues indoeuropéennes* (Wrocław-Cracow, 1958[2]), and in several comparative studies by E. Stankiewicz, e.g.,

"The singular-plural opposition in the Slavic languages," *International Journal of Slavic Linguistics and Poetics*, 5 (1962), 1–15, esp. 12 ff. For Russian, this same approach has been emphasized by G. Shevelov, "Speaking of Russian stress," *Word*, 19 (1963), 73, and utilized by Kuryłowicz, "Sistema russkogo udarenija," *Naukovi zapysky L'vivs'skoho derž. universytetu*, III ("Seryja filolohična," 2 [1946]); cf. also our "grammatical function and Russian stress," to appear in Language.

2. This view, which goes back at least to Kuryłowicz's "Sistema russkogo udarenija," is recognized by B. O. Unbegaun, *Russian Grammar* (Oxford, 1957), R. I. Avanesov, *Fonetika sovremennogo russkogo literaturnogo jazyka* (Moskow, 1956,) cf. p. 73, and accepted by most of the recent writers on Russian stress, but as Zaliznjak points out ("Uslovnoe udarenie v russkom slovoizmenenii," *Voprosy jazykoznanija* [1964], No. 1, p. 16) it has not yet penetrated all studies of Russian stress.

3. The same correspondence of phonemically mobile to morphophonemically fixed stress occurs in the gen. plur. of the fem. and neuters of this class: клеветы́, клеве́т, клеветáм = morphophonemic {klevet + í}, {klevet + ǿ}, {klevet + ám} (like стóл, столá); статьи́, статéй, статьи́м = {stat#j +í}, {stat#j + ǿ}, {stat#j +ám} (like скачóк, скачкá or ручéй, ручьи́).

4. Thus, for example, the grammar of the Soviet Academy (AN SSSR, *Grammatika russkogo jazyka*, I, [Moskow, 1952], 172, 205–207) omits вóшь, whereas V. A. Red'kin ("O variantnosti akcentnyx edinic v formax sklonenija russkogo jazyka,"

Československá rusistika, 12 [1967], 2, pp. 94–99) leaves out рóжь. Some sources add глýшь to this group, but since there is no unity in the available opinions concerning this word's stress, it will not be included here (Isačenko, *Die russische Sprache der Gegenwart*, I [Halle/Saale], 123, classes глýшь with брóвь. as having fixed stem stress throughout the sing. except for the 2nd loc., whereas the Soviet Academy grammar and Ušakov's dictionary attribute fixed end stress to this word).

5. The plural, end-stressed throughout, is irrelevant to the present discussion.

6. And, according to the Soviet Academy grammar, глýшь and (marginally) óсь and Пéрмь. Some third decl. fem. nouns have the 2nd loc. in stressed -í, but this is not to the present point.

7. Forms like пя́тью, сéмью are adverbs, derived by stress shift from the numeral noun bases.

8. The variant вóсемью is now archaic, and is included here only to show that the stress remains on the last syllable even when preceded by a mobile vowel, i.e., to emphasize the difference between the numerals and the type любóвь.

9. *Op. cit.*, pp. 172, 205–207.

10. *Die russische Sprache der Gegenwart*, p. 124.

11. L. Ďurovič, *Paradigmatika spisovnej ruštiny* (Bratislava, 1964), p. 133.

12. J. Kuryłowicz, "Sistema russkogo udarenija"; V. A. Nikonov, "Mesto udarenija v russkom slove," *IJSLP*, 6 (1963), 1–8; P. Garde, "Pour une théorie de l'accentuation russe," *Slavia*, 34 (1965), 529–59, esp. 548; M. Olexnovič, "Teoretičeskie osnovy raznomestonosti i

nepodvižnosti russkogo udarenija,'' *Russkij jazyk v nacional'noj škole*, 6 (1965), 3–11.

13. Cf. the section on "Accentology" written by V. A. Red'kin in *Osnovy postroenija opisatel'noj grammatiki sovremennogo russkogo literaturnogo jazyka* (Moscow, 1966), p. 19–49.

14. *Russian grammar*, p. 66.

15. "«Uslovnoe udarenie» v russkom slovoizmenenii," and with less theory but more Russian, "Udarenie v sovremennom russkom sklonenii," *Russkij jazyk v nacional'noj škole*, 2 (1963), 7–23.

16. "O variantnosti akcentnyx edinic ..."

17. Some problems connected with vowel-zero alternations on different levels are discussed in our papers, "Cyclical rules in derivational morphophonemics," *Phonologie der Gegenwart* (Vienna, 1967), p. 173–183 and "Vowel-zero alternations in Russian derivation," *IJSLPII* (1968), 110–231.

18. This term was introduced by R. Jakobson, "Russian conjugation," *Word*, 4 (1948), 155–67.

19. These alternations, and their relation to those in the derivational system, are discussed in "Vowel-zero alternations in Russian derivation."

20. Similar neutralizations can be observed, e.g., in the nom. plur. of fem. substantives, where the number-marking terminal → pretermial stress shift (быстрина́ → быстри́ны, долгота́ → долго́ты, etc.) is neutralized in monosyllabic stems like вдова́ → вдо́вы, compared to жена́ → жёны which has the same morphophonemic case-marking terminal → initial stress shift as голова́м → го́ловы, сковорода́м → ско́вороды, etc.

21. In a different linguistic area, cf. the extraordinary phonemic effect (practically doubling the number of consonantal phonemes and halving the number of vowels) of the relatively slight phonetic changes involves in the weakening of the *jers*.

22. On the interpretation of наём, найма and заём, займа, see "Notes on Russian stress, 3: наём and заём," *The Slavic and East European Journal*, 12 (1968), 53–58.

23. All other case-marking stress shifts are terminal → initial (голова́ → го́лову, сковорода́м → ско́вороды) or initial → terminal (бе́рег → на берегу́, сёстрам → сестёр; on this latter type, see "Grammatical function and Russian stress").